T0205205

Mastering Project Portfolio Management

A Systems Approach to Achieving Strategic Objectives

Michael J. Bible, PMP
Susan S. Bivins, PMP

J.ROSS
PUBLISHING

Copyright © 2011 by Michael J. Bible and Susan S. Bivins

ISBN-13:   978-1-60427-066-2

Printed and bound in the U.S.A. Printed on acid-free paper.

10 9 8 7 6 5 4 3 2 1

Library of Congress Cataloging-in-Publication Data

Bible, Michael J., 1966–
   Mastering project portfolio management : a systems approach to achieving strategic objectives/by Michael J. Bible and Susan S. Bivins.
      p. cm.
   Includes bibliographical references and index.
   ISBN 978-1-60427-066-2 (hardcover : alk. paper)
   1. Portfolio management. 2.   Strategic planning. I. Bivins, Susan S., 1941- II. Title.
      HG4529.5.B53 2011
      658.4'04—dc23

                                    2011032661

Phone: (954) 727-9333
Fax: (561) 892-0700
Web: www.jrosspub.com

Contents

PREFACE

BACKGROUND

Much has been written on the subject of project portfolio management (PPM). Harvey Levine, a highly regarded project management expert, defined PPM as "... the management of the project portfolio so as to maximize the contribution of projects to the overall welfare and success of the enterprise" (Levine, 2005). With PPM, projects that best support organizational goals and objectives are selected to ensure the optimal mix of projects and portfolios to achieve strategic objectives. Although many authors, including Levine, have defined "what" PPM is, it is still not broadly implemented. The authors believe that while the "what" of PPM has been effectively described by a host of PPM professionals, the process of "how" has been presented in abstract and has not received nearly as much attention. In our view, the lack of detail about "how" to perform PPM and its central role in an effective decision making process is one reason why PPM is not widely employed or used to maximum benefit. Simply put, although executives and managers may know what PPM is, many do not fully understand how to implement and practice it to make better decisions and more effectively manage project portfolios that will best achieve their objectives.

A key element of PPM is effective decision making using an organized and disciplined process. Too often projects are randomly identified, discussed to exhaustion, and then finally chosen as a means to end interminable meetings, resulting in misallocation of the organization's valued and scarce resources. Managers grapple with endless dialogue because the decision process lacks structure, and those participating fail to realize that portfolio decisions are complex enough to exceed the grasp of human cognition. Questions such as how to align projects to strategic goals and objectives, accurately determine the relative importance of conflicting objectives, evaluate the degree to which projects contribute to these objectives, decide where to allocate scarce resources for maximum benefit, and balance projects across the organization to satisfy competing demands without destroying organization morale and unity have complex answers. Such decisions cannot be made effectively using informal processes. How to eliminate fruitless discussion, improve the quality of portfolio decisions, and increase the chances of achieving the organization's strategic goals and objectives through PPM are what this book is about.

WHY PPM

Increasing competition and the need for agility in today's organizations makes a compelling case for effective portfolio selection and management through timely and sound decision making. That means getting the right information to the right people at the right time, thus increasing the likelihood of making the right decision. Many organizations fund and execute projects without using formal PPM, that is, projects are selected using ad hoc decision processes, often leading to project portfolios that are unrelated to or fail to achieve strategic goals and objectives. How projects are selected matters in terms of how well strategic goals and objectives are achieved.

Even the most basic PPM process can yield significant benefits for any organization by increasing the chances of selecting and managing project portfolios that deliver the most benefit in terms of achieving goals and objectives at a given funding level under identified organizational constraints. Making the wrong decisions and expending resources on the wrong initiatives, those that do not drive organizational achievement, are much more costly than implementing a basic, effective PPM process. Identifying, evaluating, selecting, and managing a project portfolio is a complex decision problem requiring robust processes and procedures, clear roles and responsibilities, and appropriate software tools and decision methods. While this may sound overwhelming, establishing a PPM process can be accomplished with the right guidance, effective management of change, and an understanding of what is required.

PURPOSE OF THIS BOOK

This book provides a holistic view of PPM that includes people, process, tools, and techniques that work together synergistically within the organization to produce portfolio decisions with the greatest chance of success. To accomplish this, the authors provide a PPM model that conceptually illustrates the entire process from strategic planning through portfolio evaluation and adjustment. We follow the process model through prioritizing organizational objectives; identifying and evaluating candidate projects; selecting optimal portfolios; and evaluating performance of the portfolios. To put the decision processes and tools in context, we describe roles and responsibilities, major activities, and governance concepts necessary to support the PPM process.

In addition, the book shows how members of an organization not currently using formal PPM can effectively implement processes to prioritize goals and objectives defined during strategic planning, identify and select portfolios of projects that best achieve them, and evaluate project portfolio performance. Rather than an abstract discussion, this book applies a hands-on approach using real decision support software and techniques accompanied by step-by-step illustrations to guide the reader through the process. The reader is provided temporary access to the software to reinforce the concepts described.

CONTENT AND ORGANIZATION

The book contains eleven chapters, each building on the previous one. Chapter 1 establishes a common understanding of PPM. Chapter 2 addresses the strategic planning process and its role in producing the goals and objectives that serve as critical inputs to the PPM process. Chapter 3 introduces measurement types and decision models and describes software tools used in the book's examples. These three chapters are crucial to understanding the basics of PPM and the context of decisions made within the process.

Chapter 4 introduces structuring decision models and describes the process of prioritizing the organizational objectives identified during the strategic planning process. In many organizations lacking an effective PPM process, this step is omitted and the organizational objectives are erroneously treated as though they are of equal importance.

Chapters 5 and 6 describe how to identify and screen large numbers of potential projects to produce a reduced pool of candidate projects to be considered for portfolio selection, while maintaining traceability of these projects to the organizational objectives they support.

Chapters 7, 8, and 9 address the evaluation of the candidate projects (also called alternatives) with respect to the objectives they support, thus determining relative project benefits. Additionally, the selection of the project portfolio subject to organizational constraints and risk is presented, including consideration of alternative portfolio scenarios for various sets of business assumptions.

Finally, Chapters 10 and 11 discuss the implementation of the approved project portfolio and address how to evaluate the portfolio with regard to performance against baseline plans while maintaining relevance to organizational objectives. These chapters describe the iterative nature of PPM and the cycles that drive it.

Throughout the book the material is reinforced using a notional example based on a real project portfolio situation while providing the reader access to the software used in this book in order to understand and apply it.

SOFTWARE TOOLS

It is not the intention of the authors to endorse one software product over others. However, we do make it clear that timely and effective project portfolio decisions are difficult or impossible without the right decision-making tools. In this book we do not emphasize managing projects using project management software, rather we focus on decisions involving selecting the right portfolio and effectively managing its performance to achieve strategic objectives. Accordingly, the authors use decision support software tools provided by Expert Choice to illustrate the concepts. The tools are based on the Analytic Hierarchy Process (AHP), a widely accepted approach for making complex compensatory decisions of all kinds, including those presented in this book.

This software is a logical choice to illustrate decision-making concepts because it incorporates enhanced AHP support and optimization capabilities beyond those offered by many other tools. However, other PPM software tools are available in the marketplace, including the portfolio-based enhancements for Oracle's Primavera, Microsoft's Project Server, PlanView Enterprise, and many products from smaller vendors. Some of these products, with origins in project management software, include compensatory decision-making capabilities; some require considerable resources to implement and manage. Not all of these products use AHP and the ratio-scale mathematics necessary for valid comparison of alternatives and selection of project portfolios. In any case, the decision-making concepts presented in this book using Expert Choice tools will familiarize the reader with the broad applicability of AHP for mathematically sound complex PPM decisions, including prioritizing objectives, selecting project portfolios, and evaluating portfolio performance.

AUDIENCE

The authors developed this book for use by people in any organization that relies on projects to contribute to the achievement of its vision, goals, and objectives; it is intended for those who want to implement PPM for the first time or wish to enhance their existing project portfolio processes. By providing a PPM model and the infrastructure needed to support the model, this book provides a roadmap to effectively design, develop, implement, and manage a tailored project portfolio process in a relatively short period of time without great expense. In addition to decomposing the process into easily understandable and logical phases, the book also identifies specific tools, techniques, and resources needed to support the process, together with examples throughout to show the reader how to do it. With guidance, engagement, and the support of upper management, and reasonably effective project and program management infrastructure, any organization can implement its own PPM process. Thus, they can make better decisions and increase their chances of achieving strategic objectives. People whose organizations are already using PPM might think about how to use the concepts in this book to supplement or improve existing processes.

The book is also intended for use as a textbook in a PPM course within graduate and upper-level undergraduate business degree programs. It provides a roadmap for students to understand PPM through the application of tools and techniques, using a defined process consisting of discrete phases and steps. By structuring the text to coincide with the logical progression of the PPM process and illustrating which tools and techniques to use along the roadmap, students will obtain a clear understanding of PPM.

REFERENCES

Levine, Harvey A. (2005). *Project Portfolio Management: A Practical Guide to Selecting Projects, Managing Portfolios, and Maximizing Benefits.* San Francisco, CA: Jossey-Bass Business and Management Series.

ACKNOWLEDGMENTS

The authors wish to acknowledge the contributions of Dr. Ernest H. Forman of George Washington University for sharing his outstanding expertise in decision science and portfolio management and for reviewing numerous drafts of the manuscript. As a mentor and former professor to the authors, Dr. Forman, while honest in his criticism, never wavered in his support for our idea of writing this book and always found time to provide useful and appropriate feedback to improve the quality of our writing.

We also want to thank Expert Choice Inc. (EC) for providing access to its software products in developing this book, allowing us to illustrate important concepts. In addition, by providing access to EC products with the purchase of this book, the reader receives the added benefit of practicing the concepts and increasing both the learning experience and the effectiveness of the book.

Further, we express our appreciation to Ed Hreljac founder of ProcessPower Solutions for reviewing the manuscript and providing feedback from the context of his expertise in using the Analytic Hierarchy Process and his substantial experience working with government and healthcare organizations. His perspective and suggestions were most beneficial in helping us to better organize the material and present the concepts to a more diverse audience.

We are especially grateful to our families, Sue's husband, Jim Bivins, and Mike's wife and son, Hege and Ethan Bible. Throughout this project they provided unfaltering support for our efforts. Even when we doubted our ability to finish this project, they remained resolute and steadfast. Their sacrifices and continued support allowed us to embark on this journey and realize our vision. In addition to the support of our families, Jim Bivins was invaluable in editing the graphical material in the book. Thank you!

ABOUT THE AUTHORS

Michael J. Bible, MSPM, PMP, has twenty-five years of professional and leadership experience supporting the U.S. Department of Defense, with the last twelve years dedicated to project and program management of test and evaluation programs for major defense acquisition programs. He is a project management professional with a successful history applying project management best practices to the technical field of test and evaluation for portfolios of complex defense acquisition programs and projects.

Mike specializes in the management of complex technical projects and, as a former co-owner of an engineering services firm, has applied strategic planning to establish organizational direction while utilizing project portfolio management to successfully grow the company in alignment with business initiatives.

A retired Marine Corps officer, Mike obtained his MSPM from the Graduate School of Business at George Washington University and is a member of the Project Management Institute. He lives with his wife and son in Virginia. Mike can be reached via e-mail at mb1775@gwmail.gwu.edu.

Susan S. Bivins, MSPM, PMP, has more than twenty-five years of management and leadership experience dedicated to delivering successful information technology, organizational change management, and professional consulting services projects for major global corporations. She specializes in project and portfolio management; international, multicultural and multicompany initiatives; and business strategy integration in the private and public sectors.

During her career with IBM, Sue managed multiple organizations and complex projects, including operations and support for the Olympics and a strategic transformational change program. Since retiring from IBM she has led multicompany joint initiatives with Hitachi, Microsoft, and Sun Microsystems and has served as Director of Project Management at Habitat for Humanity International.

Sue earned her MSPM from the Graduate School of Business at George Washington University where she received the Dean's Award for Excellence and was admitted to the Beta Gamma Sigma business honorarium. A member of the Project Management Institute, she served on the original PMI Standard for Portfolio Management team. She and her husband live in Missouri. Sue can be reached via e-mail at sbivins@gwmail.gwu.edu.

 Web
Added
Value™

Free value-added materials available from
the Download Resource Center at www.jrosspub.com

At J. Ross Publishing we are committed to providing today's professional with practical, hands-on tools that enhance the learning experience and give readers an opportunity to apply what they have learned. That is why we offer free ancillary materials available for download on this book and all participating Web Added Value™ publications. These online resources may include interactive versions of material that appears in the book or supplemental templates, worksheets, models, plans, case studies, proposals, spreadsheets and assessment tools, among other things. Whenever you see the WAV™ symbol in any of our publications, it means bonus materials accompany the book and are available from the Web Added Value Download Resource Center at www.jrosspub.com.

Downloads for *Mastering Project Portfolio Management: A Systems Approach to Achieving Strategic Objectives* consist of:

Background Documents and Spreadsheets for Copy and Paste

Rather than manually entering the objectives, alternatives and supporting information into the decision support software models, these files allow readers to copy and paste them while following the examples in the book. A spreadsheet illustrates the difference between an optimized portfolio and one that was chosen by the common practice of selecting projects in descending order of priority until funds are exhausted.

Sample Models in Decision Support Software

Two Analytic Hierarchy Process (AHP) models from the portfolio example used throughout the book are provided. They can be loaded into the accompanying decision support software to show how a completed model has been structured, measured (evaluated) and synthesized. (Visit the Download Resource Center for more information.)

Draft Chapter 12

The draft of a twelfth chapter suggests some unique approaches to measuring the strategic performance of project portfolios in terms of continued expectation of achieving organizational goals and objectives. While these new concepts have not yet been subjected to formal review, the authors are interested in reader comments and feedback.

Instructor Material Downloads

The following materials were developed for use by course instructors only, and access to these materials is therefore restricted. To obtain access to these materials contact customerservice@jrosspub .com.

ABU Case Study Student Paper

The student paper is an actual graduate student case study based on the fictitious American Business University (ABU) example described in the book. The paper describes the steps required to select the optimal project portfolio based upon a goal and objectives from the university's strategic plan. The process includes prioritizing the objectives, identifying and prioritizing the project candidates, establishing constraints, performing assessments of various scenarios including analysis of the efficient frontier, and selecting the optimal portfolio at a particular funding level under the specified constraints. The case study includes the use of the decision support software provided with the book to produce the desired results, in addition to narratives describing the project portfolio management process. It can be used as an example for students assigned a term project using their own real or imaginary portfolios.

PowerPoint Slide Deck for Each Chapter

A generic PowerPoint slide deck is provided covering the material in each chapter, including overview, content and summary slides. The slides can be downloaded and tailored by the instructor, or included with other lecture material.

Figures and Tables in PNG Format

All figures and tables from each chapter are provided in original color as portable network graphics files that can be copied and used in the instructor's teaching material with appropriate attribution.

Questions and Answers

Questions about the material in each chapter and sample answers are provided. Instructors can use these for homework, in-class discussions, as exam questions or simply as thought-provoking exercises.

A guide providing further information about using the ancillary material for this book is included with the downloadable materials herein described, at www.jrosspub.com.

1

Introduction to Project Portfolio Management

Many organizations fund and execute projects without using formal project portfolio management (PPM); that is, projects are selected using ad hoc decision processes, often leading to project portfolios that are unrelated to or that fail to achieve strategic goals and objectives. Other organizations practice PPM but don't know how to optimize the portfolios they select, and they may not manage portfolio execution to ensure the achievement of anticipated benefits. In today's fast-paced environment, investing in the right portfolio is imperative, but making the necessary decisions is impossible without the requisite process and tools. Selecting and managing a project portfolio is a network of complex decisions requiring a robust process, clear roles and responsibilities, and appropriate decision methods.

While no approach can guarantee the right decisions all the time, this book provides a guide to a disciplined process. It is supported by appropriate decision tools and techniques that enables people to make the complex decisions required to optimize project portfolio selection and effectively manage execution to best support the achievement of organizational goals and objectives. Between the covers is a holistic view of PPM that includes people, process, tools, and techniques that work together synergistically to produce results. We begin with a PPM model that conceptually illustrates the entire process from strategic planning through portfolio evaluation and revision. To put the decision processes and tools in context, we describe roles and responsibilities, major activities, and governance concepts necessary to deliver successful portfolios.

In this chapter we introduce the concepts of PPM that are presented in greater depth in later chapters, including the conceptual process model, the iterative phases of portfolio selection and management, and an overview of roles, responsibilities, and governance. First, however, we distinguish project management, program management, and enterprise project management (EPM) from portfolio management and provide a brief overview of the growth in acceptance of project management.

Often project management is loosely described as the processes and practices needed to *do things right*, while portfolio management is described as the processes and practices needed to *do the right things*. Project management is the business of meeting the triple constraints of schedule, cost, and quality, while at the same time, producing deliverables that meet specifications and satisfy the customer. Program management is the business of delivering multiple related projects in accordance with the same principles. EPM, in our view, is project and program management as managed consistently across the enterprise or some appropriate subset of the enterprise; it is still focused on managing enterprise resources to deliver the same results as those for an individual project, albeit rolled up into easily understood dashboards that can provide the progress results at any level of detail. Thus, project management, program management, and enterprise program management are all largely focused on *doing things right*.

Portfolio management, although related, is different from project management in the sense that projects and programs are the constituent members of a project portfolio, and these constituents are subject to the project management processes intended to yield the desired results and progress measurements. Portfolio management seeks to ensure that the selected constituents of the portfolio, taken together, are those that can best achieve the strategic goals and objectives of the organization, and that the portfolio is adjusted to ensure that it continues to do so in the face of changes in organizational strategy or the failure of constituent projects to deliver on anticipated benefits. Thus, portfolio management is focused on *doing the right things*.

1.1 ACCEPTANCE OF PROJECT MANAGEMENT

Although the roots of project management extend to ancient times, formal project management has only gained wide acceptance and traction in many organizations within the last half century. Business and government agencies have become more aware of the need to manage projects using formal practices and processes to ensure greater project success, that is, doing the work right (PMI, 2008). Meredith and Mantel (2006) provide three primary reasons to explain the emergence of project management: ". . . (1) the exponential growth of human knowledge; (2) the growing demand for a broad range of complex, sophisticated, customized goods and services; and (3) the evolution of worldwide competitive markets for the production and consumption of goods and services." These reasons have not gone unnoticed. Throughout the U.S. Department of Defense (DoD), there is a growing emphasis on program and project management as the department's acquisition personnel design, develop, and procure hundreds of billions of dollars of advanced military equipment. DoD's Defense Acquisition University (DAU) is dedicated to training and educating personnel formally in defense acquisition program and project management and establishing standards for program management career field certification (DAU, 2010). Additionally, the National Aeronautics and Space Administration established the Academy of Program/Project and Engineering Leadership, and many leading corporations have established project management training programs and project management offices (PMOs) to develop project management methodologies tailored to specific organizational needs.

The growing emphasis of project management can also be illustrated through the expansion of project management professional certification from the Project Management Institute (PMI). Founded in 1969, PMI has grown to over 420,000 members with a "primary goal to advance the practice, science, and profession of project management throughout the world in a conscientious and proactive manner so that organizations everywhere will embrace, value, and utilize project management and then attribute their successes to it" (PMI, 2010). Not only do organizations want to complete projects successfully by doing the work right, but they also want to successfully complete the *right* projects. Completing projects on time and within budget has little to no value if projects fail to contribute to the successful achievement of the organization's strategic objectives. Project connection to strategic objectives becomes even more important when the organization is undertaking many projects simultaneously that require utilization of the organization's valued resources.

1.2 OVERVIEW OF PPM

The less a project contributes to accomplishing an organization's goals and objectives, the less value it creates and the more resources are wasted, or at least inefficiently utilized. To better utilize resources and achieve desired outcomes, organizations are becoming more concerned about what projects to undertake in the first place, which has led to a more formal process called project portfolio management (PPM). Harvey Levine (2005) defines PPM as ". . . a set of business practices that brings the world of projects into tight integration with other business operations. It brings projects into harmony with the strategies, resources, and executive oversight of the enterprise and provides the structure and processes for project portfolio governance." PMI more broadly defines PPM as ". . . the coordinated management of portfolio components to achieve specific organizational objectives." (PMI, 2008) The authors of this book would also suggest that PPM is a flexible, responsive, and iterative process to select and execute the right projects that maximize achievement of the organization's strategic goals and objectives subject to physical, political, financial, and other resource constraints.

The PPM process can be thought of as the actionable management process necessary to achieve the organization's strategic objectives through project portfolio selection, implementation, monitoring and control, and evaluation. As noted earlier, PPM is not the same as EPM or the management of multiple related projects as the name might imply. A project portfolio is a group of projects selected and executed specifically because together they best help an organization to achieve its objectives. The objectives are the lowest-level output of the strategic planning process that produces the organization's mission, vision, goals, and the objectives that support each goal. The fundamental task of PPM is to select a portfolio of projects that maximizes the achievement of those objectives while achieving balance among, and coverage of, the objectives. Although effective PPM contributes to the achievement of organizational objectives, it is not the only source of achievement. The organization's ongoing business operations also contribute to the achievement of objectives, which we discuss later in this section.

Because those involved in PPM must understand how their own organizations produce goals and objectives, the authors have chosen to broadly describe the strategic planning process in this book. The PPM challenge is linking what the organization actually chooses to do with that specified in the strategic plan. As the strategic plan changes, the PPM process must allow the portfolio to change and adapt accordingly. This adaptation can be compared to the actions of a ship's crew underway on the ocean. As the captain orders course corrections, the helmsman adjusts the heading and the ship follows accordingly. The helmsman doesn't wait around wondering what he should do; he acts instinctively, because that is the disciplined process aboard the ship. As an organization's strategic course changes, so must project portfolios, and its PPM process must be adaptable, flexible, and responsive to rapidly adjust its limited resources in an ever changing global marketplace.

Every organization is resource constrained. An effective PPM process provides the structure to make reasoned trade-offs about how the resources should be allocated to maximize potential benefits. If the essence of project management is communication (Cioffi, 2002), the essence of PPM is reasoned decision making. Thus, sound decision making through a disciplined and methodical process is a crucial attribute of an effective PPM process. Through such a process the organization can make rational decisions on how best to employ constrained resources across objectives to maximize benefits of its project portfolios.

A critical point to understand about PPM is that it is an iterative process linking the strategic objectives of the organization to the projects it undertakes to achieve those objectives. This book is not intended to provide detailed guidance on how to develop an organization's strategic plan. A plethora of literature addressing different strategic planning models exists. However, this book does address the basic prerequisites or inputs to effective PPM decision making; thus, we discuss the basic process for defining the mission, vision, goals, and objectives that provide the foundation for PPM.

Once the portfolio(s) is selected and implemented, continuous monitoring and controlling of project and portfolio performance is necessary. Some projects will perform well and require no action, while others may perform poorly and require corrective action—or even termination. New projects may need to be added to address changing market conditions, exploit emerging opportunities, or react to competitors. Even projects that perform well may be considered for termination to adjust for changing strategies, market conditions, competition, and new opportunities.

1.3 PPM MODEL OVERVIEW

The PPM model conceptually illustrated in Figure 1.1 shows the authors' version of the PPM process from strategic planning through portfolio evaluation and adjustment. The model aids in visualizing the PPM process and its integration with the organization's strategic planning process; it also shows the connection to identifying, evaluating, and selecting projects for the portfolio and monitoring and controlling the portfolio once implemented. Using the model as a backdrop throughout the book, critical elements of the process show where portfolio decision making increases the chances of achieving strategic goals and objectives; specifically, we describe and demonstrate the processes and tools to prioritize organizational objectives, identify and evaluate candidate projects, select optimal portfolios, and evaluate portfolio performance.

The PPM process presented in Figure 1.1 prescribes five phases:

1. Strategic
2. Screening
3. Selection
4. Implementation
5. Evaluation

While the phases are presented in sequence, the process should not be thought of as strictly linear. Rather, PPM is an iterative sequential process with regularly planned cycles; it also requires the flexibility to adapt to external or internal factors affecting the objectives of the organization and thus to execute any phase or set of steps on demand in addition to planned cycles. Whether the external factor is a financial crisis, such as the one that occurred in 2008, or an internal factor, such as poorly

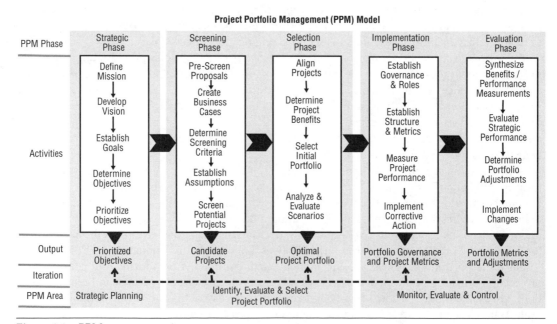

Figure 1.1   PPM process overview

performing projects, the PPM process must be responsive to timely adjustments. Although we do not suggest that dramatic portfolio changes be made on a daily, weekly, or even monthly basis, the speed of change in today's environment suggests the need for a nimble PPM process. A brief overview of each phase is provided in this chapter, with detailed information about each addressed in the chapters to follow.

The background shaded boxes in Figure 1.1 are intended to show logical groupings of the PPM phases into three PPM areas:

1. Strategic Planning delivers the prerequisite prioritized goals and objectives
2. Identify, Evaluate & Select Project Portfolio results in selection of optimal portfolios given specified organizational constraints
3. Monitor, Evaluate & Control provides the means to measure portfolio performance and adjust the portfolio contents.

1.3.1 Strategic Phase Overview

During the strategic phase, the organization establishes or revises its strategic plan, including the mission, vision, goals, and objectives. This phase provides the foundation for effective PPM as the strategic plan establishes the goals and objectives to which project portfolios contribute. Commonly, large and well-established corporations have well-defined missions, vision statements, values, goals, and objectives from previously developed strategic plan cycles, and these elements undergo periodic review and revision. However, the quality of the elements of the strategic plan can vary with the seriousness and expertise of the people who develop them. Unfortunately, even when the vision, goals, and objectives are well-defined and articulated, they may not be valid or achievable. Fuller and Green (2005) contend that "the leader sets measurable goals and objectives for the organization. A goal or objective for which attainment cannot be measured is worthless."

From a clear and unambiguous mission and vision, goals and subordinate objectives can be developed to specify how the organization will realize the vision through achievement of these goals and objectives. Attainment of objectives is a responsibility requiring contribution from all elements of the organization, including targeted achievements from operations as well as projects at all levels of the organization. Although this book is targeted at selecting the optimal portfolio of projects anticipated to achieve organizational objectives and measuring performance during implementation to ensure the portfolio maintains relevance to the strategic plan, it is important to note that attaining them is not the sole responsibility of project management. Activities from ongoing operations, including manufacturing, sales, finance, and human resources play an immense part in achieving the organization's strategic initiatives; if the organization can't efficiently manufacture a great product engineered during a new product development project, then both the project side and the operations side have failed.

The relative degree to which projects versus operations contribute to achieving organizational objectives depends on many factors such as the industry, competition, financial position, opportunities, risks, and the maturity of the company, among other factors. A newly formed company is likely to emphasize projects over operations, because it is likely that, as a start-up, it has few existing operations. The mature, well-established organization typically has a fully developed operational capability that provides a large proportion of the contribution to the achievement of strategic objectives, especially those related to revenues. This concept is illustrated in Figure 1.2 and shows projects and operations contributing more or less equally to the accomplishment of the strategic vision. In the illustration, a simplified version of PMI's Organizational Context of Portfolio Management (PMI, 2008), everything begins with a vision from which strategic goals and objectives are derived. These are denoted *strategic planning* on the right side of the pyramid. The main point of this illustration

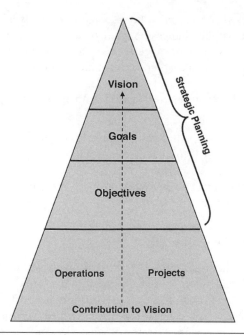

Figure 1.2   Contribution to achieving the vision (adapted from PMI organizational context of PPM)

is to show that both operations and projects play a part in contributing to the achievement of the organization's strategic vision.

To illustrate this concept, let's use this example. Starting in the early 1970s, large deposits of oil were discovered off the Norwegian coastline. One of the benefactors of this discovery was Statoil, a state-founded and -owned Norwegian oil and gas company. In the years following the discovery, Statoil relied heavily on projects to develop new offshore oil fields. As a new company in 1972, Statoil's operations contributed little (monetarily) to achieving the company's strategic objectives because the company was focused on building revenue through developing offshore oil projects (Statoil ASA, 2010). As one would expect, the company's project activities during the early years of its existence contributed heavily toward achieving the organization's future objectives. Today, as a large, well-established, profitable company with 39 steadily producing oil fields, Statoil is less reliant (proportionally) on project activities than it was in 1972. The company now has the contribution of operations by transitioning previously successful projects (i.e., developed offshore oil fields) into production. However, Statoil continuously employs research and development projects to locate and exploit new oil fields to support future revenue streams.

There are two important outputs from the strategic phase; (1) an approved strategic plan with well-stated goals and objectives that can be measured over time, and (2) prioritized goals and objectives. In Chapter 4 we discuss a process to measure and prioritize the objectives by determining the importance of each objective relative to the goal. These activities form the basis of the strategic phase and lay the foundation for follow-on PPM process activities.

1.3.2 Screening Phase Overview

With clearly articulated and prioritized goals and objectives, the screening phase begins the process of soliciting proposals for potential projects with a reasonable expectation of contributing to goals and objectives. The screening phase of the PPM process can be thought of as a funnel that channels a potentially large volume of project proposals through a formal evaluation process that reduces the pool of potential projects to a reasonable number of candidate projects. Throughout this section we discuss projects in terms of *potential* and *candidate*. Proposed projects that appear to support strategic goals and objectives and, at least initially, appear to be feasible are admitted to the list of potential projects. Further scrutiny of information about each potential project determines, through a formal screening process, a list of candidate projects that will be evaluated during the selection phase. Inevitably, some projects will be submitted that have little connection to organizational objectives; this is one of the primary reasons for performing screening. Other projects may be added to the potential pool and labeled *mandatory* such as an environmental impact analysis required by the government prior to starting construction projects on federal property. Regardless, when a project migrates from the potential pool to the candidate pool, the project is a step closer to making it into the portfolio, but its selection is still not guaranteed. The screening phase provides an opportunity to make the case for which projects should be considered for inclusion in the portfolio and is characterized by determining screening criteria, developing assumptions, and creating and examining the business case for each project against the criteria and assumptions, resulting in the list of candidate projects.

The business case contains sufficient standard information about the project to enable further assessment and represents the sponsor's rationale for including the project in the portfolio. Business cases for potential projects, also known as project proposals, are evaluated to determine the validity and feasibility of the project against the defined screening criteria. For instance, potential projects might be required to support two or more objectives or expected to cost less than a maximum specified funding level to be considered for selection into the candidate project pool. Projects that are already in progress will be assessed as well to determine whether they continue to forecast anticipated benefits relative to the current goals and objectives.

Screening criteria represent factors against which the pool of potential projects is evaluated to determine whether a business case is sufficient to include the project in the candidate project pool. Screening criteria must be well thought out and approved by senior management. Along with screening criteria, certain assumptions are often stated to form a context about the future or to provide a scenario under which the project portfolio will be selected.

While the intent of the screening phase is to reduce the number of projects to a reasonable and manageable number for evaluation during the selection phase, this phase does pose a potential problem—screening out a project that should have been included in the portfolio. Because criteria are generally specified in terms of pass or fail, they must not be so restrictive that promising projects are unreasonably eliminated. The potential for leaving out a project in the portfolio is real, but the argument can be made that, by performing a deliberate PPM process, the chances of such omission are smaller than without a PPM process at all. Ultimately, during the screening phase, the portfolio stakeholders begin making sense of which projects to move forward in the PPM process because they have the greatest potential to contribute to achieving the objectives, as well as which projects already in the pipeline may be subject to reconsideration on this basis.

1.3.3 Selection Phase Overview

The objective of the selection phase is to derive a portfolio of projects providing maximum benefit subject to resource constraints and other limitations imposed by the organization. This is accomplished by evaluating the relative contribution of each of the candidate projects to each of the objectives it supports, evaluating the relative contribution of each objective to the goal and thus deriving a mathematically sound relative priority for each of the candidates. Once this is determined other considerations can be applied such as limitations on total investment, resources, and other constraints and risk. Various scenarios can be analyzed and compared, such as different budget limits, with the purpose of deriving the optimal project portfolio. *Optimal* is defined to mean selection and implementation of a project portfolio providing maximum benefits subject to organizational constraints. Determining what is optimal is not as clear cut as some may believe; optimal means identifying the combination of projects that maximizes benefit at a specified level of funding as well as the application of other organizational considerations in addition to relative evaluated priority. The value of software tools, such as those provided by Expert Choice, and techniques, such as the analytic hierarchy process (AHP), for determining relative priorities will become clear as we progress through this book. PPM tools and techniques are critical in deriving the organization's optimal project portfolio because they facilitate responsiveness and incorporate efficiencies into the PPM system by enabling accurately applied mathematics and the rapid reevaluation of changing variables such as funding allocated for the project portfolio and risks associated with projects. Additionally, it allows the incorporation of factors that the organization deems important as well as supporting multiple *what if* scenarios wherein changes in various parameters, including risk, budget, and resource levels can be evaluated quickly. These powerful capabilities make it possible for users to determine the maximum benefit for the level of resources applied and identify optimal portfolios in real time or as conditions and assumptions change.

By developing different portfolio scenarios, users not only select optimal portfolios, but they can also prepare for contingencies. Although determining the optimal portfolio is the primary objective of the selection phase, a by-product of the selection is the identification of alternate scenarios to support contingency planning. That is, we have selected an optimal portfolio based on specified assumptions about contributions to the organizational objectives, but the organization now has a foundation to begin exploring the impacts to the portfolio should conditions change—to play *what if* in considering alternative scenarios or to analyze what might not *feel right* intuitively. No one can be certain of what will happen tomorrow, much less weeks or months from now. The ability to identify the optimal portfolio and develop alternate scenarios by applying the tools and techniques described is the essence of the selection phase. Once the optimal portfolio has been approved, it can be implemented.

1.3.4 Implementation Phase Overview

The implementation phase transitions the approved project portfolio into execution; this launches portfolio monitoring and controlling activities. Of course, with an ongoing portfolio, the launch will happen with the commencement of each project rather than all at once, as may be the case the first time an organization builds a portfolio and establishes how it will be monitored and controlled. The aims of monitoring and controlling are to measure project and portfolio performance continuously to verify that progress is consistent with baseline expectations and to detect performance deficiencies as early as possible. Corrective actions can then be taken. Monitoring, evaluating, and controlling activities are also performed to ensure that projects within the portfolio remain relevant to strategic goals and objectives and to ensure that the portfolio is on track to attain anticipated benefits as well as contribute to achieving the strategic goals and objectives.

At the beginning of the implementation phase, the organization commences activities to initiate individual projects such as identifying project managers and teams, notifying functional managers of their respective resource allocations to support the project portfolio, contracting for specialized external resources, assigning projects to program offices, if appropriate, and establishing implementation plans and timelines. As the project portfolio's management and governance are established, individual projects are initiated or transitioned into the portfolio if it is already underway. This part of the implementation phase will vary from organization to organization; the important point to remember is that certain activities must occur, once a portfolio is approved in the selection phase, to prepare the organization and the PPM system to initiate and manage individual projects in the portfolio. Ideally, this process would already be established in an organization with mature project management processes. However, for organizations newly implementing PPM, integrating project and portfolio management processes is key to their success, and proper planning is necessary to establish the required infrastructure and processes.

As implementation begins, practicing project managers will recognize activities at the individual project level such as the development of the project charter and preliminary project scope statement, building a project team, and other initiation rites. EPM personnel will address, or may have already addressed, human resource planning and acquisition, establishing the project management information system, obtaining organizational process assets (i.e., policies, procedures, standards, guidelines, etc.), and establishing project management methodologies. However, it's also important to establish appropriate project portfolio governance. PPM governance will be introduced later in this chapter and is addressed in subsequent chapters as we progress through the process. From the perspective of implementing a project portfolio under the PPM process for the first time, the activity level is intense. Organizations with greater maturity in EPM practices, such as common reporting methodologies, may find a smoother path when adding the portfolio management elements than those with less maturity.

Assume for a moment that all projects in the portfolio have been initiated and each is now in some stage of development or implementation. Practicing project management professionals are fully aware of measuring project performance through the triple constraints of scope, cost, and schedule as well as analyzing variances and making adjustments if performance is outside of tolerances. Their goal is to have successful projects that finish on time and within budget, while meeting customer expectations and specifications. This concept is equally applicable to PPM. The view from the PPM level is for the entire portfolio to perform well. Is it realistic to expect 40 to 50 projects to perform perfectly? No, not really. Some will perform well, while others will struggle for a variety of reasons. It is important that the portfolio performance be measured and analyzed to determine areas of concern, and then the information is reported to the executive level.

Project managers report their individual project performance, which is rolled up and analyzed at the program and enterprise levels. Portfolio managers, who are responsible for the successful execution of a portfolio or a segment of the organization's portfolio, report the performance of their portfolios. While the process of measuring and analyzing portfolio performance differs from that for projects, the performance measurement concept is still applicable. Reporting portfolio status and adjusting the portfolio accordingly is discussed in Chapters 10 and 11. These chapters describe the implementation and evaluation phases, respectively. As the results from individual projects are reported, they are assembled, synthesized, and analyzed to identify problem areas, and are then reported to the executive level. Portfolio performance is evaluated not only in the context of the traditional performance of member projects and programs but also in terms of how their performance may affect anticipated benefits; for example, the schedule of a new product project that must be first to market may have slipped, thus affecting its ability to achieve those anticipated benefits. This information may impact a project's ability to support its covering objectives. *Covering objectives* are the lowest-level objective or sub-objective in the hierarchy that a candidate project supports. Support is established only at that covering level and is rolled up through the hierarchy. In addition, the anticipated benefits are based on the relative importance of the organization's objectives according to the strategic plan. When the strategy changes, the changes may affect the composition of the portfolio because the relative importance of the objectives may change and new objectives may be introduced.

Not only are project portfolios expected to perform well against a static set of prioritized objectives, they must maintain relevance when the strategic plan is revised. Both of these expectations provide the basis for determining modifications to the portfolio during the evaluation phase.

1.3.5 Evaluation Phase Overview

The evaluation phase serves to evaluate the performance of the portfolio in relation to strategic objectives and to determine necessary changes or modifications. Portfolio management personnel must evaluate the portfolio's performance based on traditional measures as well as project performance against objectives. In addition, because the relative priorities of the objectives change as the strategy changes, the impact on the relative anticipated benefits of the projects within the portfolio must be evaluated. A project with high relative priority or anticipated benefit that is performing poorly has more negative impact on portfolio performance than a project with low relative priority. Unfortunately, it is hard to predict which projects within the portfolio will perform well and which will not. The evaluation phase provides the process to assemble performance results from all projects, synthesize the results in relation to their relative importance, ensure that they are on track to achieve their anticipated benefits, and understand which projects require more management focus. The second purpose of the evaluation phase considers the impact of any changes in the objectives in the strategic plan to ensure that projects within the portfolio remain relevant to the strategic plan.

In determining what changes or corrective action is required, portfolio management must consider both internal and external factors. Internally, poor project performance is one reason to make adjustments to the portfolio. Depending on the cause and impact of the poor performance, the corrective action may be termination of the project, addition of resources, or changes to scope, schedule, or cost. Also, as described, portfolio personnel must evaluate the impact of changes to the strategic plan on the portfolio. At the project level, the focus and attention are on the successful completion of the assigned project, with little attention to the forces impacting the organization strategically. For instance, if the executive committee, during a periodic review, decides to reduce the investment in construction projects due to financing uncertainties and to increase focus on improving operational efficiencies, how would this impact the portfolio? In this case, poorly performing construction projects would likely be terminated while construction projects pending initiation in the near future might not be funded. So, the performance of the portfolio is related to the performance of its constituent projects as it affects anticipated benefits and changes in the relative importance of the objectives.

1.4 ITERATIVE NATURE OF THE PPM PROCESS

Although presented here as a series of phases, the PPM process is cyclical and iterative. For example, the implementation phase and the evaluation phase shown in Figure 1.2 are executed concurrently, and the arrows are shown at the bottom to indicate that any phase can result in the re-execution of any other phase, depending on the cause. That is, as external factors influence the strategic vision, mission, goals, and objectives, the PPM process can respond quickly by incorporating appropriate organizational strategic changes and effecting adjustments to the portfolio. The same concept is true for internal factors such as poorly performing projects or reduction in available resources. Iteration is important for the real time strategic, operational, and tactical information exchange throughout the portfolio management chain where performance of individual projects may result in their cancellation or other modification of the portfolio.

Although changes to strategic objectives or failure of a particular project to meet cost or schedule or anticipated benefit targets may result in immediate changes to the portfolio, it is important to avoid the organizational *thrashing* that can result from constant change while still remaining responsive to the promise of PPM. The strategic plan is normally revised once a year on a rolling basis, at which point objectives can be reprioritized and the project portfolio reevaluated against the reprioritized objectives. However, the strategic plan may change in the interim by an internal or external imperative such as an acquisition. In that case, after due diligence, the strategic plan may be revised, and the ongoing projects of the acquired and acquiring entity are evaluated in terms of the new strategy. When objectives change in a significant way, they must be reprioritized, and then the selection, or even both the screening and selection phases, must be re-executed to reprioritize the candidate projects and apply any new constraints, funding levels, and risk.

Project performance is often reported once a week and rolled up monthly into performance reports against which action can be taken, such as the termination of unproductive projects after corrective actions have failed. When a project is terminated, the opportunity for other projects to join the portfolio may be realized. Managers responsible for PPM decisions, guided by the portfolio management plan, must specify the frequency of the evaluation of portfolio additions, which may be quarterly even though project terminations may occur at any time. Deletions or additions of projects to the portfolio often require reevaluation of relative benefits, as described in Chapters 10 and 11, because they represent relative anticipated contributions to objectives. This means re-execution of some or all of the selection phase. Many organizations will be comfortable performing this process on a quarterly or semiannual basis rather than on demand. Others, especially those in highly competitive industries, may wish to perform portfolio changes on a more frequent basis.

Of course, project management and portfolio management play intersecting roles. Project managers must effectively manage their projects and take corrective actions necessary to restore project control, while portfolio management personnel must determine whether the corrective actions are sufficient to retain the benefit anticipated when the project was selected.

So, although the phases appear to be sequential, some are concurrently executed, and they are indeed iterative as well as cyclical. The frequency of the regular cycles, and the exceptions that generate more frequent execution of those cycles, are specific to the organization and its needs, as documented in the portfolio management plan that is developed by PPM personnel early in the process.

1.5 GOVERNANCE OF THE PPM PROCESS

Throughout this book, the authors emphasize a PPM process that is iterative, flexible, responsive, and adaptable to changing situations. Additionally, it has defined responsibilities and decision authority throughout the organization—from executive management to project management—and across the functional areas to support an effective PPM process. Organizational procedures must be established to facilitate successful project portfolio governance. The Association for Project Managers (APM) in the United Kingdom introduces the subject of project management governance, including portfolio management, as, "The governance of project management concerns those areas of corporate governance that are specifically related to project activities. Effective governance of project management ensures that an organization's project portfolio is aligned to the organization's objectives, is delivered efficiently and is sustainable. Governance of project management also supports the means by which the boards, and other major project stakeholders, are provided with timely, relevant, and reliable information" (APM, 2004). Implicit in this description of project and portfolio management governance is that such governance is a subset of, and should work in unison with, organizational governance.

PMI's Portfolio Management Standard (PMI, 2008) (see Chapter 4—Portfolio Governance), focuses on portfolio governance and is an excellent source of information for its implementation. Although not referenced by the PMI standard, this governance can be described in a portfolio management plan if desired. As such, the portfolio management plan should delineate how the PPM process will be managed. The portfolio management plan:

- Clarifies roles and responsibilities
- Identifies applicable organizational policy and procedures
- Establishes communication and reporting requirements
- Identifies the relationship to strategic initiatives and how the portfolio contributes to achieving them
- Describes expectations of portfolio stakeholders (executives, project managers, project team, portfolio management group, etc.)
- Sets portfolio milestones such as cycle times
- Establishes levels of authority
- Establishes portfolio performance metrics

Other topics can be added as appropriate. However, the intent is to use the portfolio management plan to set the tone, provide management guidance, and establish approaches for all phases of PPM and for all appropriate stakeholders. Establishing PPM groups with specific roles, responsibilities, and levels of authority is key to effective governance.

1.6 ORGANIZATIONAL PPM ROLES AND RESPONSIBILITIES

Organizations must develop a PPM structure that ensures interaction among stakeholders, vertically and horizontally, within the organization to effectively oversee and manage the PPM process. These stakeholders include those who make decisions about the project portfolio, have a stake in its success or failure, and provide resources to support projects within the portfolio. The structure and composition of the groups and personnel required will vary by organization, depending on the structure and size of the organization and the complexity and scale of the projects delivered within it, as illustrated in Figure 1.3 (PMI, 2008). The illustration does not show the executives who are the primary decision makers with regard to the project portfolio. They have the ultimate responsibility and authority for both the strategy and the endorsement of project portfolios and must be committed, with a direct sense of ownership for the success of the portfolio, for any PPM structure or process to succeed.

The PPM structure provides the oversight, management, and administration of the portfolio and maintains continuity, consistency, and interaction with the executive level as well as the organization's operations activities. Whatever structure is used, it is important to establish groups that will best facilitate efficient and effective PPM. A few groups are described, but the reader is encouraged to review PMI's Standard for Portfolio Management (PMI, 2008) for a more comprehensive listing. The roles and responsibilities of the groups will also vary depending on the size of the organization. As with other disciplines, communication is integral to the success of PPM by facilitating the successful execution of roles and responsibilities, especially when reporting performance information. This topic is discussed in greater detail in Chapter 10. Each organization must have roles and responsibilities appropriate to its structure and governance that fit properly with how it performs strategic planning, PPM, and project management activities, as well as how it makes other key decisions. Of course, the names of the organizational entities with portfolio management responsibilities may differ although the roles and responsibilities are essential for effective PPM.

1.7 EXECUTIVE (STRATEGIC) REVIEW BOARD

The executive review board (ERB) provides the oversight by executive- or senior-level management for the organization's portfolio management activities. Although the CEO and his direct reports

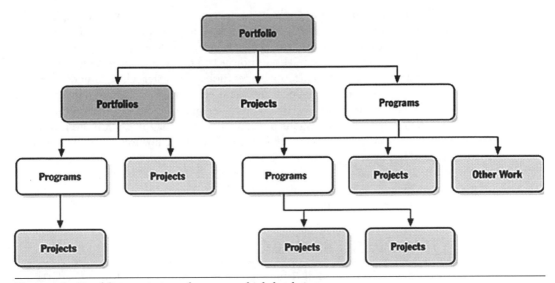

Figure 1.3 Portfolios, projects, and programs: high-level view

likely will not provide day-to-day oversight of portfolio management activities within the organization, they will delegate to a group of respected executive subordinates, while often reserving for themselves final iterative portfolio decisions. The ERB comprises selected senior managers with a direct understanding of the organization's strategic plan and who have participated in its development. In essence, they are the direct link and transition point between the executive-level and portfolio management decision makers in the organization. Accordingly, they should be empowered to provide approval authority for portfolios and projects and provide management guidance to ensure that portfolio management activities are conducted and supported in accordance with the organization's culture, or the changes to organizational culture imposed by effective PPM. In smaller organizations there may be no practical difference between the ERB and the portfolio management board (PMB), and there may be no distinction between the ERB and the C-level executives.

1.8 PORTFOLIO MANAGEMENT BOARD

The PMB is a primary player in the PPM process and is responsible for managing the portfolio selection process, supervising the portfolio process group, identifying and obtaining approval from the ERB to launch the selected portfolio, and monitoring and controlling portfolio performance. During the strategic phase, representatives from the PMB participate with the ERB in developing the strategic plan. Their participation is beneficial to the understanding of organizational strategy. The PMB drives the development of the portfolio management plan, with assistance from the portfolio process group. It also provides clear portfolio management reporting guidance to the PMO as well as to portfolio, program, and project managers responsible for executing projects within the portfolio. During screening and selection, the PMB is responsible for soliciting and consolidating projects for consideration and evaluation that results in determination of the optimal portfolio during the selection phase. During portfolio implementation, the PMB consolidates, synthesizes, and evaluates portfolio performance information and continually monitors changes to strategic objectives. During the evaluation phase, the PMB reviews and analyzes portfolio performance to determine how it conforms to or deviates from preestablished performance metrics. When performance deviates, the PMB has the primary responsibility for identifying and documenting root causes and works with the ERB and portfolio managers to enact appropriate corrective actions. The evaluation phase also provides the opportunity for the PMB to assess the impact of changes to the organization's strategic objectives on the portfolio; the PMB develops, analyzes, and recommends applicable changes.

As projects within the portfolio near completion, project and program management are responsible for their smooth transition to the organization's operations or to external customers. The PMB directs portfolio reselection when major projects are completed, or when they are eliminated, to ensure that the portfolio pipeline is appropriately full. In many organizations, this reselection is performed on a regular cycle to prevent continuous unproductive reevaluation, with more immediate action taken on an exception basis. It is expected that PMBs have a large portfolio or multiple portfolios under management. In smaller organizations, a portfolio management team might be sufficient. In any case, the PMB is responsible to the ERB for recommending optimal portfolio solutions and for obtaining and managing the necessary information to do so. Again, this is dependent on the organizational structure, resources, and culture.

1.9 PORTFOLIO PROCESS GROUP

The portfolio process group is focused on devising, developing, and implementing procedures and templates for the PPM process as well as documenting, maintaining, and administering changes to the process. This group assists in establishing ideal practices and ensuring the organization's applicable policies and procedures are incorporated into PPM governance; they assist in developing the portfolio management plan. It should be clear that this group exists to provide administrative support in establishing and enabling portfolio management that is consistent with the organization's policies, procedures, and culture. It often resides in a PPM office or is an extension of the organization's PMO.

1.10 PORTFOLIO MANAGERS AND PORTFOLIO MANAGEMENT TEAM

Portfolio managers and their supporting team are responsible for the day-to-day management of their portfolios or subsets of the organization's project portfolio and the regular interface with the project teams. The portfolio managers ensure that project teams are executing project control and reporting activities in accordance with organizational policy and procedures as well as monitoring project portfolio performance. During the strategic phase, the portfolio managers may provide key representatives to participate in ERB and PMB portfolio planning and development processes. From the portfolio perspective, the portfolio managers provide a unique perspective on how the organization might group and categorize project types to achieve balance and coverage as well as having a working perspective of the organization resources and project management capabilities. This information and experience can prove extremely useful during the early stages of portfolio selection. During PPM implementation, the portfolio managers regularly interface with the project teams to exchange information, provide administrative and management support services, and assist in resolving organizational issues affecting project teams such as resource surges and training. The portfolio managers are critical to the success of PPM by ensuring that portfolio management activities conform to organizational best practices. Additionally, they monitor and evaluate portfolio performance and then recommend and implement approved corrective action.

1.11 CONSIDERATIONS FOR IMPLEMENTING PPM

Implementing a PPM process requires commitment from the organization's leadership or senior management, a disciplined approach, and constant communication. PPM must be sponsored and championed by a senior manager and approved by the top executive. The manner in which one introduces PPM can vary and is dependent on many factors. If a senior manager recognizes the need and is the sponsor, then implementation might be easier than if the champion is a middle manager who needs to first sell it to a senior manager or leader. It is important to note that senior leaders seldom obtain their positions by luck. These individuals are primarily intelligent, hard-working, and experienced. The authors have found senior leadership to be quite receptive of ideas that are focused, organized, and presented well, especially if there is value to the organization. Nevertheless, the case must be made for how implementing a PPM process will benefit the organization.

As illustrated by Pennypacker's (2005) study of PPM maturity, documented benefits of implementing PPM include better alignment of projects to business strategy, undertaking the right projects, spending in the right areas, and PPM contribution to cost savings. As PPM acceptance has been relatively recent, most organizations have not yet achieved high PPM maturity and many are not yet using PPM software tools to manage the complex decisions that maximize the potential of PPM. According to Pennypacker (2005), of 54 organizations surveyed, over 70% had PPM processes in place for less than two years, none had a fully mature PPM process, and only 13.2% had implemented a PPM software tool. This indicates that while PPM is being adopted, there are many opportunities to more fully utilize it for maximum benefit. As organizations continue to recognize the need for PPM and increase the maturity of their PPM process, including implementing state-of-the-art software tools and techniques, they will realize greater benefits, increase their competitiveness, and improve their chances of achieving their strategic visions. The tools and techniques demonstrated in this book address the deficiencies noted by Pennypacker (2005) and support the design, development, and implementation of an effective PPM process. Another important aspect of Pennypacker's (2005) research into PPM maturity is that of the 54 organizations surveyed, 87% implemented the process themselves. This illustrates that once an organization recognizes the need for PPM most have the confidence and existing resources to implement an effective, albeit basic, PPM process that yields immediate benefits.

Implementing PPM is an organizational transformational change effort and this should be clearly understood at the outset. As with any organizational change, the task can be daunting, especially when it involves the entire enterprise. The sponsors should be cognizant of this fact beforehand and devise a methodical strategy to obtain not only approval but acceptance by the stakeholders. To explain the difficulty in implementing change, Adams (2003) states that according to ". . . Mauer, R. (1996, pg. 18) . . . a majority of organizational change efforts fail in their early stages due to insufficient buy-in." Clearly, this is not the only reason organizational change is not successful, but Adams points out how critical it is to ensure executive-level support from the beginning. Resnick (2010) notes three additional reasons to explain why success rates for organizational change are quite low. First, asking organizations to change the way they conduct their business is similar to asking individuals to change their lifestyles and it requires determination, discipline, persistence, commitment, and a clear plan for implementing the change, not to mention a clear vision. Second, resistance to change is a natural human reaction. Human beings get used to doing things a certain way; they develop habits. Deviating from the norm is quite difficult for people and results in a resistance to change. Managing that resistance is an essential part of the process. Third, change creates uncertainty. Organizations generally achieve predictable results with their existing processes. Their outcomes may not be optimal, but they are predictable. These factors must be addressed when attempting to implement a major organizational process such as PPM.

An organization not currently utilizing a PPM process must first design, develop, and implement a process that operates in unison with current processes and personnel structure. The roles and groups discussed earlier in this chapter provide initial guidance on the necessary functions by defining roles and responsibilities for the PPM process and facilitating communication and information flow. The process developers must consider how to introduce tools, such as project portfolio software, and techniques, such as AHP, to enable complex decision making into the organization's existing infrastructure.

Additionally, communication as the agent for ensuring information flow and responsiveness is essential to the PPM process. Rapid emergence of a global marketplace introduces new variables into the organizational operating environment. Whether due to reduced budgets, changing geopolitical conditions, actions by competitors, or a myriad of other factors, organizations must be able to react quickly and decisively to adjust their project portfolios to obtain maximum benefits from emerging opportunities and to minimize exposure to evolving risks. Effective and clear communication, vertically and horizontally, in the organization is critical to maintain an effective PPM system.

Harvey Levine identifies an interesting quandary for organizations not yet using PPM, but that wish to implement it. The quandary is what to do with existing projects. If an organization is considering using PPM, then it obviously has projects underway. As Levine notes, ". . . new implementers of PPM have found that a structured review and evaluation of the existing portfolio can turn up numerous instances of deficiencies in that portfolio" (Levine 2008). By evaluating existing projects, the organization can begin to understand which projects are contributing to strategic objectives and begin to restructure its portfolio as part of the PPM implementation process. Ultimately, the organization will have difficult choices to make for those projects that are not contributing as well as initially anticipated. Regardless, the organization needs to define how to handle existing projects when implementing a PPM process.

While there are many ways to accomplish obtaining support for PPM implementation, the authors suggest the development of a short (5 to 8 page) PPM implementation plan accompanied by a focused presentation (8 to 10 slides). The developers of the material should realize that they are attempting to sell upper management on an idea that they believe will benefit the organization and the burden of proof is on them. As everyone knows, senior management's time is precious. If you, as the sponsor, are not able to articulate clearly why the process is needed and how it will benefit the organization, then the chances of success are probably low. So, do your homework first and make sure you have a well thought out and clearly defined vision and roadmap for your organization that includes a timeline, cost considerations, infrastructure impacts, and an approach for implementation.

1.12 SUMMARY

As a sequential and yet iterative process, PPM provides a process to ensure linkage of projects to strategic plan objectives by developing the PPM infrastructure with a focus on selecting and completing only those projects that directly contribute to achieving the organization's strategic objectives. As a flexible, adaptable, and responsive process, PPM provides the ability to intelligently analyze factors affecting the portfolio and evaluate any changes or adjustments required to nimbly respond to business conditions. PPM thereby allows the organization to use constrained resources effectively and efficiently to maximize anticipated benefit to the organization.

Using advanced tools and techniques, PPM not only enables the selection of optimal portfolios under organizational constraints, but also supports fast and efficient contingency planning by allowing users to develop alternate scenarios based on identified risks, anticipated changes to resources levels, and emerging opportunities. In today's fast-paced global marketplace, competitive organizations, governments, and not-for-profits alike understand the importance of effective PPM in achieving strategic objectives and remaining competitive while maximizing the use of resources.

In this chapter we have introduced the PPM process and provided an overview of its elements. In Chapter 2 we establish the strategic plan as the foundation for PPM in any organization and introduce the fictitious organization upon which the examples in this book are based.

1.13 REFERENCES

Adams, John D. (2003). "Successful Change Paying Attention to the Intangibles." *OD Practitioner*, 35:4.

Association for Project Managers (2004). *A Guide to Governance of Project Management*. United Kingdom.

Cioffi, D. F. (2002). *Managing Project Integration*. Management Concepts, Virginia; from Amazon Books. Translated into Chinese, Spring 2005.

Defense Acquisition University (2010). http://www.dau.mil/default.aspx (retrieved January 23, 2010).

Fuller James N. and Jack C. Green (2005). "The Leader's Role in Strategy." *Graziado Business Report*, 8:2. http://gbr.pepperdine.edu/052/ (retrieved January 28, 2010).

Levine, Harvey A. (2005). *Project Portfolio Management: A Practical Guide to Selecting Projects, Managing Portfolios, and Maximizing Benefits*. San Francisco, CA: Jossey-Bass Business and Management Series.

Meredith, J. R. and Mantel, S. J. (2006). *Project Management—A Managerial Approach*, 6th ed. Hoboken, NJ: John Wiley & Sons.

Pennypacker, James S. (2005). *PM Solutions' Project Portfolio Management Maturity Model*, Center for Business Practices.

Project Management Institute (2008). *The Standard for Portfolio Management*, 2nd ed. ANSI/PMI 08-003-2008.

Project Management Institute (2010). http://www.pmi.org/AboutUs/Pages/FactSheet.aspx (retrieved January 22, 2010).

Resnick, Harold S. (2010). "Organizational Change Management Process A Process for Guiding Organizational Change." http://www.worksystems.com/services/organizational_change.html (retrieved February 7, 2010).

Statoil ASA (2010). http://www.statoil.com/en/About/History/Pages/default3.aspx (retrieved January 24, 2010).

2

Establishing the Foundation Through Strategic Planning

This chapter describes developing or updating the organization's strategic plan and the importance of the organization's goals and objectives to the project portfolio management (PPM) process. It addresses the first four steps of the strategic phase of PPM; the result of these steps is the strategic plan, including at minimum the vision, mission, goals, and objectives of the organization. The elements of the strategic plan are discussed. After reviewing the appropriate use of numbers and measurements in Chapter 3, the final step of the strategic phase, prioritizing objectives, is addressed in Chapter 4.

2.1 OVERVIEW OF STRATEGIC PLANNING

In Lewis Carroll's *Alice's Adventures in Wonderland*, Alice comes to a crossroads in the "Pigs and Pepper" scene and is uncertain as to which direction she should go. In a nearby tree she notices the Cheshire cat and asks the cat which way she should go. The cat responds, "That depends a good deal on where you want to get to." Alice replied that it really didn't matter. The cat replied, "Then it doesn't matter which way you go." Unlike Alice in Wonderland, an organization must have a destination in mind that leads to success and a proper roadmap to get there. In today's competitive environment an organization must take the best road that leads to continued relevance, prosperity, and success. This is the purpose of strategic planning. While strategic planning affects both the organization's operations and projects, from this point forward we discuss strategic planning only in the context of PPM, additionally, we provide an overview of strategic planning to reinforce its importance to the process.

While there are many approaches to strategic planning, we have chosen to discuss the often-used strategic planning sequence of defining or refining the organization's mission, vision, and goals followed by an assessment of the organization's ability to achieve its goals. Depending on their needs, some organizations conduct the organizational assessment before commencing other strategic planning activities. Once the goals have been identified, and once an assessment has identified gaps in the organization's ability to achieve them, we describe defining the objectives that are required to achieve each goal.

The first four steps in the strategic phase of PPM are illustrated by the outlined box in Figure 2.1:

1. Create the Mission Statement
2. Develop the Vision
3. Establish Goals
4. Determine Objectives

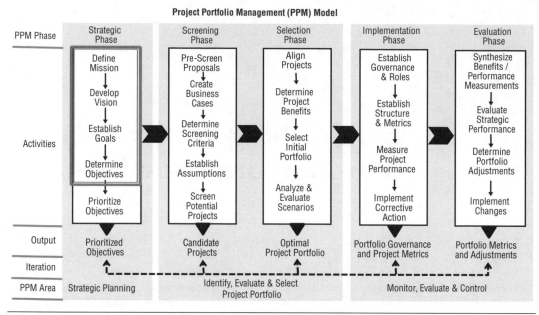

Figure 2.1   First four steps of the Strategic Phase of PPM

Mature organizations may be merely revising existing strategic plans, whereas new organizations may be conducting strategic planning for the first time. Three important points to take away from this chapter are that portfolio management personnel must:

1. Be knowledgeable about their organization's strategic planning process
2. Understand the content of the strategic plan and its relevance to the PPM process
3. View organizational strategic planning as an integral part of the PPM process

Role of Strategic Planning in the PPM Process

The foundation of the organization's PPM process is laid during the strategic phase through the development of the strategic plan that identifies the organization's destination and a roadmap to achieve desired future outcomes. A strategic plan allows an organization to (Urbanik, 2008):

- Identify its aspirations and how it will attain them to stay relevant in the marketplace
- Communicate, clarify, and align its commitments around the long- and short-term goals
- Provide consistent guidance for decision making, resource allocation, budget planning, and training

The essence of the strategic plan is to achieve an organizational state in which everyone shares a common vision for the future, understands what is required to achieve that vision, and is motivated to contribute to the organization's success. In many large organizations, strategic planning is conducted at the corporate level. Then, based on the corporate plan, each group or division in the organization's hierarchy performs its own strategic planning process, albeit at a more tactical level appropriate for the subset of the corporate goals it supports. Ideally these plans will roll up to form an integrated whole and roll down such that the goals and objectives at the lower level, and the initiatives undertaken to achieve them, all support the corporate strategy.

Those involved in PPM must play an active role as participants in the strategic planning process rather than as silent bystanders. PPM personnel can help executives better understand the organization's capability and how it can contribute to achieving the organization strategy. To be effective, portfolio and project management personnel must understand their organization's strategic planning process and know what information to provide, and when. In some organizations, executives developing the strategic plan may not fully appreciate how the portfolio and project capabilities relate to the strategic plan; the leaders in portfolio management must educate the executives in such cases.

Selection of a portfolio of projects that are best aligned with strategic objectives is contingent on a clear understanding of the organization's strategic plan and its objectives. It is also necessary to determine the anticipated contribution of candidate projects to achieve the objectives. It is easy to suggest that PPM personnel are to be involved in the organization's strategic planning process; however, the level of involvement can vary greatly depending on the organization's existing strategic planning process, its policies, and procedures. The degree to which it is willing to involve personnel throughout the organization needs to be established, including that of the PPM personnel. An effective process requires an organizational environment where information is freely exchanged and communicated both vertically and horizontally. In organizations where information is firewalled by departments, divisions, or functional areas, the PPM process can still be effective within the confines of its influence, but may be less effective on an enterprise-wide basis—as indeed may be the case with all processes, not just PPM. Far too often personnel performing projects are not sufficiently informed about why the project is being undertaken, that is, how the project is expected to contribute to strategic objectives. The managers responsible for portfolio and project management must communicate these expected contributions to those working on the projects and hold them accountable for recognizing how changes in the project scope, cost, and schedule may impact these expected contributions. A clear and concise strategic plan is the prime mechanism for defining and communicating organizational goals and objectives throughout the organization, at all hierarchical levels.

Organizational Mission and Values

In performing strategic planning, the organization considers its mission, values, vision, goals, and objectives. When assembled into a cohesive strategy, they are transformed into the organization's strategic plan that typically covers a rolling five-fiscal-year time span (e.g., 2011-2015). In Chapter 1, Figure 1.2 was presented to illustrate the concept that both operations and project activities contribute to the achievement of the vision. The illustration has been expanded to include mission and values as noted by the shaded band with "Mission & Values" surrounding the pyramid in Figure 2.2. It is intended to show that the organization's mission and values are at the core of every aspect of the organization and that they directly affect goals and objectives as well as operations and projects. The mission states why the organization exists and whom it serves, whereas values dictate how the organization will conduct itself while performing the mission. Understanding the core values of an organization is important for PPM as they serve as guiding principles for how PPM will be conducted within the organization.

2.1.1 Mission Statement—Defining Organizational Purpose

The mission states why the organization exists—its reason for being. In most cases the mission of the organization has already been explicitly defined such as with established businesses, government agencies, and military organizations. However, in other cases, including newly formed not-for-profit organizations, the mission and values may not be established, communicated, or fully understood throughout the organization. Having a clear understanding of why the organization exists, the environment in which it operates, and how it wants to conduct its activities is fundamental to effective strategic planning and increases the likelihood of developing a vision, goals, and objectives that are relevant, valid, and achievable. Even in organizations with well-established missions and

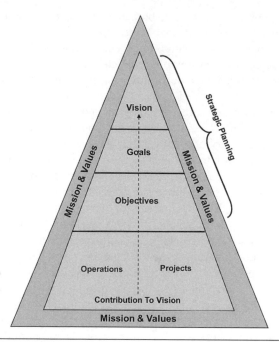

Figure 2.2   Strategic planning within mission and values

values, strategic planning provides an opportunity to reassess them in light of changes that may be required.

Why is it necessary to reassess the mission during strategic planning? There are many reasons, including mergers and acquisitions, governmental reorganizations, and changes in an organization's operating environment. In industry businesses perform mergers and acquisitions frequently; as they do, the new organization must consider the impact on future business activities—customers to be served or products to be produced. In some cases strategic alliances are formed between organizations that may impact the missions of both organizations and the portfolio of projects they undertake as part of the alliance. After the September 11th terror attacks, the U.S. federal government undertook a sizable reorganization of roles and responsibilities as well as the establishment of new agencies. In the case of the Department of Homeland Security, a new mission was created. What impact does this have on PPM? It depends. It could mean a significant change to the projects underway or it could have no impact at all. The need to answer this question is another reason to have a responsive PPM process that is mission-sensitive and closely integrated with strategic planning.

2.1.2 Establishing Values and Ethics—Defining Organizational Behavior

While the mission specifies why the organization exists and whom it serves, organizational values are the core of the organization's culture and dictate how the organization will conduct itself in performing activities, whether operations or projects. Values are the rules by which we make decisions about right and wrong, should and shouldn't, good and bad. They also tell us what values are more or less important, which is useful when we have to trade off meeting one value over another. As Harold

Kerzner (2004) states, ". . .values go beyond the normal 'standard practice' manuals and morality and ethics in dealing with customers. Ensuring that company values . . . (are) congruent is vital to the success of any project." It is important that company goals, objectives, and values be clearly understood by all members of the organization—not just by portfolio management and project teams, but every person in the organization.

While PPM is a process, it is people that make the process work; values are the principle guiding their actions as they perform their work. More specifically, values define standards that govern the actions of the organization and behaviors of individuals working in the organization. In lieu of clearly articulated values, individuals within the organization will conduct themselves in a manner that is consistent with their own values, which may be in conflict with those of the organization. This is especially true in organizations with a disparate workforce comprising personnel from various regions of the world. What might be acceptable in one part of the world may not be in another. Ultimately, well-articulated values, together with supportive measurement systems, provide the framework for encouraging norms of behavior and that support the achievement of organization's objectives, goals, and mission. It is incumbent on portfolio management personnel to ensure that portfolio activities are conducted in strict accord with the organization's values.

2.1.3 Vision Statement—Setting Long-term Direction

If Alice had been less ambivalent about her destination and had possessed the vision to know where she wanted to go, she wouldn't be stuck at a fork in the road conversing with a strange-talking Cheshire cat hanging out in a tree. On the other hand, maybe Alice was onto something. Perhaps deciding where to go isn't always that easy to determine. For organizations contemplating their vision, determining where they want to be in the future and what they want to achieve can be difficult because of uncertainty regarding the future. If we knew exactly what would happen over the next three to five years, it would be easy to develop a vision that is appropriate and achievable. Unfortunately, organizations and most senior managers have neither precognition nor psychic abilities. Instead, organizations describe where they are and state where they would like to be, or what they want to have achieved, at some point in the future. They develop this statement about the future based on known information regarding the past and present and what is assumed about the future. Sounds easy enough, right?

There's only one problem in developing the vision; we don't always know what we think we know, and, frequently, assumptions about the future turn out to be less than accurate or not as forecasted. Adding to the degree of difficulty in getting the vision right, Cohen (2002) points to internal factors such as increasing diversity, rapid technical and social change, and cynicism as challenges to overcome. As Cohen (2002) states, ". . .vision is about hope . . . there have been many colorful leaders of the past half-century whose visions have not brought the good things that they promised." So while the vision statement may appear simple, in reality a lot of work is required. Many challenges must be overcome to develop and communicate a vision that will lead to future success and that the entire organization will buy into and believe they can achieve. A classic case of a vision *gone wrong* is Motorola's Iridium concept.

With the full backing of Motorola's chairman in 1991, Motorola established the Iridium Limited Liability Corporation (Iridium LLC) as a separate company with the vision of establishing a constellation of 66 low-Earth-orbiting (LEO) satellites that would allow subscribers to make phone calls from any global location. In 1998, at a cost of $5 billion, service was launched. Unfortunately, realization of the vision of Iridium occurred at the same time as the build-out of cellular phone service. Knowing they could not compete against cellular phones, the heavier and more expensive Iridium was forced to compete where cell phones were not available. If Motorola is competing where cellular phones are not available, then they are also likely competing where there are no customers. Even when Iridium attempted to gain a cellular phone market share in urban areas, the satellite signal was lost indoors or blocked by buildings, rendering it useless. Consequently, Iridium never got off the ground and, thankfully, we aren't carrying around backpacks with our heavy satellite phones that cost a fortune and only work when we're out in the open. Of Motorola's monumental failure, Finkelstein and Sanford (2000) noted, "Iridium will go down in history as one of the most significant business failures of the 1990s. That its technology was breathtakingly elegant and innovative is without question. Indeed, Motorola and Iridium leaders showed great vision in directing the development and launch of an incredibly complex constellation of satellites. Equally amazing, however, was the manner in which these same leaders led Iridium into bankruptcy by supporting an untenable business plan." Motorola's vision for Iridium should serve as a warning to those who believe developing the vision is simple. In Motorola's case the vision was achievable, the organization was mobilized and motivated to achieve it, and it was achieved; yet the organization suffered a massive failure as a result. The vision, in this case, was based on a specific technology—the *how* rather than just the *what*—and was perhaps blind to competing technologies. Even if the vision can be achieved, it must be the right vision for the organization based on *what* is to be achieved rather than *how*. The manner in which the vision is to be achieved is part of the organizational assessment and the establishment of goals and objectives during the strategic planning.

While having a strategic vision does not automatically guarantee success, the later steps of creating goals and objectives are dependent on having something to achieve (the vision). Vision can be viewed as another tool to increase the chances of success, especially if it is clear, coherent, easily communicated, consistent, and flexible (Wilson, 2003). Flexibility might seem a strange characteristic as the vision eventually requires a defined direction supported by specific goals. However, the strategy must be flexible to accommodate uncertainty and change in the operating environment, which may require revising or redefining the vision, the anchor point for determining goals. For example, as photography became an increasingly digital-based technology, Kodak needed to refocus from the iconic Kodachrome film to digital media and cameras. In an uncertain environment, strict adherence to a static strategic plan is a prescription for disaster. Flexibility need not mean abandoning the vision, it simply recognizes the need to tune the vision continually to an ever changing business environment. As you will discover later in the chapter, or have discovered within your own organizations, the vision is the source from which all other strategic planning activity flows.

2.1.4 Setting Goals—Benchmarks for Achieving Success

Goals enable organizations to set high aspirations without actually defining the measurable objectives and initiatives that will support them. Depending on the organization and its processes, procedures, and leadership, some organizations may refer to goal setting by some other terminology such as issues and scenarios. However, as a goal-based approach is fairly common, we use the establishment of goals to describe this step of strategic planning. At this point in the strategic planning process the organization has reviewed and revised its existing vision or developed a new vision, reinforced its organizational values and ethics, and is now positioned to set goals—the next step in the process. Goals are the means to achieve the vision and are statements of the broad achievements necessary for the vision to be realized. Goals state what is to be achieved over a longer term, perhaps three to five years, while the objectives that support them define specific targets toward achievement of the goal over a shorter timeframe, perhaps one to two years.

To establish goals, the vision must be scrutinized to determine gaps between the organization's current state and where it wants to be in the future. Goals may be internal or external. For instance, an internal goal may be to improve an organizational capability or measure such as improving employee retention. An external goal, for example, may be to improve customer service. All areas of the organization are fair game for goal setting and include technology, capabilities, personnel, training, processes, projects, customers, competitors, resources, and so forth. In addition to defining new goals, organizations reevaluate previously stated goals during a strategic planning cycle, just as they reevaluate the mission and vision. The important point to consider in developing goals is to determine what is required to close the gap between the organization's current state and where it wants to be in the future. Just as a vision must be achievable and relevant to the mission, goals must also be achievable and relevant to the vision. When defining each goal, strategic planners must also determine how they will know the degree to which the goal is achieved.

Organizational Assessment

To define the gaps between an organization's current state and its vision so that goals can be derived, the organization must assess its current state. This process is also known as corporate appraisal, position audit, or assessing the present position. However, David Hussey (1998) points out "The particular terminology used is not important: the action itself is vital." The organizational assessment process can be conducted at the beginning of strategic planning, concurrently with other activities, or even after the mission, goals, and objectives have been developed, at least in preliminary form. It is not our intent to specify one approach or another for conducting the organizational assessment as that will depend on a myriad of factors. Rather, it is more important for project portfolio managers to understand the activities being performed, the reasons they are being performed, and the impact on portfolio management.

The organizational assessment begins by using a method to analyze the strengths and weaknesses of the organization. The authors describe this process using the strengths, weaknesses, opportunities, and threats (SWOT) analysis technique because it is one of the most popular and recognized methods; it is not necessarily the best method for every organization. David Hussey (1998) offers other methods, including:

- Equilibrium analysis (one way of forcing managers to make a more careful consideration of strengths and weaknesses)
- The analytical approach
- The critical success factor approach
- The core competency approach

The reader is encouraged to read Hussey's *Strategic Management: from Theory to Implementation* to gain a better understanding of these methods and how they are used.

As one would expect, organizations undertake the assessment process in a variety of ways; organizational assessment depends on many factors, including leadership, size of the organization, familiarity and experience with strategic planning, and internal processes and procedures to name a few. Nevertheless, it is typical for all organizations to employ a variety of personnel within the organization to help develop the SWOT list. One should not confuse the output of the SWOT process, a simple list of items categorized under the labels of strengths, weaknesses, opportunities and threats, as the final result. Additional analysis must be conducted to better understand the output of SWOT in terms of its meaning for the organization.

It is important to use the right people when performing SWOT analysis to ensure feedback that is useful and in context. For instance, lower-level shipping managers might assess packaging time as a weakness because it takes too long. Upper management, on the other hand, may view packaging as a strength because products are not damaged in transit, which results in a minimal replacement rate. Therefore, packaging time is less relevant to upper management. In some organizations using lower-level managers to assess opportunities and threats might be inappropriate because they lack information regarding the external business environment or the strategy in general. Lower-level managers must have a context established by higher-level management in which to perform any SWOT or other planning activities. The key point is to use those within the organization who are best positioned to provide accurate information in the right context.

Portfolio management personnel should be aware of the techniques as well as their advantages and disadvantages, and understand the types of PPM information that might be beneficial to effectively contribute to organizational assessment. Of note in this particular technique, strengths and weaknesses are internal to the organization while opportunities and threats are often, but not always, external. As the portfolio management experts within the organization, PPM personnel are in a unique position to provide valuable insight and contribute to this process. Separately from the organizational strategic planning process, portfolio managers should consider performing their own assessment of portfolio and project management to assess the capabilities and limitations of the organization's PPM process.

2.1.5 Establishing Objectives—Defining Performance Outcomes

Perform a quick review of strategic planning literature and you will find as many definitions for objectives as there are authors. Never to be outdone, the authors of this book define an objective as a specific and measurable target or initiative that supports attainment of a goal. The word *measurable* is not limited to performance targets with established quantitative parameters such as percentages and monetary or product units. In this context, measurable also includes subjective measures. In *Decision by Objectives*, Forman and Selly (2001) noted the under-appreciated value of subjective measurements when quoting Albert Einstein, "Not everything that counts can be counted and not everything that can be counted, counts." The importance of measurement in prioritizing objectives will become apparent in Chapter 4.

Objectives represent the next level of detail in the strategic plan's hierarchical structure and provide performance targets to be accomplished to meet the parent goal. Conceptually, attainment of the objectives will lead to meeting the goal that eventually and collectively leads to achieving the vision. While there is no prescribed number of objectives required for each goal, it's not uncommon to establish approximately five objectives for a single goal; perhaps more if needed. While the strategic plan often covers a rolling-wave five-year period, objectives are normally specified for completion over a one- to two-year period and can be updated during periodic review of the strategic plan. The methods for establishing objectives are many, but a common technique used to define objectives precisely is the SMART technique:

- Specific
- Measureable
- Attainable (or achievable)
- Relevant (or realistic)
- Time-Bound

Each objective should be specific and easy to understand. This reduces ambiguities and increases common understanding. Ideally, being specific would result in a number such as 200 versus the less specific *a lot* that can be interpreted differently. In other words, objectives should be measurable. Some would argue that if an objective is not quantifiable it is wrong, but Albert Einstein would disagree as has been noted. As we mentioned previously, subjective measures can be as effective as quantitative measures if using the appropriate technique and obtaining measurements from the right people. We discuss this further in Chapters 3 and 4. Objectives must be achievable; unattainable objectives can be demoralizing because those responsible will expect failure from the start if they believe that the objective cannot be achieved, at least not in the target timeframe. Would *increasing revenue 25% year-over-year* for a multi-billion dollar corporation be realistic or achievable? No, not in difficult economic conditions or when the organization has reached maturity (is not a start-up). Objectives need to be relevant by directly supporting the goal in a meaningful way. Finally, objectives must have a target timeframe. For a strategic plan covering a specific period, such as five years, one objective might specify an annual performance target, for example, revenue for the next fiscal year. Another may span the life of the five-year strategic plan, perhaps the net present value of the profits for the next five years. In general, and as mentioned previously, goals are typically longer-term (three to five years), while the objectives supporting the goal usually define shorter-term performance targets (one to two years) to achieve the goals. Although the manner or method used by the organization to derive objectives may differ, portfolio managers must clearly understand the objectives as well as how they contribute to meeting the goals. This is because project portfolios are selected as the combination of projects that best support the objectives, and, through them, the goals.

2.1.6 Strategic Plan—Charting the Course

At the beginning of the chapter, the strategic phase of PPM was shown to be comprised of five steps. The first four steps produce the strategic plan. To be effective, it must not only have been carefully prepared, it needs to be communicated throughout the organization. While the organization wants to develop the right strategic plan to ensure future success, the plan needs to be constructed in a way that can be communicated effectively and interpreted uniformly throughout the organization, especially if the organization is distributed across many geographies and cultures. The strategic plan must contain a focused message to prevent any ambiguities or misunderstandings. Before we move to Chapters 3 and 4 and begin discussing the process of measuring and prioritizing objectives, we provide a few examples to illustrate the extreme differences by which organizations construct their strategic plans.

Environmental Protection Agency Strategic Plan Approach

The reality is that not all strategic plans are created equal. Some organizations believe it necessary to develop lengthy and detailed strategic plans. An example of a strategic plan that is less than effective, in the authors' view, is one developed by the Environmental Protection Agency (EPA) in 2003. While beautifully packaged and visually attractive, the EPA's 2003-2008 strategic plan (EPA, 2003) contains ambiguous and contradictory statements, lacks a cohesive and focused message, is verbose, and is not conducive to communicating a clear message throughout the organization. A short passage from the introductory section of this plan confuses the reader about what the agency's leadership wants to accomplish. "EPA leaders believe that taking this broader approach of establishing five goals focused on environmental results and streamlining EPA's planning and budgeting structure will facilitate the Agency's ability to promote multimedia, cross-program approaches to solving environmental problems. . . . Establishing goals that are less rigorously aligned with Agency programs or organizational units will provide greater flexibility. . .[1]" (EPA, 2003). Although subject to interpretation, suggesting that goals should not be rigorously aligned with programs, or perhaps programs with goals, seems counter to the aims and benefits of PPM. The plan then stretches on for 239 pages, which appears to be inordinately long for effective communication.

Ian Wilson (2003), former employee of General Electric (GE) and author of *The Subtle Art of Strategy*, relays his thoughts on strategic plans. "The principal mistake that many strategic plans make is overkill, that is, including in their analyses and conclusions just about everything that could be said about the business, its markets and competition, and then overlaying that with endless pages of financial projections (the dollar sign being taken as evidence of certainty!). In the process any vestige of strategic thinking that may have been present is lost in this traditional labyrinth of corporate planning. I had occasion to allude to this failing a number of years ago when I was lecturing at my corporate alma mater, GE's Management Development Institute in Crotonville, New York; at the end of my presentation I was asked what I *really* thought, now that I had left the company, of GE's vaunted strategic planning system. After detailing my criticism of what I felt was overly bureaucratic and burdensome documentation that cloaked rather than highlighted any vestige of strategic thinking, I concluded that, in my opinion, 'A truly strategic (as opposed to operational) plan can be presented in some twenty or so pages.'" In this same speech, Wilson described an unexpected encounter with then CEO of GE Jack Welch who had slipped into the back of the room, "At this point a voice came from the back of the class saying, 'I would say, rather, a half dozen pages—followed by three hours of discussion!' The voice was that of Jack Welch, who had just arrived to give his version of a commencement address to this class." This is not to suggest that a strategic plan must be of a prescribed page length or cannot be broad in its approach, but it must convey a clear vision and path forward for members of the entire organization to understand. In our opinion, clearly communicating the contents of 239 pages across a large organization such as the EPA is difficult.

The EPA's plan was certainly lengthy and perhaps unclear about aligning objectives. Resources are valuable and limited, even for the EPA, and the approach specified by the strategic plan implies projects will be selected at random or with some ill-conceived ad hoc process. As PMI (2008) notes, "If a portfolio's components are not aligned to its organizational strategy, the organization can reasonably question why the work is being undertaken. Therefore, a portfolio is a true measure of the organization's intent, direction, and progress."

PPM is effective when project portfolios are selected that specifically align to the objectives of the organizations and can adapt to unexpected changes and circumstances. As you can see, when the strategic planning process is flawed, the negative effects ripple through PPM.

Siemens AG Strategic Plan Approach

Siemens, a global electronics and electrical engineering company operating in the industry, healthcare, and energy sectors, managed to effectively and clearly lay out its Fit4 2010 strategy in 11 PowerPoint slides (Siemens, 2009). Even Jack Welch would appreciate the efficiency and effectiveness of this approach. As a short and concise presentation, this brief can be e-mailed to every employee in the company, placed on the bulletin board in break rooms, and used as part of new employee training. As a global company employing over 405,000 employees in nearly 100 countries, the ability to present the corporate strategy in a clear and concise manner to unify the focus of effort of the organization is a major advantage. Equally impressive is the manner in which Siemens structured the information to relate the story to its employees and other stakeholders.

In Figure 2.3, Siemens opened its presentation by showing how the company progressed from past strategies to Fit4 2010 and how they are building toward the future. The reader will notice the major changes from the previous strategy to Fit4 2010 that include new organizational values, ambitious target margins, and updated portfolio priorities. This simple graphic tells the strategic story of where the company came from, where it is today, and where it intends to go from a top-level view.

While Figure 2.3 illustrates the path from past to present, Siemens then provides Fit4 2010 strategic guidance in Figure 2.4 in four areas: (1) people excellence, (2) operational excellence, (3) corporate responsibility and (4) portfolio with performance targets stated inside the Siemens' bull's-eye. Notice Siemens' leadership is providing high-level guidance that specifies where the organization should focus its efforts and what the organization wants to achieve through the establishment of performance targets. It does not tell the organization how to do it. Regardless of whether an employee is in production, human resources, project management, or some other area of the company, this graphic relays the principles of the strategy and what the strategy is aiming to accomplish.

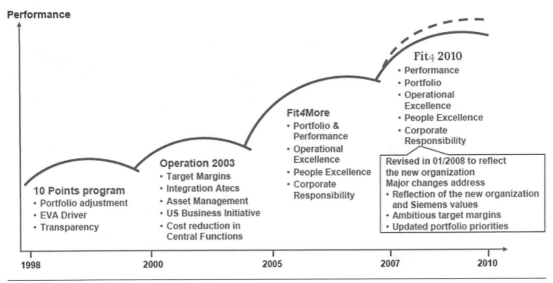

Figure 2.3   Siemens strategic programs from Siemens Fit4 2010 strategy slide presentation

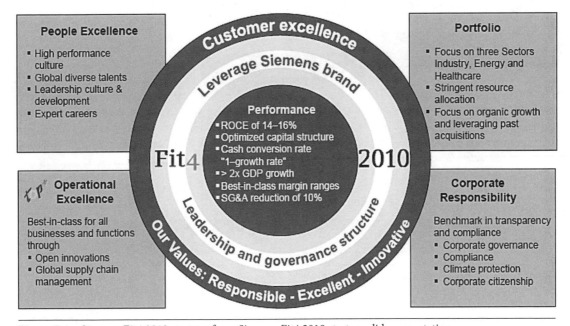

Figure 2.4   Siemens Fit4 2010 strategy from Siemens Fit4 2010 strategy slide presentation

As we discussed earlier, performance objectives that are measureable are preferred. Siemens has established precise performance targets, and, although not shown in Figure 2.5, these targets were further separated in an additional slide by business sector: industry, healthcare, and energy. On closer examination of the metrics, Siemens has established *ranges* for most performance targets rather than specific point estimates targets.

In Figure 2.6 Siemens provides guidance by specifying what is important to the organization in capital allocation—organic growth, streamlining to the company's core businesses, and being

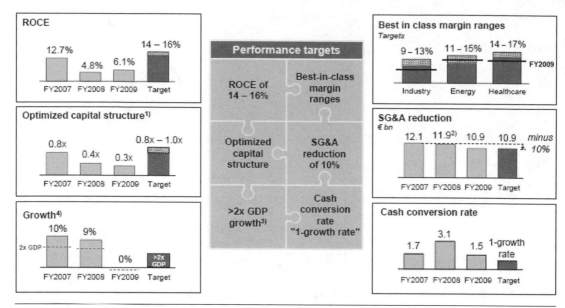

Figure 2.5   Siemens Fit4 2010 performance targets from Siemens Fit4 2010 strategy slide presentation

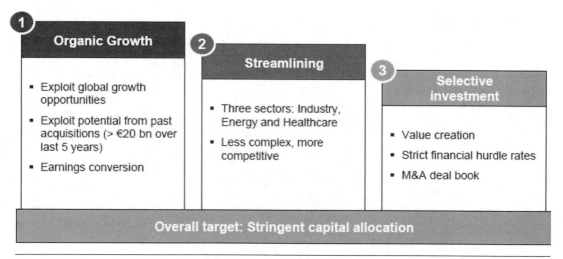

Figure 2.6   Siemens Fit4 2010 priorities from Siemens Fit4 2010 strategy slide presentation

selective in investment. This information supplies subordinate divisions and departments with adequate guidance to derive their own priorities while recognizing that each business segment may have a differing level of importance (e.g., the healthcare segment may conclude organic growth is slightly more important than the energy segment).

From the corporate perspective, organic growth is most important followed by streamlining and selective investment. This is in stark contrast to the EPA's approach and a step above many other strategic plans that typically imply all goals and objectives are equally important. This information is invaluable for the organization when making portfolio trade-offs.

In the Siemens strategic plan approach, the message was articulated at a high level in a clear and concise manner in order to focus the efforts of a globally distributed organization employing nearly

500,000 people. From this clearly delivered message, major business units within Siemens had sufficient guidance to begin crafting their plans and taking action necessary to achieve the Fit4 2010 strategy. Having completed the Fit4 2010 program in fiscal 2010, in fiscal 2011 Siemens replaced Fit4 2010 with a new vision and strategy called One Siemens. The EPA and Siemens examples illustrate two totally different approaches for strategic plans and methods for communicating those plans to their organizations.

2.1.7 Strategic Planning and Project Portfolio Management

The output of the organization's strategic planning efforts, and that of the first four steps in the PPM strategic phase, is a strategic plan that clearly articulates the organization's mission, vision, goals, and objectives. Preferably project portfolio managers have been afforded the opportunity to participate in this process. While the differences in styles and approaches for developing and communicating the organization's strategic plan are many, project portfolio managers must understand the strategic plan and apply its intent to the PPM process by ensuring that the projects selected will best support the achievement of organizational goals and objectives. Ultimately the purpose of the organization's PPM capability is to contribute to the organization's success. That's not possible if the strategic plan, vision, goals, and objectives are not clearly understood by those who help to select and manage the portfolios.

Although the strategic planning process is performed by the organization's executive-level management, portfolio management needs the results of strategic planning as an integral input to the PPM process. The better that those driving portfolio management understand the organization's strategic planning process and the goals and objectives defined by it, the better equipped they are to design, develop, and implement a flexible and responsive PPM process, that is, one that can select the optimal portfolio and react quickly to future strategic changes. As more organizations embrace PPM, more involvement will be sought from those who can perform it.

2.1.8 Completing the Strategic Phase

Armed with a freshly approved strategic plan, the process of transitioning from the strategic phase to the screening phase can begin. The form and function of this transition will vary by organization. This process requires considerable coordination and interaction by PPM with senior executives as well as with the organization's operations to determine the combination of projects that will best contribute to achieving the objectives. After developing the strategic plan, many organizations do not then take a formal step to prioritize the defined objectives. Specifying the relative importance of the objectives with respect to the goal is a prerequisite for effective portfolio selection; we have elected to identify it as a fifth major step in strategic planning. Those who participate in evaluating the relative priorities of the objectives are generally the same people who played key roles in the development of the strategic plan. Part of determining the anticipated contribution of a project that is a candidate for portfolio selection is the relative importance (in terms of achieving the goal) of the objectives that it supports. Thus, before the relative anticipated contribution of a project can be determined, the objectives hierarchy must be prioritized.

In Chapter 4 we discuss the process of prioritizing objectives using PPM tools and techniques in preparation for transitioning to the screening phase of the PPM process. Prioritizing objectives provides valuable insight to the organization when trade-offs such as allocation of constrained resources have to be made. The authors have deliberately included this step, because the objectives are not equally important. It is more likely that some objectives will contribute more to accomplishing the goal than others. After prioritizing objectives, the portfolio management process can progress to screening and selecting the combination of projects that maximizes benefit to the organization.

From this point forward in the book, the organization's portfolio management team or group, as stewards of the PPM process, guide the portfolio management process; the ultimate portfolio decisions and approval are the responsibility of executive management, but managing the process is the responsibility of these PPM stewards.

As we discussed earlier in this chapter, typically multiple goals are defined in the strategic plan, each supported by multiple objectives. We have chosen to use only one of the goals from the fictitious organization's (American Business University) strategic plan to illustrate the concept without overly complicating the material. The same process described in the remainder of this book can be expanded to include all of the organization's goals and their objectives, or to perform multiple levels of portfolio selection and management. Like the process, the tools and techniques used are also suited to support as many goals and objectives as identified in the strategic plan and can be used to support as many levels of strategic plans and portfolios as required by the organization.

To demonstrate the concepts of portfolio candidate identification, selection, implementation, and evaluation using PPM tools and techniques, we use a fictitious organization, the American Business University (ABU), based on a real academic institution's strategic plan. An introduction to ABU and its strategic plan is provided. This information sets the stage for prioritizing objectives in Chapter 4.

2.2 AMERICAN BUSINESS UNIVERSITY BACKGROUND & STRATEGIC PLAN

Founded in 1928, the ABU has become one of the leading business schools in North America. With its academic success, and the subsequent rise in academic prestige, ABU has experienced an 8% increase in year-to-year applications. However, its outdated campus infrastructure and facilities are not adequate to support these enrollment increases and thus threaten the university's ability to continue to deliver the necessary degree of academic quality. As a result, the university's Board of Trustees has authorized the development of the ABU Campus Revitalization Program. Approved in 2010, this plan intends to revitalize the university's campus infrastructure and facilities to meet its mission, vision, and strategic objectives. The plan will be governed by the university Board of Trustees and executed under the guidance of the University Facilities team.

2.2.1 ABU Mission

The mission of ABU is to educate leaders who will shape the practice of business across the country and around the world, teaching them how to put into action both the knowledge and the analytical skills that they receive.

The mission of the University Facilities team is to plan, build, operate, and maintain the physical infrastructure of the university to provide students, faculty, staff, and guests with a safe, clean, and secure environment in which to live, work, learn, and succeed.

The purpose of the Campus Revitalization Program is to modernize and revitalize the educational, residential, athletic, and recreational infrastructure in a manner that best supports ABU's mission, goals, and objectives.

2.2.2 ABU Vision

The vision of ABU is to become the leading business school by 2016 by "attracting and retaining faculty with a passion for teaching, experience in working with organizations worldwide, and the insights gained from their research . . ." (Harvard Business School, 2008); by increasing student applications by 20% per year while growing the student population by 10%, thus becoming increasingly selective; and by providing the best facilities for living, working, and learning on campus.

The vision of the Campus Revitalization Program is to deliver the optimal infrastructure and facilities during the next five years to support the vision of ABU.

2.2.3 ABU Goal

At ABU, research, teaching, learning, and campus-community interaction occur with synergy and integration. This environment fosters innovation, critical thought, academic exploration, and creativity. ABU serves the nation and the world by advancing education across a range of business disciplines.

Heretofore, we have discussed the mission and vision of the university and the mission and vision of the Campus Revitalization Program separately. Henceforth, our discussion is confined to the Campus Revitalization Program that draws its goals and objectives from a single ABU strategic plan goal that was refined during the strategic planning session conducted by the president and academic officers and approved by the Board of Trustees. That goal is:

> *Campus facilities and surroundings will contribute to shared learning, collaborative research, and a sense of community by providing an environment that is conducive to dynamic interchange and that enhances the quality of life on campus.*

2.2.4 ABU Objectives

The facilities objectives are divided into the following five major areas of focus or categories:

1. Academic Land Use and Facilities
2. Services and Administration Facilities
3. Intercollegiate Athletics Facilities
4. Recreation Services Facilities
5. Residential and Conference Facilities

The objectives and sub-objectives for each of these are described in some detail. They will become the basis for an Analytic Hierarchy Process (AHP) decision model to support the selection and management of the portfolio of facilities projects nominated or underway as part of the Campus Revitalization Program.

ABU Objectives and Sub-objectives:

1. Academic Land Use and Facilities objectives and sub-objectives

   Meet the academic needs identified in the space needs analysis conducted by University Facilities under the updated guidelines of the State Commission on Higher Education.
   a. Provide high quality facilities to meet institutional needs by renovating or replacing obsolete facilities
   b. Use technology to improve learning, teaching, and research
      i. Facilitate interactive, participative, and project-based learning
      ii. Provide distance learning technology capability
   c. Accommodate a projected enrollment growth of 10% per year through academic year 2013-2014 for both undergraduate and graduate populations
   d. Address needs of nontraditional and community audiences
      i. Enhance evening class facilities
      ii. Provide concert, presentation, and conference facilities
   e. Use campus buildings for continuing and distance education

2. Services and Administration Facilities objectives and sub-objectives

   Restructure existing delivery system facilities to meet current and future demands for convenient and efficient service.
   a. Improve existing and add new facilities for administrative and student services staff
      i. Centralize front-office *high touch* student transaction services such as registration and financial aid
      ii. Relocate back-office administrative services to perimeter locations
   b. Provide food, health, and other student and employee services efficiently and in a customer-oriented manner
   c. Improve services, transportation, and communication systems linking various parts of the campus

3. Intercollegiate Athletics Facilities objectives and sub-objectives

   Help student-athletes succeed in both venues and advance the institution's winning spirit and drive.
   a. Improve facilities for intercollegiate competition to be comparable to others in the prestigious Big Kahuna conference
   b. Enable compliance with federal Title IX requirements by ensuring facilities for women's sports teams
   c. Improve athletic support facilities (restrooms, concessions, media support facilities, and food service areas) and ingress-egress in the stadium complex

4. Recreation Facilities objectives and sub-objectives

   Help students, faculty, and others achieve a healthy mind/body balance by providing quality recreation programs and facilities.
   a. Upgrade existing outdoor facilities to accommodate increased demand
   b. Improve student support facilities and recreation center

5. Residential and Conference Facilities objectives and sub-objectives

   Create a living and learning environment outside of the classroom and provide affordable housing for students.
   a. Provide student, staff, and faculty housing and related facilities to meet the diverse needs of single and family populations
      i. Provide affordable student housing for at least the current percentage of students (30%) living on campus as enrollment grows
      ii. Provide residence facility lounges, meeting spaces, and wireless high speed network access
      iii. Modernize dining service facilities
         1. Meet dining service capacity goals
         2. Support a community experience in the dining facilities
      iv. Provide family housing with childcare facilities
   b. Provide conference, lodging, and specialized dining facilities
      i. Establish sufficient conference facilities to accommodate meeting, lodging, and dining facilities for year-round conferences
      ii. Provide seasonal conference facilities with sufficient lodging and dining

2.3 SUMMARY

In this chapter we have:

- Described the process and the outputs of strategic planning
- Described strategic plans
- Discussed the role of project portfolio managers as stewards of the PPM process who must understand the strategic plan
- Expressed what remains in the strategic phase of PPM
- Introduced the portion of the ABU strategic plan that will be used in the examples in future chapters.

As more organizations move toward a collaborative environment in conducting their strategic planning, active participation by PPP stewards will enhance not only the substance and quality of the strategic plan, but also provide a better understanding of what the organization is trying to achieve to those responsible for its success.

Before we proceed to the final step in the PPM strategic phase—prioritizing the objectives established during strategic planning—it is necessary to review certain concepts that are crucial to understanding how to measure and how to interpret the measurements. Many organizations inadvertently rely on meaningless numbers to make all kinds of critical decisions, including the selection of their project portfolios. In Chapter 3 we address making complex decisions and how to get results that are mathematically and intuitively sound, and we also introduce the widely used AHP and supporting tools. The material in Chapter 3 provides prerequisite knowledge for future chapters for those unfamiliar with structuring and evaluating complex decisions using AHP.

2.4 REFERENCES

Cohen, Allan R. (2002). *The Portable MBA in Management*, 2nd ed. Hoboken, NJ. John Wiley & Sons.

Environmental Protection Agency (2003). "2003-2008 EPA Strategic Plan: Direction for the Future." http://www.epa.gov/ocfo/plan/2003sp.pdf (retrieved February 7, 2010).

Finkelstein, S. and S. H. Sanford (2000). "Learning from Corporate Mistakes: The Rise and Fall of Iridium." *Organizational Dynamics*, 29:2, 138-148.

Harvard Business School Mission (2008).

http://www.hbs.edu/about/ (retrieved October 5, 2008).

Hussey, David (1998). *Strategic Management: From Theory to Implementation*, 4th ed. Oxford, UK: Butterworth-Heinemann.

Kerzner, Harold (2004). *Advanced Project Management—Best Practices on Implementation*, 2nd ed. Hoboken, NJ: John Wiley & Sons.

Project Management Institute (2008). *The Standard for Portfolio Management*, 2nd ed. ANSI/PMI 08-003-2008.

Siemens AG (2010). http://www.siemens.com/about/en/index/strategy.htm (retrieved February 10, 2010).

Urbanick, Janice (2008). "Strategic Planning Essentials for Construction and Design Firms." http://www.nawic.org/images/nawic/stratplanningess.pdf (retrieved February 10, 2010).

Wilson, Ian (2003) *The Subtle Art of Strategy: Organizational Planning in Uncertain Times* Westport, CT: Greenwood Press. (Reproduced with permission of ABC-CLIO, Santa Barbara, CA.)

3

Introduction to Ratio-scale Measurements and the Analytic Hierarchy Process

Some of the most important, and most complex, decisions made by organizations are those that determine which projects will be executed to maximize return to the organization. The ability to structure decisions, measure options, and synthesize the measurements to derive priorities is critical to implementing and maintaining an effective PPM process and in selecting optimal portfolios. These capabilities must be embedded in the tools and techniques used. How choices are made can be the difference between good decisions and bad ones. Understanding how to measure, and how to interpret the measurement, are crucial skills in making good decisions. Therefore, just before embarking on the project portfolio decision journey, we examine some common decision practices in use today and plot a smoother course through the rocky shoals of such decisions.

In many cases, when making choices among alternatives, individuals and groups assign weights and scores with absolute numbers; for example, when scoring vacation spots from lowest to highest (1 to 5) you might give a Mediterranean destination 5 and a Caribbean destination 4. How are these absolute numbers different from 4.3 versus 4.8? Suppose you live in Toronto and have five vacation spots in the United States in mind. You decide to rank them from first to last choice based on desired average temperature for the month you intend to take your vacation. After looking up the mean temperatures, you might rank these destinations (1) Orlando, (2) Los Angeles, (3) Denver, (4) San Francisco, and (5) Anchorage. These rankings tell you the order in which you would choose these locations based on temperature, but they do not reflect how much better Orlando is than Los Angeles. What if you have other objectives beside warmest mean temperature in July? Now the decision becomes more complicated. You could have another objective of access to nature to view many species of wildlife. The objective of seeing wildlife in its natural setting would likely result in ranking the cities (1) Anchorage, (2) Denver, (3) San Francisco, (4) Los Angeles, and (5) Orlando, unless you only want to see alligators. Table 3.1 shows a typical approach taken by some groups and many businesses to make a decision in a case like this.

As you can see, after averaging the rankings for the two objectives, Denver would be the selected destination and all other destinations, except San Francisco, would be considered equally acceptable for second place. Denver ranked in the middle for both objectives, not first in anything. As will be seen later, performing arithmetic operations on ordinal numbers yields meaningless results. The rankings are ordinal numbers and indicate just that, order. If graduate students line up for caps and

Table 3.1 Vacation destination selection based on average ranking

Destination	Warmest High Temperature	Access to Wildlife	Average Rank	Resulting Average Choice
Orlando	1	5	3.0	2
Los Angeles	2	4	3.0	2
Denver	3	2	2.5	1
San Francisco	4	3	3.5	5
Anchorage	5	1	3.0	2

gowns, how much more important (or smarter) is the first student in line than the tenth? Yet many organizations insist on averaging or adding rankings on multiple factors to make important business choices. In addition, we have not distinguished how much more important average high temperature might be than access to wildlife. Even if access to wildlife were twice as important as temperature, applying weights to ordinal scores also yields meaningless or invalid results.

Most business decisions involve multiple objectives, making the assignment of weights and scores difficult, arbitrary, and with no sound basis for differentiation. In addition, these assessments may involve different orders of magnitude, that is, how does one really compare the relative importance of an alternative with a weight of 0.06 to another with a weight of 60.00. Can human intelligence really differentiate items by thousandths and be consistent about these differentiations? For human beings to make complex decisions, as we discover, the complexity must be reduced by grouping the objectives and by breaking the groups into sub-groups; in other words, creating a hierarchy. Just as the deliverables of a project are decomposed into a deliverable work breakdown structure, complex decisions must be addressed by breaking them into manageable portions defined in a hierarchy. In addition, within the hierarchy, decision makers need a way to assign priorities to objectives that are mathematically meaningful when compared to other objectives at the same level so that we know, for example, that the wildlife objective is, perhaps, 2.5 times as important as the warm temperature objective; these are called ratio-scale priorities.

Many businesses, academia, government agencies, and not-for-profits expend days if not weeks of executive and management time developing strategic plans for their organizations and defining goals and objectives by which to achieve those strategies. These goals and objectives may be numerous and are often competing. This chapter discusses current decision making techniques and their shortcomings and introduces a rational approach for structuring and measuring such decisions—the analytic hierarchy process (AHP). It provides the means and the mathematics for decisions to be hierarchically structured, and for ratio-scale priorities to be derived to support meaningful decisions under conditions of complexity. For now, let's take a look at some commonly used decision making approaches.

3.1 DECISION MAKING WITH B.O.G.S.A.T.

A common method for making complex decisions is called BOGSAT, an acronym for a *Bunch of Old Guys/Gals Sitting Around Talking* that Encarta defines as "decision making by committee: the management practice of using often inexperienced committee members to make the most important decisions" (Encarta, 2009). Even experienced senior management has been known to use BOGSAT in the absence of any alternative approaches, often resulting in unproductive, tension-producing, lengthy meetings with outcomes sometimes based on the undue influence of the leader or hurried by the clock that is approaching the lunch hour or the end of the business day. BOGSAT decisions are hampered not only by fruitless discussion, but also by poor measurement techniques and poor collaboration practices.

A major reason for the failure of BOGSAT as a decision making technique is that, as psychologists have found, the human brain is limited in both its capacity to discriminate among only seven things, plus or minus two, and its ability to remember for the short term only seven things, plus or minus two (Miller, 1994). In other words, we can remember about seven numbers in the order read to us and can discriminate or make judgments about, for example, seven musical tones, with each sound associated with a letter or number. Most business decisions can involve dozens of elements such as ". . . issues, pros, cons, objectives, criteria . . ." (Forman, 2001, p. 6). If these complex decisions can be broken down into simpler parts and restructured in the form of hierarchies, each level of which has no more than seven—plus or minus two—elements, a more feasible and rational decision process can be used. So, we can use hierarchies to break down complex decisions into manageable pieces.

3.2 THE IMPORTANCE OF HIERARCHIES IN COMPLEX PROBLEMS

Herbert Simon recognized that large organizations are structurally hierarchical; they create units that are divided into smaller and smaller units. He noted that hierarchical subdivision occurs in all complex systems, and it is how humans with limited cognitive powers can address complexity (Simon, 1960). Lancelot Whyte declared that hierarchies are ". . . the most powerful method of classification used by the human brain-mind in ordering experience, observations, entities and information" (Whyte, 1969). As described later, AHP provides us with a method to structure major decisions into hierarchies of objectives and alternatives and compare them to arrive at any complex decision, including the selection of an optimal project portfolio for an organization.

3.3 COMPARISON OF WAYS TO USE NUMBERS

Now that the need to decompose complex decision factors into hierarchies is understood, let's consider another important aspect of decision making—the use of numerical identifiers or scores to compare alternatives. As Darrell Huff pointed out, statistics don't lie, people do (Huff, 1993). Even if there is no intent to misuse numbers, numerical representations are not always what they seem and may be used, accidentally or purposely, to give credence to nonsense. We discuss briefly the four ways that numbers are used as levels of measurement and select one of the four as the basis for comparing the importance of objectives and alternatives for complex decision making and, specifically, for selecting project portfolios. As identified in social science research (Sable, 1999; Trochim, 2006), the four numerical scales of measurement are nominal, ordinal, interval, and ratio. Each scale retains the properties of all the prior scales while adding some unique properties.

3.3.1 Nominal Scale

The nominal scale uses numbers in name only, thus the term *nominal*. Nominal numbers are used for identification such as Region 1 as the Western Region, Region 2 as the Southern Region, and so on. Student identification numbers and zip codes are other types of nominal numbers. Performing any mathematical operations on nominal scale numbers such as adding zip codes or region numbers produces nonsense.

3.3.2 Ordinal Scale

The ordinal scale retains the properties of the nominal scale and adds the property of ranking; the numbers indicate the order of the evaluation, whether increasing or decreasing. For example, a group of 10 employees can be ranked from 1 to 10 to indicate their perceived performance or value to the organization. However, this does not mean that the difference between the performance of the top- and second-ranked employee is the same as the difference between the eight- and ninth-ranked employee. In other words, these numbers assign rank order and can be used to sort data, but they say nothing meaningful about the size of the intervals between them. Performing mathematical operations on ordinal numbers also results in nonsense, or, at least, misleading information. However, think of the surveys you've seen that rank cities or vacation destinations on ten features, for example, and then average or add the rankings as described. The results are enthusiastically accepted because they are numeric. However, they are mathematically meaningless.

3.3.3 Interval Scale

The interval scale retains the properties of the ordinal scale and adds the property that the intervals between numbers are meaningful. For example, the difference between 10 and 20°F is the same as the difference between 70 and 80°F. So, computing an average temperature for a location is meaningful. However, this does not mean that 80° is four times as hot as 20°, even though the number 80 is four times as large as the number 20. Averages make sense for interval scale numbers, for example, the average daily temperature in Los Angeles on March 1 might be 55°F because the average low on that date is 40°F and the average high is 70°F; however, ratios with interval numbers are meaningless. Arithmetic operations such as addition and subtraction, or multiplication and division, require at least interval scale meaning. Interval level numbers can be multiplied by constants or by a ratio level number, but not by another interval level number (Forman, 2001).

3.3.4 Ratio Scale

The ratio scale retains the properties of the interval scale and adds the property that ratios are meaningful, for example, twice as many customers bought Pepsi as Coca Cola, and zero customers bought Dr. Pepper. Ratio scales have a fixed zero point. Numbers or units on the scale are equal over all levels of the scale. Time is a good example of a ratio scale because the difference between 3 hours and 6 hours is the same as the difference between 9 hours and 12 hours (an interval scale), and 6 hours is twice as long as 3 hours (a ratio scale). In addition, 12 hours is twice as long as 6 hours and thus four times as long as 3 hours. No restrictions are placed on the use of mathematical operations on ratio level numbers. Because of this, decision methods based on ratio scale numbers are mathematically sound as well as the most flexible and accurate (Forman, 2001). The ratios can be absolute, as in the example just given of 6 hours being twice as long as 3 hours. They can also be relative, as in comparing the size of one rectangle to another in terms of area, as shown in Figure 3.1.

Box A, with a width of 3 units and a height of 3 units has an area of 9 square units, while Box B, with a width of 6 units and a height of 3 units has an area of 18 square units. So, Box B is twice as big, in relative terms, as Box A. Even if the absolute measurements are not known, relative measurement can be as accurate as, or more accurate than, absolute measurement. If the absolute height and width or other absolute measurements are not provided, people can produce accurate relative comparisons of size readily, as demonstrated by the estimates of the relative areas of five geometric shapes.

Figure 3.1   Absolute and relative size ratios

In an experiment performed by a group of 15 business graduate students at the George Washington University in 2008, and repeated many times by other groups in other settings, students were asked to allocate $100.00, representing the relative size of five illustrated shapes, including a circle, a triangle, a square, a diamond, and a rectangle. The estimates were performed using comparisons of each object to the other objects by asking, for example, Circle A is _____ times larger than Triangle B, and so on, until Circle A had been compared to each of the other four objects. The process was repeated by comparing Triangle B to each of the other four objects, then Square C to each, and so on until each object had been compared in relative size to each of the other four. Comparing an object to one other object at a time is known as a *pairwise comparison*, and the entire process is known as performing pairwise comparisons. When the individual dollar amounts estimated by the group were averaged, the results were accurate to two decimal places and within one percent of the actual relative sizes of the five objects (Forman, 2008). Further, the group result was more accurate than the estimates of any individual in the group—which is nearly always the case—indicating that multiple qualified evaluators can make more accurate decisions than individuals.

With relative measurement, it is possible to determine preferences without the need for absolute measurements such as the known sizes of the boxes. AHP uses and produces ratio-scale numbers that represent the relative importance of objectives and alternatives to the achievement of the objectives. This means that qualitative measurements can be made and applied in decision making along with quantitative measurements to indicate the relative importance of objectives and alternatives.

We have already stated that BOGSAT, although *well* practiced in terms of frequency, is not a *good* practice for making complex decisions because of the cognitive limitations of the human brain. Forman (2001) cited Max Bazerman (1986) on the economist's model of rationality that assumes that decision makers follow a specific set of logical steps that require a perfectly defined problem and knowledge of all relevant information and criteria. Since humans have cognitive limitations that prevent such perfect, unaided ability to find the optimal solution, they will settle for what is sufficient or good enough, which Herbert Simon called *satisficing* (Simon, 1960). Later in this chapter, we show how using AHP, along with appropriate computer-based tools, can help decision makers reach optimal solutions in less time than a decision making process using BOGSAT can reach satisficing solutions. First, it is important to understand the concept of compensatory decision making and why it is superior to non-compensatory decision making.

3.4 COMPENSATORY AND NON-COMPENSATORY DECISION MAKING

Robin Hogarth, a distinguished researcher in the field of behavioral decision making, has categorized *decision rules* for choice into two groups:

1. Strategies that confront the conflicts inherent in the choice situation
2. Strategies that avoid the conflicts

Conflict-confronting strategies are compensatory. That is, they allow you to trade off a low value on one dimension against a high value on another. Conflict-avoiding strategies, on the other hand, are non-compensatory. That is, they do not allow trade-offs (Hogarth, 1987).

Compensatory decisions are rational decisions that require identification of the complete set of attributes that could positively or negatively affect the success of the options, assigning a relative importance to each attribute, computing a value for each option based on the model, and, finally, selecting the option with the best value. "In compensatory decisions, when the final values for attributes are computed, negative attributes can be compensated for by equal or higher value positive attributes. For instance, a plane ticket that costs $50 more (negative attribute) may ultimately be the better choice because it is a direct flight (positive attribute)" (Straub, 2003). Using a non-compensatory approach, the decision maker would not be able to consider the trade-off value of convenience against price.

Hogarth identifies the linear compensatory model as the most comprehensive strategy for making choices; however, until recently, its use has been infeasible because the complexity of the calculations and the number of alternatives to consider is beyond human cognitive abilities. Thus, people have generally made and continue to make non-compensatory decisions, taking the first adequate option, as in satisficing.

Now, however, because of AHP and software tools and available computer technology to support it, people can make compensatory personal and organizational decisions with relative ease, using not just the linear compensatory model recommended by Hogarth, but a multi-linear model because of the AHP's ability to multiply priorities from one level to the next (Forman, 2001).

3.5 ANALYTIC HIERARCHY PROCESS

Developed by Dr. Thomas Saaty at the Wharton School of Business in the 1970s, AHP is a conceptual process that allows people to structure complex decisions and to incorporate both qualitative and quantitative assessments as well as intuition into the process of decision making. AHP helps people to:

- Structure complexity by organizing the various elements of a problem into a hierarchy.
- Assess, via pairwise comparisons, the relative importance of the objectives and the relative preference for the identified alternatives.
- Derive priorities by combining intangible information from experience and intuition, and tangible information such as quantitative data.
- Synthesize the results of competing objectives and different points of view (Forman, 2008).

Through a series of complex mathematical calculations that are easily performed today by widely available computer software, AHP allows comparisons of objectives to establish their relative importance and comparisons of alternatives to establish the relative degree to which each alternative satisfies the objectives.

The use of AHP involves three basic steps (Forman, 2006):

1. Decomposition or structuring
2. Comparative judgments or measuring
3. Combining or synthesizing

The structuring or decomposition step breaks down a complex problem into hierarchies or related clusters much like a deliverable work breakdown structure is created to refine the products for a large project. The measuring or comparative judgment step compares the relative importance of each element in a cluster to each of the other elements of the cluster with respect to the parent of the cluster (Forman, 2001) to derive the local priorities of those elements.

AHP is based on four axioms:

1. Reciprocal
2. Homogeneity
3. Lack of feedback among objectives
4. Adequate representation of ideas to ensure the appropriate use of AHP

Only the first two are discussed here. For further information about the AHP axioms, refer to Thomas Saaty's journal article on this subject (Saaty, 1986).

The reciprocal axiom requires that if a pairwise comparison of Element A to Element B is made with regard to how much more (or less) A supports the parent attribute X than B, then the reciprocal is also true. For example, if A is evaluated to be three times as important as B in supporting X, then B is 1/3 as important as A in supporting X. For example, if A is three times the size of B, then B is 1/3 the size of A. If X = 12, then B = 3 and A = 9.

The homogeneity axiom requires that elements in a cluster of the hierarchy differ by no more than one order of magnitude, otherwise large errors in judgment may occur. For example, if the elements in a cluster weigh between 1 and 10 pounds, then pairwise comparative judgments can be made with much greater accuracy than if the elements weighed between 1 pound and 1 ton. Following this axiom results in greater consistency because evaluators are less likely to make consistency errors such as A is greater than B and B is greater than C, but A is less than C.

3.6 PAIRWISE COMPARISON

Pairwise comparisons can be made using verbal, numeric, and graphical methods to derive ratio-scale priorities and allow the evaluator to structure decisions with limited data. These comparisons are used to derive priorities for each objective with respect to the goal, the importance of sub-objectives with respect to each of the other sub-objectives at the same level with respect to each objective, and the preference of each of the alternatives with respect to those objectives and sub-objectives. Finally, the information is synthesized and an overall *best* choice is indicated, with a benefit calculated for each alternative.

"Pairwise comparisons are basic to the AHP methodology. When comparing a pair of factors, a ratio of relative importance, preference or likelihood of the factors can be established. . ." (Forman, 2001, p. 62). The factors can be any two elements at the same level in a hierarchy, including objectives, sub-objectives, or alternatives. Interestingly, the ratio does not need to be found on a standard absolute scale such as minutes or meters, but can be based on subjective judgment, as described in the experiment on the relative sizes of five polygons. AHP synthesizes these results using mathematical processes for computing eigenvectors, methods which have been subjected to testing and have proven to be extremely accurate (Forman, 2001). Thus it is possible to use both subjective and objective data and observations in pairwise comparisons. We suggest that the reader consult textbooks on linear algebra for more information about the mathematics underlying AHP.

3.7 OVERVIEW OF AHP IN PROJECT PORTFOLIO MANAGEMENT

The initial step in a project portfolio decision process is to develop a top-down hierarchical evaluation structure characterized by a goal and objectives. If desired, these objectives can be further decomposed as sub-objectives. For an organization, these goals and objectives are normally identified as part of the organization's strategic planning process as described in Chapter 2. Once the goal is established and the objectives hierarchy defined, AHP allows comparison of each objective with each other sibling objective at the same level using pairwise comparisons to derive ratio-scale priorities between objectives. This establishes which objectives are considered more meaningful than others by the stakeholders assigned to evaluate them. If sub-objectives are identified, the same pairwise comparison process is followed to derive ratio-scale priorities for the sub-objectives with respect to the parent objectives.

The next step is to identify alternatives, or projects, to be considered as part of the organization's project portfolio. AHP allows comparison of each alternative project against each of the other alternative projects with respect to how well that project satisfies each objective and thus can calculate ratio-scale priorities among the alternatives; these priorities provide more meaningful information than the arbitrary and often misleading traditional weighting scales and ordinal rankings. Finally, these multiple attribute priorities are synthesized (combined) to determine the optimal portfolio of projects within defined limitations such as maximum budget.

AHP is used worldwide today in thousands of organizations, including corporations, universities, and governments for various complex decisions from hiring employees to evaluating mergers and acquisitions. One of the rapidly growing application areas is the selection and evaluation of the optimal portfolio of projects, the subject of this book.

3.8 INTRODUCTION TO EXPERT CHOICE SOFTWARE TOOLS

Multiple software tools are available to support the AHP for structuring, measuring, and synthesizing complex decisions; any such reputable tool can be used to provide the accurate complex calculations required. We have chosen tools provided by Expert Choice. A temporary software license accompanies this book to allow readers to follow along with the examples. Expert Choice is a leading software and consulting organization that for more than a quarter of a century has developed software and helped improve complex decision making for business, government, educational institutions, and not-for-profit organizations. The examples in this book show the reader how to apply the PPM process step-by-step using the supplied software at appropriate stages in the process. Thus, readers learn the processes along with premium AHP-based tools that they can apply to improve PPM and other complex decision making in their respective organizations, and even in their personal lives. Expert Choice software tools employed in this book include:

- Comparion™ Suite to structure the AHP model and prioritize objectives and alternatives
- Expert Choice Desktop™ with the Resource Aligner™ module for portfolio optimization
- Periscope for dashboard illustration purposes only

Temporary licenses for limited versions of Comparion™ Suite and with the Resource Aligner module are provided with the purchase of a new copy of this book to enhance learning and provide you with hands-on experience in the processes described in the book. To obtain access to this software navigate to http://ppmbook.expertchoice.com. The terms of use are described and you will be asked to provide contact and login information and to verify that you are eligible to use the software. In this section we briefly introduce each of these tools. In subsequent chapters detailed step-by-step examples are provided to support the selection and optimization of the sample project portfolio.

3.8.1 Comparion™ Suite

Comparion™ Suite is a web-based solution for building AHP models, conducting evaluations, and analyzing results. It enables asynchronous or synchronous real time collaboration to structure and synthesize decisions based on quantitative data and intuition for geographically dispersed or collocated teams. Like ECD, Comparion Suite allows consideration of trade-offs and what-if scenarios. Because it is web-based, Comparion is often preferred to collect evaluator input for virtual teams dispersed across geographies or time zones.

We have chosen a simple example to illustrate the use of Comparion that provides verbal and graphical modes of comparison. In the example we use graphical pairwise comparison mode. The goal is to select the best ice cream based on the following three objectives for a good dish of ice cream:

- Most flavor (qualitative based on participant subjective assessment)
- Healthiest (quantitative based on expert nutritional assessment)
- Best price (quantitative based on price per unit)

The objectives have not yet been prioritized. In addition, there are five alternatives or choices for ice cream:

- Nonfat vanilla frozen yogurt
- Ultra-rich chocolate ice cream
- Lowfat coffee ice cream
- Melon sorbet
- Coconut cream gelato

Figure 3.2 shows the objectives and the alternatives after they have been entered into Comparion.

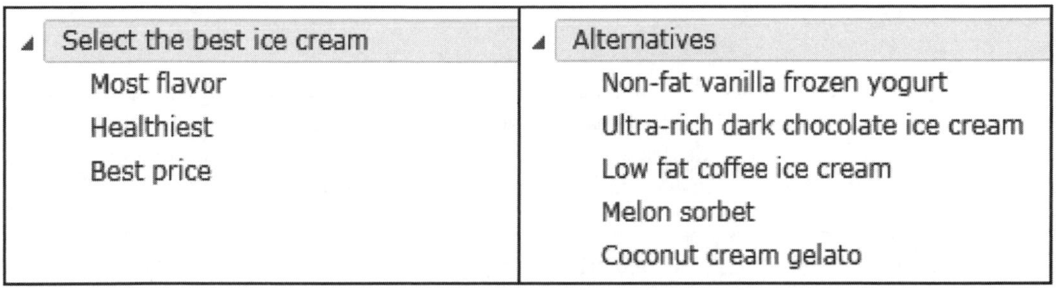

▲ Select the best ice cream	▲ Alternatives
Most flavor	Non-fat vanilla frozen yogurt
Healthiest	Ultra-rich dark chocolate ice cream
Best price	Low fat coffee ice cream
	Melon sorbet
	Coconut cream gelato

Figure 3.2 Objectives and alternatives for selecting the best ice cream (Expert Choice Comparion)

When a participant logs in to Comparion, he is presented with a series of pairwise comparisons to provide judgments about the relative importance of the objectives. In Figure 3.3 the participant is asked to consider the goal of selecting the best ice cream and then to compare one objective to another—in this case to determine whether *most flavor* or *healthiest* is more important and how much more important. This evaluator used the slider to indicate that flavor is twice as important as healthfulness.

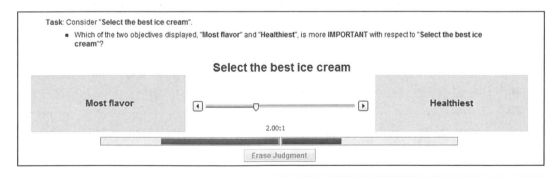

Figure 3.3 Pairwise comparison of "Most flavor" versus "Healthiest" objectives

When each objective has been compared to each other objective, the priorities derived from the participant's judgments can be displayed as shown in Figure 3.4.

Priority of Objectives for 'Select the best ice cream'

Name	Participants Results	Graph Bar	
Most flavor	54.97 %	▬▬▬▬▬▬	
Healthiest	26.63 %	▬▬▬	
Best price	18.40 %	▬▬	

Figure 3.4   Priorities of objectives for a participant

This participant determined that flavor is about twice as important as healthfulness and about three times as important as price when selecting the best ice cream. Next, participants evaluating the five different types of frozen dessert representing the alternatives are asked to rate how well each alternative supports each of the three objectives as shown in Figure 3.5.

Rate the PREFERENCE (or contribution) of each alternative with respect to 'Most flavor'.

C Non-fat vanilla frozen yogurt	Good (47%) ▼
C Ultra-rich dark chocolate ice cream	Outstanding (100%) ▼
C Low fat coffee ice cream	Very Good (69%) ▼
C Melon sorbet	A Tad (4%) ▼
C Coconut cream gelato	Excellent (86%) ▼

Figure 3.5   Participant evaluation of how well each alternative satisfies the "Most flavor" objective

As can be seen, this evaluator thinks that ultra-rich dark chocolate ice cream is more than twice as preferable as nonfat vanilla frozen yogurt. The evaluator likes the flavor of coconut cream gelato nearly as much, but doesn't find the flavor of melon sorbet appealing when selecting ice cream. In Figure 3.6 the relative priority of the alternatives for the *most flavor* objective is shown.

Priority of Alternatives for 'Most flavor'

No.	Name	Participant results ▼	Graph Bar
2	Ultra-rich dark chocolate ice cream	32.69%	▬▬▬▬▬▬▬
5	Coconut cream gelato	28.18%	▬▬▬▬▬▬
3	Low fat coffee ice cream	22.56%	▬▬▬▬
1	Non-fat vanilla frozen yogurt	15.27%	▬▬▬
4	Melon sorbet	1.31%	▪

Figure 3.6   Relative preference of alternatives with respect to "Most flavor" objective

When all participants have completed their evaluations, the results are combined, or synthesized, to produce the overall decision results as shown in Figure 3.7. As can be seen, the relative priorities of the three objectives are *most flavor* at 54.97%, *healthiest* at 26.63%, and *best price* at only 18.40% in terms of relative importance to the goal. Given the combined preference for flavor over healthfulness, and healthfulness over price, the group decision for the alternative that most meets the goal of best ice cream is the ultra-rich dark chocolate ice cream.

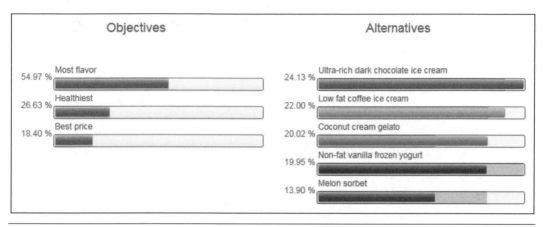

Figure 3.7   Synthesized results for all participants

Sensitivity analysis allows us to play *what if* by changing certain parameters such as the relative priorities of the objectives to see what the result would be if they were different. Figure 3.8 shows how the results change when the healthiest objective is increased to about 45%, thus reducing the relative importance of the other objectives. In this case, it would take a considerable increase in the importance of healthfulness to change the results, meaning that the decision result is not sensitive to changes in the importance of that objective.

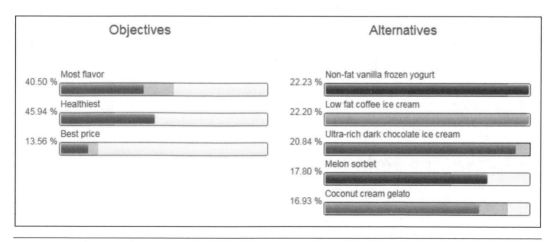

Figure 3.8   Changing the importance of the objectives changes the decision result

Although the ice cream selection example is a simple decision, the same process can be applied to more complex personal decisions and to the most complex decisions in business, academia, government, and not-for-profit organizations by structuring the objectives hierarchy and identifying the

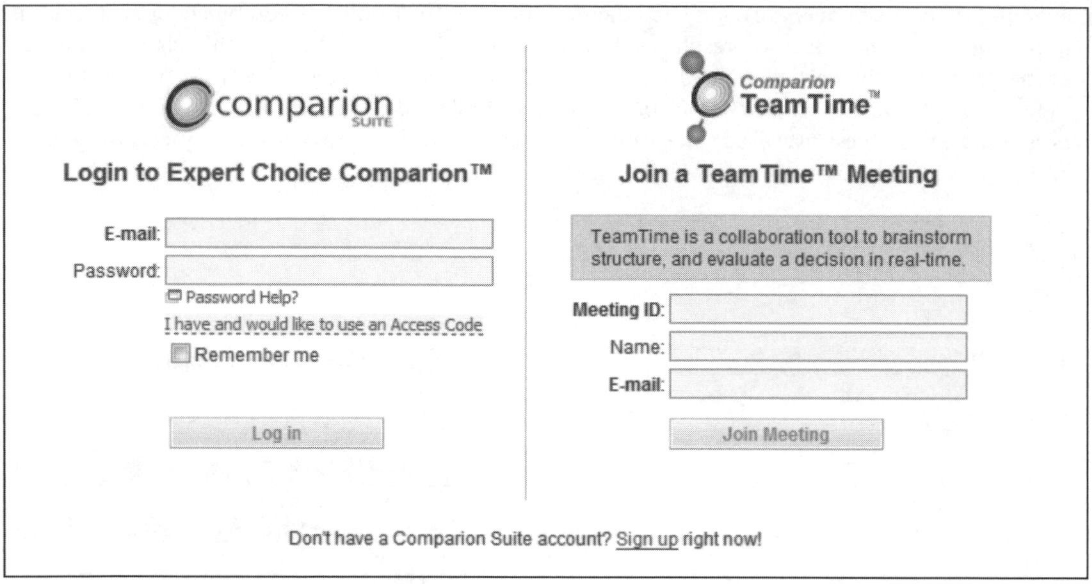

Figure 3.9   Login screen for Comparion™ Suite

alternatives, measuring using pairwise comparisons or other methods to remove the complexity of multiple competing factors, and synthesizing the results to be reviewed with the participants.

Comparion and tools with similar capability are essential to prioritize objectives and alternatives during the strategic and selection phases of the PPM process. Such tools enable structuring complexity, managing compensatory decision making, and deriving ratio-scale measures of relative importance of objectives and alternatives.

In addition to the asynchronous model building and evaluation capabilities, Comparion TeamTime™ can be used for web-based synchronous evaluation meetings and brainstorming or decision-structuring meetings at the invitation of a facilitator. Such meetings can be conducted with geographically dispersed or collocated participants or a combination of remote and local participants.

To gain an introductory understanding of Comparion Suite, go to the website link using the user name and password provided. You will see a login screen similar to the one shown in Figure 3.9.

In later chapters detailed step-by-step guidance is provided for using Comparion during relevant steps in the process.

3.8.2 Expert Choice Desktop

ECD is a Windows desktop-based software tool that, like Comparion Suite, models the decision-making process based on the complex mathematical calculations that are the foundation of AHP and allows for iterative development of a decision hierarchy by requiring the identification of a goal, objectives, and alternatives. Both ECD and Comparion include additional tools to perform sensitivity analysis and provide graphical information that can be used to enhance communications and the human commitment to the resulting decisions. Sensitivity analysis allows the user to graphically assess how the preferred alternatives change with respect to changes in the importance of the objectives or sub-objectives contained in the model.

In addition to supporting structuring, measuring, and synthesizing of AHP models, ECD supports an additional module, the Resource Aligner, to enable project portfolio selection and optimization at specified budget levels and under constraints specified by the organization. With the Resource Aligner, multiple portfolio scenarios can be easily saved and compared.

Both Comparion Suite and ECD software support multiple modes for entering judgments. Each judgment compares two elements in a cluster and produces a ratio-scale result. The same objectives and alternatives, prioritized in the same way, yield the same results in either tool.

We'll use the simple ice cream selection example from Comparion to show how the same evaluation screens can appear in ECD. It allows comparisons to be presented to evaluators in three modes— numerical, verbal, and graphical.

Numerical Mode

If we want to prioritize the objectives in numerical mode, Figure 3.10 shows the first screen presented by ECD asking the evaluator to compare the relative importance of *most flavor* to *healthiest*. The user can choose the tab labeled 3:1 to obtain this mode.

In one evaluator's opinion, if you're going to eat ice cream the most important objective is to get the best flavor. In fact, this person thinks that flavor is six times as important as the healthiness objective for a bowl of ice cream and, therefore, pushed the slider bar to the number 6.0 toward *most flavor*. Other evaluators may choose the health objective as being several times as important as the flavor or price objectives. The result of the mathematical calculations of all the evaluators' pairwise comparisons for all the objectives will yield the priorities for each of the three objectives.

Verbal Mode

Making the same comparison in verbal mode, Figure 3.11 asks the evaluator to compare the relative importance of *most flavor* to *healthiest*. By moving the slider toward *most flavor* to between *strong* and *very strong* indicators on the verbal scale, the same evaluation is achieved in the verbal mode, as can be seen in the pairwise comparison cell between *most flavor* objective and *healthiest* objective. The user can choose the tab labeled ABC to obtain this mode.

Graphical Mode

Once again, making the same pairwise comparison in graphical mode looks like the screen in Figure 3.12 in which the evaluator drags a bar to the right for *most flavor* or to the left for *healthiest* until the pairwise comparison shows about the right area of the pie, or circle, to indicate the appropriate ratio

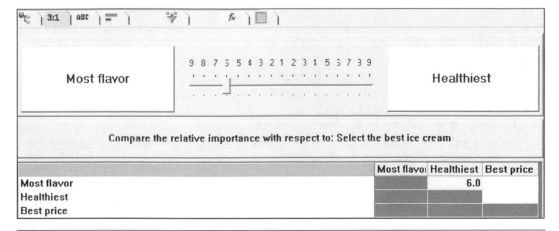

Figure 3.10 Expert Choice numerical pairwise comparison

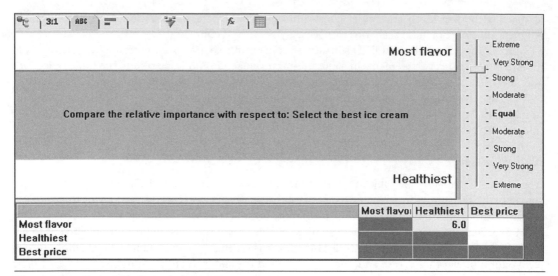

Figure 3.11 Expert Choice verbal pairwise comparison

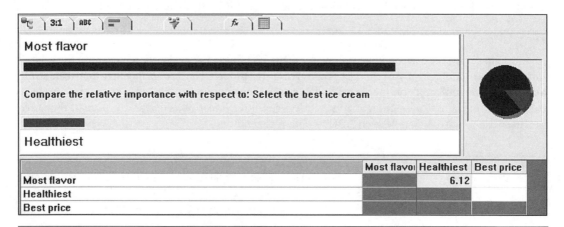

Figure 3.12 Expert Choice graphical pairwise comparison

of importance to the goal of selecting the best ice cream. The user can choose the tab labeled with a blue and red bar chart to the right of the ABC tab to obtain this mode.

Note, the numerical and graphical modes result in integer ratios, while the graphical mode does not necessarily do so. These are three different ways for ECD to present pairwise comparisons to evaluators. Thus, the developer of the model can tailor it for the evaluation audience and the specific decisions to be made. Not shown here for ECD are the evaluations of the ice cream alternatives in terms of how well each one satisfies each of the objectives, which is the next step in reaching a suggested decision for the best ice cream. These steps are covered in detail using the sample project portfolio selection process in subsequent chapters.

To gain an introductory understanding of the ECD product, download the software using the user name and password provided. After downloading, install the software using the serial number provided. Once you have installed the software, double-click on the ECD icon created on your desktop, and, from the pop-up window shown in Figure 3.13, choose either the Quick Overview or the Full Overview.

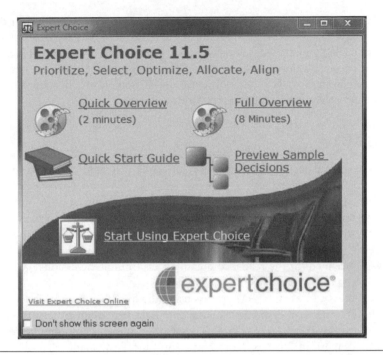

Figure 3.13   Expert Choice start-up window

Depending on the version, you may see the word Desktop after Expert Choice at the top of the screen, instead of the version number 11.5. After you have seen the overviews, you may wish to check the *Don't show this screen* again box at the lower left (to avoid seeing this screen again) and go straight to Start Using Expert Choice. If you wish to see the Quick Start Guide or Tutorials after you have disabled the initial window, simply select the Help menu, and choose the Quick Start Guide or Tutorials option.

Both Comparion Suite and ECD provide audit trails showing how each decision was reached. These are essential to the process of reviewing the integrity of decisions and for explaining the reasons for them to others. Both tools also support sensitivity analysis and allow iteration as necessary. Either tool can be used to structure a decision, to measure and collect evaluator input, and to synthesize results. ECD contains enhanced capabilities for interfacing with other software such as Oracle, Excel, and MS Project, and additional options for risks, constraints, and portfolio optimization. Models can be easily exchanged between the two software programs through uploading and downloading. At present, to implement risks, constraints, and portfolio optimization, the Resource Aligner module of ECD is required. Any synthesized Comparion model can be downloaded to a desktop computer with the appropriate software module for this purpose. Eventually, Expert Choice plans to deliver the capabilities of its Resource Aligner via enhancements to Comparion. Although examples of use are provided for both Comparion and ECD, readers with access to the internet are encouraged to use Comparion for structuring the model and prioritizing the objectives and alternatives.

3.8.3 Periscope

Periscope is a sample dashboard tool that supports progress reporting and management of project portfolios. Data from ECD or Comparion can be imported into Periscope to develop a periodic portfolio performance report card. A dashboard uses project status data to create a visual display of project and portfolio progress at a point in time, or across time periods, with drill-down from the portfolio to the project level. As you will see during the implementation and evaluation phases of the PPM process, such a tool can help decision makers determine where action is needed to adjust the portfolio. The results produced by Periscope reflect the evaluated potential strategic benefits of the selected project alternatives. For this book, Periscope is used only to illustrate performance dashboards in the final chapters and is not available for download.

3.9 SUMMARY

This chapter has described decision making techniques and the benefits of ratio-scale measurements to provide background for understanding complex decisions and factors necessary for making them accurate. It has also introduced AHP as a leading process for structuring decisions, synthesizing results, and making trade-offs that result in optimal decisions for people and organizations. The tools needed to manage the complex calculations underlying AHP were introduced in the form of software from Expert Choice, through which the implementation steps in this textbook are illustrated. Instructions were provided for the reader to obtain access to limited versions of the software tools along with the purchase of a new book.

Subsequent chapters address the PPM process using the five-phase approach described in Chapter 1. We show how to establish, implement, and maintain the process in an organization through the use of a sample portfolio of projects. The sample portfolio candidates represent projects from the fictitious university—American Business University—introduced in Chapter 2 and is used to provide step-by-step guidance in applying the supporting tools and techniques. In Chapter 4 the objectives hierarchy is established and the objectives defined during strategic planning are prioritized using AHP and Comparion Suite as the final step in the strategic phase of PPM.

3.10 REFERENCES

Encarta® World English Dictionary (North American Edition) (2009). Microsoft Corporation. http://encarta .msn.com/dictionary_561532773/BOGSAT.html (retrieved January 30, 2010).

Forman, E. H. and M. A. Selly (2001). *Decision by Objectives*. River Edge, NJ: World Scientific. (Reproduced with permission from World Scientific.)

Forman, E. H. (2008). "Project Prioritization and Portfolio Management," Lecture 3 (PowerPoint). George Washington University, Washington, D.C.

Hogarth, Robin (1987). *Judgment and Choice*. New York, NY: John Wiley & Sons, 72.

Huff, Darrell and Irving Geis (1993). *How to Lie with Statistics*. New York, NY: W. W. Norton.

Introduction to Measurement Scales and Data Types (1999). *Sable*. http://simon.cs.vt.edu/SoSci/converted/ Measurement/activity.html (retrieved January 23, 2010).

Lee, Lorraine and Rita Anderson (2009). "A Comparison of Compensatory and Non-Compensatory Decision Making Strategies in IT Project Portfolio Management." International Research Workshop on IT Project Management 2009. Paper 9. http://aisel.aisnet.org/irwitpm2009/9 (retrieved February 1, 2010).

Miller, G. A. (1994). "The Magical Number Seven, Plus or Minus Two: Some Limits on Our Capacity for Processing Information." *Psychological Review*, 101:2, 343-352.

Saaty, Thomas L. (1986). "Axiomatic Foundation of the Analytic Hierarchy Process." *Management Science*, 32:7 (July), 841-855.

Simon, Herbert A. (1960). *The New Science of Management Decision*. New York, NY: Harper and Brothers.

Straub, K. and C. Gaddy (2003). "Decisions, Decisions . . . What's a Poor User (and Designer) To Do?" Human Factors International. http://www.humanfactors.com/downloads/oct03.asp (retrieved February 1, 2010).

Trochim, William M. (2006). "The Research Methods Knowledge Base," 2nd ed. http://www.socialresearch-methods.net/kb/ (version current as of October 10, 2006).

Whyte, L. L. (1969). *Hierarchical Structures*, New York, NY: American Elsevier.

4

Prioritizing the Objectives Hierarchy Using Analytic Hierarchy Processes

In completing the first four steps of the strategic phase of PPM, the organization has developed its strategic plan with a new or updated mission, vision, goals, and objectives. Prioritization of these objectives is the responsibility of top management and is their primary way to exercise control in guiding the organization to achieve the strategic objectives. Determining the relative importance of the objectives provides the foundation for selecting a portfolio of projects that, together, maximize the total anticipated benefit to the organization.

Most people have had to buy an automobile at one time or another. When they approach such decisions either intuitively or methodically, they develop a set of objectives such as comfort, acceleration speed, capacity, safety, fuel economy, price, and maintenance costs, and they then determine the relative importance of the objectives. A young, single person may determine, for example, that acceleration speed is three times as important as capacity, while the parents of two young children decide that safety and capacity are equally important and twice as important as fuel economy. These prioritized objectives help buyers to consider alternative automobile models not only in terms of how well each model supports each of the objectives, but also how important each objective is in making their selections.

Prioritizing objectives provides similar advantages for organizations, but with considerably more complex decisions. To prioritize the objectives, executives make difficult but informed and reasoned judgments about the relative importance of the objectives in achieving the goal. This chapter addresses the process of prioritizing the organization's objectives and the techniques that provide accurate results used for doing so.

Determining relative priorities when selecting project and operational portfolios requires tools that deliver improved accuracy through mathematically sound ratio-scale results and increase the probability of making the right decision. The use of Analytic Hierarchy Processes (AHP) provides ratio-scale results such that mathematical operations can be performed on them without changing the portfolio selection. Other leading techniques provide only ordinal and interval-scale results and, as mentioned in Chapter 3, produce mathematically meaningless results with misleading conclusions and unintended consequences. The correct tools are crucial for supporting the process of prioritizing the objectives as well as for other critical steps in the PPM process.

4.1 PPM ROLE IN PRIORITIZING OBJECTIVES

PPM personnel play an active and facilitative role in the process of prioritizing objectives. Once the strategic plan is developed with specified objectives, PPM personnel structure the objectives evaluation model, seek identification of evaluators from among senior executives, and facilitate the process. The process by which these actions occur must be designed by the organization's PPM personnel in consultation with and approval by executive management. It is incumbent on the team to collaborate with executive management to establish a process for prioritizing objectives that best fits within the organization's existing governance models.

This chapter describes the process of prioritizing the objectives using AHP and software from Expert Choice. We recognize that learning new software can distract the reader from the primary goal of this book, that is, to understand how to apply tools and techniques to effectively implement and maintain a PPM process. We have therefore included step-by-step guidance for using the software and tips to help the reader through the process. The screenshots and the supporting text provide ample guidance for the novice to easily navigate through the software and its capabilities while focusing on the process. As introduced in Chapter 2, the fictitious American Business University (ABU) is used as an example to illustrate the concepts throughout the remainder of this book.

4.2 PRIORITIZING OBJECTIVES

During the strategic planning process, objectives were defined by the participants, hopefully through a collaborative and iterative process that included brainstorming, grouping related elements into clusters, eliminating or combining redundant ideas, and carefully determining descriptive phrasing such that all parties arrived at a common understanding of their meaning. This chapter describes the process of prioritizing the defined objectives and demonstrates how to use AHP and supporting software tools to do so. During this process, each objective is compared to every other objective, in a pairwise comparison, to establish the relative importance or ratio-scale priority of each objective with respect to the goal. To accomplish this it is necessary that:

- The objectives hierarchy is structured in the chosen tool.
- The appropriate evaluators and their roles are selected.
- The individual evaluations are conducted.
- The results are synthesized by combining the evaluator responses.
- Open discussion is facilitated among the evaluators to confirm the results, iterating as necessary.

Figure 4.1 indicates that this chapter addresses the final step in the strategic phase of PPM, prioritizing objectives.

To prioritize objectives, PPM personnel coordinate with the organization's senior leadership who identify and select personnel in the organization with the appropriate perspective. Recall that the evaluators of objectives are generally senior executives who participated in the development of the goals and objectives. Evaluators should understand the organization's vision and objectives thoroughly and represent the major stakeholders for achievement of the goal. Buy-in at the senior executive level of the organization (or the part of the organization that is implementing PPM) is critical to the success of every subsequent step.

First, the process and its major steps are described followed by an example using the ABU objectives and the software from Expert Choice provided with this book.

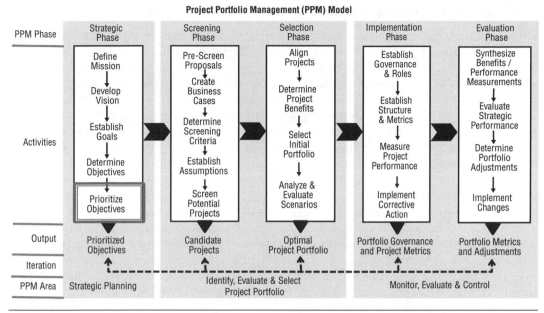

Figure 4.1   Completing the Strategic Phase by prioritizing objectives

4.3 STRUCTURING THE OBJECTIVES HIERARCHY

The objectives hierarchy is defined during strategic planning and represents the goal(s) at the top followed by the objectives and their supporting sub-objectives. Structuring the objectives hierarchy is simply identifying the goal, objectives, and sub-objectives already established in the strategic plan and then replicating them in an AHP model. A generic objectives hierarchy is shown:

Objective I
    Sub-objective A
    Sub-objective B
    Sub-objective C
        Sub-sub-objective 1
        Sub-sub-objective 2
    Sub-objective D
Objective II
Objective III
Objective IV

Once the objectives hierarchy is structured as an AHP model, the next steps in the process are to *select and invite participants*, *establish their roles* in terms of who will evaluate which objectives and sub-objectives, and *conduct the evaluation*.

4.4 MEASURING BY CONDUCTING THE EVALUATION

Prior to conducting the evaluation of the relative importance of the objectives, the measurement method to be used and how the evaluation will be conducted are determined, and the participants are prepared through appropriate orientation.

4.4.1 Select Measurement Methods

Only two measurement methods are available for prioritizing objectives: (1) pairwise comparison or (2) direct entry. Direct entry of priorities is used only rarely, when, for example, they represent priorities that have been derived elsewhere and are being restated for this model, or when they represent pre-determined allocation of relative importance such as for elements of a request for proposal. In most cases, priorities are derived using pairwise comparisons of the importance of each objective to each other objective, with respect to the goal, and each sub-objective compared to each other sub-objective in a cluster with respect to the parent objective or sub-objective. A cluster is the set of children at a given level of the hierarchy that have the same parent. When pairwise comparison is used, each evaluator is asked to compare each objective's contribution to the goal, relative to each of the other objectives, and each element of a cluster to each other element of the cluster. The results of each evaluator's input are combined to calculate ratio-scale relative priorities for the objectives.

Pairwise comparisons can be presented to evaluators either verbally or graphically. An example of a verbal pairwise comparison is shown in Figure 4.2. When performing a verbal pairwise comparison, the evaluator is presented with a screen that asks her to consider the goal and determine which objective is more important, and how much more important, by selecting the appropriate verbal descriptor from among the choices. The verbal descriptors are shown in Figure 4.2. The participant in this case evaluated that Services and Administration Facilities are "Strongly" more important than Academic Land Use and Facilities when asked:

> *Which of the two objectives displayed, "Academic Land Use and Facilities" and "Services and Administration Facilities", is more important with respect to "Campus facilities and surroundings will contribute to shared learning, collaborative research, and a sense of community by providing an environment that is conducive to dynamic interchange and that enhances quality of life on campus"?*

Comparison between two objectives measures the evaluator's preference as well as the ratio-scale degree of preference for one objective over another. The verbal scale ranges from "Equal" (one times as important) to "Extremely" (nine times as important).

An example of a graphical pairwise comparison is shown in Figure 4.3. Although graphical comparisons provide more precision, verbal comparisons make more sense when judging qualitative factors. This is because graphical comparisons can yield values that convey a false sense of accuracy,

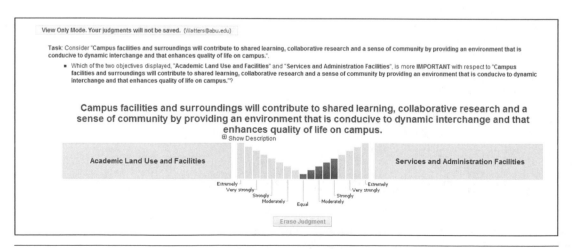

Figure 4.2   Example of a verbal pairwise comparison between two objectives

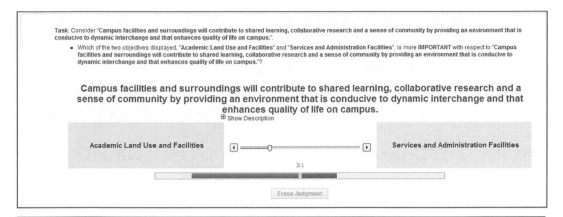

Figure 4.3   Example of a graphical pairwise comparison between two objectives

whereas verbal comparisons yield specific values for a single judgment on a nine-point scale. Distinguishing among nine points is perhaps as accurate as a human being making a qualitative comparison can be, because it falls within the seven plus or minus two cognitive limitation and represents approximately one order of magnitude.

4.4.2 Additional Pairwise Comparison Concepts

When performing pairwise comparisons, the priority of each objective is determined by comparing it to each other objective until all objectives have been compared to all other objectives. After each objective has been compared to each other objective once, such as comparing A to B, the process starts over and repeats itself to compare B to A. The point during an evaluation at which the objectives (and later, alternatives) begin to be compared a second time is known as the pairwise comparison diagonal.

The second set of comparisons is known as redundant comparisons. They help to establish the degree of consistency of each evaluator and improve the accuracy of the evaluation as a whole. A completely consistent evaluation would appear in pairwise comparisons as, for example, *A is three times as important as B* when comparing A to B, and *B is one-third as important as A* when comparing B to A.

You can calculate the number of pairwise comparisons needed for full redundancy using the formula $(n \times (n-1))/2$, and for first and second diagonals only using the formula $(n-1) + (n-2)$. As n becomes larger, the difference between the two options becomes more dramatic. When there are sub-objectives in the hierarchy, the same formulae can be applied to each cluster, and the sum of the number of comparisons for each cluster is the total number of comparisons to be offered.

4.4.3 Preparing the Participants

To perform measurements and determine the relative priorities of the objectives, the facilitator notifies the selected participants and prepares them by conducting an orientation to familiarize them with the process and the use of any software tools. Additionally, the facilitator makes them aware of their roles and responsibilities and ensures a common understanding of the objectives that they are evaluating. The facilitator also communicates the logistics of the evaluation and the deadline or timeframe by which all evaluations are to be completed.

Once that has been done, the evaluation can be conducted by gathering judgments from the participants either synchronously or asynchronously. Synchronous evaluation meetings enable discussions and clarifications to take place but, of course, require that all participants be available at the same time regardless of location or time zone. They are useful vehicles for conducting orientations, reviewing roles and responsibilities, and ensuring a common understanding of the items to be evaluated. Asynchronous evaluation allows participants to conduct evaluations at a time and place that is convenient for them. It is time to conduct the evaluation and obtain the individual judgments.

4.5 SYNTHESIZING TO DERIVE PRIORITIES FOR THE OBJECTIVES

When all evaluators have completed their input, the results are synthesized to produce the ratio-scale relative priorities for each objective and sub-objective.

4.5.1 Local and Global Priorities in an Objectives Hierarchy

When evaluation results are synthesized, local and global priorities are derived for each element in the objectives hierarchy. The local priority represents the relative priority of the element in a cluster with respect to its siblings. Recall that a cluster is the set of children at a given level of the hierarchy that have the same parent. Local priorities for any given cluster will sum to 1.000, or 100%. Global priorities are the product of the local priority of the node and its parent node's global priority. The global priorities of sibling child nodes, or cluster, will sum to the global priority of the parent node.

Figure 4.4 shows the generic objectives hierarchy as an example of local and global priorities after a mock evaluation of a sample objectives hierarchy with sub-objectives. It contains a diagram of a sample decision hierarchy with a goal and four objectives. One of the objectives, Objective II, has four sub-objectives, and one of the sub-objectives, Sub-objective C, is broken down even further into two lower-level sub-objectives.

The local and global priorities resulting from the evaluation are displayed next to each objective or sub-objective. The local priorities are the priorities that are derived for each element of a cluster (sibling children of the same parent or node) with respect to their parent and are preceded in the diagram by L: that indicates *local*. In the diagram in Figure 4.4, in the branch for Objective II, Sub-objective C, Sub-sub 1, the local priority is 0.600. The local priority for its sibling is 0.400. So, within Sub-objective C, the local priorities are 0.600 for Sub-sub 1 and 0.400 for Sub-sub 2. On a ratio-scale basis, that means that Sub-sub 1 was considered in the combined evaluations to be 1.5 times as important (0.600 / 0.400 = 1.5) as Sub-sub 2 with respect to their parent Sub-objective C, and, together, the local priorities add to 1.00, representing all of the consideration for Sub-objective C.

On the other hand, the global priorities are the priorities that are derived for a given node (objective, sub-objective or, in this case, sub-sub-objective) with respect to the goal. The global priorities of a cluster sum to the global priority of their parent node. In the example, the global priorities of Sub-sub 1 and Sub-sub 2, at 0.144 and 0.096, respectively, sum to the global priority of Sub-objective C, which is 0.240. The global priorities are derived in AHP by multiplying the global priority of the parent node by local priority of the child node; for example, the global priority of Sub-objective C is obtained by multiplying its local priority of 0.600 by the global priority of its parent, Objective II, which is 0.400, to obtain 0.240. As you can see, the global priority of Sub-sub 1 with respect to the goal is 0.144, so, by itself, it is more important in this decision than the entire Objective IV that has a global priority of 0.100; in fact, because these priorities are ratio-scale, it is considered by the decision evaluators to be 1.44 times as important as Objective IV when the individual results for all evaluators are combined.

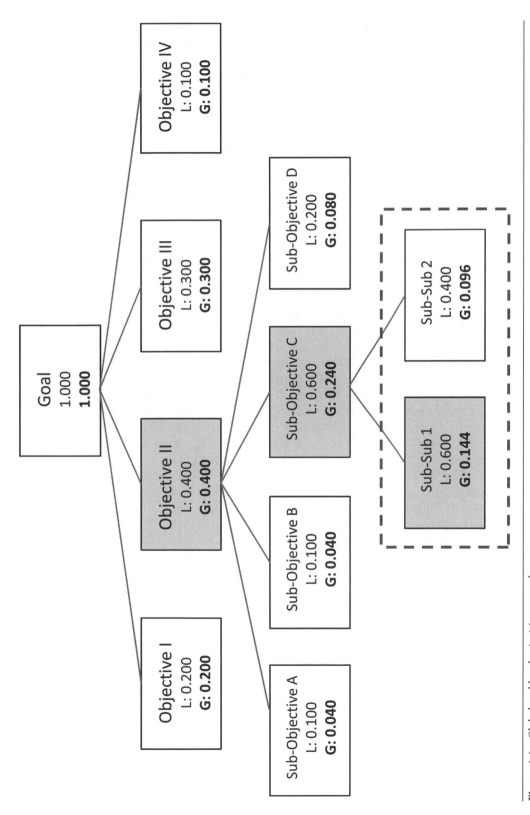

Figure 4.4 Global and local priorities example

Of course, the global priorities of all the lowest-level nodes add to 1.00 or 100%. The synthesis step that combines the results of the individual evaluators multiplies the local priorities of each element within the cluster by the global priority of the parent and yield an overall global priority for each of the objectives. The synthesis results in the perceived ratio-scale relative importance of each node in achieving the overall goal.

4.5.2 Ideal versus Distributive Mode

Using AHP, synthesis can be performed in two modes: (1) ideal or (2) distributive. When prioritizing objectives, either mode is appropriate since pairwise comparisons yield the same results in both. Further discussion of this subject is provided in Chapter 7 where the choice of mode can matter when prioritizing alternatives or candidate projects.

4.5.3 Consistency

When evaluators are presented multiple pairwise comparisons, they may be more or less consistent in their judgments. Accurate decisions are usually based on consistent judgments, but some degree of inconsistency is tolerable. Being entirely consistent means that for every judgment entered, comparative relationships are maintained; for example, if Shape A is larger than Shape B, and Shape B is larger than Shape C, Shape A is always judged to be larger than Shape C. An inconsistency ratio of 0.00 would represent perfectly consistent choices. For example, if an evaluator said that an Objective A were two times as important as Objective B, the same evaluator would also say that Objective B is only half as important as Objective A. The axiom of transitivity (Saaty, 1986) states that if A is twice as preferred as B and B is twice as preferred as C, then A is four times as preferred as C. Deviations from the axiom of transitivity contribute to the degree of inconsistency.

An inconsistency ratio of 1.00 represents what would be expected with judgments made at random rather than intelligently. AHP and Expert Choice products measure the degree of inconsistency in every set of judgments (Forman, 2001). AHP allows some degree of inconsistency. An inconsistency ratio of 0.10 or less for the combined evaluator results is considered acceptable. With the right tools, the facilitator can easily review inconsistencies for each evaluator as well as for the combined results.

High rates of inconsistency may indicate that either particular individuals, or the group, may have different interpretations of the meaning of the elements in the objectives hierarchy. Clarification may be necessary. The facilitator reviews the inconsistencies and identifies solutions to discuss with the evaluators in a follow-up session. We recommend that the evaluators make any changes with the guidance of the facilitator or evaluation model project manager.

4.6 ITERATING AS NECESSARY

When inconsistency is high or, more importantly, when the results of the evaluation do not coincide with intuition, iteration may be necessary. The facilitator reviews the result with evaluation participants to determine their level of comfort. In the end the output should agree with the intuitive perceptions of the group. When a group member disagrees with the relative priorities because of a factor that was not considered, for example, it might be necessary to return to structuring the model to add a sub-objective or even an omitted objective. In another example, it may become clear that evaluators had different interpretations of the meaning of some of the objectives or sub-objectives, in which case reprioritization can be performed after clarification.

Because prioritizing organizational objectives is an important executive decision process, and a complex one at that, multiple iterations may be required. Iteration should be expected and thus sufficient time allotted in the process schedule to allow for it. This is especially true in the early stages of performing such evaluations when members of the evaluation team are new to the process or when the organizational strategy has changed dramatically.

4.7 PRESENT RESULTS AND MAINTAIN GOVERNANCE OF THE PROCESS

Once the results have been reviewed with the evaluators, and any necessary adjustments made, including iterations, the PMB and ERB present the objectives evaluation outcome to senior executives for the purpose of communicating the results and obtaining approval for the path forward. The most important results are the ratio-scale priorities for the objectives; they are proportional measures of relative importance of the objectives from the strategic plan. During these sessions, senior management approves the prioritization of the objectives and assigns action items to be resolved. They also provide guidance to the ERB and PMB about resources and distribution of projects across objectives, project categories, or strategic buckets.

Additionally, the PMB and ERB convey that the next steps include:

- Soliciting and pre-screening the project proposals to select potential projects
- Soliciting and screening the business cases to select the candidate projects
- Conducting the evaluation of the candidates to prioritize them in terms of anticipated benefit to the organization
- Obtain approval from senior management

4.8 ABU CAMPUS REVITALIZATION PROGRAM EXAMPLE

As described in Chapter 3, decision support tools from Expert Choice demonstrate the use of supporting software during key stages of project portfolio selection and optimization. Readers are provided a temporary software license to use with the examples provided in the book or to allow them to apply their own data to support the learning process.

Although the AHP model can be created, evaluated, and synthesized in either Expert Choice Desktop or Comparion Suite, each has unique capabilities as described in the previous chapter. Most of the functions can be performed in either the desktop Expert Choice or the web-based Comparion. Some functions are better accomplished, or can only be accomplished, in one of the platforms, and we will point these out as we progress through the process. In the examples in this textbook we have chosen to create the model and perform the evaluation in Comparion to simulate the asynchronous collection of data from geographically dispersed personnel. It is then downloaded to Expert Choice Desktop for portfolio selection and analysis. This approach is one of many suitable for a distributed organization where data is required from personnel who are in multiple locations.

Two appendices are included with this chapter to demonstrate other approaches to accomplishing parts of the objectives evaluation in Expert Choice Desktop instead of Comparion. Appendix 4A: Using Expert Choice Desktop to Create the Model demonstrates how to use it to create the objectives hierarchy. Appendix 4B: Synthesizing in Expert Choice Desktop demonstrates how to perform synthesis and reporting.

Step-by-step instructions provide guidance for using the software throughout the examples. As revisions to software occur regularly, use the help functions provided to supplement the instructions herein and visit the publisher's website for the book to obtain information about major revisions and enhancements.

Recall that we are using the fictitious ABU as the sample organization throughout the book. We now apply ABU's facilities goal and the objectives that support it to demonstrate how the process works using software tools.

4.8.1 ABU Campus Revitalization Program Goals and Objectives

As described in Chapter 2, one of the goals developed during the most recent strategic planning session forms the basis for the objectives of the Campus Revitalization program. That goal is:

Campus facilities and surroundings will contribute to shared learning, collaborative research, and a sense of community by providing an environment that is conducive to dynamic interchange and that enhances quality of life on campus.

This chapter begins the process of establishing project portfolio selection and management for the ABU goal associated with revitalizing the university's facilities to support its mission and vision. Not all portfolios selected to support a goal have a program name but, in this case, the plan to support this goal is called the ABU Campus Revitalization Program. Here, the word program is not used in the sense of a group of related projects but, instead, represents the activities required to choose and manage the portfolio of projects that best meet the objectives supporting the facilities goal of ABU. To support the goal, five major areas of focus were identified, one for each of the five types of university facilities:

1. Academic land use and facilities
2. Services and administration
3. Intercollegiate athletics
4. Recreation services
5. Residential and conference

Identify Objectives and Sub-objectives

The objectives and sub-objectives for each of these were described in detail in Chapter 2. These become the basis for the objectives hierarchy portion of an AHP decision model to support the selection and management of the portfolio of facilities projects nominated or underway as part of the ABU Campus Revitalization Program.

Organizations may classify their objectives by product type (e.g., established products and emerging markets for pharmaceuticals; or services, software, and hardware for a technology company), by enterprise hierarchy (e.g., geographies or divisions), or by what some organizations are calling strategic buckets or areas of focus. ABU has chosen to classify its facilities objectives by facility type or major use categories.

Determine the Level of Objectives To Be Evaluated

Because the objectives supporting a goal do not share equal importance, a methodology for prioritizing them is required to gain a better understanding of their importance relative to each other. This is necessary to ensure that the perceived relative value of the objectives influences the ultimate anticipated relative benefit of the candidate projects.

While the top-level objectives shown were expanded further to lower-level sub-objectives, for purposes of illustrating the concepts and application of AHP supported by Expert Choice tools, only top-level objectives are prioritized. The process described in this section for prioritizing the objectives can also be applied to each level of sub-objective. At the top level, ratio-scale priorities are established for each objective with respect to the goal. The same process is then applied within each objective, for each level of sub-objective, to establish the ratio-scale priority of each sub-objective with respect to the objective, or with respect to the parent sub-objective if multiple levels of sub-objectives are defined.

The names of the objectives for the Campus Revitalization Program have been shortened so the names are easily readable and associated with the objective for each type of facility. For example, *Academic Land Use and Facilities* is:

> *Meet the academic needs identified in the space needs analysis conducted by University Facilities under the updated guidelines of the State Commission on Higher Education.*

For ease of entry into and readability for the software tools, the objective is shortened to *Academic Land Use and Facilities*. In like manner, each of the five objectives is shortened for use in the examples and step-by-step guidance as provided in the following list:

Academic Land Use and Facilities
Services and Administration Facilities
Intercollegiate Athletics Facilities
Recreation Services Facilities
Residential and Conference Facilities

Although all five objectives support the ABU goal for campus facilities, the objectives are not of equal importance and require a prioritization methodology to determine the relative importance of each objective with respect to the goal. Later, the alternative projects that contribute to an objective will take on the priority of the objectives they support.

4.8.2 Prepare to Evaluate the Objectives Using AHP and Comparion

In this section we prepare the evaluation model for the ABU objectives in the Comparion Suite software:

- Learn to login to Comparion
- Create a new project in Comparion to evaluate the objectives
- Establish the AHP objectives hierarchy
- Elect participants and their roles and notify them
- Select options for guiding the evaluation process

Screen shots with explanations are used throughout this portion of the chapter to demonstrate how the software tool supports the concept of prioritizing objectives within a structured, methodical process. As software is frequently updated, use Comparion help should the instructions appear different from what is shown on your screen. Again, the illustrations are intended to make it easy for novices or the technically challenged to move comfortably through the ABU example with the software while focusing on the process of making complex decisions. To reinforce the learning experience, we encourage you to log on and perform each of the steps while reading the material. The material to be entered can be copied and pasted from the supplied Word document (ABU_Objectives_Candidates_Copy_Paste .docx in the WAV material) or can be entered by hand using the material from the end of Chapter 2 in Section 2.2; alternatively, you may wish to use your own real or hypothetical objectives.

Login to Comparion and Create a New Project

To begin this process, go to the Comparion Suite site at the link provided and log on with the credentials (e-mail address and password) supplied as shown in Figure 4.5.

After supplying the authorized e-mail address and password, click on the "Log In" button. Note that this is the same screen that is seen when invited to join a TeamTime meeting, but, in that case, the participant supplies credentials on the right side of the screen and chooses the type of meeting to be joined. After login, your home screen is seen similar to that in Figure 4.6 that also shows any

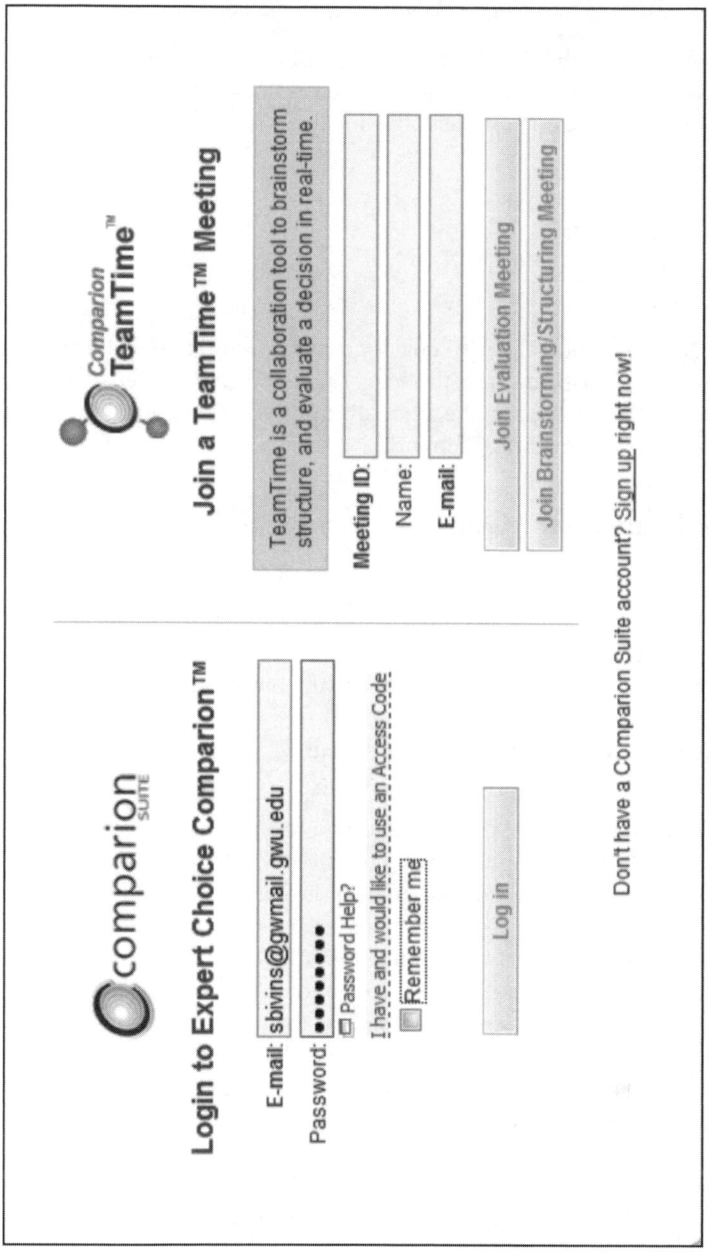

Figure 4.5   Login to Comparion Suite

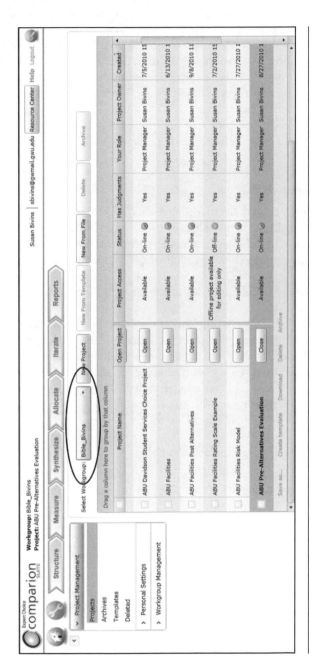

Figure 4.6 Comparion home screen

existing projects in the selected workgroup. If there are multiple workgroups, choose the workgroup provided with the book or by your instructor by selecting it from the drop-down list next to "Select Workgroup."

Any projects currently underway will be shown together with the status information about each. "Select New Project, New from Template" to create a project from a template. Templates are projects that contain skeletal information for evaluation projects that are to be repeated frequently such as evaluating potential new employees or even project portfolios. The template contains the objectives, and sometimes the alternatives but no actual evaluation information, and has been saved using the "Create template" link seen as one of the choices at the bottom of the screen in Figure 4.6. In this case, create a new project by selecting the "New Project" button at the top of the screen shown in Figure 4.6. Note that a pop-up window opens to allow a file to be selected; therefore, pop-ups must be enabled in your browser for this website. The pop-up window asking you to enter a "Project name" is shown in Figure 4.7. Type a meaningful name (the example uses "ABU Objectives Evaluation") and click on "OK."

Basic Navigation in Comparion

A screen that allows you to structure the model appears as shown in Figure 4.8. Note the two icons at the upper left of the screen. The icon resembling a house returns the user to the home screen, while the one that resembles a wrench allows you to manage information about the project. The left arrow icon under the house icon is used to hide or unhide the steps menu at the upper left to provide more screen space.

Selecting "Help" at the upper right provides context sensitive help, while the *Resource Center* button provides text and video help.

The arrow tabs across the top, including "Structure, Measure, Synthesize," provide a framework for building the AHP model, while the steps in the menu at the left are specific to the stage of the framework that is highlighted. To structure the model, highlight the "Structure" tab; the menu at the left shows the steps that can be taken while structuring the model. If the software license includes TeamTime, a "TeamTime Structuring" box can be seen at the upper right that enables the user to invite participants or start a meeting in which participants can help to structure the objectives or alternatives when either one of those is selected in the steps menu.

Preliminary Project Management Information

Before creating the actual model, establish some basic information about the new project by selecting the wrench icon at the upper left that displays the project management screen shown in

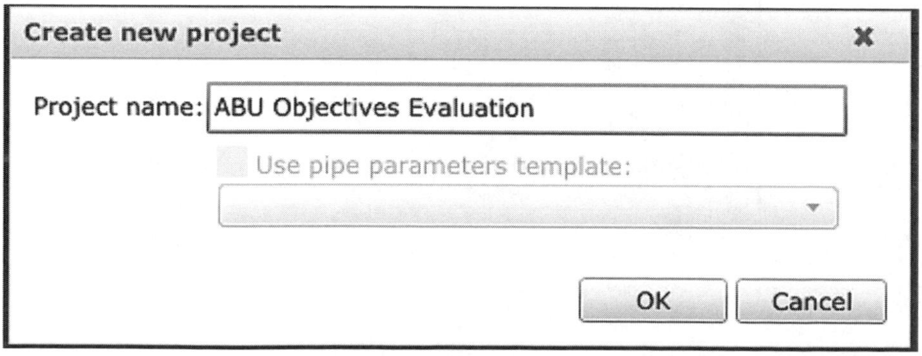

Figure 4.7   Creating a new Comparion project

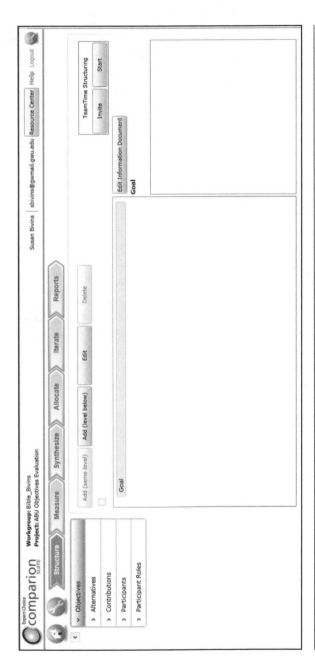

Figure 4.8 New model ready for the structuring steps and basic navigation

Figure 4.9. In this screen, the project manager (you) provides a description of the new project and creates a meaningful access code that is later supplied to evaluators and other participants.

Key in a description of the project such as that shown and change the access code from the automatically generated random string of characters to something more relevant, in this case "ABU Objectives." Check the box next to "Available by access code" to enable its use and then select "OK." Later, the access code will be used by evaluators to go straight to their evaluations from log-on without going through the home screen to select the project. When more information is available about objectives and evaluators, the project manager can come to this menu to obtain project status and to download and save the model in either Comparion or Expert Choice Desktop format. Downloading can also be accomplished from the home screen by clicking on the project name, selecting "Download," as shown in Figure 4.10, and choosing the format and location. Downloading is used to save

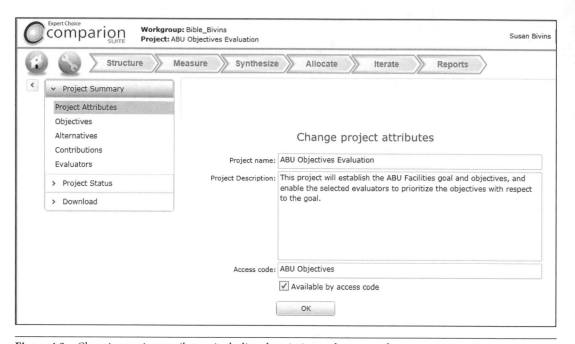

Figure 4.9   Changing project attributes, including description and access code

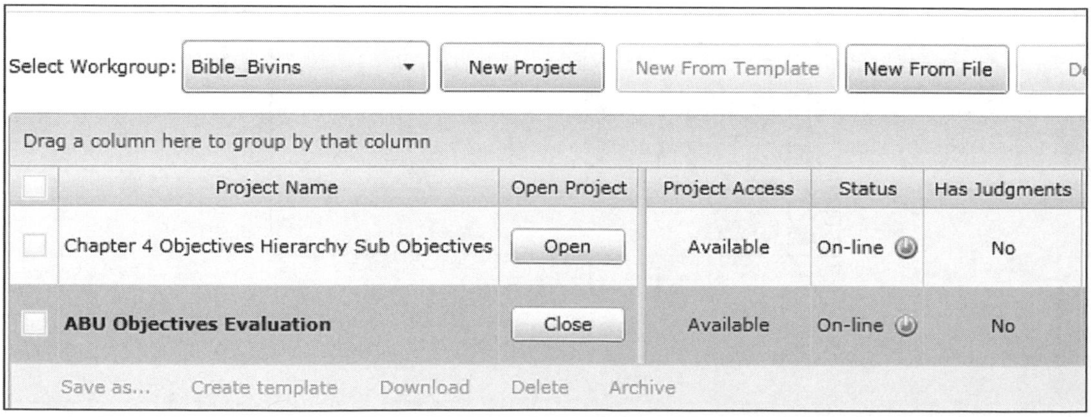

	Project Name	Open Project	Project Access	Status	Has Judgments
☐	Chapter 4 Objectives Hierarchy Sub Objectives	Open	Available	On-line ⊙	No
☐	**ABU Objectives Evaluation**	Close	Available	On-line ⊙	No

Select Workgroup: Bible_Bivins ▾   New Project   New From Template   New From File   D

Drag a column here to group by that column

Save as...   Create template   Download   Delete   Archive

Figure 4.10   Download from the home screen

the model on a local computer for later use as a backup to the online version or for re-upload to Comparion if desired.

As can be seen in Figure 4.10, the model can also be saved with a different name, used to create a template, deleted, or archived. Use the "Help" button for more information about the home screen and its features. Note: to make a decision inactive, select the "On-line" symbol in the "Status" column shown in Figure 4.10. This changes the status to "Off-line." In the case of a software license with a limited number of active decisions, this capability allows several models to be created while establishing only the online models as active for evaluation purposes. Select the "Off-line" symbol to change the status back to "On-line."

4.8.3 Structure the Model

With some basic navigation and preliminary project management information steps complete, begin structuring the model by selecting the "Structure" tab at the top of the screen to return to the structuring steps shown in Figure 4.8. Structuring the model includes entering the objectives hierarchy and the alternatives, mapping the alternatives to their covering objectives, and selecting the participants and defining their roles. In this chapter only the objectives are being evaluated, and only the portions of the model related to how objectives will be evaluated are completed. In Chapter 7 prioritizing alternatives, or candidate projects, will be addressed.

Structure the Model—Entering the Goal and Objectives

To enter the goal, click on the "Edit" button and either type it in or copy the goal from a document and paste it from the clipboard as shown in Figure 4.11. Also, by selecting "Edit Information Document," a new window opens to allow additional information to be typed or pasted; the information entered will be shown on the right side of the screen after closing the window.

With the goal defined, select the "Add" (level below) button that opens a new window as shown in Figure 4.12. Enter the objectives in their abbreviated form by typing them or by copying them from a document and selecting "Paste from clipboard."

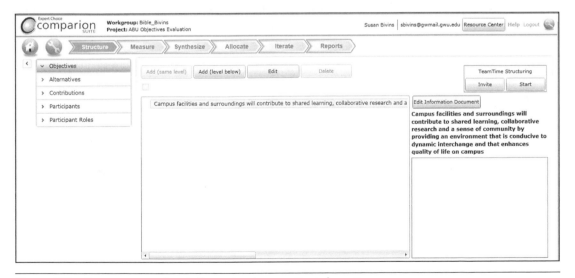

Figure 4.11   Type or copy and paste the goal and supporting information

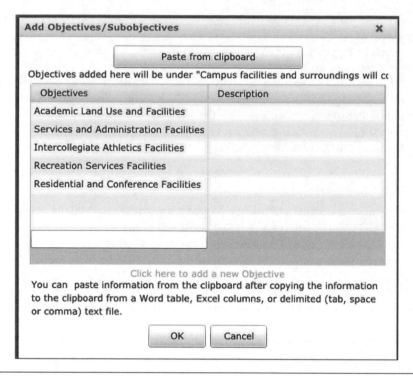

Figure 4.12   Adding the five ABU facilities objectives

When adding objectives, descriptive information is added as in Figure 4.12 by including it in the second column of a two-column Word table or Excel worksheet, or can be added by highlighting each objective and selecting "Edit Information Document" as shown in Figure 4.13.

A new window will open, as it did to allow descriptive information to be entered for the goal, and the description can be typed or pasted as before as shown in Figure 4.14. Since the evaluators must all have the same understanding of the objectives to produce valid relative priorities, additional

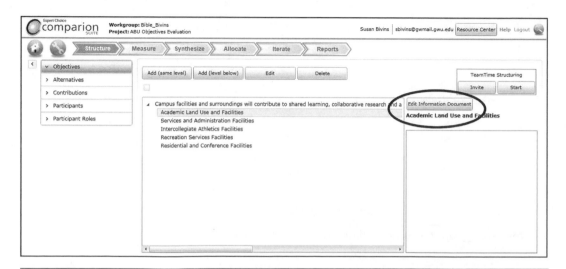

Figure 4.13   Add descriptive information for an objective

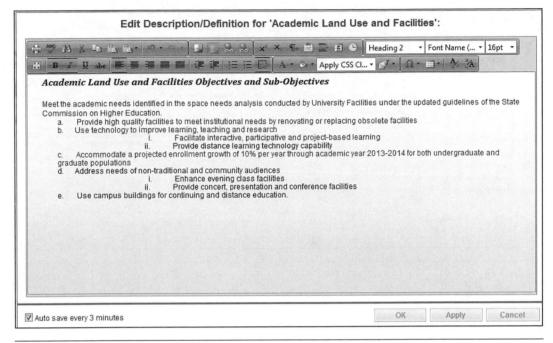

Figure 4.14   Adding additional description for academic facilities objective

descriptive information can be used to clarify the objective, and collaborative meetings can be conducted to achieve such common understanding.

Click on "Apply" to save what has been entered, and "OK" to exit the Comparion Suite Rich Editor. A screen appears that looks similar to the one shown in Figure 4.15, showing the goal and the objectives hierarchy.

Including Sub-objectives in the Objectives Hierarchy

To include the sub-objectives, apply the same process just used to enter the objectives. Bear in mind that the evaluations of the alternatives described in a later chapter are performed at the lowest level of the sub-objective for each objective. Sub-objectives can be copied and pasted, and their placement in the hierarchy will be in accord with their indentation in the source document or spreadsheet. Recall from Chapter 3 that human beings cannot accurately compare more than seven, plus or minus two, elements. When constructing the objectives hierarchy, no cluster should exceed this guidance. A cluster is all the elements at a particular level of the hierarchy that have the same parent.

An example of the AHP model with sub-objectives entered only for the Academic Land Use and Facilities objective is shown in Figure 4.16; elements that have sub-elements are denoted by an indicator at the left. The highlighted sub-objective "Use technology to improve learning, teaching and research" has a cluster of two sub-elements. The "Academic Land Use and Facilities" objective has a cluster of five sub-objectives, two of which have further sub-objectives.

When establishing evaluation options, the objectives hierarchy can be evaluated bottom up—meaning that the pairwise comparisons for the lowest-level clusters will be presented first—or top down—meaning that the highest-level pairwise comparisons will be presented first. The remainder of this chapter uses the AHP model that includes only the five high-level objectives to facilitate learning the process and the tools while minimizing the complexity of the decision process. However, the same PPM process and tools can be applied with a more complex decision model.

Expert Choice
comparion SUITE
Workgroup: Bible_Bivins
Project: ABU Objectives Evaluation
Susan Bivins
sbivins@gwmail.gwu.edu
Resource Center
Help
Logout
Structure
Measure
Synthesize
Allocate
Iterate
Reports
Objectives
Alternatives
Contributions
Participants
Participant Roles
Add (same level)
Add (level below)
Edit
Delete
TeamTime Structuring
Invite
Start
Campus facilities and surroundings will contribute to shared learning, collaborative research and a
Academic Land Use and Facilities
Services and Administration Facilities
Intercollegiate Athletics Facilities
Recreation Services Facilities
Residential and Conference Facilities
Edit Information Document
Campus facilities and surroundings will contribute to shared learning, collaborative research and a sense of community by providing an environment that is conducive to dynamic interchange and that enhances quality of life on campus

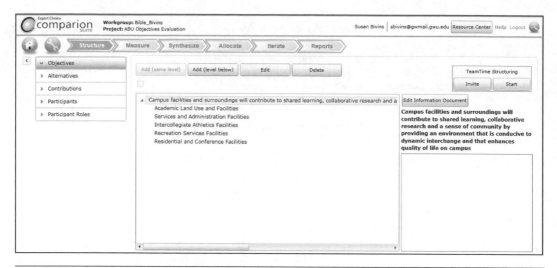

Figure 4.15 The ABU facilities objectives hierarchy

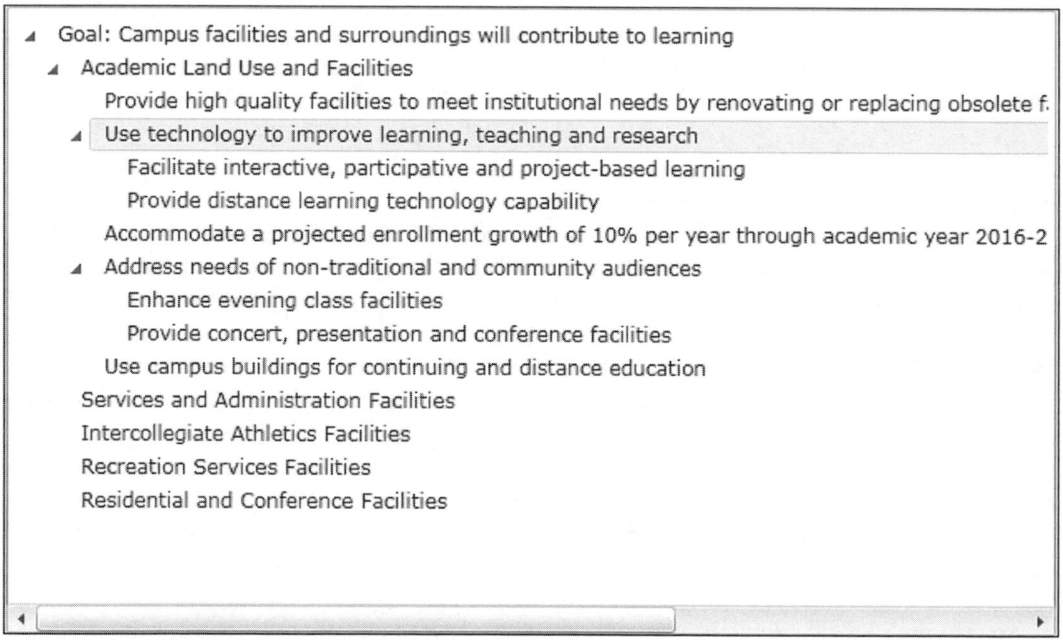

Goal: Campus facilities and surroundings will contribute to learning
Academic Land Use and Facilities
Provide high quality facilities to meet institutional needs by renovating or replacing obsolete f.
Use technology to improve learning, teaching and research
Facilitate interactive, participative and project-based learning
Provide distance learning technology capability
Accommodate a projected enrollment growth of 10% per year through academic year 2016-2
Address needs of non-traditional and community audiences
Enhance evening class facilities
Provide concert, presentation and conference facilities
Use campus buildings for continuing and distance education
Services and Administration Facilities
Intercollegiate Athletics Facilities
Recreation Services Facilities
Residential and Conference Facilities

Figure 4.16 Example of one objective with sub-objectives

Structure the Model—Participants and Their Roles

Now that the objectives hierarchy is created, the next steps in the menu for the structuring process are "Alternatives and Contributions." "Alternatives" are the candidate projects to be evaluated. The "Contributions" step allows us to identify which objectives or sub-objectives are supported by which candidate projects. Both are discussed in Chapter 7. For now, skip these two steps and go on to establish the objectives evaluators and their roles.

Table 4.1 Participants selected to prioritize the objectives

Name	Title	Representing	email
Ms. Cynthia Watters	Chairman	Board of Trustees	Watters@abu.edu
Mr. David Tollson	Vice Chair	Board of Trustees	Tollson@abu.edu
Dr. Robert Collins	Chairman	Steering Committee	Collins@abu.edu
Mr. Stewart Jones	Faculty Director	PMO	Jones@abu.edu

To prioritize objectives, PPM personnel coordinate with the organization's leadership and management to identify and select personnel in the organization who have the appropriate perspective to evaluate the objectives. Recall that the evaluators of objectives are generally senior executives who participated in the development of the goals and objectives. Evaluators should understand the organization's vision and objectives thoroughly and represent the major stakeholders for achievement of the goal.

In the ABU example evaluators include representatives of the Board of Trustees, the Campus Revitalization Program Steering Committee, and the Director of the Program Management Office (PMO). The list of evaluators for the facilities objectives is provided in Table 4.1. The names of the participants in the ABU example are, of course, fictitious.

To perform measurements and determine the relative priority of the objectives, the PMB establishes a means to prepare the evaluators, after they have been identified, and determines a method for collecting data and synthesizing results. In preparation for the evaluation of the priority of the objectives, selected participants are notified of the data collection process and assembled for an orientation to familiarize them with the process and to ensure that they are aware of their roles and responsibilities. By performing their evaluation roles, participants establish the relative priorities of the objectives with respect to achieving the goal. To perform this role effectively, participants must develop a common understanding of the objectives. To that end, the facilitator conducts a real time session with all participants present before making the evaluation model available to them.

Add Participants to the Model

To enter the chosen participants, select "Participants" from the structuring steps menu to see the screen shown in Figure 4.17. Select "Add Participants" to obtain the screen shown in Figure 4.18, choose the option "Enter or paste from clipboard" to enter the participants directly or "From existing workgroup members"—that provides a list of all members of the workgroup—from which the desired evaluation participants can be selected. In most cases an administrator in the organization will have established a workgroup with potential participants. In the case of fictitious evaluators, as in this example, it may be necessary to add them directly as shown in Figure 4.18, or from the clipboard.

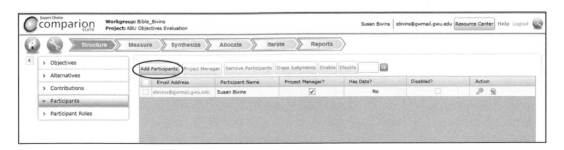

Figure 4.17 Participants menu

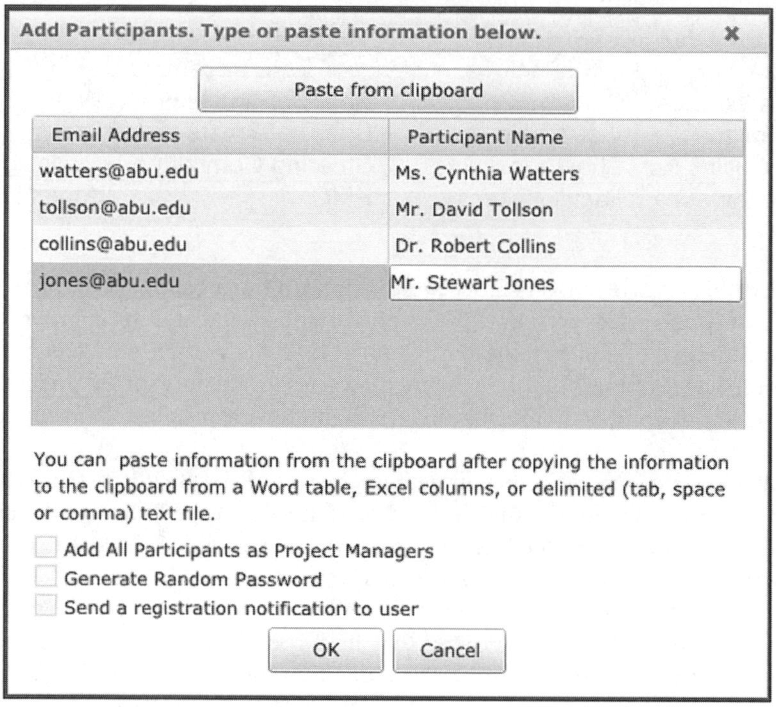

Figure 4.18 Adding the participants who will prioritize objectives

In this case, do not assign project manager privileges for the evaluation model and do not generate a password and send it via e-mail, since these are fictitious evaluators—leave the boxes unchecked. In a real situation, these boxes can be checked to have the system provide a randomly generated password for each participant and send a registration notification that you, as the project manager, can tailor. As the creator of the project, your e-mail address and name are already there and you have project manager privileges. After clicking "OK," the participants who will evaluate the objectives have been added but have not yet provided any input, as shown in Figure 4.19. When a participant has provided at least some of the judgments, the indicator "Has Data?" changes to "Yes" from "No."

One or more participants can be selected by checking the boxes to the left of their e-mail addresses. When selected, the project manager can remove them from the project, erase their judgments (necessitating that they reevaluate, so use this option with caution), and enable or disable their participation in the evaluation.

Establish ABU Participant Roles

Now that the participants have been added, specify the role(s) they will perform during the evaluation by selecting "Participant Roles" from the step menu under the "Structure" tab. This functionality allows for the executives on the ERB and portfolio management leaders on the PMB to be specific about not only who will participate in the candidate project evaluation process, but also what they will each evaluate. This is an important benefit of using project portfolio decision tools such as Comparion. Having the capability to tailor the specific roles for selected evaluators allows the organization to leverage the experience and expertise of specific individuals for only that part of the evaluation for which they are qualified. Naturally this also prevents personnel from evaluating areas for which

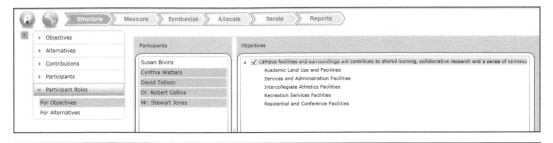

Figure 4.19   Objectives evaluators added to model

they are not qualified. This team of participants evaluates the relative importance of the objectives with respect to the goal and includes two members of the Board of Trustees, the Chairman of the Steering Committee, and the Faculty Director of the PMO—people with a high-level perspective of the organization, its goal, and objectives.

The software allows the roles of evaluators to be tailored to evaluate only objectives, only alternatives, or both alternatives and objectives. In addition, participants can be assigned to evaluate only specific objectives or only specific alternatives. Select each of the objectives evaluators in turn by highlighting the evaluator's name. To assign roles simultaneously, hold down the CTRL key and select each of the alternatives evaluators in turn so all four are highlighted as shown in Figure 4.20.

The default setting is for all four ABU participants to evaluate all objectives and all alternatives against all objectives. In this case, the four participants are to evaluate all the objectives and only the objectives. Note that roles "For Objectives" and roles "For Alternatives" can be specified separately. In this example, all four evaluators have exactly the same role—to prioritize the objectives with respect to the goal and not to evaluate any alternatives. That will be assigned to a separate group in a later chapter. When "For Objectives" is selected under "Participant Roles," as is the case in Figure 4.20, the box next to the goal "Campus facilities and surroundings will contribute to". . . is checked by default. A check in this box indicates that the highlighted participants will evaluate the objectives listed under the goal; thus, they will see all of the objectives evaluation steps during the evaluation.

The project manager, as the facilitator, may or may not be assigned to perform evaluations, depending on his role in the decision. Since the default is for everyone to evaluate everything, highlight the project manager(s) and change the role assignments as necessary, if the project manager's evaluation role is different from that of other participants. In this case, the project manager will not enter any judgments, so highlight your name and that of any other project managers and uncheck the box next to the goal. Failure to do so will cause Comparion to consider the judgments incomplete.

Tailoring evaluation options, customizing information for the participants, and inviting the participants are functions of the next tab "Measure."

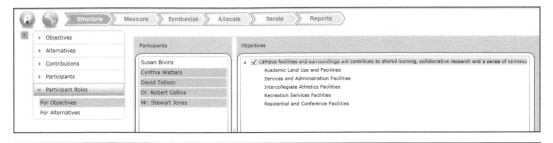

Figure 4.20   Setting evaluator roles for participants to evaluate objectives

4.8.4 Measure—Establish the Evaluation Approach

With alternatives entered and roles assigned, priorities are derived to determine the relative importance of the objectives with respect to each other. To determine priorities it is necessary to define the measurement methods, select options for presenting the material to participants, and conduct the actual evaluation. Select the "Measure" tab as shown in Figure 4.21 to begin this process.

Select Measurement Methods

Only two measurement methods are available for prioritizing objectives: (1) pairwise comparison or (2) direct entry. Direct entry of priorities is used rarely. For example, it may be used when it represents priorities that have been derived elsewhere and are being restated for this model or when it represents a pre-determined allocation of relative importance such as for a request for proposal. In most cases priorities are derived using pairwise comparisons of the importance of each objective to each other objective, with respect to the goal. Select "Measurement Methods, For Objectives" and the drop-down menu for the goal to obtain access to the two choices, as shown in Figure 4.22.

In this case there is only one cluster, the cluster of the five objectives; all the elements of the cluster must use the same measurement type that is specified in the drop-down box next to the cluster parent. The parent of the five objectives in the cluster is the goal, displayed as the "Cluster Parent Objective." Choose "Pairwise Comparison" in the drop-down list.

This selection causes Comparion to ask each evaluator to compare each objective's contribution to the goal relative to each of the other objectives. Comparion will use these pairwise comparisons to calculate ratio-scale relative priorities for the objectives.

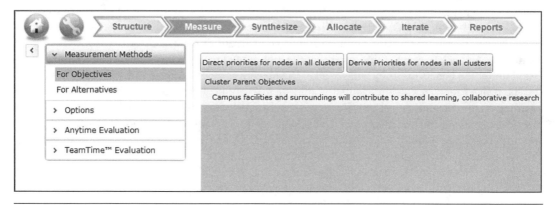

Figure 4.21   Establishing the evaluation approach using the measure tab

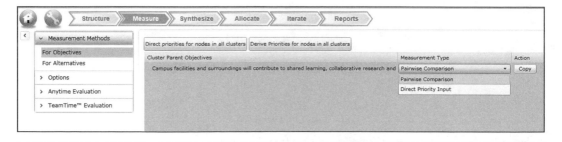

Figure 4.22   Select measurement type for each cluster parent

Next we will choose among available options for how the evaluation will be presented to participants for evaluation, navigation, and display.

Choose Evaluation Options

In this section the project manager specifies "Evaluation" options that determine what to evaluate, the order and manner in which the evaluation takes place, and how the steps are shown to participants, including "Navigation" options that guide and support the progress of the participants and "Display" options that specify what information and results to show to the participants.

Navigate to the "Measure" tab, select "Options" and then "Evaluation" as shown in Figure 4.23. This section identifies what to evaluate, the order of the evaluation, and how to evaluate alternatives that have rating scales. It also allows trade-off of accuracy versus number of comparisons for pairwise comparisons and allows the selection of either graphical or verbal for pairwise comparisons.

For "What do you want to evaluate," choose "Objectives," although we could have chosen both. When some evaluators are evaluating both objectives and alternatives, and the PMB wants to perform them in separate phases such as all objectives first and then later all alternatives, only one of these can be checked. "Order of Evaluation" applies to evaluators who will evaluate both objectives and alternatives and thus does not apply in this example. However, see Comparion "Help" for rationale that is used in making these choices. Usually, as in this case, the objectives are evaluated first.

Although sub-objectives are not included at this time, the "Order for evaluating hierarchy of objectives" applies to whether the relative importance of the sub-objectives is presented first before presenting the relative importance of the higher-level objectives, "Bottom up"; or the reverse, evaluating the relative importance of the higher-level objectives and working down the hierarchy, "Top down." Expert Choice recommends bottom-up evaluation of the objectives hierarchy to give participants a better appreciation of the significance of the elements that contribute to the higher-level objectives before they are evaluated.

"Evaluation of alternatives having rating scales" is grayed out because alternatives are not being evaluated at this time. "Make a choice for trade-off between accuracy and # of comparisons (Pairwise diagonals to complete)" determines the number of comparisons required in cases where pairwise comparisons are used. Recall the discussion of additional pairwise comparison concepts earlier in the chapter. In Figure 4.23, the option to "Use the most comparisons for the best accuracy (All)" option was chosen. Choosing this option provides greater redundancy and thus produces the most

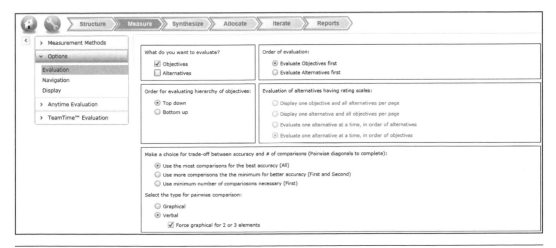

Figure 4.23 Establish evaluation options

accurate results, but it also takes more time. With five objectives, this option results in $(5 \times 4)/2 = 10$ comparisons using the formula $(n \times (n - 1))/2$ to calculate the number of comparisons. With only five objectives, the added accuracy makes this the best choice.

Choosing the option "Use more comparisons than the minimum for better accuracy (First and Second)" provides a compromise between the maximum number and the minimum number. Using this option generates, for each objective cluster, $(n - 1) + (n - 2)$ comparisons, where n is the number of objectives in the cluster. The sum of the number of comparisons for each cluster is the total number of pairwise comparisons required. Thus, if pairwise comparisons were used for the five objectives, this would result in $(5 - 1) + (5 - 2) = 7$ pairwise comparisons. If the first objective has three sub-objectives and no other objective has any sub-objectives, then the number of pairwise comparisons for the cluster of three sub-objectives is $(3 - 1) + (3 - 2) = 3$ and the total number of comparisons would be $7 + 3 = 10$. The maximum number of comparisons is calculated as $(n \times (n - 1)/2)$. The minimum number of comparisons is $(n - 1)$; this minimal option should be used only when pairwise graphical judgments can be made with confidence that the result will be accurate.

The option "Select the type for pairwise comparison" results in a display of pairwise comparisons in either "Graphical" or "Verbal" mode. An example of both a verbal and a graphical pairwise comparison is shown in Figures 4.24 and 4.25, respectively.

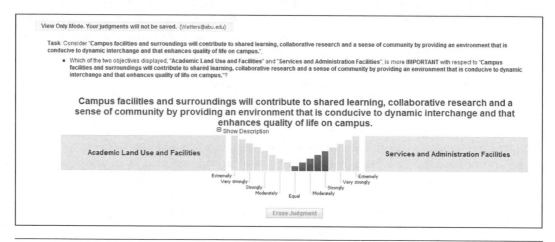

Figure 4.24   Example of a verbal pairwise comparison between two objectives

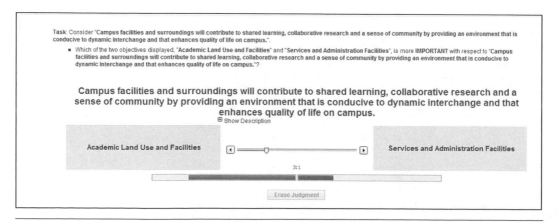

Figure 4.25   Example of a graphical pairwise comparison between two objectives

Although graphical comparisons provide more precision, we are choosing verbal comparisons because they make more sense when judging qualitative factors, as is the case with the ABU example.

Recall that when performing a verbal pairwise comparison, the evaluator is presented with a screen that asks her to consider the goal and determine which objective is more important, and how much more important, by selecting the appropriate verbal descriptor from among the choices. The verbal descriptors are shown in Figure 4.24. The participant in this case evaluated that Service and Administration Facilities are "Strongly" more important than Academic Land Use and Facilities when asked:

> *Which of the two objectives displayed, Academic Land Use and Facilities and Services and Administration Facilities, is more important with respect to campus facilities and surroundings will contribute to shared learning, collaborative research, and a sense of community by providing an environment that is conducive to dynamic interchange and that enhances quality of life on campus?*

Comparison between two objectives measures the evaluator's preference and the ratio-scale degree of preference for one objective over another. When the objective presented on the left is considered more important than the objective presented on the right, Comparion shows columns representing the scale, up to and including the relative importance chosen, in blue on the left. When the opposite is true, columns representing the scale up to and including the relative importance are shown in red on the right. When the evaluator considers the two to be of equal importance, only the "Equal" column is highlighted in gray. The verbal scale ranges from "Equal" (one times as important) to "Extremely" (nine times as important).

Choose Navigation Options

To see the navigation options shown in Figure 4.26, select "Navigation" under "Options."

Unless the option to "Hide navigation box" is selected, the evaluator will see the navigation box shown at the lower left of Figure 4.27 that enables navigation forward and backward through the evaluation. By selecting "Show next unassessed" in Figure 4.26, the evaluator is able to jump directly to the next uncompleted step, which is helpful when not all steps can be completed in one session. Selecting the "Auto advance" in Figure 4.26 automatically advances the participant to the next evaluation step when the current step is completed. To force the evaluator to complete a step before going to the next, and thus not allow any steps to be skipped, check the "Don't allow leaving an evaluation step unless input is complete box" shown in Figure 4.26. This option can frustrate evaluators who may wish to give more thought to a particular step even though they are ready to proceed to subsequent steps. A participant can be directed to a particular URL after the evaluation is complete by checking the "Redirect after collecting input" box shown in Figure 4.26 and supplying a URL address in the box or automatically log the participant off after the evaluation is complete by checking

Figure 4.26   Setting navigation options

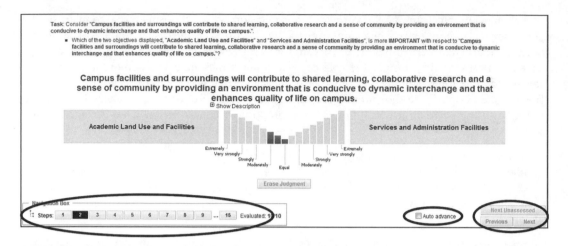

Figure 4.27   What the evaluator sees—Navigation Box and Advance options

the "Log-off after collecting input" box. These options provide more or less control of the evaluators' navigation. For inexperienced evaluators, check "Don't allow leaving an evaluation step unless input is complete," "Auto advance," and "Log-off after collecting input."

Choose Display Options

The display options allow for selecting which results to show the evaluators. Navigate to the display options by selecting "Display" under "Options" as shown in Figure 4.28.

On this screen, select what to show participants during the evaluation for intermediate and overall results. You can choose whether to display sensitivity analysis graphs and, if so, for the individual or combined results. Additionally, you can decide whether or not to show the welcome page, thank you page, inconsistency ratio, information documents associated with objectives and alternatives, and the full path of the objectives. Also, participants can be allowed to enter comments during the evaluation such as those that might explain or support a certain choice for later discussion or clarification.

We recommend showing individual intermediate and overall results as well as the individual's inconsistency ratio to allow the evaluator to reevaluate elements that do not feel right or are highly inconsistent. Showing combined results should be left unchecked when there is concern about unduly

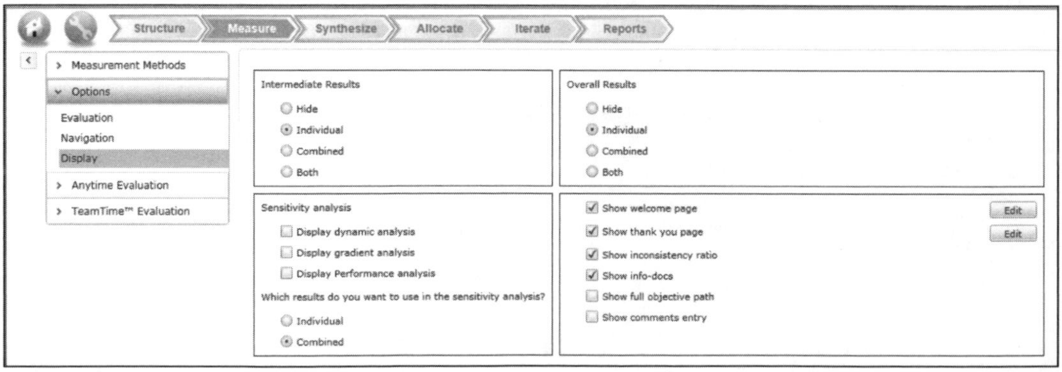

Figure 4.28   Setting display options

influencing the participant based on what others have said. We also recommend that "Show welcome page" and "Show thank you page" are checked as well as supporting information documents. These pages can be customized by selecting the "Edit" button next to each of these two options. The full objective path should be selected when necessary to distinguish similar sub-objectives for multiple different objectives, but otherwise tends to clutter the screen. The "Show/allow comments" entry should be checked to enable evaluators to note the reasons for their selections or to indicate confusion about any decision elements.

The example in Figure 4.29 shows a participant his own results, for example, when a cluster or meaningful subset of the evaluation is finished such as completing pairwise comparison of the objectives. The evaluator is asked whether the results make sense, and, if not, she can navigate back to reevaluate her responses. The note on the right about insufficient information to calculate overall priorities is shown because this evaluator is evaluating only objectives and, therefore, has no personal results about the priorities of the alternatives with respect to the objectives.

Choosing the Participation Method

The evaluation model project manager (facilitator), with guidance from the Steering Committee (PMB), determines whether each individual logs into the evaluation model and provides judgments asynchronously (without the rest of the group present) or whether the entire team is present to provide a consensus judgment synchronously after deliberating, or some combination of the two.

Anytime Evaluations for Asynchronous Participation

When the model is ready, invite participants to begin their evaluations asynchronously by selecting the "Measure" tab, and the "Anytime Evaluation, Invite Participants" step to generate invitations for an asynchronous evaluation, as shown in Figure 4.30.

In this case we only want to invite the four objectives evaluators. While the invitation can be tailored, in its default state it resembles the e-mail in Figure 4.31, substituting the project name and the actual link for the parameters shown in Figure 4.30. If the target timeframe for completion is not clear to the participants, add it while tailoring the e-mail invitation. Because these participants are fictitious and have fictitious e-mail addresses, they will not see this invitation. With a real decision project, the invitations would be directed to actual people. Check your name as the project manager to actually receive the e-mail and use the link.

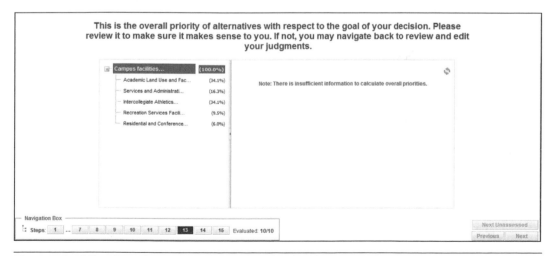

Figure 4.29   What the evaluator sees—personal results after objectives evaluation

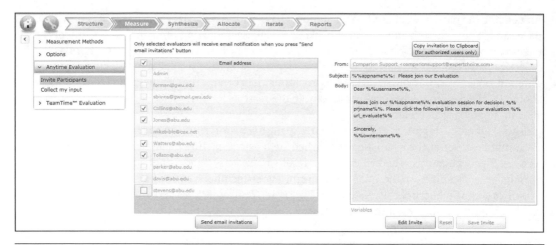

Figure 4.30   Tailor invitations and invite participants to asynchronous evaluation

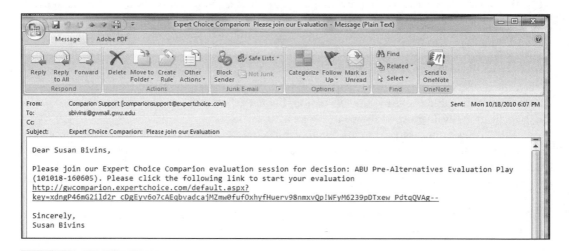

Figure 4.31   Email invitation received by selected participants

A participant who clicks on the e-mail link will be taken directly to the first evaluation screen, conveniently bypassing login and the use of an access code, if any. In this example the project manager will log in as each of the evaluators to simulate the evaluation and experience the process as the participants. An asynchronous evaluation can be conducted after ensuring that all participants have a common understanding of their roles as well as the meaning of the objectives.

TeamTime Evaluation for Synchronous Participation

To invite the objectives evaluators to a synchronous evaluation session, whether collocated or geographically dispersed but online concurrently, under "Measure" select the "TeamTime Evaluation, Select Participants" step and check the four evaluators as shown in Figure 4.32. Note that additional participants can be invited in "View Only" mode, as shown for Professor Forman.

Check the "Use keypads" if participants are collocated and using TeamTime Assistant. Check the "Allow joining TeamTime evaluation by logging into Comparion with Meeting ID as well as with a

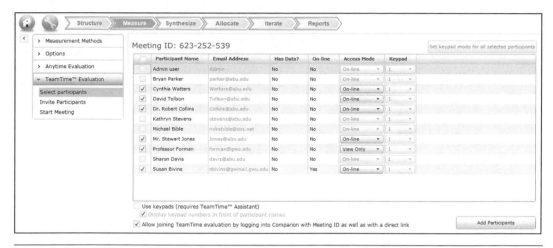

Figure 4.32   Preparing for TeamTime synchronous evaluation session

direct link" if desired, then press "Add Participants" to add any participants not previously part of the evaluation.

Move to "Invite Participants" to tailor the invitation, especially to supply the date and time as well as a direct link to the meeting to be sent via e-mail as shown in Figure 4.33. At the scheduled date and time, move to "Measure," "TeamTime Evaluation," "Start Meeting." You can elect to show users with "View only" access, and show or hide judgments from the participants, show participants with identities or anonymously, and show or hide the project manager, as shown in Figure 4.34.

Check the Progress of the ABU Evaluation

Once invitations have been sent, use the "Manage Project" wrench symbol, "Project Status" menu, and select "Evaluation Progress" to determine the progress of each evaluator.

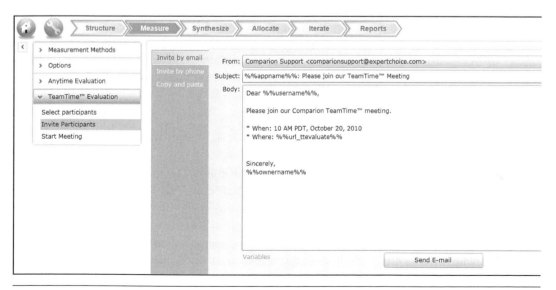

Figure 4.33   Inviting participants to a TeamTime evaluation meeting

Figure 4.34   Starting a TeamTime session with options

Determine the Status of the Evaluation

The current status of each of the evaluators is shown in Figure 4.35. The four evaluators of the objectives have not yet started their evaluations. As expected, the project manager and the "Admin" users will not be contributing comparisons for the evaluation. In some cases the project manager or person managing the evaluation process may also be one of the active contributors, but here that is not the case. If an evaluator has partially completed judgments, the percent of judgments completed will be shown. One advantage of the asynchronous evaluation capability in Comparion is that evaluators can log on at a convenient time and can also interrupt their evaluations, if necessary, and resume them later.

Verify the ABU Alternatives Evaluation Steps

Use the "Evaluation Progress" screen shown in Figure 4.35 to verify that what the participants will see corresponds with your intent. Perform this after all options are selected but prior to inviting the participants and placing the project online. Click on the numbers at the right of the participant in Figure 4.35 whose steps you want to verify; in this case, to check the path for Dr. Robert Collins, click on the "0% (0/10)" that goes directly to the first screen he will see when he begins his evaluation, as shown in Figure 4.36.

The first step is the welcome screen shown in Figure 4.36. Note the message in the upper left corner when viewing the evaluation steps. It indicates that although judgments may be entered, they will not be saved. In addition, it indicates which evaluator's path is being viewed. At the lower left, the "Navigation Box" shows how many steps the evaluator will see and can be used to move forward or backward through the steps, or to jump to any particular step. At the lower right, select the "Next Unassessed" item or the "Next" item to progress forward. The "Previous" button allows the evaluator to return to the last step. If the participants have different roles, verify that the steps for each role or individual are correct. When satisfied that the evaluator steps, in this case to evaluate all objectives and only the objectives, together with the options selected are as intended, proceed to notify the participants.

Status When Objectives Evaluation Is Complete

After the evaluations have begun, use the same project management icon to check on the progress of the evaluation by selecting the wrench icon, "Project Status" and "Evaluation Progress." Based on the information shown in Figure 4.37, all objectives evaluators have completed their evaluations and the model is ready for the "Synthesize" stage.

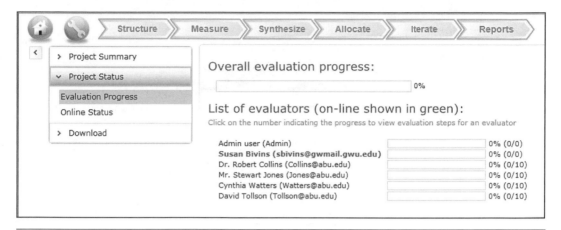

Figure 4.35   Showing the progress of the evaluations—not started

Figure 4.36   View the evaluation steps—welcome screen and navigation

4.8.5 Perform the Evaluation—Collect Data and Prioritize Objectives

To perform measurements and determine the relative priorities of the objectives, the ABU facilitator prepares the four evaluators, after they have been notified of their selection, by conducting an orientation to familiarize them with the process and use of the software tool, make them aware of their roles and responsibilities, and ensure a common understanding of the objectives they are evaluating. The facilitator also communicates the access code, if any, and the deadline or timeframe by which all evaluations are to be completed. Once that has been done, it is time to conduct the evaluation and obtain the individual judgments. TeamTime and other collaboration tools are useful vehicles for conducting orientations, reviewing roles and responsibilities, and ensuring a common understanding of the items to be evaluated.

Collect Data

With evaluators notified and orientation complete, each evaluator logs in to Comparion using the e-mail address established in the model; for example, Dr. Robert Collins will log in as Collins@abu .edu and click on "I have and would like to use an Access Code" that opens the Access Code window,

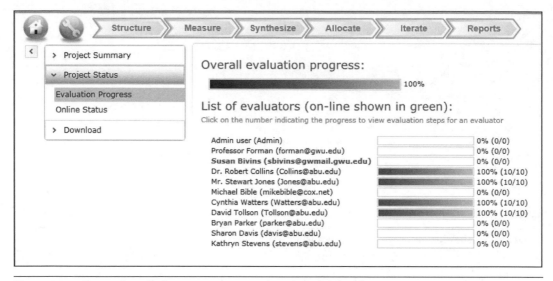

Figure 4.37 Status when all objectives participants have completed evaluation

as shown in Figure 4.38. Recall that the access code established in this version of the model is "ABU Objectives." If a participant does not specify an access code, he is shown all the projects in the workspace in which he is a specified evaluator, and he can choose the specific project by selecting the "Evaluate" indicator next to the one for which he will now enter judgments. In this example the evaluation is conducted asynchronously.

As Dr. Collins, complete all steps of the evaluation using the navigation boxes or auto advance—whichever is most comfortable. The evaluator is taken through the steps you reviewed during "View

Figure 4.38 Login to Comparion as an evaluator

Evaluation Steps," but now judgments are recorded for the participant. To make the entire evaluation screen visible, select the magnifying glass icon at the upper right corner of the screen, as shown in Figure 4.39. As Dr. Collins, enter a comment to explain why you evaluated this step in this manner (available if the option was selected during "Measure").

During the evaluation, after pairwise comparisons have been completed for the objectives, the evaluator will see an interim review screen that shows the relative priorities established by his responses for the importance of the objectives. The review screen asks the evaluator to either confirm that the priorities make sense or to navigate back to the previous judgments and edit them, as shown in Figure 4.40.

The evaluator can return to any step in the evaluation from the results screen and reenter or even erase the judgment. If Dr. Collins erases any of his judgments, the project status will be updated to indicate that he has not completed his evaluation. As shown in Figure 4.41, Dr. Collins has erased

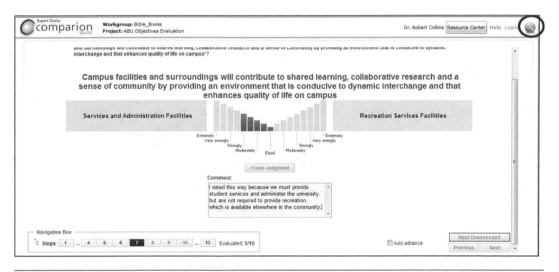

Figure 4.39   Using the magnifying glass and the comment field

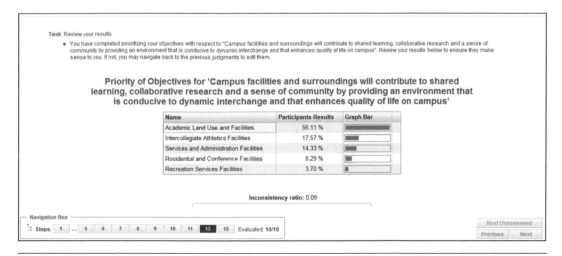

Figure 4.40   Individual results after prioritizing the objectives

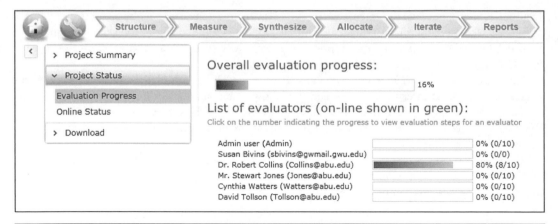

Figure 4.41   Change in project status after participant erases judgments

two of his judgments. To prevent a participant from changing his input once it is complete, the project manager for the model can disable the user in the "Structure" menu, "Participants" step. However, in an actual evaluation, the facilitator or responsible manager contacts the individual to determine when the results will be complete or why they were changed before taking other action.

It is important to note that what the evaluator is seeing on these review screens are the individual local priorities he has assigned to the alternatives for the given objective. After the evaluations are complete, his results are synthesized with those of the other objectives evaluators to determine the combined relative priorities of the objectives.

When the evaluator is satisfied with the relative priorities established for the objectives, the evaluator moves to the final screen that displays a thank you message. It is displayed to the evaluator if that option was chosen. The evaluator is also informed that he can navigate back to and change previous judgments. Once he is satisfied that his individual results represent his perceptions, the evaluator may log out.

To complete the example ABU evaluation, log in as each participant in turn and complete the judgments on behalf of the fictitious participants.

4.8.6 Synthesize the Results to Produce Relative Priorities

Once all individual judgments have been entered, the results are synthesized to produce mathematically accurate ratio-scale relative priorities of the objectives with respect to the goal and based on the combined judgments of all participants. In a real situation, once assured that all participants have completed their evaluations, the project owner views the results. In this example, select the "Synthesize" tab and select "Overall Results" to view the display shown in Figure 4.42. By default, "Overall Results" shows the objectives in the left pane and the alternatives in the right pane. Because they have not been entered or evaluated, no priorities are available for alternatives at this time.

Drag the vertical bar separating the objectives hierarchy and alternatives to the right, if necessary, to obtain a more complete view of the objectives. To view the combined results of the objectives evaluations, select the two left icons above the objectives, as shown in Figure 4.43. The first icon on the left displays the "Local" priorities and the second icon from the left displays the "Global" priorities.

Of course, if you have been following along and performing the steps presented, your specific priorities will be different from those in the example. Look carefully at Figure 4.43 or at your own results and note that the priorities for the goal are shown as "[Local: 100.00%] [Global: 100.00%]."

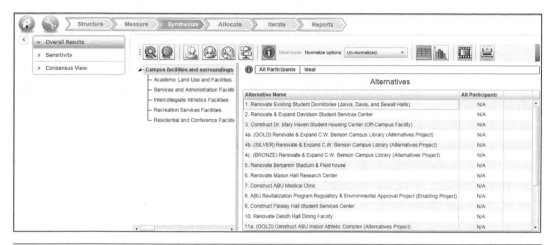

Figure 4.42   Synthesize and view overall results after evaluation of objectives

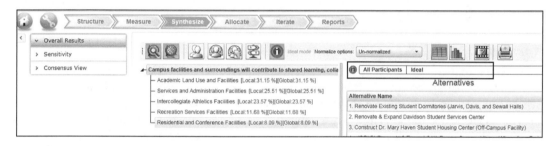

Figure 4.43   View local and global priorities for the objectives

This signifies that the priorities or importance of all the objectives add up to 100.00% and, after evaluation, each objective has a relative importance, after pairwise comparisons, of between 0% and 100% to signify their ratio-scale priority or contribution to the achievement of the goal as seen by the evaluation team. Depending on the length of the goal statement, it may be necessary to use the scroll bar at the bottom of the screen underneath the objectives to see the priorities displayed to the right of the goal.

The local and global priorities resulting from the evaluation are displayed next to each objective. As stated, local priorities are the ratio-scale weights of a child node with respect to the parent node and the local priorities of the cluster sum to 100%. Global priorities are the ratio-scale weights of any node with respect to the goal. The global priorities of all the lowest-level nodes sum to 100%. In this case, because there is only one level in the hierarchy of objectives, the local and global priorities will be the same.

Ideal versus Distributive Mode

An important concept in AHP is the mode of synthesis, ideal or distributive. Because this is shown as an option in the "Synthesize" menu, as shown in Figure 4.44, we discuss briefly the distributive mode versus the ideal mode.

In general the ideal mode is used in PPM. Forman (2010) recommends that the ideal mode always be used with PPM except when deriving probability distributions for risk. Its use ensures that the

Figure 4.44   Ideal versus distributive mode switch

ratio-scale relative anticipated benefits of the alternatives do not change with respect to each other when projects are added to or removed from the portfolio, even though the absolute global priorities would change. This is discussed further in Chapter 7 when the alternatives are evaluated. Since pairwise comparison is the measurement method for evaluating objectives, no difference in results is seen here between the ideal and distributive mode.

Consistency

Recall the discussion of consistency earlier in the chapter, indicating that an inconsistency of less than 0.10 is generally acceptable. In this case, the overall inconsistency of 0.04 indicates that inconsistency in this ABU example set of judgments is acceptable. If that was not the case, Expert Choice provides suggestions in the help topic "Examining and Improving Inconsistency" for lowering inconsistencies. This capability is expected to be added later for Comparion. The facilitator reviews the inconsistencies as necessary and identifies solutions to discuss with the evaluators in a follow-up session. The Expert Choice software can suggest a best fit, or the affected judgments can be changed by making new pairwise comparisons. However, we recommend that the evaluators themselves be asked to make any changes with the guidance of the facilitator or project manager.

Other Functions Available for the Synthesize Tab

On the "Overall Results" step, four icons can be seen above the objectives as shown in Figure 4.45, one each for selecting the results for one or more participants, selecting groups, managing groups, and selecting alternatives. These icons apply to overall results only, so because the alternatives have not yet been evaluated, these icons, although active, do not provide useful information until that has been completed. The "Normalize options" drop-down menu also does not apply until all work is complete. These are powerful functions for calculation and the display of subsets of the results (discussed further in Chapter 7).

The letter "i" icon toggles the information bar on and off. The information bar can be seen above the alternatives shown in Figure 4.46 and indicates for which participants the synthesized results are displayed and whether the mode is "Ideal" or "Distributive."

Synthesizing also includes sensitivity analysis in the "Sensitivity" step. The "Consensus View" step affords the opportunity to determine the degree of consensus for judgments that use other than pairwise comparisons. These are not applicable until after the alternatives are evaluated in Chapter 7. For now we will skip the "Allocate" workflow tab. It is used in Chapter 7 to download the results of the evaluation to the Resource Aligner of Expert Choice Desktop.

Figure 4.45   Viewing results for individuals, groups, and alternatives

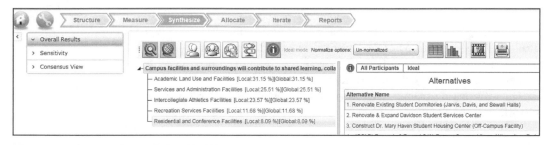

Figure 4.46   Information bar specifying which results and the current mode

4.8.7 Iterate

After evaluator input is synthesized, the project owner and other members of the PMB review the output or call the evaluators together for a meeting. They discuss the validity of the results and raise any questions such as whether the objectives with the highest priority seem to be the right choice or whether any objectives might be missing from the model (Forman, 2010). A missing objective in the case of objectives developed during strategic planning might require a decision by the ERB to revisit or revise the strategic plan.

Another reason to iterate might arise when the objectives are evaluated prior to the alternatives (Forman, 2010). In many cases the evaluation of the alternatives can influence the priorities of the objectives because of what is learned during alternatives evaluation, a phenomenon known as feedback. This is why, when the same participants evaluate alternatives and objectives, we recommend evaluating alternatives first so that the feedback from prioritizing alternatives influences the prioritization of objectives.

In the case of ABU, however, the evaluators were assigned specific roles, either to evaluate objectives or to evaluate alternatives, so such feedback does not apply. Forman (2010) states that, "With adequate iteration, the results of an AHP model will be intuitive." Forman goes on to explain that the results agree with intuition as it is experienced after the evaluation and any needed iterations, but do not necessarily agree with intuition as it was before the evaluation.

The prioritization of objectives is an important decision. When the evaluators agree that the results are right, and there is consensus, then the decision probably makes sense. Often, though, there is a need to revisit the objectives hierarchy to make sure it is complete, or the participants need to

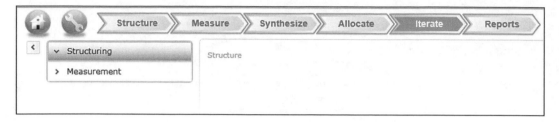

Figure 4.47   Using the iterate tab to return to structuring or measuring

revisit their judgments or roles. The "Iterate" tab provides a rapid means of returning to either structuring or measurement, as shown in Figure 4.47.

4.8.8 Reports

To create ad hoc reports or to use the predefined reports provided with Comparion, select the "Reports" workflow tab and then select the "Predefined Reports" step to see the list of standard reports available. The reports can be saved, printed, or exported in a variety of formats. A search capability is provided to find words or strings of characters within the reports. Select the "Priority of Objectives" predefined report to see the report shown in Figure 4.48.

The information from the reports is used to help prepare for the presentation of results and for historical documentation of the process and the outcome of the evaluation.

4.8.9 Review and Present for Approval

Once the results have been reviewed with the four evaluators and any necessary adjustments made through iteration, they can be presented by the Steering Committee to the Board of Trustees or other senior management as necessary. The next steps include nomination of ABU facilities projects, solicitation of business cases, and selection of the candidate list for the portfolio. This concludes the ABU example for prioritizing objectives. It will be continued in Chapter 7 with the prioritization of the candidate projects or alternatives.

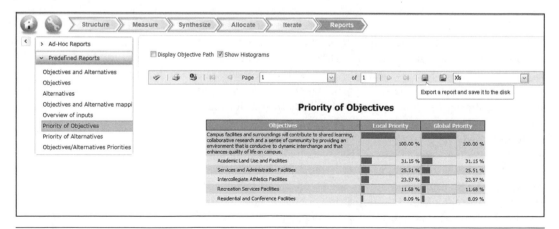

Figure 4.48   Using the priority of objectives predefined report

4.9 PRIORITIZED OBJECTIVES—A MAJOR STEP

Synthesized results of the objectives evaluation provide the relative priorities of the objectives and sub-objectives with respect to achieving the goal of the organization. These prioritized objectives form the foundation for establishing the priorities of the eventual candidate projects that support them during the project prioritization process. They also round out the strategic plan with the important addition of establishing the relative importance of the objectives it contains.

4.10 SUMMARY

In this chapter we established the objectives hierarchy and created the AHP model, identified and invited the participants, and collected their input using a web-based tool and verbal pairwise comparisons. After completing the evaluations, results were synthesized to derive local and global priorities of the objectives. During this process we discussed concepts associated with measurement methods and their presentation, reviewed the meaning and calculation of local and global priorities, and provided an overview of inconsistency. This led to a prioritized objectives hierarchy.

This completes the strategic phase of the PPM process. In Chapters 5 and 6, we describe how candidate projects are identified and screened for entry into the actual portfolio selection process. This is known as the screening phase. In Chapter 7 we build on the model established in this chapter. The priorities of the objectives are applied to the evaluations of the project alternatives that support them, producing a meaningful and mathematically sound assessment of the anticipated benefit of each alternative project with respect to the goal.

4.11 APPENDIX 4A—USING EXPERT CHOICE DESKTOP TO CREATE THE MODEL

The purpose of the material presented here is to demonstrate how to use Expert Choice Desktop rather than Comparion to create the objectives hierarchy. In this section you will learn to open it, create a new Expert Choice AHP model, open and save an existing model, and specify the AHP goal and objectives for the model. This appendix progresses through the same process as presented in the main text. However, the steps to complete this process are substituted for Comparion.

4.11.1 Building the Expert Choice Desktop Model

Screen shots with explanations are used throughout this appendix to demonstrate how the software tool supports the concept of prioritizing objectives within a structured, methodical process. As software is frequently updated, use the Expert Choice Desktop and Comparion help functions should the instructions appear different from what is shown on your screen. Again, the illustrations are intended to make it easy for novices or the technically challenged to move comfortably through the ABU example with the software while focusing on the process of making complex decisions. To reinforce the learning experience, we encourage you to log on and perform each of the steps while reading the material. The material entered for the ABU example can be copied and pasted from the supplied Word document "ABU_Extracts.docx" or can be entered by hand using the material from the end of Chapter 2 in Section 2.2.

Open Expert Choice Desktop

If you still have the welcome screen that provides tutorials, shown in Figure 4A.1, select the "Start Using Expert Choice" link at the lower left. You may also wish to check the box in the lower left

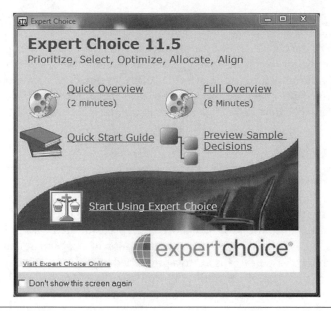

Figure 4A.1 Start using Expert Choice

corner labeled "Don't show this screen again." Depending on the version of Expert Choice Desktop you have, you may see "Expert Choice 11.5" at the top of the welcome screen.

Create the Expert Choice AHP Model

Select the "Create New Model" button and choose the "Direct" modeling method as shown in Figure 4A.2. This will allow you to specify the goal and begin to enter the objectives hierarchy. After clicking

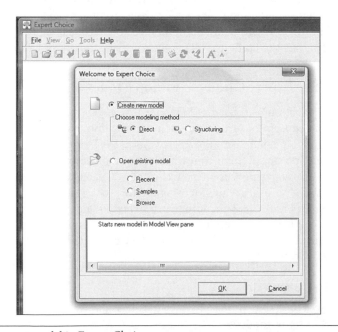

Figure 4A.2 Start a new model in Expert Choice

"OK," Expert Choice presents a dialog box to allow the user to select a directory and folder (or create a new folder) and type in a filename. Here we have chosen to create a new folder named "Chapter_4" and the filename "Chapter_4_Objectives_Hierarchy." Expert Choice automatically provides the file type suffix of ".ahpz." Provide the filename and location as shown in Figure 4A.3 and click on "Open" to create the file.

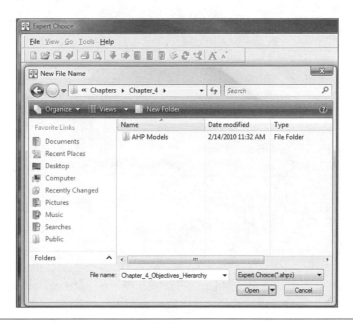

Figure 4A.3   Create the Expert Choice AHP model file

Entering the Facilitator's Email Address

If you plan to upload the Expert Choice model to Comparion for easy evaluator access, as discussed later, the facilitator's e-mail address must be entered into the model. In many instances Comparion will be used at some point, thus, it is a good practice to enter this address. To do so select "Facilitator" in the drop-down box on the right of the row of icons as shown in Figure 4A.4 and then click on the "Participants" icon (that looks like two heads) just to the left of the drop-down box.

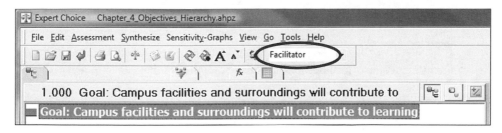

Figure 4A.4   Select facilitator and click on the participants icon

A pop-up window opens showing a column for "Email." Enter the facilitator's e-mail address as shown in Figure 4A.5 and select "Close" at the lower right of the pop-up window. In this case we have entered a sample e-mail address name@domain.com. What you will enter is the e-mail address of the

PPM person responsible for facilitating the decision process represented by the model. In this case, enter your own e-mail address.

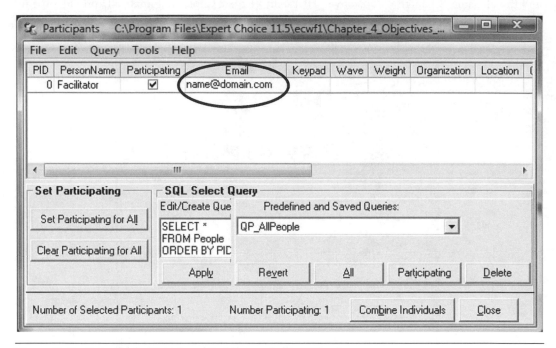

Figure 4A.5   Enter the facilitator's email address and select "Close"

Saving the Model

Once the model has been created, save it on a regular basis to preserve your work. This can be accomplished by clicking on the disk icon (third from the left in the row of icons) or clicking on "File" and then "Save." Both are shown in Figure 4A.6 and will save the model in the directory from which you opened it or in which you first created it.

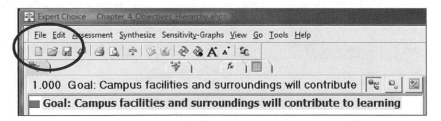

Figure 4A.6   Saving the Expert Choice model

If you wish to save the model in a new location, select "File" and then "Save As" to obtain the dialog box shown in Figure 4A.7. The default contains the prior filename and directory locations, but you can change them by navigating in this dialog box. Save the model now, either with the same name and location or by changing the location, filename, or both. After you have saved the model, you can exit Expert Choice by clicking on the X symbol at the far upper right of the window.

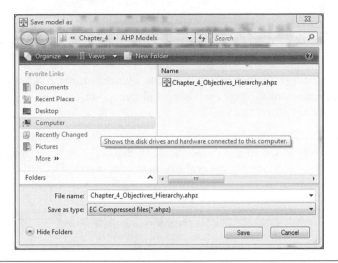

Figure 4A.7   Saving the model in a new location or with a new name

Opening an Existing Expert Choice Model

If it is not already open, start the Expert Choice program as described earlier in this section. The default dialog box will open with the buttons selected for "Open existing model" and "Recent." As can be seen in Figure 4A.8, you can select the "Create new model" or for existing models you can open one you have used recently by selecting (or allowing the default for) the "Recent" button. You can open sample files provided by Expert Choice by selecting the "Samples" button or you can look for other models by selecting the "Browse" button. In this case, open the model you saved earlier by double-clicking on the filename or by highlighting it and clicking *OK*.

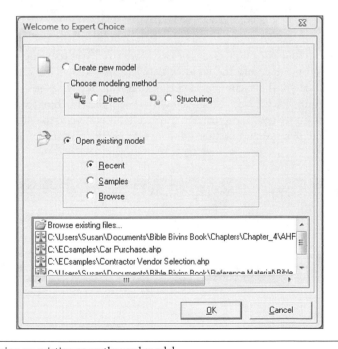

Figure 4A.8   Opening an existing recently used model

Establish the Goal

When you open the model, Expert Choice Desktop will request a description for the goal. As stated, the ABU strategic goal related to facilities is:

> *Campus facilities and surroundings will contribute to shared learning, collaborative research and a sense of community by providing an environment that is conducive to dynamic interchange and that enhances quality of life on campus.*

Although Expert Choice Desktop will allow the entire goal to be entered, only an abbreviated version will be visible on the screen and in reports, as shown in Figure 4A.9, but bear in mind that it represents the entire goal statement. During the evaluation, to be completed later, the entire statement will be visible to the evaluators.

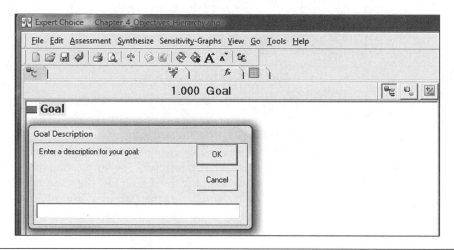

Figure 4A.9   Enter the goal description

After typing in the goal description, click on "OK." If desired you may copy the description from another document and paste it into the window using the Windows copy and paste functions—Ctrl-C and Ctrl-V. Once you have completed this, Expert Choice will show you the goal that you typed, as shown in Figure 4A.10. Notice that you will see only as much of the goal as can be shown in the window, but the entire goal is captured in the model. If you want to edit what you have typed, either right-click on the item or click on the "Edit" menu to bring up the dialog box shown in Figure 4A.11.

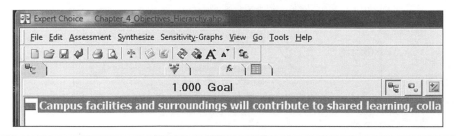

Figure 4A.10   Goal established

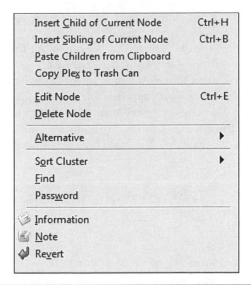

Figure 4A.11   Select "Edit" node to modify the selected node

In the dialog box select "Edit Node" and another dialog box will open to allow you to modify what you have typed, as in Figure 4A.12. Note that the dialog box in Figure 4A.12 is "Edit Objective Name." You can use the same editing capabilities for modifying the text for the goal or for objectives that we enter later. Place the cursor in the box to make any changes needed, then select "OK" and the statement will be modified accordingly.

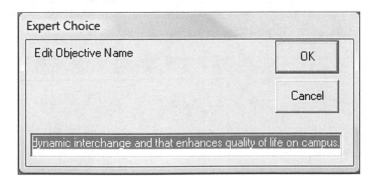

Figure 4A.12   Edit text in goals or objectives

Establish the Objectives Hierarchy

Now that the goal has been defined, we are ready to enter the five objectives as abbreviated in Section 4.8.3. For easy reference they are repeated here, but without the numerals:

Academic Land Use and Facilities
Services and Administration Facilities
Intercollegiate Athletics Facilities
Recreation Services Facilities
Residential and Conference Facilities

The objectives can be entered one at a time by right-clicking on the goal node and selecting "Insert Child of Current Node," backspacing over the default number (e.g., "1st" and typing a descriptive objective name followed by pressing the "Enter" key. When you hit the "Enter" key, a new line will appear for the next objective with the default number "2nd." Backspace over the number and type the second descriptive objective name followed by the "Enter" key. When you have typed and pressed "Enter" for all the objectives under the goal, press the "Esc" key to indicate that you are finished. See Figure 4A.13 for entering the objectives by typing them. As you can see, two of the objectives have been typed, and the default third is about to be revised to say Intercollegiate Athletics Facilities. Continue this until all five have been entered and the "Esc" key is pressed to tell Expert Choice that there are no more objectives.

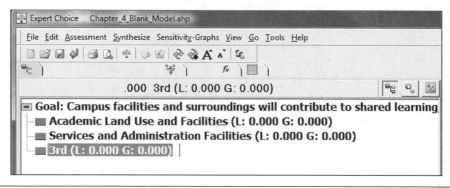

Figure 4A.13   Entering the objectives by keying directly

However, the fastest and most straightforward way to enter all the objectives is to copy them to the clipboard from Word or another application, right-click on the goal, and select "Paste Children from Clipboard," as shown in Figure 4A.14.

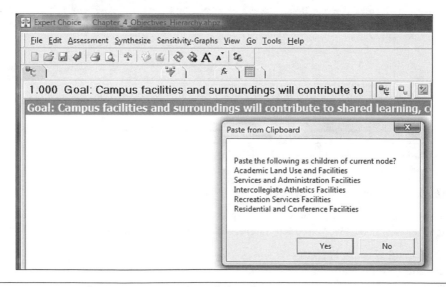

Figure 4A.14   Entering objectives by pasting from clipboard

By selecting "Yes" in the dialog box, all five objectives will be entered, as shown in Figure 4A.15. Once the objectives have been entered, save the file.

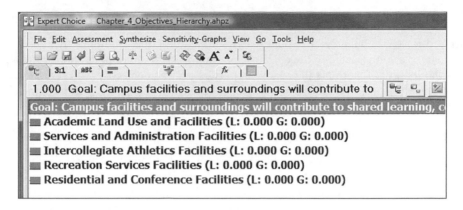

Figure 4A.15   AHP model with goal and objectives

Including Sub-objectives in the Objectives Hierarchy

To include the sub-objectives, apply the same process just used to enter the objectives. Bear in mind that the pairwise comparisons or ratings performed by the evaluators will be performed at the lowest level of sub-objective for each objective. An example of the AHP model with sub-objectives entered for only the Academic Land Use and Facilities objective is shown in Figure 4A.16. The shaded boxes to the left of a node indicate that it has subordinate objectives or *children*, while those with grayed boxes represent the lowest level of a particular branch of the hierarchy. The remainder of this appendix will use the AHP model that includes only the five high-level objectives to facilitate learning the process and the tools while minimizing the complexity of the decision process. However, the same PPM process and tools can be applied with a more complex decision model.

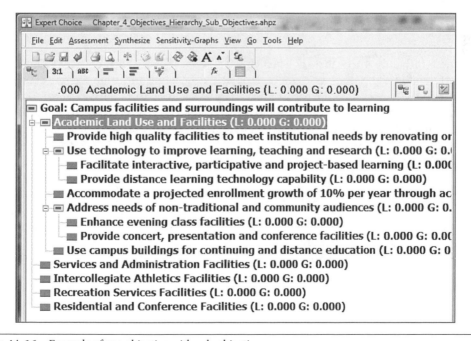

Figure 4A.16   Example of one objective with sub-objectives

4.11.2 Complete the Model and Upload to Comparion

As described earlier, although all five objectives identified describe conditions that enable ABU to meet its goal for campus facilities, the objectives are not of equal importance and require a prioritization methodology to determine the relative importance of each objective with respect to the goal. Later, the alternative projects that contribute to an objective will take on the priority of the objectives they support.

Local and Global Priorities

Before proceeding, look carefully at Figure 4A.17 and note that the line item selected is the "Goal" and "1.000" appears in front of it. This signifies that the priorities or importance of all the objectives will add up to 1.000. After evaluation each objective will have a relative importance, after pairwise comparisons, of between 0.000 and 1.000 to signify their ratio-scale impact or contribution to the achievement of the goal, as seen by the evaluation team.

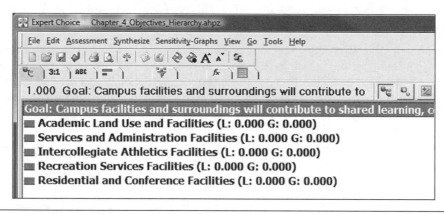

Figure 4A.17   Local and global priorities before evaluation

Also note in Figure 4A.17 that (L: 0.000 G: 0.000) appears after each objective. These indicate the local (L) and global (G) priorities for each objective. Local priorities are the ratio-scale weights of a child node with respect to the parent node. They will add up to 1.000. Global priorities are the ratio-scale weights of any node with respect to the goal. The global priorities of all of the lowest-level nodes will sum to 1.000. In Figure 4A.17 all the values are zero initially because no evaluations have been entered. Also, because there is only one level in the hierarchy of objectives, the local and global priorities will be the same.

Figure 4A.18 provides an example of local and global priorities after a mock evaluation of a sample objective hierarchy with sub-objectives. Local priorities for any cluster will sum to 1.000. Global priorities are the product of the local priority of the node and its parent node's global priority. The global priorities of sibling child nodes in a cluster will sum to the global priority of the parent node. Also note that the priorities are ratio-scale weights. In the example the evaluators have considered Objective II to be twice as important as Objective I in achieving the goal, and four times as important as Objective IV. Likewise, Sub-objective C is considered three times as important as Sub-objective D and six times as important as Sub-objectives A and B in terms of achieving Objective II. Sub-sub 1 was evaluated as 1.5 times as important as Sub-sub 2 in terms of achieving Sub-objective C, and so on. The ratios are the same whether using global or local priorities. For more information see the discussion of local and global priorities in the "Synthesize" discussion in the main part of this chapter.

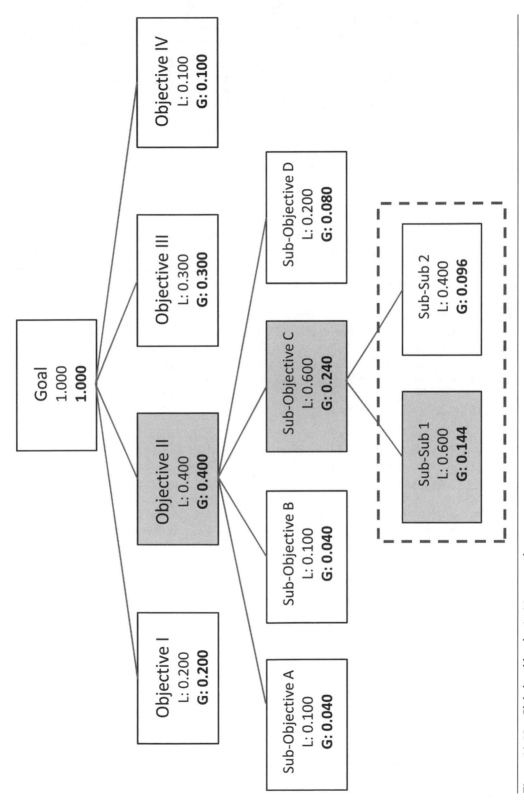

Figure 4A.18 Global and local priorities example

Table 4.A1 Participants selected to prioritize the objectives

Name	Title	Representing	email
Ms. Cynthia Watters	Chairman	Board of Trustees	Watters@abu.edu
Mr. David Tollson	Vice Chair	Board of Trustees	Tollson@abu.edu
Dr. Robert Collins	Chairman	Steering Committee	Collins@abu.edu
Mr. Stewart Jones	Faculty Director	PMO	Jones@abu.edu

Armed with this understanding, in the remainder of this section you will establish the objective evaluation environment, notify participants of its availability, perform the evaluation on behalf of the participants, and analyze the results.

Selecting the Participants

To prioritize objectives, PPM personnel will coordinate with the organization's leadership and management to identify and select personnel in the organization who have the appropriate perspective to provide an assessment of each objective. The evaluators should understand the organization's vision and objectives thoroughly and represent the major stakeholders for the achievement of the goal. The organization's equivalent of the ERB and the PPG will likely select the appropriate evaluators. In the ABU example, evaluators include representatives of the Board of Trustees, the Campus Revitalization Program Steering Committee, and the Director of the PMO. The list of evaluators for the facilities objectives is provided in Table 4A.1. The names of the participants in the ABU example are fictitious. In this example, the personnel providing data are not all residing locally. Thus, Comparion provides the best option to collect data as it allows for web-based access.

Upload the Model to Comparion

Each evaluator will use Expert Choice's associated web-based evaluation tool, Comparion, to compare each objective's contribution to the goal relative to each of the other objectives. Comparion will use these pairwise comparisons to calculate ratio-scale relative priorities for the objectives. As stated earlier, although the actual evaluation can be done in EC, Comparion provides remote access through the internet and guides the participants step-by-step through the process. Thus, to use the workstation it does not require the participants to be in the same location. Comparion Suite offers both synchronous and asynchronous meeting capability. The synchronous meeting capability allows an entire group to meet online and exchange ideas and thoughts in real time; the asynchronous capability allows a team member or evaluator to go online at his or her convenience to complete assigned activities. Most PPM groups will use both capabilities.

To establish the evaluation environment, the AHP model created in Expert Choice can be uploaded to Comparion. To upload a model to Comparion, the Facilitator's e-mail address must have been entered in the model. To begin this process, go to the Comparion Suite site at the link provided by your instructor and log on with the credentials (Email Address and Password) supplied, as shown in Figure 4A.19.

After supplying your authorized e-mail address and password, click on the "Log In" button. Note that this is the same screen you will see if you are invited to join a TeamTime meeting, but, in that case, you would supply your credentials on the right side of the screen and choose the type of meeting you are joining. After login, you will see your home screen like the one in Figure 4A.20 that shows any existing projects you may have. If you have multiple workgroups, select the workgroup provided with the book or by your instructor by selecting it from the drop-down list next to "Select Workgroup."

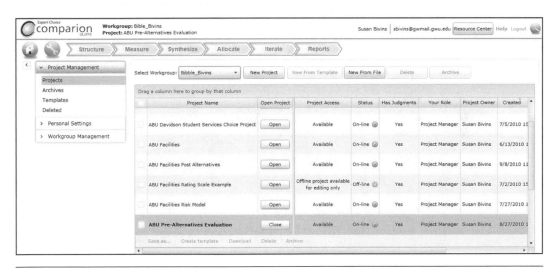

Figure 4A.19   Login to Comparion Suite

Figure 4A.20   Comparion home screen

If you already have projects underway, they will be shown together with status information about each. You can also select "New Project, New from Template," if any templates have been created. In this case, though, we want to use the Expert Choice model you created that already contains the goal and objectives. Select the "New From File" button on the screen in Figure 4A.20. Note that a pop-up window will open to allow you to select the file as shown in Figure 4A.21, therefore, pop-ups must be enabled for this website in your browser.

Browse to the directory folder that contains the Expert Choice file with the goal and objectives created earlier, select the filename, and click "OK." The file will be uploaded to Comparion and shown

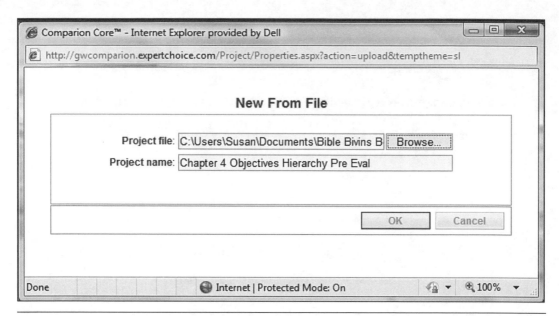

Figure 4A.21 Select New from File to upload Expert Choice model

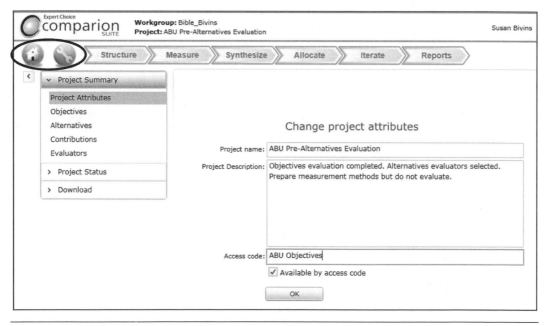

Figure 4A.22 Manage the project to change project attributes

at the top of your list of projects on the home screen. Select "Open" under "Open Project." If you want to manage the attributes of the project (e.g., name, description, or access code) or check the box to make the project available by access code, select the icon that resembles a wrench at the upper left corner of the screen, as shown in Figure 4A.22.

You can go back to the home screen shown in Figure 4A.20 by selecting the icon that looks like a house, also in the upper left corner of the screen. Unless you have changed it, the "Access code" box contains a randomly generated mix of letters and numbers that can be given to your participants so they can go directly to the specific project. Change this to a meaningful access code such as "ABU Objectives" and check the "Available by access code" box.

Now the model you created in Expert Choice Desktop has been uploaded to Comparion where we will complete structuring it by assigning participant roles, and then we measure and synthesize as described in the main section of this chapter.

4.12 APPENDIX 4B—SYNTHESIZING IN EXPERT CHOICE DESKTOP

In the main section of this chapter synthesis and reporting were performed in Comparion. The purpose of this appendix is to demonstrate performing similar functions in Expert Choice Desktop. We have elected, in this example, to perform an analysis of results on a workstation.

Screen shots with explanations are used throughout this appendix to demonstrate how the software tool supports the concept of prioritizing objectives within a structured, methodical process. As software is frequently updated, use the Comparion and Expert Choice Desktop help functions should the instructions appear different from what is shown on your screen. Again, the illustrations are intended to make it easy for novices or the technically challenged to move comfortably through the ABU example with the software while focusing on the process of making complex decisions. To reinforce the learning experience, we encourage you to log on and perform each of the steps while reading the material.

When all participants have completed their evaluations, download the model to Expert Choice Desktop. This can be done when the model is open by selecting the "Manage Project" wrench and then selecting "Download" as shown in Figure 4B.1.

Comparion will display the "Download Project" window with a choice of Expert Choice Desktop or Comparion format for the downloaded file. Click on the "EC Desktop File (.ahpz)", and then click the "Download" button at the lower right, as shown in Figure 4B.2.

A window will open asking whether you want to "Open" or "Save" the file; select "Save," navigate to your directory location of choice and select "Save" at the lower right. If you wish you can change the filename of the model before saving.

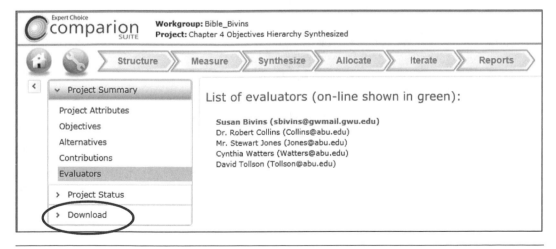

Figure 4B.1   Download the model from Comparion to Expert Choice for analysis

Figure 4B.2   Select "File" format and download the project

4.12.1 Combining and Synthesizing the Results

Although the participants have completed their individual evaluations of the priorities of the objectives, they need to be combined in the Expert Choice model to provide a single relative priority for each of the five objectives with respect to the goal; in other words, what is the relative contribution of each type of facility to the achievement of the goal for campus facilities and surroundings? Open the Expert Choice file that was saved in the last section. As you can see, the local and global priorities of the objectives are still zero as shown in Figure 4B.3. However, by selecting each participant in turn, using the drop-down list next to the Participants icon, Expert Choice will display the individual evaluator results, as shown in Figure 4B.4.

Selecting "Combined" in the drop-down list shows zeros because the individual results have not yet been combined. To combine the evaluation results, select the "Assessment Menu" and then select "Combine Participants Judgments/Data" as shown in Figure 4B.5.

As can be seen, the user can choose to combine judgments and data for the entire hierarchy, for the plex (the currently highlighted node and its children) or for the current highlighted node. In this case, select "Entire Hierarchy" and then "Both." You will then see the local and global priorities for each objective as determined by the team of evaluators and shown in Figure 4B.6.

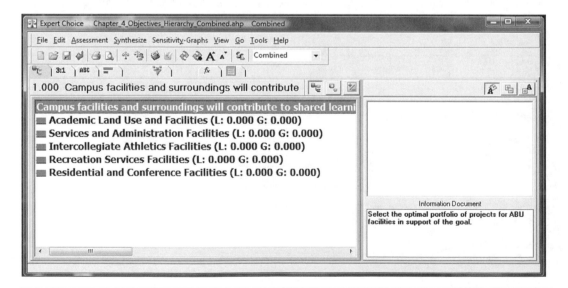

Figure 4B.3   Expert Choice model before combining evaluator information

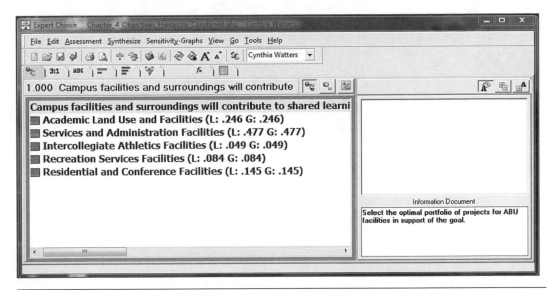

Figure 4B.4   Individual evaluator results

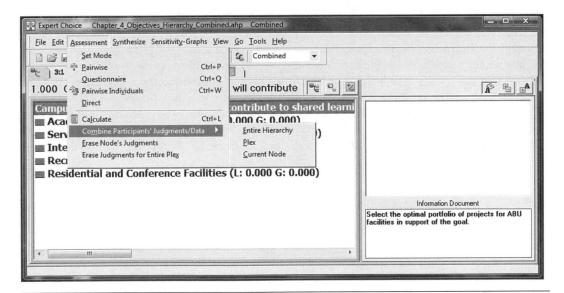

Figure 4B.5   Combining evaluator judgments

The combined results are established in AHP by obtaining the geometric mean of the individual results for each judgment. Although it is possible to assign different weights to individual evaluators—for example, if we want the CEO's judgment to count twice as much as the CIO's judgment—the weights would be applied to the individual results before calculating the geometric mean. In this case all the evaluators were considered equal, and the geometric mean for Academic Land Use and Facilities is 0.311. Recall the discussion in the "Synthesize" section of the main chapter about the meaning of local and global priorities. In this case, since there is only one level for the objectives, the local and global priorities are the same for each objective, as would be the case for the highest-level

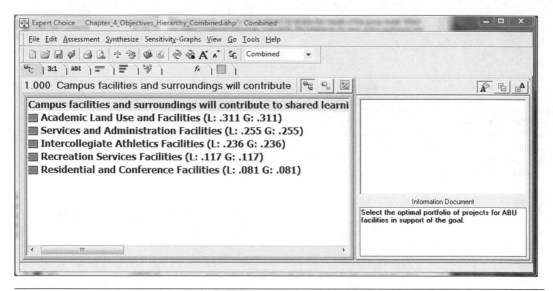

Figure 4B.6   Local and global priorities for each objective as evaluated

objectives in any hierarchy. Note also that they add to 1.000, thus providing a ratio-scale comparison of the relative contributions of each objective to the goal, as evaluated by the selected team. With careful structuring of the model, the time for each evaluator to get online and complete the evaluation was a few minutes. Imagine how long it would have taken the group to produce these results using BOGSAT!

Now that the results have been combined, it is possible to examine them and represent them graphically by synthesizing them. Synthesis is the process of combining priorities to obtain global priorities for each node. The synthesis process will be more meaningful after we have added and prioritized alternatives (projects that are candidates for the portfolio) in a later chapter. To synthesize the results just for the objectives with respect to the goal, from the "Synthesize" menu select "With Respect to Goal" as shown in Figure 4B.7.

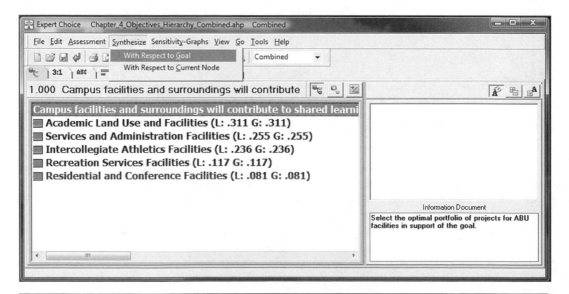

Figure 4B.7   Synthesizing the results of prioritizing the objectives

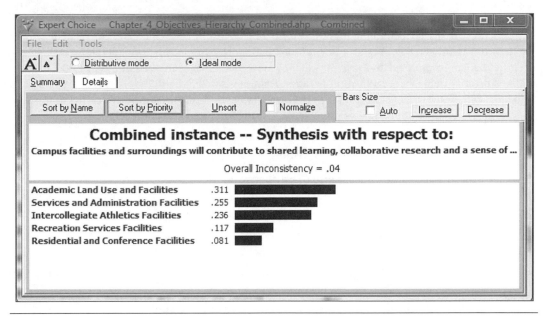

Figure 4B.8   Synthesized objectives by priority

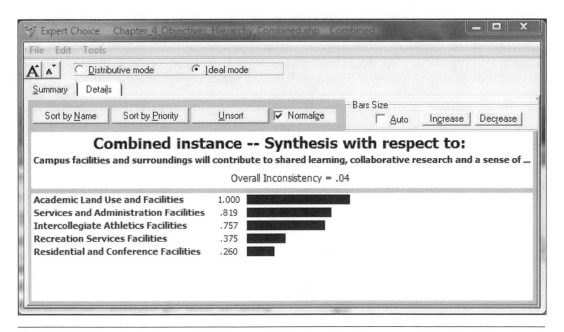

Figure 4B.9   Normalized objectives priorities

Expert Choice will graphically display the combined, synthesized results as shown in Figure 4B.8. In this case, the default is to "Sort by Priority," although there are options to sort the objectives alphanumerically by name and to leave sorted in the original order. In this case, quite by accident, the original entry order is the same as the order when sorted by priority. It is also possible in this synthesized view to change the size of the bars to be visually more attractive.

To enable the ratio-scale priorities to be seen more easily, check the box next to "Normalize." Expert Choice assigns 1.000 to the highest priority objective and then calculates the relative priority for each of the other objectives as a portion of 1.000. For example, since Academic Land Use and Facilities had an original relative priority of 0.311, now that it has been normalized to 1.000, the normalized priority of Services and Administration Facilities is 0.255 divided by 0.311, or a normalized value of 0.819. Thus, as can be seen in Figure 4B.9, Services and Administration Facilities are seen by the evaluation team as about 82% as important as Academic Land Use and Facilities.

4.12.2 Ideal versus Distributive Mode

Please see the discussion of "Ideal versus Distributive Mode" in the "Synthesize" section of the main chapter, as the material applies equally to both the Comparion and Expert Choice Desktop approaches.

4.12.3 Consistency

The topic of consistency was discussed in the "Synthesize" section of the main chapter and the concepts apply equally here. Recall that an inconsistency ratio of 0.00 would represent perfectly consistent choices; for example, if an evaluator said that an Objective A were two times as important as Objective B, the same evaluator would also say that Objective B is only half as important as Objective A. The axiom of transitivity (Saaty, 1986) states that if A is twice as preferred as B and B is twice as preferred as C, then A is four times as preferred as C. Deviations from the axiom of transitivity contribute to the degree of inconsistency.

An inconsistency ratio of 1.00 represents what would be expected with judgments that are made at random rather than intelligently. A consistency ratio of 0.10 or less is considered acceptable. The "Overall Inconsistency" shown in Figure 4B.9 is 0.04, indicating inconsistency at an acceptable level.

To inspect inconsistency for any individual in Expert Choice Desktop, using any pairwise comparison window, select the "Inconsistency" menu and choose a number from the drop-down list, as shown in Figure 4B.10. Here, we have selected the responses from evaluator Cynthia Watters.

By selecting "1st" from the list, Expert Choice will show the most inconsistent (least consistent) judgment in the set. In this case the most inconsistent comparison is between Academic Land Use and Facilities and Services and Administration Facilities, as shown by the highlighted comparison in Figure 4B.11.

Likewise selecting "2nd" from the dropdown will show you the next most inconsistent judgment, and so on. In this case the overall inconsistency of the individual of 0.20 indicates that inconsistency in this set of judgments is acceptable. If that was not the case, Expert Choice provides suggestions for lowering inconsistencies in the help topic "Examining and Improving Inconsistency." As the facilitator, review the inconsistencies as necessary and identify solutions to discuss with the evaluators in a follow-up session. Expert Choice can suggest a best fit, or you can change the judgment by making a new pairwise comparison. However, we recommend that, with your guidance, the evaluators make any necessary changes.

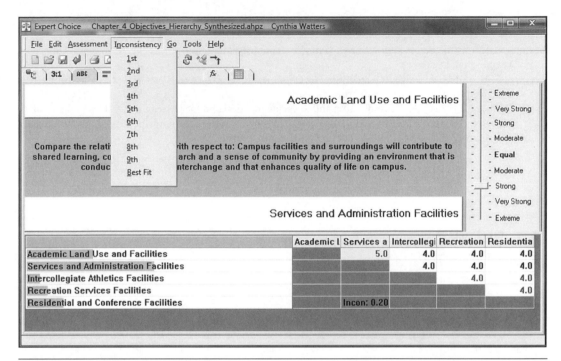

Figure 4B.10   Inconsistency selection list

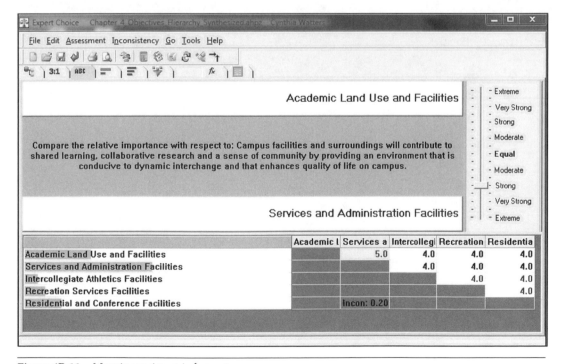

Figure 4B.11   Most inconsistent judgment

4.13 REFERENCES

Forman, E. H. (2010). *The Analytic Hierarchy Process.* Unpublished manuscript, George Washington University, Washington, D.C.

Forman, E. H. and M. A. Selly (2001). *Decision by Objectives.* River Edge, NJ: World Scientific Publishing. (Reproduced with permission from World Scientific.)

Saaty, Thomas L. (1986). "Rank Preservation and Reversal: the Ideal and the Distributive Modes in the Analytic Hierarchy Process." http://www.docstoc.com/docs/26622975/The-Ideal-and-the-Distributive-Modes-in-the-Analytic-Hierarchy-Process (retrieved February 27, 2010)

5

Building the Pool of Potential Projects

This chapter focuses on the project portfolio management (PPM) actions necessary to solicit project ideas to build a pool of potential projects for further consideration during the screening process. As mentioned previously, potential projects are defined as those project proposals that pass the feasibility test; that is, ideas for projects that have merit when compared against broadly defined pre-screening criteria. The assumption during pre-screening is that a significantly large number, possibly hundreds, of new project proposals require pre-screening to determine the likelihood of contributing to the objectives in the strategic plan. Buried among the mass of project proposals are golden nuggets waiting to be discovered. If mined properly, these golden project nuggets eventually make their way along the screening process and into the portfolio of projects to enrich the organization in the future. Pre-screening, or methodically sifting through project proposals, begins the process of determining project feasibility. Excluded from consideration during pre-screening are the organization's ongoing existing projects that are automatically included in the potential project pool for further scrutiny during the screening process. Once the pool of potential projects is identified during pre-screening, it is screened against more stringent criteria to identify candidate projects for possible inclusion in the portfolio. Figure 5-1 indicates that this chapter addresses the first step in the screening phase of PPM, pre-screen proposals.

During the strategic phase we discussed that PPM personnel participate in the organization's strategic planning process by providing subject matter expertise regarding the organization's portfolio and project management capabilities. While participation in strategic planning gives PPM personnel the opportunity to help shape the strategic plan, they also gain valuable insight and a clear understanding of what the organization is attempting to accomplish. This insight is further enhanced through the objectives prioritization process (see Chapter 4) by providing PPM personnel information about the relative contribution of objectives with respect to the goal and the relative contribution of the goals with respect to the vision. Participation in strategic planning and prioritization provides a frame of reference, or context, for developing portfolio selection criteria. With the release of the strategic plan, opportunities arise for the organization to solicit and identify new project ideas to support the current strategy and begin sifting out those that clearly do not contribute to the accomplishment of current goals and objectives.

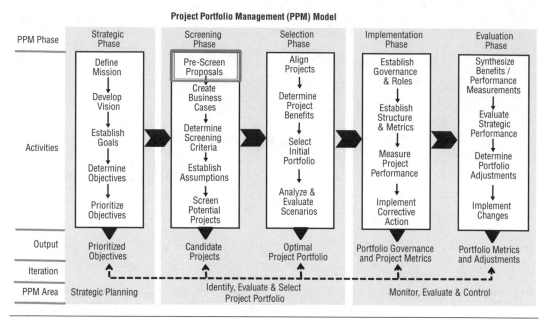

Figure 5.1   Pre-screening proposals—Screening Phase of PPM

5.1 PRE-SCREENING PROCESS

The pre-screening process described in this chapter assumes the organization is instituting a new PPM process and anticipates a large volume of project proposals to evaluate. There may be little discernable difference between pre-screening and screening (Chapter 6) in organizations with an existing PPM process working from an updated strategic plan often only slightly changed from the previous version. The goal of pre-screening is to cast a wide net to solicit as many project proposals as possible and compare them to pre-screening criteria to eliminate any proposals that fail to meet them.

The pre-screening process includes establishing broad pre-screening criteria (in alignment with expected screening criteria), soliciting project proposals from within the organization, reviewing proposals to determine feasibility, and developing a pool of potential projects for further evaluation during the more deliberate and thorough screening process. The objectives of pre-screening are to:

- Identify project ideas that have a reasonable chance of contributing to the achievement of strategic objectives
- Reduce the number of projects to a manageable number by eliminating projects that do not contribute to goals and objectives
- Eliminate those projects that have no chance of making it into the portfolio because they are not feasible, and
- Develop the pre-screening alignment matrix

Therefore, pre-screening provides a process to methodically reduce the number of project proposals, thus allowing more attention and scrutiny for feasible project proposals during the screening process.

Once the strategic plan is approved and released, a pre-screening group must distribute project proposal submission guidance, direct the activities to solicit project proposals from the organization, review submissions, determine proposal feasibility, and develop the potential project list that must be approved by executive management representatives. In short, the pre-screening group is responsible for distributing project proposal guidance and coordinating the process for consolidating and reviewing the proposals. For those organizations instituting PPM, pre-screening cannot occur until the pre-screening group is formed, roles and responsibilities are established, and the responsible parties are empowered to act on behalf of the organization. This group is expected to have long-term additional responsibilities within the PPM process.

5.1.1 Pre-screening Roles and Responsibilities

The group responsible for pre-screening projects is the Portfolio Management Board (PMB) or similar group. The name of this group is not important as it varies by organization; however, it is important to identify the group and its members and define their roles and responsibilities. Specifically, the PMB:

- Designs and develops a method for soliciting project proposals throughout the organization
- Provides guidance on the breadth and depth of information required for the PMB to evaluate each new proposal
- Defines screening criteria from which to evaluate project proposals in concert with executive management or their designated representatives (Executive Review Board)

As discussed later in this chapter, pre-screening criteria cannot be random. They are a high-level and relaxed interpretation of the eventual screening selection criteria. After proposals are received, members of the PMB evaluate each proposal against the pre-screening criteria to determine which are suitable for further consideration. While the organization wants to solicit as many project proposals as possible by soliciting input from throughout the organization, the PMB only selects those with a reasonable or likely chance of making it into the eventual portfolio. Determining which projects are suitable can be difficult.

5.1.2 Soliciting Project Proposals

There's an old saying "be careful what you ask for, you just might get it." This is true when soliciting project proposals. It is important to specify what and how much information is required to support the pre-screening process, and why. Accordingly, project proposal submission guidance from the PMB must be clear and unambiguous. Determining whether a project is worthy of further scrutiny against more stringent screening criteria requires some information from which to evaluate the project. Yet, there has to be a balance between how much time and effort the sponsor spends collecting information and the amount of information actually needed to make the evaluation. For purposes of pre-screening, a simple project proposal is all that's needed to determine suitability for further consideration, containing information that is correct and in the right context (what is known and unknown). As discussed in Chapter 6, once a project proposal has been approved by executive representatives, the sponsor commences drafting the more detailed business case in which additional information is required. While the specific template used for project proposals depends on the nature of the organization, each proposal should contain, at a minimum, the following elements:

- Title
- Sponsor with contact information
- Project objective(s)
- Description of the project's final deliverable
- Statement about how the project contributes to organizational goals and objectives

- Cost estimate
- Risks
- Critical resources

Ideally the proposal contains only a few (1 to 3) pages. The aim is to make a yes/no decision on each proposal without overburdening the organization with additional administrative tasks. Guidance for project proposal submission should be provided along with a template that contains a section for pre-screening disposition of the proposal by the PMB. The disposition section provides a location on the proposal to document the determination of the PMB, whether the project has been approved for further consideration, rejected, or requires additional information; the PMB must communicate the outcome to the sponsor.

5.1.3 Project Proposal Submission Methods

Three basic approaches for soliciting project proposals are top-down, bottom-up, and collaborative methods. In the top-down method, senior executives or managers suggest, or even direct, specific projects to be considered. Executives have their own perspective on which projects to include for further screening and selection. Given their high-level positions within the organization, their strategic view of the organization's operations, and their knowledge and understanding of what the organization is trying to accomplish, these executives generate proposals for projects that lower-level personnel may not have considered due to their lack of strategic perspective. The form in which these proposals are initiated might be a scribble on a piece of paper, an e-mail, or a brief conversation in the hallway. Nevertheless the PMB should solicit as much information about the proposed project as possible and, if needed, assist the executive representative or staff to prepare the project proposal for the executive and include it for consideration.

In the bottom-up method, project proposals are submitted, using the same template and instructions described in the top-down method, from lower levels of the organization through their respective organizational hierarchies to the pre-screening group. Managers at each higher level of the organization conduct preliminary screenings of the proposals being submitted from their organizational units. This review is the first line of defense to eliminate project proposals that do not contribute to any stated goals and objectives. To play this role successfully, these managers must understand both the strategic plan and the PPM process. In accordance with guidance and timelines disseminated by the pre-screening group, project proposals are filtered on the way up to the pre-screening group where each proposal is further reviewed and evaluated for a determination of suitability. Proposals approved by their respective organizational units are reviewed by the pre-screening group. This group determines which project proposals are suitable for further consideration as well as those that the pre-screening group recommends for elimination. This information is then communicated to the sponsoring managers.

In the collaborative method, organizations establish working groups from various functional areas, departments, or business segments to work together to identify projects proposals that support organizational goals and objectives. By establishing working groups comprised of various departments and levels of the organization, different perspectives are employed to identify potential project ideas that have an impact across the organization beyond just the department or functional area. Similar to the bottom-up method, project proposals resulting from the collaborative approach are filtered to the PMB through the working group leaders. In this regard the working group uses a consensus building process to filter out project ideas that they determine to be unsuitable, and they identify project proposals worthy of additional consideration. The end result is project proposals, using the same template as the other two methods, that are submitted to the PMB for further review and evaluation.

5.1.4 Receiving, Reviewing, and Evaluating Project Proposals

In disseminating project proposal guidance, the PMB also needs to specify a submission deadline for receiving proposals. Additionally, the PMB must devise a method for recording receipt of the proposal and for tracking its progress, not just during pre-screening, but throughout the process; even a basic Excel spreadsheet works nicely. However, the ideal tracking system includes real time access by authorized personnel to update the status of the project proposal and allows sponsors to check the progress of their submissions. Additionally, the system incorporates convenient features such as automatic updates to the sponsor as the project proposal record is changed. Organizations with existing workflow and document management systems can take advantage of them to manage project proposals. When project proposals have been received, the PMB commences reviewing and evaluating each proposal.

In reviewing project proposals, the PMB convenes and performs a cursory review of each project proposal to ensure each contains all of the information specified in the guidance disseminated for proposal submissions. Any ambiguities or areas with incomplete information require the sponsor to provide supplemental information or it may result in an automatic rejection of the proposal. The aim is to scan each proposal to ensure it contains all the necessary information from which to pre-screen the proposal during evaluation. In larger organizations this review is performed by knowledgeable administrative personnel. Assuming the proposal is complete and contains all the information, it is moved forward for evaluation.

PMB personnel evaluating project proposals require a clear understanding of the proposed project, the pre-screening criteria, and the strategic plan, along with other relevant organizational factors. Determining feasibility, discussed later in this chapter, is the process of pre-screening each project proposal to determine whether the proposed project is within the realm of the possible and if it supports the objectives and goals stated in the strategic plan. The process of review and evaluation is accomplished in a variety of ways and is usually dependent on the organizational structure, the PPM process implemented, the number of proposals, and the number of pre-screening criteria. For instance, all proposals could first be reviewed for completeness and then considered one at a time by the entire pre-screening group. While this process requires more time, it ensures all pre-screening personnel have visibility and input for each proposal. This process decreases the chances of a proposal being wrongfully eliminated from further consideration during the pre-screening. For organizations expecting a small number of proposals to be pre-screened within a few days, this process is the better option.

However, for organizations considering hundreds of proposals, this approach can be grueling and requires significant time to complete. Faced with days of proposal evaluations, many members may be inclined to *just go along* in an effort to finish the process. Instead, an approach that divides up the groups and the proposals may work more efficiently and requires less time. The sub-groups can be specialized by objective or by discipline. The entire group must then review the results, looking for wrongfully rejected proposals especially. This is a common pitfall with pass-fail criteria.

The evaluation approach used is also dependent on the number of pre-screening criteria. The more pre-screening criteria, the more time it will likely take to review each proposal against each criterion. Some proposals will meet all pre-screening criteria; some will not. Others may require additional deliberations by personnel who are performing the evaluation.

Regardless, when determining which approach best suits an organization's needs and situation, consideration must be given to the quantity of proposals expected for evaluation, the number of members participating in the pre-screening group, and the number and type of pre-screening criteria used to evaluate the proposals. Whatever approach is used, it must balance the time to complete the process with the quality of the evaluation for each proposal. Each proposal must be afforded the amount of time and discussion needed to make the appropriate determination without overburdening the organization or unnecessarily delaying the PPM process.

5.1.5 Identifying the Pool of Potential Projects

The pre-screening evaluation is performed not only to sift out project proposals that do not have merit and stand no chance of making it into the eventual portfolio, but also to align each successful pre-screened project proposal to the goals and objectives it primarily supports. The result is the pre-screening alignment matrix, containing a more manageable list of projects with a preliminary alignment to organizational goals and objectives. Table 5.1 provides an example of such an alignment matrix. In the example, two goals from the strategic plan are represented, each of which is supported by two objectives. The alignment matrix is easily expanded to support as many goals and objectives as are defined in the strategic plan or are applicable to the organizational unit (division, department, sector, etc.). The primary function of this matrix is to ensure connectivity and the relationship between the project proposal and the goal and objective(s) it supports.

The Project number column corresponds to a project proposal number assigned to the proposal when it is submitted by the PMB. In addition to a short title, the proposed project is aligned with the goal and objective it supports. It should be noted that this alignment is preliminary because it is based on the project proposal that does not provide as much information as will later be required during screening in the project's business case. The Mandatory column indicates project proposals that are mandated by the organization's leadership or that must be performed for regulatory, operational, or other necessities. These projects should be identified as early as possible in the PPM process because they take on special significance in determining which projects make it through to the screening process.

As shown in Table 5.1, some projects may contribute to multiple goals and objectives. As discussed in Chapter 6, some of the preliminary alignments may change as more information is provided in the business case. The point is to ensure that each project proposal contributes to at least one objective or has been identified as mandatory. One responsibility of the PMB is to identify multiple instances of similar projects. In the case of Project A in Table 5.1, three project proposals are assigned to a single project. In this instance, the PMB determined, after a discussion with the sponsors, that three separate proposals were similar and could be combined into a single project; for example, three different departments submitted proposals using the bottom-up method and all three described a

Table 5.1 Pre-screening project alignment matrix (example)

			Goal 1		Goal 2	
Project #	**Short Title**	**Mandatory**	**Objective 1**	**Objective 2**	**Objective 1**	**Objective 2**
1a, 1b, 1c	Project A		X		X	
2	Project B		X	X		X
3.1	Project C.1			X		
3.2	Project C.2		X	X		
3.3	Project C.3		X		X	X
4	Project D	X	X			

Note: Header spanning row reads "Strategic Plan 20xx-20xx (Organization Name/Unit)"

similar customer service project to increase customer satisfaction. Instead of listing these projects as separate projects, they were combined into one project for the time being. During the screening phase, the sponsors of these projects could be requested to collaborate in a working group to develop a single business case for this project.

A different annotation is used to denote different approaches, also called activity levels, for the same project. For instance, the purpose of Project C is to build an athletic facility. As part of the broad project proposal, the sponsor has roughed out three alternative concepts (Projects C.1, C.2, and C.3) with increasing levels of estimated required funding, along with increasing size and capability of the facility. Annotation methods for these kinds of projects can use words such as GOLD, SILVER, and BRONZE to denote the decreasing value in terms of cost and contribution to achieve a particular objective. The advantage of allowing multiple alternatives is to provide flexibility to decision makers rather than presenting the proposal as an all-or-nothing approach.

5.1.6 Obtaining Buy-in and Approval of Pre-screened Projects

Although the PMB performs the actions of soliciting, receiving, reviewing, and evaluating project proposals, concurrence with or approval of the pre-screening alignment matrix must be obtained from the Executive Review Board (ERB) prior to moving into screening. The PMB presents the results of the pre-screening process to executive representatives who either approve the matrix, direct changes, or require additional information. This can result in several iterations before the final pre-screening alignment matrix is approved. Presenting the pre-screening alignment matrix allows the PMB to receive buy-in and approval from executives prior to moving to the screening phase while ensuring that executives maintain their authority to decide how to invest organizational resources in accordance with the governance of the PPM process. As part of this presentation, project proposals excluded from further consideration should be covered. This allows executives or upper management to understand the rationale for rejection and to concur with the PMB's actions. Approval of the pre-screening alignment matrix by the ERB marks the end of the pre-screening process and the beginning of the screening process described in Chapter 6. However, developing an appropriate list of potential projects and an accurate alignment matrix depends on the PMB members' ability to determine what is feasible. That is based on an understanding of relevant organizational factors and the development of a pre-screening model or approach.

5.2 DETERMINING FEASIBILITY

Feasibility is an interesting term to apply to pre-screening. The American Heritage Dictionary (2002) defines feasible as "capable of being accomplished or brought about; possible . . . likely." Unfortunately, what an organization or individual determines to be doable is in the eye of the person or group making the determination. Even with pre-screening criteria, the act of determining feasibility is largely subjective and requires information from which to judge feasibility; a well-developed strategic plan and clearly articulated objectives and goals make the process much easier.

The idea or concept of feasibility is more easily explained using an example such as buying a new house. At any given point in time there are literally hundreds of thousands of new houses for sale across the country that span a variety of characteristics: cost, style, location, size, colors, and finishes. The sheer volume of new houses for sale prevents potential buyers from visiting every house. Even with the advantages of the internet, time constraints prevent new home buyers from visiting as many houses as they would like. Furthermore, why would someone in California want to view new homes in Montana unless, of course, they were moving there. Instead, new home buyers establish broad criteria from which to reduce the large volume of new homes for sale down to a manageable number.

What one considers a manageable number can vary greatly, but it's reasonable to suggest the number is less than a hundred, and likely much less. Certainly attempting to view 100 new homes would be much more manageable than attempting to view 1000 new homes, assuming all the homes were within the same local area. Location, price, and the size of the home are used as common criteria for reducing the number. The buyer might select a specific location first. If this yields a number of new homes that the buyer deems as unmanageable, then additional pre-screening criteria are added to further reduce the pool of prospective new homes. For instance, the potential new home buyer might set pre-screening criteria for house size as no larger than 3000 square feet, and for price, cost of no more than $500,000 to purchase. Houses larger than 3000 square feet and costing more than $500,000 would be excluded from consideration. These pre-screening criteria establish boundaries beyond which the buyer is unwilling to consider or beyond what the buyer determines as feasible. Of course, there is always the chance that the perfect home might cost $500,001 or be 3001 square feet in size, and the buyer would not know that because these homes were excluded. Unfortunately, the outer limits or bounds of what an individual or organization consider feasible must be established. In the case of our new home buyer, without these pre-screening criteria, the buyer could spend the rest of eternity looking for the perfect house. Remember the compensatory decision making discussion from Chapter 3. In setting criteria limits, the buyer should keep in mind that strength in one screening criterion limit might offset exceeding the limit of other criteria, for example, the value of a house located in an outstanding school district might be worth considering paying slightly over $500,000.

If after applying these pre-screening criteria the number of new homes is still not manageable, then additional criteria are added or the existing criteria adjusted. For instance, the buyer could add the style of the home to pre-screening criteria or constrict the existing pre-screening criteria. If the buyer decreased the cost to $400,000, this would result in more new homes being excluded. Ultimately, the new home buyer must determine the number of new homes that is manageable and continue to develop and enforce increasingly strict criteria until the number of options is deemed manageable. The broad criteria discussed are meant as a method for reducing the large volume but at the same time are consistent with the criteria the buyer anticipates when selecting the new house to buy. It would not be logical to establish pre-screening criteria for a cost at $1M if the buyer were only pre-approved by the bank for $400,000. Unless the buyer were the recipient of an unexpected inheritance, it is unlikely that he could afford to buy a house costing $1M; that is not a feasible alternative. In setting broad pre-screening criteria, the buyer framed the bounds of acceptability or what was feasible. Anything beyond these bounds was considered to be infeasible, or at least beyond what the buyer was willing to consider purchasing.

In the PPM process, applying subjective judgment to determine feasibility during pre-screening results in the identification of project proposals that are likely to contribute to accomplishing the objectives of the organization, can be reasonably accomplished within the capabilities of the organization (and potential partners), and are not clearly outside the bounds of more stringent criteria to be applied during the screening process.

5.3 OTHER CONSIDERATIONS FOR PRE-SCREENING

Understanding the organization's situation and the context in which the project proposals are evaluated is important to ensure that the right projects survive pre-screening. In the home buyer example, even before considering which houses to preview, the prospective home buyers likely understood the context in which they wanted to purchase a new home. For instance, the home buyer was aware of his circumstances and reasons for making the new home purchase, that is, confident in long-term job security, could afford a house within a certain price range, and expected to live in the local area for many years. The same is true for organizations and pre-screening project proposals. To know which project proposals are feasible, those responsible for performing pre-screening need to be aware of certain aspects of the organization. This awareness provides a position from which to make an accurate disposition of each proposal and ensure that only those project proposals that clearly do not contribute, or are infeasible, are excluded from further consideration. In the following sections we'll touch on some major areas to consider when pre-screening projects, including:

- Organizational risk tolerance and attitude
- Influence exerted by senior leadership
- Portfolio budget considerations
- Organizational capabilities and resources
- Project and portfolio management capabilities

5.3.1 Organizational Risk Tolerance and Attitude

In the PPM process, determination of feasibility must include assessing project risk against the organization's risk attitude or tolerance. The more that is known about how the organization views risk, the more likely it is that the portfolio management board (PMB) will pre-screen projects into the potential project pool that are consistent with the organization's risk values. Understanding the risk tolerance also helps to determine which project proposals are clearly outside the bounds of that tolerance. While the project proposal may appear sound and meet quantitative pre-screening criteria, an objective high-level risk assessment of the proposal by the sponsor and the PMB can eliminate proposals that are clearly not in line with the organization's risk attitude.

Risk is defined as "a measure of the probability and consequence of not achieving a defined goal . . . and involves uncertainty" (Kerzner, 2006). Probability of occurrence assesses how likely risks are to occur while consequences assess the impact if the risk event is realized. An event with a high probability of occurring and serious (detrimental) consequences would obviously be considered riskier than an event with low probability of occurrence and no consequences. The amount of risk an organization is willing to accept is dependent on the expected reward from taking the risk.

There are three generally accepted risk tolerance personality types: (1) risk avoider, (2) risk neutral, and (3) risk seeker. The risk avoider is conservative by nature. That is, the risk avoider prefers certainty over uncertainty and is less willing to choose great reward at the expense of high risk. Instead, the risk avoider prefers to accept lower rewards in exchange for more certainty that the reward will be realized. The risk neutral personality is neither overly conservative nor overly aggressive. Instead, a person or organization with a risk neutral attitude seeks to accept rewards that are commensurate with the amount of risk taken. In comparison, the risk seeker is aggressive in undertaking risk if the reward is deemed of adequate value relative to the amount of risk being taken. Every organization has its own risk attitude or tolerance and is influenced by many factors, including industry sector, government regulations, evolving market conditions, and the stage of the organization's existence, among other factors.

The industry in which the organization is operating impacts the risk attitude of the organization. Firms operating in industries based on new technologies such as information technology and renewable energy generally take more risk because their products require significant upfront investment, and they cannot be certain how the intended market will react. In 1990, developing hybrid cars was seen as too risky for some car manufacturers because the consumer market was demanding full-sized sport utility vehicles. However, those willing to take the risk such as Toyota are market leaders in the hybrid car market and are realizing the return on their investment. Government policy and regulation can also impact organizations' risk attitudes. Over the last few decades, a virtual tidal wave of companies has surged into China to produce and sell products. This is primarily the result of the Chinese government revising its policies to allow increased foreign investment in China. As illustrated with Statoil in Chapter 2, the operating stage of the organization can impact the organization's risk attitude. Newly formed entrepreneurial organizations may be willing to accept more risk in the hope of achieving aggressive growth while mature organizations are not likely to be as willing to bankrupt their companies on excessively risky undertakings. While excessively risky projects and ventures can bring great rewards, they also can inflict great penalties when risks are realized and can have a devastating financial effect on the organization and its stakeholders. The balance of risk versus reward is an ever changing dynamic for any organization, and evaluators must be conscious of this fact as they pre-screen project proposals.

5.3.2 Senior Leadership Influence

Those performing project proposal pre-screening should expect to receive some level of input from senior leadership within the organization. While personnel at lower levels of the organization have ideas about which projects should be undertaken, so will senior management. Senior management may direct inclusion of specific projects or may simply provide general guidance such as specifying a new business sector, for example, healthcare or information technology. Stating the obvious, this guidance and direction cannot be ignored even when evaluators determine that a project clearly falls outside of the bounds of the organization's capabilities or what is feasible. This situation poses a dilemma; on one hand the senior executive wants the project, yet the potential project may not be feasible or support an objective. If the project is not screened out, then it could potentially make its way into the portfolio and waste valuable resources without contributing to accomplishing the objectives. Still, some executives may take exception to having their ideas summarily dismissed without due diligence. This is not an easy situation for any organization and the outcome largely depends on the personalities involved, the culture of the organization, and the level of organizational PPM maturity. These situations should be the exception rather than the rule.

However, one course of action to prevent any ill-will and uncomfortable situations with senior executives is to let the PPM process work. Since the pre-screening process is intended to identify feasible projects, inclusion of projects suggested by senior management could be reasonably deemed to meet that requirement. If senior management believes a project has merit, then proceed to include it in the potential pool and pass the project on for further consideration during screening. As will be seen in the screening process and PPM selection phase, one of the added benefits of using PPM is to highlight projects that do not support the accomplishment of objectives. Although pet projects (sacred cows) do occasionally make it into the potential project pool, the PPM process will clearly identify whether they actually contribute to achieving objectives. At the very least, the PPM process exposes these projects to further scrutiny. If a project does not have merit (does not contribute to objectives), then the PPM process will provide ample justification to argue for its exclusion from further consideration during the selection phase.

5.3.3 Anticipated Portfolio Budget

The reality is that the major need when implementing a portfolio of projects is funding, which is not unlimited. As one would expect, every organization establishes some level of funding for implementing the project portfolio. Determining the feasibility of a project proposal also relies on assessing the estimated cost for the project by comparing the estimate against the expectations for project cost limits or pre-screening criteria for project cost. Inevitably, some project proposals result in estimated costs that are either woefully underestimated or are outside the bounds of what an organization is willing to spend on a single project. It is not inconceivable for the project sponsor to underestimate the cost of a project in the proposal. On rare occasions the sponsor understands that if the project is too expensive that its chances of making it into the portfolio are reduced. Accordingly, it may be tempting to deflate the estimated cost of the project to something more palatable. More often though, cost estimates are performed with incomplete information and that leads to estimate inaccuracies. Consult the AACE table of cost estimates provided as an appendix to Chapter 6, sources within the organization, or external references for information about the degree of accuracy of cost estimates at various stages of project definition.

Cost estimates provided in project proposals must be assessed with some skepticism during the pre-screening process, especially if they are not accompanied by supporting documentation. During the screening process, described in Chapter 6, the business case provides a mechanism to ensure a more robust process for developing cost estimates and ensuring the estimates are accurate. The eventual portfolio may consist of only a few high-cost projects, many low-cost projects, or a combination of the two. It is common for organizations to set funding limits such as not to exceed amounts for single projects of specific types. That is, an organization may not be willing to undertake a project that is too costly or that requires a large portion of the portfolio budget. While the final budget for the portfolio may not be precisely known during pre-screening, a rough estimate should help to determine whether an individual project is too costly to be considered feasible. Evaluators should work with executive management or their representatives to determine individual project cost boundaries. By setting cost ceilings for different types of projects, evaluators can determine whether the project proposal exceeds the organization's cost expectations.

5.3.4 Understanding the Organization's Capabilities and Resource Pool

What an organization would like to accomplish and what it can actually accomplish are largely influenced by its existing capabilities and resources and its access to capabilities and resources it does not have internally. Evaluators must have a thorough understanding of the organization's capabilities and resources to determine whether it is competent to undertake a proposed project. While resources and their impact on the portfolio are discussed later during the selection phase, all projects require resources and those resources need to be of sufficient quantities and types for the proposed projects. More importantly, an expectation must be established that the resources can be reasonably accessed or obtained to support the project during implementation. A proposal requiring the utilization of specialized processes or expertise not available to the organization, and with limited availability on the open market, could be reasonably considered beyond what the organization is capable of undertaking.

Projects can also be included in the portfolio that support accomplishment of short-, medium-, and long-term goals and require different durations to complete—from weeks to years. An important consideration is the expectation of availability of the resources and capabilities at the start of the project at some point in the future. If a project is not envisioned to start for a year or is dependent on the completion of another project and the organization does not presently have specific resources to support it, the PMB and the sponsor must determine whether there is a reasonable expectation of procuring the resources in the future. It would be a wasted opportunity to dismiss a project proposal because of the lack of current resources without considering how those resources could be obtained in the future.

5.3.5 Project Management Capabilities

As organizations undertake increasingly complex projects, the organization's project management capability must increase as well. According to PMI (PMI.com, 2010), "research has shown that project failure rates have increased, and that those rates correspond directly to the size of the project; a staggering 39% of project with budgets over US $10 million failed." It may be tempting to undertake new complex projects as part of the portfolio, but if the organization does not have the capability to successfully manage these more complex projects, then the portfolio may be doomed to fail before it starts. Every organization has at least a few key people who maintain a rare capacity for success no matter what they are assigned. However, the organization must maintain a project management capability commensurate with the scale and scope of projects being undertaken in the portfolio. The PMB must be keenly aware of the organization's project management capability rather than assuming more capability than is actually available.

An organization considering a shift to large-scale construction projects when its existing project managers specialize in small-scale information technology projects would not be wise. Arguably, it is incorrect to assume that an organization can easily transfer specialized project management from one industry to another. While the basic principles of project management apply, each industry maintains its own unique standards and requires knowledge and expertise of that specific industry. The organization's leaders, who are typically less familiar with the intricacies of project management, may not realize the significant differences in managing projects across different industries. Evaluators and others in the organization need to match the scale, scope, and complexity of the projects the organization proposes to undertake against the existing project management capability and expectations of, or plans for, improved maturity in the near future.

One method for assessing the organization's project management capability is through an organizational project management maturity model. PMI's Organizational Project Management Maturity Model (OPM3) is a best-practice standard for assessing an organization's current project management capability as well as identifying steps to expand and improve existing capabilities. More information on OPM3 can be obtained from PMI at http://opm3online.pmi.org/. In addition, David Hillson (2001) devised the Project Management Maturity Model "in order for an organization to be able to determine whether its project management processes are adequate, agreed measures are required to enable it to compare its management of projects with best practice or against its competitors. As with any organizational change program, benchmarks and maturity models can play an important part in the process by defining a structured route to improvement." Hillson's method is divided into four practical project management capability levels: (1) naïve, (2) novice, (3) normalized, and (4) natural. Expectedly, the naïve organization has no project management capability and does not see the need for project management, nor does it have a structured approach for managing projects. The novice organization has started to experiment with project management through small projects but does not have a structured approach for project management. The normalized organization has implemented project management practices across the organization although they may not be understood by everyone in the organization. In the natural organization, the organization has a project-based culture with a proactive approach to managing projects. The benefit of Hillson's simple assessment method is the ease with which an organization can baseline its existing capabilities. Although the result of the assessment is somewhat crude, it does provide an immediate method to roughly determine its existing project management capability with minimal effort.

The author's prefer the project management maturity model developed by Ibbs and Kwak (2000). The primary advantage of this model is that it is not industry-specific. The model consists of 148 questions divided into six processes/life-cycle phases:

1. Initiating
2. Planning
3. Executing
4. Controlling
5. Closing
6. Maintaining a project-driven organizational environment

Additionally, it contains eight Project Management Body of Knowledge (PMBOK) areas:

1. Scope
2. Time

3. Cost
4. Quality
5. Human resources
6. Communication
7. Risk
8. Procurement

The model allows an organization to drill down within areas or project stages to better identify specific deficiencies.

Even when using these project management maturity models, the organization, and specifically the PMB, must understand the limitations of the current project management capability. In pre-screening projects, a careful balance must be struck between the capabilities that exist today and those that the organization hopes to have in place in two to three years. During pre-screening, this enables elimination of those project proposals that greatly exceed current internal or accessible external capabilities, while preserving proposals that contain achievable capabilities.

5.3.6 Portfolio Management Capabilities

Inevitably, organizations that undertake projects to contribute to achieving strategic goals and objectives must realize the importance of implementing a PPM capability as well as to continue to increase the maturity of the process as the organization grows and matures. Mistakenly, many organizations view PPM as management of multiple projects that are undertaken as a portfolio because they sound like a good idea or as a result of an edict from a senior executive. As with project management capability, the organization must have an awareness of its PPM capability and maturity. As organizations undertake an increasing number of projects with increasing complexity and scope, its process must mature to ensure the right projects are undertaken and managed while adapting to changes in the strategic plan.

For those who do not have an existing process but want to consider implementing one, the benefits have been well-established. As illustrated by Pennypacker's (2005) study of PPM maturity, documented benefits from its implementation include better alignment of projects to business strategy, undertaking the appropriate projects, spending in the right areas, and PPM contribution to cost savings. As adoption of PPM is relatively new, many organizations have not yet achieved a high degree of maturity and have yet to maximize the potential by using appropriate PPM software tools. As organizations continue to recognize the need for and increase the maturity of their PPM processes, including state-of-the-art software tools and techniques, they will realize greater benefits, increase their competitiveness, and improve their chances of achieving their strategic visions.

5.4 ABU CAMPUS REVITALIZATION PROGRAM PRE-SCREENING

To reinforce the discussion in this chapter, the American Business University (ABU) example is used to illustrate the pre-screening process in action.

5.4.1 Pre-screening Process

In the ABU example the university decided to undertake a Revitalization Program consisting of a portfolio of projects to support the university's strategic goals and objectives. In Chapter 2, the university developed and released its strategic plan and established specific goals and objectives. As mentioned in Chapter 4, only one goal and its supporting objectives are addressed by the example project portfolio discussed from this point forward. The essence of this portion of the strategic plan is to transform the ABU campus facilities to provide a better learning, living, and teaching environment for its students and staff. Like many organizations, the university has previously undertaken small scale and relatively simple projects. These were typically additions to existing buildings, replacing new walk paths, and upgrading electrical and plumbing in older buildings. Large or more complex projects such as the design and construction of a new campus building were contracted externally with oversight provided by the university's Facilities Office. However, the scale and scope of the Revitalization Program means that the university must undertake projects of much greater complexity, scope, and scale. In addition, the timeline for these projects will span many years and greatly exceed the organic capabilities of the university. In consultation with the university's principal staff—deans, vice presidents, and legal counsel—the university president requested the Board of Trustees to oversee the Revitalization Program.

5.4.2 Establishing Roles and Responsibilities (Governance)

Board of Trustees (Executive Review Board)

Acting on behalf of the university for the Revitalization Program, the Board of Trustees is analogous to the ERB in Chapter 1. The Board of Trustees, among its other duties, approves operating and capital budgets, supervises investment of the university's endowment, and oversees campus real estate and long-range physical planning. In essence, along with its other duties, the Board of Trustees provides governance for the Revitalization Program and the process supporting its achievement. As such, the Board of Trustees will approve the portfolio of projects under this initiative and will conduct quarterly reviews and make decisions about the addition or launch of new projects and the termination of existing projects, and it will evaluate the continued funding of projects in progress in accordance with the balanced scorecard reporting process. Recognizing the need to institute a PPM process to manage the portfolio of projects, the Board of Trustees established the ABU Steering Committee to manage the PPM process and work with the Board of Trustees to identify, screen, select, implement, monitor, and control a portfolio of projects aimed at accomplishing the university's strategic goals and objectives.

Steering Committee (Portfolio Management Board)

The Steering Committee comprises appointed representatives from across the university, including selected vice presidents and deans as well as faculty senate, student association, and alumni association representatives. It is responsible for identifying projects for consideration, ensuring their association with Campus Revitalization Program goals and objectives, and for the actual prioritization recommendations for the Board of Trustees. The Steering Committee is charged with performing the routine work required to facilitate identification, selection, implementation of the portfolio of projects, and acts as a conduit between the Board of Trustees and the Program Management Office (PgMO), which is discussed later in this chapter. Accordingly, the Steering Committee engages the appropriate project sponsorship to provide project nominations and defines the necessary artifacts for entering a project into the pipeline for consideration. These members provide a diverse perspective of the university as well as unique institutional knowledge and experience. However, these members are part-time participants and lack the necessary project and portfolio management skills necessary to implement and manage the PPM process. To supplement the Steering Committee, project management professionals from within the university as well as project management personnel obtained through consulting services providers were added to the Steering Committee to design, develop, and implement a PPM process tailored to support the Revitalization Program and act as the Steering Committee's permanent personnel.

University Facilities Office

The university's Facilities Office is responsible for maintaining all existing campus facilities and, through representation on the Steering Committee, participates in the pre-screening process. The Facilities Office maintains the resident knowledge of the university's existing infrastructure; it provides perspective and expertise when assessing projects affecting the university's existing facilities or potential new facilities. As discussed in more detail in later chapters on PPM implementation, project managers from the Facilities Office work closely with the Steering Committee to gather and report relevant project data and information to monitor the performance of projects and maintain close coordination with the PgMO and Steering Committee throughout the execution of the Revitalization Program.

5.4.3 Establishing the Program Management Office

During strategic planning, the Board of Trustees and Steering Committee recognized the need to establish a PgMO to manage projects comprising the eventual Revitalization Program portfolio. Coordination with the Facilities Office was begun to ensure that at least the core membership is in place by the end of the pre-screening process. A PgMO was determined to be more appropriate than a project office because the portfolio of projects is unified to support a single organizational program. The PgMO is responsible for instituting project management practices for ABU and delivering day-to-day management of projects comprising the portfolio, including all project management areas throughout each project's life cycle. In addition to obtaining key PgMO personnel, the Steering Committee also began to identify office space to house the PgMO and future project teams, and to assess software tools to effectively manage the portfolio and project management activities. The intent is to locate the PgMO on campus and provide sufficient space to co-locate key members of the various contractor project management teams with the PgMO staff to facilitate communication and coordination, identify program-related issues quickly, and to ensure effective management. While PgMO personnel will be contracted specifically to support the university's Revitalization Program, project management teams are expected to be comprised of personnel from various contractors responsible for completing respective projects within the portfolio. In this case, the PgMO acts to establish uniform and consistent project management practices and to standardize information and reporting requirements as well as to facilitate a smooth and efficient turnover of completed projects to the Facilities Office.

5.4.4 Implementing a PPM System

Concurrent with the Steering Committee's efforts to solicit, review, and evaluate project proposals, it was also focused on implementing a PPM system to support the process over the life of the Revitalization Program. The first action taken was to supplement the Steering Committee with project and portfolio management expertise by contracting these services through a professional company specializing in these services to supplement the Steering Committee and establish the PgMO. ABU does not maintain a robust organic project portfolio or program management capability nor is it expected to permanently require this capability beyond the Revitalization Program. Accordingly, it is more economical and advantageous to contract this service than to establish a permanent capability. ABU was familiar with revitalization efforts of another local university and received referrals to companies who performed similar services. While market research identified numerous firms specializing in these services, referrals from a known and respected organization provided ABU with the confidence that they would select the correct service provider with experience in a similar program. The other advantage of this approach is the reuse of templates, software products, processes, and procedures from a similar program that can be easily tailored to ABU's Revitalization Program. In essence, ABU's approach was to obtain a temporary, mature PPM process quickly through outsourcing.

5.4.5 Preparing to Pre-screen Project Proposals

To this point, the following actions have been taken and decisions made:

- ABU has released its approved Strategic Plan.
- The Board of Trustees (aka Executive Review Board) has agreed to oversee the university's Campus Revitalization Program.
- The Steering Committee (aka Portfolio Management Board) has been established to implement the PPM process and has led the process of prioritizing objectives (see Chapter 4).
- The Steering Committee has decided to establish a PgMO.

In coordination with the Board of Trustees, the Steering Committee priorities were established to begin the process of soliciting project proposals, develop a project selection model with selection criteria, implement a PPM system, and complete preparations to establish a PgMO. While the primary focus of the Steering Committee is to begin the pre-screening process, actions must also be taken to develop an adequate PPM infrastructure necessary to implement the portfolio after it is selected and implemented. Those actions must start as early as possible. Accordingly, the Steering Committee set goals to have a PPM system and core infrastructure of the PgMO established by the end of the pre-screening process, which is marked by completion of the approved pre-screening alignment matrix. Expectedly, the infrastructure activities occur in parallel with pre-screening activities and in coordination with the Board of Trustees, which has oversight of the Campus Revitalization Program. The Board of Trustees maintains governance responsibilities and must be consulted on major activities and decisions affecting the Campus Revitalization Program.

5.4.6 Soliciting Project Proposals for the ABU Revitalization Program

Following the release of the Strategic Plan and the prioritization of strategic objectives, the Board of Trustees, using the top-down project proposal approach, submitted a list of projects to the Steering Committee for inclusion in the alignment matrix. This list encompassed major project suggestions focused on athletics and technology that were discussed by major stakeholders during the strategic planning process and requested by major alumni association donors. These projects included suggestions for new athletics facilities, library, and technology center. Given the scale and scope of the project proposal ideas, the Steering Committee and Board of Trustees worked collaboratively with other university offices, facilities, and the Athletic Department to obtain necessary information to complete the project proposal documentation.

In an effort to obtain project ideas from throughout the university, the Steering Committee, through the various university departments and associations, disseminated project proposal guidance for submitting project proposals, including the submission timeline and template information. This bottom-up approach ensured that each department, functional area, and key group were provided a means to submit proposals that affect their groups or areas. A proposal by university faculty may not take into account the specific needs of students or desires of alumni. The bottom-up approach ensures all groups have a means to provide input on projects that are proposed for the Revitalization Program. As proposals are submitted, each group was responsible for determining how the proposals would be evaluated within their groups and was then approved for submission to the Steering Committee. In general, each proposal was reviewed at each level within the group's hierarchy and eventually submitted by the leader (faculty president, president of the student association, etc.) of each group. In addition, the Steering Committee formed working groups to solicit project proposals from other stakeholders.

The purpose of the working groups was to survey campus personnel and citizens surrounding the campus to ascertain what they believed would provide benefit to the university. ABU has maintained good relationships with the surrounding community and, given the close proximity and interaction with university personnel, the Steering Committee wanted to ensure that ideas from these stakeholders were considered. Three working groups were formed to solicit information from the community, local businesses, and university vendors and suppliers. Through these working groups project proposals were developed and reviewed within the groups. Each in turn evaluated the proposal before submitting it to the Steering Committee. The example project proposal represents a synopsis of the project proposal information submitted to the Steering Committee:

- *Title:* Davidson Student Center Renovation Project Proposal
- *Sponsor:* Mr. Jack Notion, President of the ABU Student Association
- *Sponsor contact information:* phone: 805-432-9999, e-mail: jnotion@abu.edu
- *Strategic plan objective:* Services and Administration Facilities
- *Project goal:* Meet current and future student demands for convenient and efficient service.
- *Project objective:* Improve existing facilities for administrative and student services staff.
- *Overview:* This project requires complete renovation of the existing building to modernize the structure while retaining the architectural details. The renovation will incorporate new features and technology, including high-speed internet access and student self-help kiosks, construction of student-advisor counseling rooms, and electronic information terminals.
- *Strategic Objective:* The Davidson Student Center Renovation project contributes to the achievement of the following strategic objectives: Services and Administration Facilities, Recreation Services Facilities, Residential and Conference Facilities, and Academic Land Use and Facilities.
- *Cost (rough order of magnitude):* $5.2m (Cost roughly estimated based on an analogous estimate derived from a similar project completed by another local university adjusted for inflation and increase in construction labor costs).
- *Benefits:* Increase staff ability to effectively and efficiently resolve student services issues, reduce wait time by students, reduce issues requiring staff attention, and provide students access to information through multiple mediums.
- *Alternatives:* Not applicable.
- *Risk:* Short-term disruption caused by construction, identification of hazardous material from original construction, cost overruns from unforeseen damage resulting from age of existing structures and subsequent schedule delays if unforeseen problems are discovered.
- *Critical Resources:* Temporary facility to conduct student services during the renovation project.

5.4.7 Evaluating ABU Revitalization Program Project Proposals

As project proposals were received, the Steering Committee identified specific members to receive and perform a cursory review of the proposals. Each proposal was logged in and a confirmation of the proposal's receipt was e-mailed to the sponsor. In reviewing each proposal, the group ensured that all fields were filled in and that the information was clear and understandable. As the Steering Committee was comprised of both full- and part-time personnel, the Steering Committee decided on an evaluation approach. The Steering Committee evaluated one proposal at a time with all personnel present.

A total of 67 project proposals were submitted for review that allowed ample time to consider each proposal, compare the proposal against the pre-screening criteria, and discuss the proposal. Decisions to screen-out project proposals were determined by consensus. Table 5.2 provides a partial listing of the 67 project proposals determined to be feasible after evaluating each proposal against pre-screening criteria. The only pre-screening criterion was that a proposed project must contribute to at least one objective. Of the initial 67 proposals received, a total of 34 were selected for inclusion in the alignment matrix to be presented to the Board of Trustees for concurrence and approval. Those not selected were determined to be duplicates of those already listed within the pre-screening matrix or did not align to any of the objectives determined to support the stated strategic goal.

Table 5.2 ABU Revitalization Program pre-screening project alignment matrix

Strategic Goal: *Campus facilities and surroundings will contribute to shared learning, collaborative research and a sense of community by providing an environment that is conducive to dynamic interchange and that enhances quality of life on campus*					
Project Proposals	**Objectives**				
	Academic Land Use and Facilities	**Services and Administration Facilities**	**Intercollegiate Athletics Facilities**	**Recreation Services Facilities**	**Residential and Conference Facilities**
1. Renovate Existing Student Dormitories (Jarvis, Davis & Sewall Halls)	X				X
2. Renovate & Expand Davidson Student Services Center	X	X		X	X
3. Construct Dr. Mary Haven Student Housing Center (Off-Campus Facility)	X	X			X
4a (GOLD). Renovate & Expand C.W. Benson Campus Library (*Alternatives Project*)	X	X			X
5. Renovate Benjamin Stadium & Field house	X		X	X	
6. Renovate Mason Hall Research Center	X				X
7. Construct ABU Medical Clinic	X	X			
8. ABU Revitalization Program Regulatory & Environmental Approval Project (*Mandatory/Enabling Project*)	X	X	X	X	X
9. Construct Paisley Hall Student Services Center	X	X		X	X
10. Renovate Deluth Hall Dining Facility	X			X	X
11. Construct ABU Indoor Athletic Complex (*Alternatives Project*)	X		X	X	X
12. Construct ABU Distance Learning Center	X				X
13. Expand Campus Share Ride Services		X		X	X
14. Construct Campus Theatre	X			X	
15. Construct ABU Faculty Technology & Research Center	X	X			X

5.4.8 Obtaining Pre-screening Alignment Matrix Approval

To maintain proper governance of the Revitalization Program, the Steering Committee is required to seek a concurrence and approval for the pre-screening alignment matrix from the Board of Trustees. This serves to ensure that the Board of Trustees is advised early of project proposals submitted from organizational stakeholders, provide the Board of Trustees an opportunity to verify that the Steering Committee is acting to identify projects consistent with intent of the strategic plan, and ensure that the Board of Trustees agrees with projects excluded from further consideration. After several adjustments, the pre-screening alignment matrix was approved by the Board of Trustees. That marks the end of the pre-screening process and the beginning of the screening process.

This process resulted in the identification of 67 project proposals that were systematically evaluated to identify the project proposals deemed to be feasible and, therefore, to move forward for additional consideration during the screening process. In performing pre-screening, the university was able to ensure maximum involvement by soliciting projects from throughout the university, the community, and from businesses that rely on the university while implementing a process to ensure that only those proposals that directly related to contributing to strategic objectives were selected for additional consideration.

5.5 SUMMARY

The pre-screening process is essential if the organization is expecting a large volume of project proposals, because it provides a method for sifting through and weeding out project proposals that will not directly support the accomplishment of goals and objectives. By casting a wide net, the organization can capture many project proposals, exploit resident talent, and receive feedback from all stakeholders and yet retain the ability to quickly eliminate proposals that do not support the strategic plan or, if present, other pre-screening criteria. As expected, there is no idle time between phases, and preparations are ongoing to properly prepare for the next phase of the process. In the ABU example, we see an institution that does not have an existing PPM process and lacks mature project management capabilities; however, it devised a solution to meet the specific needs of the situation. The organization was able to leverage its existing structure and knowledge to implement an effective PPM process and begin the process of quickly improving project and portfolio management maturity.

Based on the pre-screening criteria and the pre-screening alignment matrix containing the potential projects, the selection model will be developed and the potential projects will be screened in Chapter 6 to produce a shorter list of projects that are realistic candidates for the portfolio.

5.6 REFERENCES

American Heritage College Dictionary (2002), 4th ed. Boston, MA: Houghton Mifflin.

Hillson, David. (2001), *Benchmarking Organizational Project Management Capability, Proceedings of the Project Management Institute Annual Seminars & Symposium* November 1–10, 2001, Nashville, Tenn., USA.

Ibbs, C. W. and Y. H. Kwak (2000). "Assessing Project Management Maturity." *Project Management Journal* (March).

Kerzner, Harold (2006). *Project Management A System Approach to Planning, Scheduling, and Controlling*, 9th ed. Hoboken, NJ: John Wiley & Sons.

Pennypacker, James S. (2005). *PM Solutions' Project Portfolio Management Maturity Model*, Center for Business Practices.

Project Management Institute (2010). http://www.pmi.org/BusinessSolutions/Pages/OPM3.aspx (retrieved April 10, 2010).

Steyn, Nicholas (2008). *Project Management for Business, Engineering, and Technology*. Oxford, UK: Butterworth-Heinemann.

6

Determining Candidate Projects and Making the Case

In Chapter 5 we identified potential projects to be considered for the portfolio and applied pre-screening criteria to reduce the large number of project proposals and thus giving us the ability to identify a manageable number of potential projects. During the screening process described in this chapter, these potential projects undergo additional evaluation and scrutiny by the portfolio management board (PMB), assessing each project's business case against specific screening criteria. This chapter addresses the remaining steps in the screening phase of PPM, including developing business cases, establishing screening criteria, defining organizational assumptions, and screening potential projects, as indicated in Figure 6.1. The result of the screening phase is a pool of candidate projects that are viable options for achieving the organization's objectives; the candidate pool will be used during portfolio selection in chapters 7, 8, and 9 to identify the optimal project portfolio.

This chapter focuses on the project portfolio management (PPM) actions necessary to further qualify and more strenuously evaluate potential projects such that they become candidate projects or are eliminated. The purpose of the screening process is to select the portfolio candidate projects by:

- Combining the potential projects selected during pre-screening with the existing projects to be considered.
- Assessing the combined list against the screening model(s).
- Refining and verifying the alignment of projects with objectives.
- Producing the project candidate list along with a refined project alignment matrix after evaluating the business cases against screening criteria.

6.1 SCREENING PROCESS

The screening process reduces the list of pre-screened potential projects to a smaller number of serious contenders that become the pool of candidate projects to be considered for inclusion in the portfolio. Many organizations perform nominations, pre-screening of potential projects, and the screening of candidate projects on an annual basis after the strategic plan is updated and communicated. Some smaller organizations, or those in which technology is changing rapidly, may perform this process more frequently. Within this nomination and screening cycle, much more frequent evaluation of current projects is performed with perhaps a weekly assessment of scope, cost, and schedule performance. A monthly or quarterly evaluation of the project's continued relevance to goals and objectives may also be performed (Shenhar, 2007). Some organizations subject new product projects

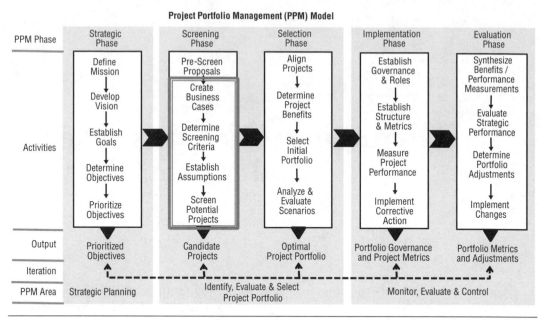

Figure 6.1   Screening potential projects to identify candidates

to stage gates through which these projects must pass in accordance with their own schedules rather than at specified intervals.

6.1.1 Screening Activities

Major activities during screening include establishing project portfolio categories, establishing screening models for each category, soliciting business cases from the sponsors of potential projects identified during pre-screening, reviewing the business cases to assess strategic alignment and achievability, revising the alignment matrix between projects and objectives, and developing a pool of candidate projects for consideration for portfolio selection.

At the end of pre-screening, the PMB has developed a consolidated list of potential projects and added existing projects to be screened. Project sponsors then develop more detailed business cases from the initial proposals for each potential project and review the business case and progress for each existing project to be considered for portfolio candidacy. The selection of portfolio candidate projects from among the potential projects is based on comparing the business case to the organization's selection model. The selection model is a refinement of the pre-screening criteria described in Chapter 5 and must be consistent with the organization's strategy. An organization may have multiple selection models, depending on the categories or classifications of projects. Before the business cases can be completed, the organization needs to specify the portfolio categories and identify the screening criteria for each category. The screening criteria for each category will be unique. For example, an organization would not require the same level of net present value (NPV) for a regulatory compliance project as it would for a new product project.

6.1.2 Screening Roles and Responsibilities

Several groups play key roles and undertake specific responsibilities for the screening process, including the PMB, the project sponsors, the executive review board (ERB), and the project management office (PMO). The role of the PMB is to act as the interface between the organization's executives and the PPM process. During the screening process, the PMB directs project sponsors to prepare business cases for each potential project that passed the pre-screening process, evaluates the business cases against the appropriate screening models, and prepares a list of candidate projects to be reviewed with and approved by the ERB. The PMB also refines the pre-screening alignment matrix and is responsible for notifying the sponsors of the results of candidate selection as well as keeping stakeholder management informed.

The role of the project sponsors for PPM is to promote the projects within their spheres of influence that they believe best support the objectives of the organization and to serve as the interface for their staffs to the PMB, and, as necessary, the ERB. During the screening process, the project sponsors prepare, or direct their staff to prepare, a business case for each potential project, review the business cases for compliance with information requirements and for accuracy, submit the completed business cases to the PMB, and respond to requests for clarification from the PMB or the ERB. Project sponsors are also responsible for representing the strategic interests of the organization to their staffs, thus preventing overstated business cases or the submission of unworthy projects at any time during the PPM process. Once informed by the PMB of the candidate selection status, project sponsors are responsible for notifying their staffs of the results.

The role of the ERB is to establish organizational strategy and to ensure that it is executed as established, and that it is modified as conditions warrant. During screening, the responsibilities of the ERB is to verify the project portfolio investment categories, review the project candidate list and rationale provided by the PMB, and assist in the resolution of screening disputes when they cannot be resolved at the appropriate lower levels.

The role of the PMO, with regard to PPM, is to manage and provide progress data about existing projects. The primary responsibility of the PMO during screening is to prepare the business case information relevant to project performance for each existing project as specified in the business case template. With close coordination between the PMB and the PMO, this process is simplified by requiring the same or similar data as that reported when measuring and reporting the progress of existing projects in the PMO dashboard. While the PMO dashboard is discussed in more detail in Chapter 11, the dashboard provides status reporting information for projects and programs in progress as part of the current portfolio. Preparation of business case performance data requires collaboration by the PMO with the PMB. If an inventory of existing projects does not exist, the PMO is also responsible for preparing such an inventory to be used for the screening process, as well as for future progress reporting. In rare instances in which no standard means of project progress measurement and reporting exists, progress measurement and reporting must be initiated to ensure that the organization considers both new and existing projects when making portfolio decisions.

6.1.3 Screening Prerequisites

Prior to the first time an organization undertakes screening for PPM, the methods and structure for screening must be established. Prior to screening the PMB develops a template for business cases and devises a method for soliciting business cases from the sponsors of each potential project, as well as for evaluating the submitted business cases. In addition, the PMB continues to work with executive management to define project categories and screening models. Meanwhile, Executive management ". . . establishes organization-wide allocation of assets among investment categories in line with the strategy and establishes overarching performance goals for the portfolio" (Levine, 2005).

Project categories and screening models are developed only once. They are then refined as frequently as the goals and objectives in the strategic plan are revised or when major organizational structure changes as a result of mergers, acquisitions, and divestitures dictate. If the PPM process is new to the organization, the PMO will establish an inventory of current projects with additional parameters in the business case regarding cost and schedule performance. Note that estimate to complete is used in place of estimated cost for projects already in progress for reasons described later in this chapter.

6.2 BUSINESS CASES

The main objective of the business case is to identify the purpose of the project, specify the anticipated benefits to be realized, and define the resources needed. The purpose of the project includes what it will produce, which organizational objective(s) it supports, and specifically how it supports the objective(s). The anticipated benefits define the financial and nonfinancial return to the organization if the project is undertaken and is successful.

Quantitative benefits use the same financial or other quantitative metrics adopted by the organization (e.g., NPV, estimated improvement in customer satisfaction survey results, or a decrease in levels of contaminant emissions by a plant). Qualitative benefits are as important, or more important, as quantitative benefits (e.g., enhanced community relations, better quality of life, or improved partnership opportunities). In any case, the benefits must relate directly to a goal and one or more objectives of the organization. If that is not the case, most likely the nominated project has no strategic value and should be eliminated from further consideration. However, the examination of stated benefits that do not contribute to an organizational objective can sometimes identify an organizational objective that was missed in the strategic planning process.

Some organizations might allow mandatory projects that do not meet any organizational objective, such as those required to meet regulatory directives. On the other hand, many organizations do include an explicitly stated goal or objective for regulatory compliance, sometimes as part of an overall objective addressing community service or good corporate citizenship. For those that do not have such a stated goal or objective, a project category and screening model can be established just for mandatory projects. This screening model for the mandatory project category would identify the potential types of compliance that might be required, for example, compliance with EPA regulations, human resources legislation (e.g., minimum wage), or even an ability to compete (e.g., a product feature offered by a direct competitor).

6.2.1 Developing Business Cases

For any *proposed* project to become a *potential* project as a result of pre-screening, project sponsors are required to develop a high-level project proposal (see Chapter 5). The portfolio governing body will normally ask the sponsors of each potential project to prepare a complete business case for the new projects that remain on the list after scrutiny for combining or separating project proposals. Thus, only qualified projects, those that have passed pre-screening, will require preparation and scrutiny of a business case.

The business case provides project justification information that enables the proposal to be evaluated by decision makers such as the PMB. Many organizations use standardized templates for this purpose—business case templates are available on the internet, free or for a fee, that organizations can tailor for their own purposes. As discussed in Chapter 5, a method must be devised to solicit and filter project proposals from within the organization's structure to the PMB. Clear guidance and communication between the PMB and those preparing business cases must be established to ensure business cases are submitted through the organizational chain of commands and in accordance with directed timelines and formats.

While the specific template used is dependent on the nature of the organization, the business case should require, at minimum:

- Description of the project and background information
- Rationale for the project (in other words, what needs it satisfies, what benefits the project provides, and why that is important)

- Anticipated quantitative and qualitative benefits to be obtained
- Alternatives considered and the rationale for selection
- A work breakdown structure that describes expected deliverables
- Estimated costs
- Estimated resources, including labor, equipment, and materials
- Anticipated risks with likelihood, impact, and strategies for addressing them
- Constraints associated with the project, for example, night work only
- Assumptions about the project, for example, that building permits will be received or that a prerequisite product will be available

The business case template, in addition to providing a place for relevant information about a project, includes a designated entry item for every element in the screening models. This may appear to be a great deal of information and require considerable effort. However, it is not unreasonable for personnel within an organization, especially those with lengthy tenure and intimate familiarity with the organization's capabilities and resources, to be able to assemble this information quickly.

Organizations that support the relationship between their strategic plans and their project and operations portfolios prominently identify in the business case which goal(s) and, specifically, which objective(s) is addressed by the project. Projects that fail to support any organizational goal and its supporting objectives do not become portfolio candidates unless they are mandatory projects. This relationship is the foundation for PPM and is intended to ensure that the organization's resources and capabilities are utilized to achieve the strategic vision of the organization.

The quantitative benefits specified in the business case are expressed in the same terms that the organization uses in its screening models and for measurement purposes, for example, NPV, net cash flow, or return on investment.

A sample of a high-level business case from the American Business University (ABU) Campus Revitalization Program is included in Appendix A of this chapter. In an actual screening process much more detail should be required (e.g., an architect's drawing, a deliverable work breakdown structure, and a detailed cost estimate.

6.2.2 Special Considerations for Cost Estimation

Affordability of a project always requires special scrutiny by evaluators. The business case provides the first real opportunity to assess whether the project's cost estimate is reasonable in terms of both accuracy and affordability. The cost estimate's portion of the business case identifies assumptions about costs, for example, the estimated rate of growth in personnel costs and materials. For the actual estimates, the organization should establish a means to classify the cost estimate. Many organizations use the guidelines developed by the Association for the Advancement of Cost Engineering (AACE) International and supported by a practice guide. Appendix 5C in this chapter describes the five classes of estimates developed by the AACE based on the degree to which the project is defined, from Class 5 at the highest level to Class 1 when the project is well-defined (AACE, 1997). For each class, AACE provides an expected accuracy range for the cost estimates, and recommends Class 5 for "screening or feasibility," Class 4 for "concept study or feasibility," Class 3 for "budget authorization, or control" (AACE, 1997), and so on. This classification also provides a context for cost estimate accuracy for those evaluating the project's affordability and the accuracy of the cost estimate provided in the business case.

The expected cost accuracy range for each class of estimates is largest for the earlier estimates and smaller for the later, more accurate estimates because more is known about the project. With assistance from finance, the PMB provides guidance to project sponsors about when to use which type of estimate, based on how much is known about each project, with consideration for the level of effort required to produce accurate estimates. For existing projects there will be less uncertainty in estimating remaining cost, while there may be considerable uncertainty in the projected costs for projects at the conceptual stage.

6.2.3 Business Case Elements for Existing Projects

A business case for existing projects, in addition to the standard elements for proposed projects, including alignment with organizational objectives, also contains relevant information about progress to date. It can include the performance against major milestones and actual performance measurements such as cumulative schedule performance, cost performance, and other earned value statistics. The cost evaluated for existing projects is only the remaining cost or the estimated cost to complete. In addition to traditional performance metrics, business cases for existing projects should contain risk history, with the disposition of risk events as well as remaining risks with likelihood, as well as the impact and strategy for each. When the organization establishes and is using metrics for performance against anticipated benefits as described in Chapter 11, these elements should be added to the business case for existing projects.

The degree to which this information is available is dependent on the project and portfolio management maturity of the organization. As discussed in later chapters addressing the implementation and evaluation phases, a PMO is normally assigned responsibility for tracking and reporting project performance metrics for an organization. The PMB and PMO collaborate during the establishment of project performance metrics to identify the right metrics and ensure that the PMO monitors the appropriate metrics and reports useful performance information to decision makers, including schedule and cost performance and schedule and cost estimates to complete as well as performance against anticipated benefits. For poorly performing projects, the business case provides an opportunity to justify why the projects should not be terminated.

6.3 EXISTING PROJECTS

All projects currently in progress and managed by the organization's PPM process form the existing projects portion of the list of candidates for portfolio selection. During the implementation and evaluation phases discussed in later chapters, existing projects are subjected to monitoring and control with adjustments made as needed to determine whether these projects fulfill their promise and continue to be a part of the portfolio. As part of this ongoing evaluation, existing projects may be terminated at any time in accordance with the evaluation process. Those that are in progress during the periodic portfolio selection process are reevaluated along with the new candidate projects.

The issue of what to do with existing projects is always difficult for decision makers. In some instances projects may be nearly completed but may be thought to have little value to the newly revised strategic plan. Should this kind of project be terminated? A poorly performing project that has recently started and is not aligned to any goal and objective could conceivably be removed during screening. On the other hand, a project that has traditionally performed poorly with regard to cost and schedule, is nearly complete, passes the screening model criteria, and supports at least one objective will probably be allowed to complete, or at least to compete during the selection phase (after screening). The information to make these screening decisions needs to be resident in the existing project business case. It is also likely that poorly performing projects already under the auspices of an effective PPM process will be culled as part of the regular performance assessments and will not, therefore, be subject to screening after the first round of successful implementation.

Again, changes to the strategic plan, especially to goals and objectives, will have a ripple effect throughout the organization's existing projects. Informed decisions need to be made as to whether or not these projects continue to support the new or revised strategic plan (goals and objectives). Inevitably, these difficult judgments must be made in the best interest of the organization, and with respect to morale.

6.3.1　Inventory of Existing Projects

An organization that does not have an established PPM process begins by creating an inventory of current projects. Such an inventory will likely identify projects that are not meeting, and may never meet, their performance targets for cost and schedule, and some that bear no relationship to any goal or objective identified in the strategic plan (Levine, 2005). Eliminating such projects not only saves significant dollars spent on something other than organizational priorities, it also frees resources to work on projects that will meet those priorities.

One organization with which the authors are familiar undertook an inventory of existing projects; the inventory identified 1,000 projects, while top management, newly educated in PPM, believed only about 60 projects could be resourced effectively. The employees in that organization experienced considerable stress because more projects were being initiated than could be accomplished, with more always arriving. Employees had no way to distinguish priorities because the organization had specified none. Managers and subordinates were *thrashing*. Thrashing, in this instance, means that managers and subordinates were spending more time and effort running from task to task than getting those tasks completed and little useful work was getting done. Strategic planning and the introduction of PPM gave the senior management of the organization the necessary traction to select a manageable number of the right initiatives and allow employees to focus on completing them. A common question to ask managers is whether they would rather accomplish 60 percent of each of 100 projects or 100 percent of each of 60 projects. The operational benefit of projects is generally not realized until the product or outcome is delivered, so accomplishing only part of a project rarely delivers the expected results or benefits.

The inventory of existing projects adopts the same format as the high-level project summaries described in Chapter 5, because the same information is needed. In addition, it should contain schedule, cost, and risk performance information. However, because the projects are in progress, the estimates are expected to be more accurate. It is important to note that the estimated costs should reflect only the cost to complete rather than the entire cost. This is because we are looking at a portfolio investment now, at the present time, and thus should not consider and are not affected by *sunk cost* that cannot be recovered despite the eventual disposition of the project. This also means that existing projects are somewhat favored from a cost point of view. However, if they fail to satisfy organizational goals and objectives, these projects are killed or terminated before their remaining cost is considered. If an existing project qualifies under the screening criteria, then it should receive this slight advantage because it may require less new financial or personnel resource investment to produce its expected return.

6.3.2　Organizational Change Management

If the concept of reevaluating existing projects for potential termination is new to the organization, significant resistance should be anticipated because it interferes with the status quo, can disrupt existing resource commitments, and defies the perceived human virtue of finishing what you start. The PMB, supported by top management, needs to effectively communicate the value of PPM to the owners of these projects. If this is a transformational concept, the introduction must be treated as an organizational change management initiative. This book is not meant to provide instruction in leading organizational change as there are many excellent references on the subject. The authors recommend, in particular, the chapter "Leading Change: Why Transformation Efforts Fail" by John

Kotter in the book *Business Leadership* (Gallos, 2008) and the chapter "Leading Positive Change" in Whetten and Cameron's *Developing Management Skills* (Whetten, 2007). Those within the organization's PPM process should be aware of the need to reevaluate existing projects and the potential disruption this will create for the organization. Sponsors of existing projects that are being terminated will not likely be as understanding because they are personally and professionally invested in their projects. As an organization grows in PPM maturity, project sponsors more readily identify with alignment of project portfolios to organizational strategy and more readily support the termination of projects that no longer support it or that fail to deliver.

6.4 ESTABLISHING PROJECT CATEGORIES OR CLASSIFICATIONS

According to Levine, an effective PPM process accomplishes three major goals: (1) ensure that the selected projects are aligned with the business strategy, (2) maximize the value of the portfolio for a given target spending level, and (3) attain balance in the portfolio in accordance with classifications or parameters established; for example, short- versus long-term projects, across product lines, high-versus low-risk projects (Levine, 2005). To achieve any of these goals, an organization must classify its projects. How it does so is dependent on the nature of the organization, but the classification is primarily a reflection of organizational objectives in combination with organizational hierarchy and must be consistent with the strategic plan. The important element is that the project classifications selected are congruent with both how senior management wants to allocate spending and the screening criteria for each classification.

A company designing and manufacturing innovative products might classify its projects by type of product. Apple might classify projects by product line such as personal computing, portable digital music, and mobile communications. It might further classify projects by target market—academia, creative professionals, corporations, government agencies, and consumers (Apple, 2008). In Chapter 2, Siemens classified its projects and target measurements by sector—industry, energy, and healthcare—and set separate performance targets for each. Other companies classify projects by geography—Asia, North America, and so on. However, with more organizations becoming truly global, with projects and virtual teams spanning geographies, classification by geography is becoming less prevalent.

Many organizations categorize their projects in accordance with the goal or objective they best satisfy. These organizations will usually explicitly state goals or objectives that result in mandatory projects, in addition to the goals intended to maximize business growth, reduce cost, or support infrastructure. As stated earlier, project categories for the organization are defined once prior to project screening and revised as necessary in accordance with changes to the strategic plan.

6.4.1 Common Categories of Projects

Potential common classes of projects include mandatory projects, research and development, new product development, incremental product or service enhancements, and cost reduction. Mandatory projects are those that are necessary to achieve legal or regulatory compliance, even though they may not themselves contribute to the achievement of explicit organizational objectives. Research and development projects are those that are intended to advance knowledge and perhaps find promising new technology breakthroughs that may, in the future, become new product development projects. Because they are not, by themselves, expected to produce a profit, they are generally screened against a different set of criteria than new product development projects.

New product development projects can range from introducing an entirely new product, such as Apple did with the iPad, or enhancing an existing product, as many automobile manufacturers do when they introduce the next year's model. Incremental product enhancement projects are simply at the less inventive and smaller scope end of new product development.

Cost reduction projects are those intended to reduce the cost of producing or delivering a product or service. Some common examples include outsourcing of call centers, strategic placement of warehouses to reduce transportation costs, or conversion to renewable sources to reduce energy costs, in addition to having potential environmental benefits. The objective of service enhancement projects is often to increase customer satisfaction and, because of increased satisfaction, perhaps to attract additional customers.

Each category of projects supports different organizational objectives, and the expected measures of success are unique for each. As we discover, the screening criteria are adapted and customized for each project type.

6.4.2 Strategic Buckets

A concept known as strategic buckets can be used to categorize projects; it has been applied mainly in new product development portfolio management practices, but the authors believe it has broader applicability. Strategic buckets are a way of allocating the overall portfolio budget into smaller and more specific portfolio budgets (Chao, 2008).

In new product development, strategic buckets are allocated to particular strategies to achieve a competitive advantage, such as innovative research and development, cost reduction, existing product enhancements, and the like (Chao, 2008). The use of strategic buckets enables senior management to determine how much resource to allocate to each bucket. "The strategic buckets model operates from the simple principle that implementing strategy equates to spending money on specific projects. . . . Thus, operationalizing strategy really means setting spending targets" (Levine, 2005). Executive management is responsible for establishing these spending targets and should be asked to provide such guidance to the PPM process.

6.5 DEFINING SCREENING MODELS FOR PROJECT CATEGORIES

Ideally, the organization's leadership and PPM personnel share a common understanding of what is required for a project to be accepted as a candidate. Although screening potential projects to derive a pool of candidate projects is dependent on sound business cases, project categories, screening models, and assumptions, other considerations must also be taken into account in determining whether a project is feasible. Whether a potential project becomes a candidate project is dependent on more than quantitative metrics such as its anticipated NPV. Regardless of how well prepared the business case, screening also considers other factors, including the organization's risk attitude, anticipated budget for the portfolio, organizational resources, project management maturity, and portfolio management capability (see Chapter 5). The presumption during the screening phase is that those individuals selecting projects already have established the project categories and screening models against which the project will be screened.

 During screening each project is considered individually against the set of criteria defined in the screening model for that type of project, and a determination is made as to whether it should become a candidate for the portfolio. Projects eliminated at this stage do not meet the screening criteria, for example, perhaps the expected NPV is below the minimum required or the budget exceeds prescribed limits. A project can also be eliminated because an incomplete business case provides insufficient information to enable the project to be screened; the PMB would first, of course, notify the sponsor of the additional information required and provide a deadline for responding. Eliminating projects that fail to meet the screening model criteria further reduces the number of projects to be considered for the portfolio and simplifies downstream portfolio evaluation (Morris, 2007). Although the number of candidate projects should be reduced considerably during screening in order to support more accurate decisions by evaluators during portfolio selection, it is important to avoid eliminating projects with considerable potential by setting the screening model criteria targets too high (Morris, 2007). Some examples of potential screening model criteria, both quantitative and qualitative, are described in the next section.

6.6 POTENTIAL SCREENING MODEL CRITERIA

With project categories defined, criteria for screening are selected and combined into a screening model for that project category. For new product development, for example, the screening model criteria might be cost, expected NPV, and risk. For cost reduction projects, the screening model criteria could be expected cost savings and availability of resources. Using the suggested screening model criteria, a screening model for new product development could resemble the following:

Project category	New product development
Expected cost	< $20M development costs at AACE Class 3
Expected NPV	> $80M over 5 years
Risk	> 70% probability of success

The business cases for new product development projects in this example would contain information justifying the attainment of or exceeding the screening model criteria minimum values.

Screening models are developed by the PMB with a review and approval by the ERB. They are specific to the organization and its goals and objectives, as well as to its budget. A not-for-profit organization might use improvements in donations and an increase in the number of beneficiaries of its service for its new products screening criteria. On the other hand, a high-tech computer company might use anticipated market share and return on investment for its new products screening criteria. All organizations might include regulatory compliance for their mandatory projects. In the case of mandatory projects, the screening process simply ensures that the project qualifies as mandatory, and then it is automatically placed in the list of candidates.

Screening model criteria can be quantitative or qualitative, numeric or nonnumeric. Examples of nonnumeric screening criteria are regulatory requirement, operating necessity, and competitive necessity; examples of numeric screening criteria are payback period, internal rate of return (IRR), and NPV. They must, in any case, align with the organization's strategy, except possibly when it comes to mandatory projects. Although an organization may not have a stated objective for mandatory regulatory projects, it likely has an implicit goal of compliance with the law and will therefore support such projects.

The following section includes a brief description of common numeric and nonnumeric screening model criteria used by organizations for portfolio screening.

6.6.1 Nonnumeric Criteria

Nonnumeric criteria for screening models are qualitative in nature and are sometimes binary, meaning that if the characteristic exists, the project is automatically included in the candidate list, and if it does not then it is excluded. However, the criteria in a screening model may be prioritized; thus, the decision on whether to include a project would be made in a compensatory manner.

In this section, common types of nonnumeric screening criteria are discussed. In some organizations, these screening criteria are considered project categories or project types, each of which would have its own screening criteria. When used as screening criteria, they are considered pass-fail measurements, not necessarily for selection into the portfolio but for status as project portfolio candidates.

Sacred Cow

A sacred cow project is one that is undeservedly safe from elimination or criticism, often because it is the pet project of a senior executive. The term sacred cow alludes to the Hindu respect and reverence for cows and thus their protected status. However, in business such projects tend to drain resources without necessarily producing great benefit or organizational value. In organizations with mature PPM practices, such projects do not prevail because senior executives and other managers believe in selecting the portfolio with the most value within organizational constraints. Early in the establishment of practices, these projects should be identified by the PMB and subjected to the same rigorous standards as other projects. However, this can be accomplished only after senior executives have recognized and accepted the value of PPM. When that is the case, the governance of the project portfolio process determines the validity of proposed projects (Levine, 2005).

Operating Necessity

Projects considered operating necessities include those that must be implemented for the organization to function properly. Typically, these are projects undertaken to achieve legislative or regulatory compliance. In addition, in some organizations projects such as implementation of replacement technology at the end of a lease period, or replacement of assets that have been fully depreciated, may be considered operating necessities. Other types of projects classified as operating necessities include facility upgrades that are required because of related projects, such as when increased manufacturing capacity is needed to satisfy production needs for a new product to be released or the consolidation of IT systems for a merger or acquisition.

Competitive Necessity

Organizations identify projects needed to remain competitive in their industries as competitive necessities. This criterion is applied to a project to outsource a noncore business process, for example, thus freeing internal resources to focus on core competencies or reducing costs. Other examples of applying the competitive necessity criterion are a retail chain's need to establish a web sales presence through electronic commerce or a technology firm's need to build a new production facility for mass customization to satisfy customer demands for variety. Imagine how long a PC producer would remain in business if it offered only one model or charged exorbitant prices for customization. How would a large brick and mortar retailer survive in this e-commerce world without a virtual store?

Product Line Extension

Established organizations that produce products or offer services do so by product line. Apple, for example, offers computers, music-related products (iTunes, iPod), phones (iPhone), multipurpose products (iPad), and others. An Apple product line extension project might be to release a new version of the iPod. Accenture offers multiple services, including consulting services, technology services, and outsourcing. Accenture might choose to add a new specialty to its strategic consulting services offerings. Product line extensions can usually be accomplished using existing resources. Such projects are common and often compete for similar resources. Rather than a criterion stated as *the project must be a product line extension or be eliminated*, product line extension projects might be considered a project category or classification. Some organizations consider multiple types of product line extensions, including major revisions, incremental changes and simply remarketing, or repackaging or promoting existing products in a new way.

True Innovations

Projects meeting this criterion are either new to the organization or truly innovative in the sense that they will deliver something the world has not yet seen (e.g., the launch of Sputnik I by the Soviet Union in 1957, ushering in space exploration). A 2003 benchmark study of new product performance and practices by the American Productivity and Quality Center (APQC) found that the best performing companies have a higher percentage of new to the organization or new to the world projects in terms of investment funding when compared to the worst performing companies that tend to have a higher percentage of small incremental product or packaging change projects (Levine, 2005). If an organization creates products, an important new product portfolio consideration is determining the best mix by type of development projects. The APQC study showed that this mix is a strong predictor of business performance (Levine, 2005).

6.6.2 Numeric Criteria

Numeric criteria have discrete or continuous values. Frequently an increase in the value of a criterion in terms of desirability may be linear, such as NPV. In other instances, the increase or decrease in desirability may not be linear, in which case utility functions can be assigned. A utility function assigns values in terms of usefulness or desirability to differences in a commodity or characteristic. For example, if a graph is plotted in which the x-axis represents increased hunger and the y-axis represents the value or desirability of eating a Big Mac, it might resemble the graph shown in Figure 6.2.

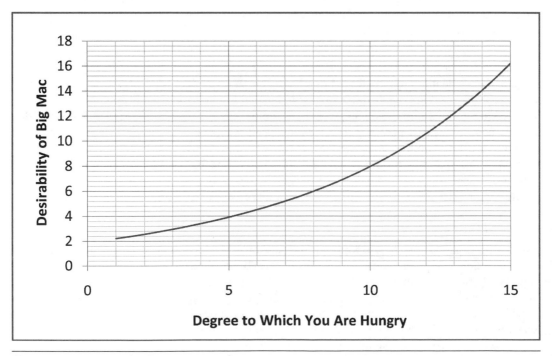

Figure 6.2   Exponential utility curve example

The utility curve shows that the hungrier that one is, the greater the desirability, or perceived value, of having a Big Mac (or, perhaps, any food at all). In this case, the utility function is not linear but exponential, and it shows that the desire grows exponentially as hunger increases. In cases in which the relationship between increments in value is not linear, the organization may consider building a utility function. Another example is the utility value of winning a $10M lottery. To the impoverished, it would be a life-changing boon; to a billionaire, it would seem a drop in the bucket. In another example, although the value of increased space in a building may be linear in terms of increasing value up to the point at which it satisfies all space needs, beyond that point additional space has no value (and probably involves increased costs). A utility function is created to represent the increased desirability of space up to a point and with no value beyond that point.

Thus, numeric values may stand on their own for evaluation purposes or may be assigned a utility value based on the organization's perspective. Following are common financial criteria often used to evaluate project investments.

Payback Period

The payback period is simply the length of time a project takes to return the investment or the cost incurred to deliver it. The shorter the payback period, the more preferred the project, according to this criterion. Table 6.1 shows the calculation of the payback periods for two mutually exclusive projects, A and B. Although the total cash inflow is much greater for Project B, if a payback period of two years or less was used as the only criterion, Project A would be selected and Project B would be eliminated.

The payback period is easy to calculate and is an attractive criterion in companies for which the cash position is one of the most important measurements. However, since the payback period does not consider earnings beyond the payback timeframe (e.g., for Project B, the $500 earnings in just the portion of Year 3 beyond the payback period), the organization would select Project A rather than the greater cash contribution of Project B (Weaver, 2001).

The example in Table 6.1 did not take into account the time value of money. More realistically, the discounted payback period can be used to determine the number of time periods required to return the original investment based on discounted estimated future cash flows. Table 6.2 shows the discounted payback periods for the same two projects, A and B, with a sample discount rate of 10%.

Table 6.1 Payback periods for Project A and Project B

	Year	Project A	Project B
Cost (Cash Outflow)	0	$ (600)	$ (600)
Cash Inflow	1	400	200
Cash Inflow	2	300	300
Cash Inflow	3	200	600
Accumulated Cash Flows			
	1	$ 400	$ 200
	2	700	500
	3	900	1,100
Payback Period		**1.67 YRS**	**2.17 YRS**

Table 6.2 Discounted payback periods for Project A and Project B

		Project	
	Year	A	B
Cost (Cash Outflow)	0	$ (600)	$ (600)
Cash Inflow	1	400	200
Cash Inflow	2	300	300
Cash Inflow	3	200	600
		10% Assumed Discount Rate	
PV of Year 1 Cash Inflow		$ 364	$ 182
PV of Year 2 Cash Inflow		248	248
PV of Year 3 Cash Inflow		150	451
		Accumulated Discounted Cash Flows	
	1	$ 364	$ 182
	2	612	430
	3	762	881
Payback Period		**1.39 Years**	**2.19 Years**

Average Rate of Return

The rate of return for a single time period, such as one year, is the ratio between the periodic gain or loss and the amount invested; if the amount invested was $100 and the gain in one year was $5, the rate of return = 5/100 or 0.05 or 5%. Note that the amount of capital available for the second year in this case is $100 + 5 = $105. So, if the return in the second year is also $5, the rate of return is not $5/100, but, instead, $5/105, resulting in a return of only about 0.0476 or 4.76%.

The arithmetic average rate of return, most commonly shown as the arithmetic average of the rates of return over several time periods, is calculated by dividing the sum of the rates of return over multiple periods by the number of periods. Thus, if the rates of return on the original $100 investment were 0.05, 0.07, 0.09, and 0.07, respectively, for each of four years, the arithmetic average rate of return can be calculated as (0.05 + 0.07 + 0.09 + 0.07)/4 = 0.07 or 7%. However, since the rates of return are based on the available capital at the beginning of the time period, rather than the original investment amount, the actual dollar amounts of the return are not visible. When the gains or losses are large, or the time periods are many, the arithmetic average rate of return can be misleading.

When calculating the average rate of return over a large number of time periods, that is more than two years, use the geometric or compound average rate of return. This calculation generates the percent return actually produced at the end of the time period against the original investment. To obtain the compound rate of return, use the following formula: ((capital/return) ^ (1/n)) − 1, where n is the number of time periods.

To illustrate the difference between the arithmetic average rate of return and the geometric average rate of return, let's suppose you initially invest $100. At the end of the first year, the investment is valued at $200, but at the end of the second year the investment has lost $100, leaving the original investment of $100. Using the arithmetic average rate of return calculations, the rate of return for the first year is (($200 − $100)/$100) × 100% = 100%. The rate of return for the second year is (($100

– $200)/$200) × 100% = −50%. The arithmetic average of the rates of return for the two-year period is (100% + −50%)/2 = 25%. For the geometric average or compound rate of return, we know that (($100/$100) ^ (1/2)) − 1 = (1 ^ 0.5) − 1 = 0%, so the compound rate of return is 0% versus 25% for the arithmetic average rate of return (ThinkQuest, 2010). Since we know that at the end of two years we have only the $100 we started with, the return is $0, and thus the compound rate of return calculation makes more sense than the arithmetic average. Given that two years have passed, the investment has probably lost money because of the time value of money discussed in the next section.

Discounted Cash Flow

Discounted cash flows are used in finance to calculate the value of a future sum of money if the funds were available today, or the present value (PV) of a future sum of money. Businesses developing and selling products use some form of discounted cash flow analysis to compare the anticipated value and to measure the actual value of projects their executives are considering for the project portfolio.

Most financial decisions are based on the time value of money, considering that funds in hand now are worth more than the same amount of money in the future (Weaver, 2001). This is for three reasons: (1) inflation reduces the purchasing power of a given sum of money, (2) uncertainty about receiving a sum of money in the future tends to increase with the distance into the future we expect to receive it, and (3) because if we wait until the future to invest a current sum of money, we are forgoing the opportunity of investing it today (Higgins, 2007). The opportunity cost, as this is known, is what would have been the return had it been invested today.

Although this book is not intended to provide an exhaustive discussion of the time value of money, a brief overview of some key concepts is included because these concepts are employed by most organizations when placing value on competing potential and existing projects.

Future Value and Present Value

If you invest $100 today and anticipate a 10% return in one year, you can expect to have $110 at the end of that first year. If the expectation for the return is the same for the second year, by investing the $110 and at the end of the second year, you expect $121. So, the 10% interest has been compounded. By the same token, if you expect to have $121 at the end of two years, and want to know what the equivalent value of that $121 is today, instead of compounding, discount the value of $121 by the discount rate. In this example, you expect a rate of return of 10% per year, so use 10% as the discount rate. To perform the calculation, if you will have $121 at the end of (in this case) two years, $121/1.10 = $110 to determine how much you would have at the end of the first year of discounting; for the PV, perform the calculation again as $110/1.10 = $100.

As seen in the last paragraph, compounding yields the future value (FV) of a current investment, while discounting yields the PV of a future sum of money. So, the PV of $121 at a discount rate of 10% is $100, and the FV of $100 at a compound rate of 10% is $121. An important concept to understand is that the PV of future cash flows is considered to be equivalent in value to the future cash flows (Higgins, 2007).

Computer spreadsheet software, such as Microsoft Excel, contains functions to automatically calculate these values with parameters specified by the user, as do most financial calculators. Many finance textbooks also contain tables for FV at a particular compounding rate and for PV at a particular discounting rate corresponding to a particular number of periods.

Net Present Value

When organizations undertake projects lasting more than a few months, or projects that generate cash flows to be realized over a period of years, the evaluation must take into account the time value of money, or discounted cash flows. As Higgins stated, "The chief determinant of what a company will become is the investments it makes today" (Higgins, 2007). We believe that the most common quantitative measurement or criterion applied to candidate projects, including those already underway, is the project's expected or actual NPV. It is the result of calculating the sum of the PVs of all cash inflows minus the sum of the PVs of all cash outflows; thus the moniker *net* present value. The NPV assesses how much value is created, expressed in terms of today's funds, by undertaking a certain project or portfolio of projects.

When NPV is positive at a particular discount rate, value is created; when it is negative, value is lost. The larger the positive NPV, the greater the value created at that discount rate. Keep in mind that not all projects are comparable. Some projects, such as those undertaken to meet legislative requirements, may have negative NPV but are mandatory members of a portfolio. In that case, if NPV is calculated at all, the purpose would be to determine the highest value negative NPV, or lowest cost approach to the project. Also, in not-for-profit and many government portfolios, the anticipated value often does not include consideration of NPV. Screening models for each project category may include different NPV targets. For example, for a new product development project category, the NPV screening target criterion may be much larger than the NPV screening target criterion for product enhancement projects, and mandatory projects may exclude NPV altogether.

Benefit–Cost Ratio

Another way to express the time-adjusted value of an investment is the benefit-cost ratio (BCR), often used in the government sectors (Higgins, 2007). The BCR is calculated as the (present value of cash inflows/present value of cash outflows). An investment is attractive when its BCR is greater than 1.0 and unattractive when it is less than 1.0. One advantage of BCR over NPV is that it allows a comparison of investments that are not similar in size. However, as mentioned during the discussion of NPV, projects with NPVs that vary widely may not be classified in the same project category.

Internal Rate of Return

The IRR is a popular measurement used to determine the discount rate at which the NPV for an investment is zero. Whereas the NPV for an investment might be positive at, for example, a 10% discount rate, it might well become negative at a 15% discount rate. The IRR is calculated to determine the discount rate percentage at which NPV = 0. When the expected discount rate is higher than the IRR, the NPV will be negative, and when the discount rate is lower than the IRR, the NPV will be positive. Of course, as the discount rate is reduced, NPV rises; contrarily, when the discount rate is increased, NPV falls. This is because the PV of future cash inflows increases as the discount rate falls and decreases as the discount rate rises. In many cases the discount rate is considered equivalent to the cost of capital to an organization. When IRR is selected as a criterion, then the opportunity cost of capital (K) is compared to the IRR to determine how to evaluate the investment (Higgins, 2007) as follows:

IRR > K (accept the investment)
IRR < K (reject the investment)
IRR = K (investment is marginal)

In most cases, the NPV and the IRR result in the same recommendation for a project. The IRR is interpreted to be the rate at which funds can be reinvested. However, it is considered by many to be a flawed criterion because funds cannot always be reinvested at the same rate as they are earned; it also doesn't consider the cost of capital. In addition, if positive cash flows are followed by negative cash flows, a given project can have multiple IRRs (Weaver, 2001).

Modified IRR

The modified IRR (MIRR) or terminal rate of return (TRR) is considered to be superior to the IRR because it takes into consideration the rate at which intermediate cash flows can be reinvested. The

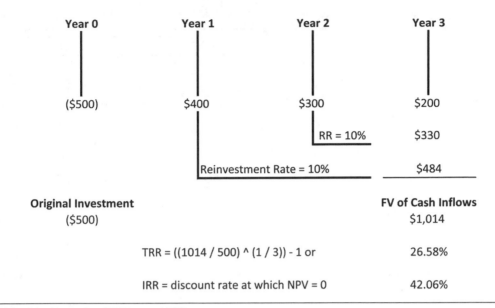

Figure 6.3 Example of TRR versus IRR

TRR is the discount rate at which the cost of the investment is equal to the FV of intermediate cash flows that are reinvested, not at the IRR, but at some suitable risk-adjusted cost of capital. TRR is calculated in a two-step process. The first step reinvests each intermediate cash flow at the organization's cost of capital, for example, 10%. The second step calculates the TRR by comparing the accumulated FVs of the projected cash flows reinvested at the assumed rate (Higgins, 2007). It reasonably presumes that the interest rate paid by the organization to fund the investment is different from the rate it receives when reinvesting the cash flows.

A graphical example is shown in Figure 6.3. As can be seen, the TRR that considers the actual rate the organization expects to obtain as a result of reinvesting the cash flows is much lower than the IRR that presumes that reinvestments of intermediate cash flow amounts can produce returns equivalent to the IRR. In the example shown, the TRR was obtained using the MIRR function in Excel, and the IRR was obtained using the IRR function. When calculated by hand, this example yields:

$$\text{TRR} = ((1014/500) \wedge (1/3)) - 1 = 26.58\%$$

Excel calculates IRR using a trial and error function. This can be done with a financial calculator or by hand as well.

For reasons stated, the TRR (MIRR) is usually preferred over the IRR as a criterion for assessing financial return rates of project portfolio candidates.

Profitability Index

The profitability index (PI) is related to the NPV. It shows the ratio between the total PV of future cash flows and the original investment. Table 6.3 shows the calculation of both NPV and the PI for projects A and B.

Table 6.3 shows that for each dollar invested in Project B, the return is $1.47 as opposed to $1.27 for Project A. Both the NPV and the PI indicate that Project B is preferred over Project A. Had our selection been based on the discounted payback period shown earlier in Table 6.2, Project A would be selected because of its shorter payback period and the fact that it missed the larger discounted

Table 6.3 NPV and PI for Projects A and B

	Year	Project	
		A	B
Investment in Year 0	0	$ (600)	$ (600)
Cash Inflow	1	400	200
Cash Inflow	2	300	300
Cash Inflow	3	200	600
		10% Assumed Discount Rate	
PV of Year 1 Cash Inflow		$ 364	$ 182
PV of Year 2 Cash Inflow		248	248
PV of Year 3 Cash Inflow		150	451
Total PV of Cash Inflows		$ 762	$ 881
Investment in Year 0		(600)	(600)
NPV at 10% (Total PV - Investment)		$ 162	$ 281
Profitability Index (Total PV / Investment)		1.27	1.47

cash inflows, NPV and PI of Project B. Note that the NPV takes into account both the size of the investment and the actual returns, while the PI considers only the ratio between them. To avoid the risk of eliminating projects with smaller profitability indices but much larger returns, use the PI only when the sizes of the investments and cash flows for a group or category of projects are similar.

NPV Advantages

Some financial textbooks have selected NPV as the preferred financial criterion for selecting project portfolios or ranking projects because it considers discounted cash flows at a selected rate, or opportunity cost of funds, and helps to maximize the value of the organization (Weaver, 2001).

NPV can be misused, for example, when comparing projects with widely varying cash flow durations. Evaluators might be tempted to take the larger NPV of a five-year project over the small NPV of a project with only two years of returns, when, in fact, completing the two-year project might free resources for yet another project in the third year with an even larger NPV. Ross points out that one should undertake a project with a positive NPV "as long as doing so doesn't interfere with the ability to take on a competing project" (Ross, 1995). Choosing a portfolio from among competing projects is, of course, what PPM is all about. Ross also warns that NPV is calculated at a point in time (Ross, 1995); although it is unlikely, a project may be just as viable next year, albeit with a different NPV.

With these caveats in mind, NPV is arguably the preferred and most common financial measurement of project value and is often used as a screening criterion for portfolio selection. Of course, it applies only to those projects expected to deliver financial returns. For many projects, such as those dedicated to research and development, regulatory compliance, and many public sector projects, NPV may not apply.

6.6.3 Screening Model Considerations

Criteria in screening models may be used as binary, yes/no decisions, such that a project failing to meet any criterion would be excluded from further consideration. When used in this manner, an otherwise stellar project might be arbitrarily excluded. Rather than using a strictly binary approach to screening, some organizations use spreadsheet ratings, and others apply the analytic hierarchy process (AHP) to enable compensatory decision making during the screening process. Recall from Chapter 3 that compensatory decisions allow trading off of good and bad characteristics and allow a project that fails to meet one of the screening criteria to continue to be considered because of outstanding expected performance on other criteria.

One approach to compensatory screening is to create a ratings spreadsheet model. Organizations extract the screening criteria results from each project's business case to create worksheets that contain the relevant comparative information for the projects in each project category. Weights are assigned to criteria to indicate that they do not all have the same value to the organization. Each project is then given a weighted overall screening score. With a spreadsheet model, projects can be sorted by various criteria to give the PMB and others a simplified view of how the projects stack up against each screening model criterion.

When a large number of potential projects of certain types are under consideration to become portfolio candidates, such as operating or competitive necessity, it may be sufficient to rate or rank them or perform an analysis of comparative benefit. In other cases, the use of ratio-scale comparisons with AHP and Comparion tools is useful for prioritizing the screening criteria as well as for narrowing the list of projects that become portfolio candidates. For the new product development screening model example, AHP is suitable to prioritize the three criteria of expected cost, NPV, and risk in much the same way the objectives were prioritized in Chapter 4.

Another use is to define and prioritize the objectives for the project category, for example, operating necessity. Why are projects considered to be operating necessities? Would they include replacing computer equipment that has been fully depreciated, repairing infrastructure required to sustain heating and cooling, or an increase in plant capacity to enable increased product demand? Projects that fall into the category of operating necessity satisfy several different kinds of objectives.

If operating necessity projects are numerous and competing for organizational resources or funding, a separate evaluation is warranted using the same tools being used to select the project portfolio. Organizations with an overwhelming number of projects in a certain category should analyze the objectives for that project category. If the category is too broad, it can be split into multiple categories, each of which has differing objectives. To improve the portfolio decision processes by clarifying and simplifying project categories, and making the screening model criteria for each category more relevant, the PMB recommends changes in project categories and screening models be given to the ERB for review and approval.

6.7 DEVELOPING THE LIST OF CANDIDATE PROJECTS FOR ABU

By evaluating the common set of data provided in the business cases, each project on the list of potential projects is assigned to a project category and evaluated against the screening model for the category. As a result, the list of potential projects is reduced to those that satisfy the screening model(s). Earlier, the Steering Committee (SC) developed the ABU Campus Revitalization Program project categories and the screening model to be applied to the business cases.

6.7.1 ABU Campus Revitalization Program Project Categories

The ABU Board of Trustees (the ERB for this portfolio) elected to align the portfolio project categories with the type of facility to be built or enhanced to satisfy the university's goal for campus facilities and surroundings. This aligns directly with the five objectives identified to satisfy the goal, as described in Chapter 2. Thus, the five project categories are:

1. Academic Land Use and Facilities
2. Services and Administration Facilities
3. Intercollegiate Athletics Facilities
4. Recreation Services Facilities
5. Residential and Conference Facilities

6.7.2 ABU Campus Revitalization Program Screening Model

Since all five project categories represent campus facilities projects, all related to the goal of campus revitalization through appropriate facilities, only one screening model was developed for the portfolio. Remember that in this example, the ABU Campus Revitalization Program was initiated as the result of a $200M endowment from prominent alumni. The Board of Trustees initially envisioned utilizing the endowment to start all of the projects at the same time or as soon as possible.

The screening model was developed by the Steering Committee (analogous to the PMB), with review and approval by the Board of Trustees (analogous to the ERB). The model takes into account the risk-averse nature of the Board of Trustees, the lack of experience of university facilities' staff in managing major new construction projects, and an interest in encouraging local employment.

As discussed, screening criteria in real organizations are often compensatory in nature, and the screening criteria may possess different degrees of importance. In this case, for the sake of simplicity, the screening criteria are binary and considered to be of equal value. Thus, a potential project must satisfy all four criteria to be carried forward as a candidate for portfolio selection. The model consists of the following criteria:

- A project must support at least one of the defined objectives.

  Indicate in the designated area in the business case which strategic objective(s) is (are) supported and provide a description of how and to what extent.

- A single project must cost less than the amount of the endowment, which in this case is $200M.

  Indicate in the designated area in the business case the anticipated cost for the project, including the costs for major deliverables and their timeframes. Indicate the stage of cost development in accordance with the AACE and include the cost ranges accordingly.

- The project must utilize local resources if available; otherwise resources must be readily available on the open market.

  Describe the major resources required and intended source from which to obtain each of them. If the resources are to be obtained from outside of the university metropolitan area, identify and include necessary estimated costs for transport, living expenses, or other expected peripheral costs.

- The probability of success must be at least 0.75.

  Identify and describe each risk in the risk section of the business case. For each one, provide the likelihood of occurrence (low, medium, or high) and the impact on the project should the risk be realized. For each substantive risk (impact or likelihood medium or above), identify the risk strategy as (1) accept, (2) avoid, (3) transfer, or (4) mitigate. For those risks to be transferred or mitigated, describe how this will be accomplished and include the estimated cost of transfer or mitigation.

Just as the information to support pre-screening criteria must be available in the initial project proposals, information to support the screening criteria must be readily identifiable in the business cases. Everyone involved must have a common understanding of the meaning of each criterion as specified in the definitions below each one. Executives, project sponsors, and the PMB are encouraged to be honest in their assessments of cost and risk, as well as benefits, by rewarding the achievement of benefits of selected projects rather than merely rewarding the selection.

6.8 ABU CANDIDATE PROJECTS

As discussed in Chapter 5, 67 projects were proposed during pre-screening; of that number, 34 passed the pre-screening process and became potential projects to enter the screening process. The list of candidate projects includes those already in the pipeline (started but not completed) and new initiatives. Pipeline projects are denoted as such in the business cases. As is common practice, the budgets for pipeline projects represent only the incremental costs to complete the project, not the original cost estimate.

6.8.1 Evaluating ABU Campus Revitalization Project Business Cases

As business cases were received, the Steering Committee logged them in and established a small group to perform a cursory review of the business case for completeness. It then notified the sponsor electronically to confirm receipt and request any missing information. The Steering Committee also determined that it would require all business cases to be submitted and reviewed prior to performing the business case evaluation. The review team included experts in cost, risk, and each type of facility; all were intimately familiar with the content and intent of the strategic plan and its goals and objectives. Part of the responsibility of the review team was *to identify potential inconsistencies* with regard to cost and risk, *to request clarification of business cases*, to *apply the screening criteria* to eliminate projects failing to qualify, and *to select the portfolio candidate projects*.

The Steering Committee reviewed the candidate list with the Board of Trustees to identify which projects to select and which to eliminate from further consideration, and why. When approved by the Board of Trustees, the Steering Committee notified the project sponsors of the disposition of each business case. Recall that the Steering Committee is the ABU equivalent of the Portfolio Review Board, and the Board of Trustees is the ABU equivalent of the Executive Review Board, or senior management.

6.8.2 ABU Campus Revitalization Program Portfolio Candidates

For the ABU example organization, the portfolio selection committee chose 15 candidate projects from among a much larger number (34) of potential projects, as shown in Table 6.4.

Notice in the discussion that follows that Projects 4 and 11 have alternative approaches. Project 8 is termed an *enabling project* because although it does not enhance campus facilities, it enables the other projects to happen. This project must be undertaken in order to facilitate the entire program, so it can be considered in a manner similar to mandatory projects in the screening process.

Table 6.4 List of ABU candidate projects

ABU Candidate Projects
1. Renovate Existing Student Dormitories (Jarvis, Davis, and Willard Halls)
2. Renovate & Expand Davidson Student Services Center
3. Construct Dr. Mary Haven Student Housing Center (Off-Campus Facility)
4. Renovate & Expand C.W. Benson Campus Library* *(Alternatives Project)*
5. Renovate Benjamin Stadium & Field house
6. Renovate Mason Hall Research Center
7. Construct ABU Medical Clinic
8. ABU Revitalization Program Regulatory & Environmental Approval Project *(Enabling Project)*
9. Construct Paisley Hall Student Services Center
10. Renovate Deluth Hall Dining Facility
11. Construct ABU Indoor Athletic Complex * *(Alternatives Project)*
12. Construct ABU Distance Learning Center
13. Expand Campus Share Ride Services
14. Construct Campus Theatre
15. Construct ABU Faculty Technology & Research Center

6.9 ALTERNATIVE APPROACHES TO A SPECIFIC PROJECT

Multiple approaches to a given project are often identified during the nomination process. The project sponsor may ask the developers of the business case to offer two or more alternatives that vary in scope and cost. Projects 4 and 11 in our example have three alternative approaches each dubbed GOLD, SILVER, and BRONZE. These terms can be anything meaningful within the organization. In this case, the GOLD alternatives have the largest scope and cost; the BRONZE alternatives have the smallest scope and cost; the SILVER alternatives are in between in terms of scope and cost. Multiple alternatives may be considered for portfolio selection and that is how ABU decided to deal with these two projects. Within specified constraints and evaluated priorities, a second or third approach might be selected when the first alternative causes the selected portfolio to exceed its allocated funding. This approach is recommended when the selection of any of the alternatives is considered an integral part of the entire portfolio selection process.

Another way to deal with a project having multiple alternatives, however, is to build a software decision model, using a tool such as Comparion from Expert Choice. One can then select one of the approaches prior to nominating the project as a candidate for the portfolio. This approach is recommended when the sponsor of the project, and other decision making stakeholders, want to choose the best alternative among themselves rather than having one selected as a result of other considerations in choosing the portfolio. In other words, these stakeholders want to agree on the scope and cost and present only one alternative as a candidate. The sponsor of the project for the Davidson Student Services Center elected to follow this process. Project 2, to Renovate & Expand Davidson Student Services Center, is aligned with the objective: "Improve existing facilities for administrative and student services staff." As with many projects, there are multiple ways it can be performed. In Appendix 6B we present an analysis of the alternative approaches considered and demonstrate that AHP and software tools can be used to evaluate project alternatives when the group owning the project wishes to reach a decision internally and then carry forward only one alternative. See Appendix 6B in this chapter to see how we arrived at the suggested renovation and expansion project put forth as a candidate for the project portfolio for the ABU Campus Revitalization Program.

In Chapter 4 the use of Expert Choice and Comparion demonstrated how to prioritize objectives. The process of entering and prioritizing objectives for this evaluation is exactly the same as that described in Chapter 4. However, we have not yet described the processes of entering alternatives, synthesizing the evaluation results, and performing sensitivity analysis. These are addressed in Chapter 7 where the portfolio candidate projects are prioritized and sensitivity analysis is performed to test the sense of rightness of the results. For purposes of this chapter, however, we simply wish to show that the same process and software can be used to decide among alternatives. The main difference between choosing a portfolio and choosing the best alternative is that for the portfolio, multiple alternatives are selected that taken together represent the selected portfolio; when choosing the best alternative, only the top alternative is chosen. Those wanting to experiment with the sample project alternatives might want to read ahead in Chapter 7 for an understanding of the concepts presented.

6.10 ALIGNING PROJECTS TO OBJECTIVES—THE ALIGNMENT MATRIX

During screening, as business cases are developed, part of the case for each project identifies the objectives supported and documents specifically how the project does so. Also, some projects are combined, split, or otherwise modified.

The screening process eliminates some potential projects; not all potential projects become candidate projects. For instance, a project proposal may have been deemed to support a specific objective during pre-screening, but it is eliminated after more information provided in the business case showed the project would not contribute to the objective or to any other objective. Also, analysis of anticipated project benefits while preparing the business case may result in modifications to a project's anticipated impact on objectives. This necessitates revising or rebuilding the alignment matrix to clearly illustrate which objectives are supported by which projects. This information is used to establish the relationships between projects and objectives in the AHP model and demonstrate continued alignment to the strategic plan. Thus, changes to the alignment matrix arise because of new information from the business cases, greater understanding of the objectives, or both. Ensuring sufficient documentation and discussion of the meaning of the objectives to yield a common understanding of the meaning of each objective is critical to properly create the alignment matrix. This common understanding eliminates ambiguity that is crucial throughout the PPM process.

After the projects are selected as candidates during the screening process, the objectives supported by each are identified in a refined alignment matrix, containing only candidate projects as shown in Table 6.5. Cells marked X indicate final alignment of proposed projects (row) contributing to the corresponding objective (column). Note that several changes to the matrix have been made since it was created during pre-screening in Chapter 5; these changes are due to an improved understanding and interpretation of the objectives as well as new information from the business cases. It is quite common for the alignment matrix to become considerably more specific during screening. In this case, the Steering Committee and the project sponsors realized that most often a project contributes in a meaningful way to only one objective or at most two. Failure to be specific about project alignment with objectives tends to dilute the portfolio selection process, as noted in Chapter 7. In this case, after verification of the proposed projects alignment matrix, the X marks are fewer for certain candidate projects. In Table 6.5, candidate projects removed from their initial alignment are identified by O.

Table 6.5 Alignment matrix of candidate projects to objectives

Candidate Projects	Objectives				
	Academic Land Use and Facilities	Services and Administration Facilities	Intercollegiate Athletics Facilities	Recreation Services Facilities	Residential and Conference Facilities
1. Renovate Existing Student Dormitories (Jarvis, Davis, and Sewall Halls)	O				x
2. Renovate & Expand Davidson Student Services Center	O	x		O	O
3. Construct Dr. Mary Haven Student Housing Center (Off-Campus Facility)	O	O			x
4a. (GOLD) Renovate & Expand C.W. Benson Campus Library	x	O			O
4b. (SILVER) Renovate & Expand C.W. Benson Campus Library	x	O			O
4c. (BRONZE) Renovate & Expand C.W. Benson Campus Library	x	O			O
5. Renovate Benjamin Stadium & Field house	O		x	x	
6. Renovate Mason Hall Research Center	x				O
7. Construct ABU Medical Clinic	O	x			
8. ABU Revitalization Program Regulatory & Environmental Approval Project (**Enabling Project**)	x	x	x	x	x
9. Construct Paisley Hall Student Services Center	O	x		O	O
10. Renovate Deluth Hall Dining Facility	O			x	x
11a. (GOLD) Construct ABU Indoor Athletic Complex	O		x	O	O
11b. (SILVER) Construct ABU Indoor Athletic Complex	O		x	O	O
11c. (BRONZE) Construct ABU Indoor Athletic Complex	O		x	O	O
12. Construct ABU Distance Learning Center	x				O
13. Expand Campus Share Ride Services		x		x	x
14. Construct Campus Theatre	O			x	
15. Construct ABU Faculty Technology & Research Center	x	O			O

- An x denotes that the project is aligned with an objective.
- An O denotes that the project was no longer aligned after clarification of objectives.
- A blank indicates that the project was never considered to be, and is not, aligned with an objective.

The creation and approval of this matrix represents the final step in the screening process. The matrix is used to prepare the evaluation model for project prioritization in Chapter 7 and portfolio selection in Chapter 8. Identifying the impact of the relative priorities of the objectives and the degree to which each project satisfies the objectives it supports are crucial elements of portfolio selection.

6.11 SUMMARY

In this chapter we defined the project types and the screening criteria that are defined by an organization only once, at the inception of PPM. Thereafter, these are revised as the strategic plan and needs of the business change. The PMB worked with appropriate project sponsors to revise project proposals that needed to be combined, split, or otherwise modified. We created the business cases to be evaluated against the screening criteria and performed the evaluation. Multiple ways to handle alternative approaches to a given project were described.

The result of these activities is a list of candidate projects that were used to create a revised project alignment matrix with only the selected portfolio candidates mapped to the objectives they support. As we move into the selection phase, the potential projects have now been formally screened against the criteria for selection as candidates for the portfolio; the list of candidate projects represents serious contenders for inclusion in the portfolio. While pre-screening and screening projects are presented as two distinct processes, they can be combined. Ensuring consistency between the two requires considerable forethought about the requirements necessary for projects to be selected.

6.12 APPENDIX 6A—SAMPLE HIGH-LEVEL BUSINESS CASES

Appendix 6A presents two sample high-level business cases for ABU projects, Renovate & Expand C. W. Benson Library, and Construct ABU Indoor Athletic Complex. By coincidence, these two sample business cases support projects that happen to have alternative proposed solutions.

6.12.1 Renovate and Expand C. W. Benson Campus Library

Project Name

Renovate & Expand C. W. Benson Library

Screening Criteria Overview

Details are provided in the sections following the screening criteria information (see Table 6A.1).

Background

As one of the original buildings, the C. W. Benson Library has served as the focal point for the university since 1935. The library's evocative and picturesque neo-classic architecture served as the basis for subsequent building construction on campus through the 1950s. Although the library still retains its original detail and charm, the building requires a continual maintenance effort and has not been refurbished since 1960. It has become increasingly difficult to house the university's substantial collection of literature due to the lack of an environmental control system. Damage to existing literary inventory has required the university to include substantial funding in the annual budget to replace damaged inventory. Further, studies conducted by graduate students over a 10-year period (1995-2004) reveal a year-over-year decline in usage by the student body. Students have noted difficulty in finding works from the archaic and antiquated cataloging system. Students have also noted the

Table 6A.1 Business case screening for C. W. Benson Library Renovation and Expansion

Project Name	Renovate and Expand C.W. Benson Library			
Objective(s) Supported	Academic Land Use and Facilities			
Cost Data ($ Millions)	**Expected**	**Accuracy**		
GOLD				
Project Management	$ 0.5			
Exterior Main Structure	$ 1.8			
Interior Main Structure	$ 3.3			
Library Addition	$ 3.0			
Total	$ 8.6	± 15%		
SILVER				
Project Management	$ 0.5			
Exterior Main Structure	$ 1.8			
Interior Main Structure	$ 2.1			
Library Addition	$ 2.1			
Total	$ 6.5	± 15%		
BRONZE				
Project Management	$ 0.3			
Exterior Main Structure	$ 1.8			
Interior Main Structure	$ 2.1			
Library Addition	$ -			
Total	$ 4.2	± 15%		

Major Resources
See Resource Estimates section of business case
Costs for transport and living included in estimate

Probability of Success (Risk Analysis)	0.90		
Risks	**Likelihood**	**Impact**	**Strategy**
Hazardous materials	H	M	Avoid
Schedule delays	M	M	Mitigate
Historical Society approvals	L	H	Mitigate

less than pleasing interior and echoing sounds generated from the slightest noise. Consequently, the Benson Library has become a liability that is avoided by the students.

Project Rationale

The central campus location of this grand building is conveniently close to the students' residences and also serves as an immediate focal point for visitors. The renovation of the C. W. Benson Library includes modernizing the building with the latest technological advances without sacrificing the building's original architectural design. This project seeks to blend the old neo-classic structure with modern conveniences, including state-of-the-art technology.

Project Objectives and Goals

The primary objective of the project is to provide high-quality facilities to meet institutional needs and contribute to a living and learning environment.

Anticipated Benefits

- Protect the literary collection from environmental damage.
- Improve students' quality of life.
- Create a living and learning environment outside of the classroom.
- Maintain and strengthen a range of study environments conducive to individual needs and learning styles.
- Strengthen online access to information resources campus-wide.
- Improve physical access to the library during times when access to other university facilities might not be available.
- Expand information resources from global sources.
- Enhance the visibility of library services at the university centers.
- Improve regional and national prominence for the university.
- Build inclusive and diverse campus communities that promote intellectual inquiry and encourage civility, mutual respect, and cooperation.
- Strengthen collections that encompass diverse beliefs and perspectives.
- Enrich the university community by collaborating with instructional faculty and staff in the design, development, and production of instructional programs and materials.

Project Alternatives

This project provides three cost alternatives:

- GOLD alternative. The GOLD alternative will fully renovate the existing 55,000 square feet library building to include the incorporation of state-of-the-art technology such as research portals and electronic cataloging system. Additionally, the entire library will be fully refurbished from floor-to-floor. This project also includes the construction of a 10,000 square feet addition to the existing library. Construction will be conducted using green building technologies.
- SILVER alternative. The SILVER option includes everything inclusive of the GOLD alternative minus green building technology.
- BRONZE alternative. The BRONZE option includes only the renovation and refurbishment of the existing library building.

Project Work Breakdown Structure

The product of the project will result in a completely renovated library building and a newly constructed 10,000 square feet addition. The complete work breakdown structure (WBS) is illustrated in Figure 6A.1.

Cost Estimates

Cost estimates were derived using a parametric cost estimation technique for similar projects and alternative approaches. The final estimates were subjected to expert review by other selected university facilities departments. As the data used to develop these estimates is recent and similar in scope to other library renovation projects, these approximate estimates are thought to have an accuracy of ±15%, thus approaching an AACE Class 2 estimate. The cost estimates for each of the three alternative approaches are shown in the Screening Criteria Overview.

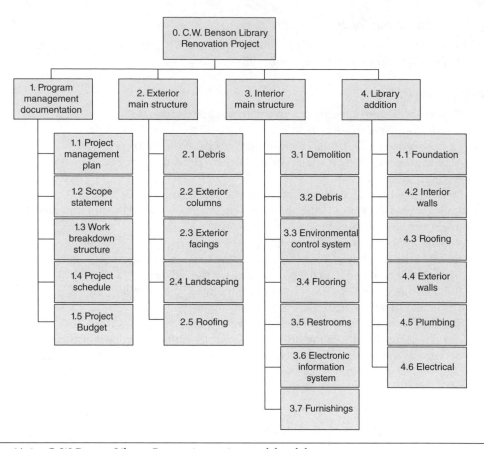

Figure 6A.1   C. W. Benson Library Renovation project work breakdown structure

Resource Estimates

As a result of the severe winter conditions in the region, major construction projects are scheduled mainly during the spring through fall period. Accordingly, this project will be competing for resources with other major construction projects in the area. Specific resources have been identified that are expected to be scarce or have a limited availability during project execution.

People

- Crane operators. There is an existing short supply of crane operators that will be required for the renovation of the main building exterior as well as the library addition.
- Architecture expertise. Architects with expertise in neo-classic architecture are in short supply in the local area.
- Neo-classic craftsman. Supply of craftsman skilled in neo-classic restoration is in short supply due to ongoing restoration projects in the local area.

Equipment

- 20-ton cranes. Due to the expense required to operate and maintain these cranes, only two are available locally. This crane is required for work on the exterior section of the main building.

Material

- Byzantine marble. Local quarries have been closed for some time and no other local source is available to supply this material. This marble is required to replace existing front exterior columns that have been deteriorating rapidly.

Risks and Mitigation Strategies

Primary risks to the Benson Library Renovation have been identified and a mitigation strategy developed. Risks affecting this project include:

- Hazardous materials—Original construction incorporated materials that have since been identified to be hazardous (e.g., asbestos). This risk will be avoided by requiring construction personnel to wear protective equipment, and the construction area will be cordoned off during demolition.
- Schedule delays—Delays in completing the project may impact the fall semester and disrupt campus as students return and fall classes commence. This risk will be mitigated by preparing a plan to house the library in another campus facility temporarily.
- Historical society—As a registered historical building, the Historical Society Council (HSC) requires approval of the changes to the building. This risk will be mitigated by identifying a representative from the HSC and conducting coordination with the council prior to the start of construction.

Constraints

The primary constraints for the renovation of the C. W. Benson Library are:

- Work must be conducted during the summer session.
- Work must be completed prior to the start of the fall semester.
- Restoration experts in neo-classical architecture must oversee the exterior work.
- Restoration of exterior surface must use original materials.
- Key decision makers may be difficult to contact during project period (summer session).
- The project is required to be conducted in accordance with environmental approvals.
- Vehicles weighing more than 5-gross vehicle tons require advance approval to enter campus grounds.

Assumptions

The following assumptions are germane:

- Approval will be received for all environmental and building permits.
- Project can be completed during summer semester.
- Expertise in neo-classic construction will be available during project execution.

6.12.2 Sample Business Case for ABU Indoor Athletic Complex Project

Project Name

Construct ABU Indoor Athletic Complex

Screening Criteria Overview

Details are provided in the sections following the screening criteria information (see Table 6A-2).

Table 6A.2 Business case screening for construction of indoor athletic complex

Project Name	Construct ABU Indoor Athletic Complex		
Objective(s) Supported	Intercollegiate Athletics Facilities		
Cost Data ($ Millions)	**Expected**	**AACE**	
GOLD			
Project Management	$ 2.5		
Main Structure	$ 25.2		
Concession Area	$ 5.3		
Lounges	$ 6.7		
Competition Courts	$ 5.5		
Total	$ 45.2	± 35%	
SILVER			
Project Management	$ 2.0		
Main Structure	$ 19.9		
Concession Area	$ 3.1		
Lounges	$ 5.5		
Competition Courts	$ 5.0		
Total	$ 35.5	± 35%	
BRONZE			
Project Management	$ 1.3		
Main Structure	$ 14.2		
Concession Area	$ 2.1		
Lounges	$ 3.2		
Competition Courts	$ 3.4		
Total	$ 24.2	± 35%	

Major Resources

See Resource Estimates section of business case

Costs for transport and living included in estimate

Probability of Success (Risk Analysis)	0.95		
Risks	**Likelihood**	**Impact**	**Strategy**
Schedule delays	M	L	Mitigate
Raw material cost increases	L	H	Mitigate
Environmental	M	H	Mitigate

Background

In 2005, the university's Athletic Department submitted a request to the Board of Trustees to expand its sports programs to include tennis and volleyball (men and women's programs). The Big Kahuna Conference has seen robust growth in student enrollment since the 1970s. In turn this has led to a significant increase in year-over-year growth in alumni contributions to the university. This has afforded the university the opportunity to expand its athletic programs to keep pace with other athletic departments in the conference. These programs are scheduled to begin competition in the

2012-2013 season. However, the university presently lacks the facilities to support the programs in the long term.

Project Rationale

This complex provides the facilities necessary to adequately support the volleyball and tennis programs and to ensure they are competitive with other programs. The new complex will be state-of-the-art and attract top-tier athletes that ABU had not previously been able to recruit. The complex will continue to strengthen the university's relationship with the local community through interaction programs such as athletic camps and youth sporting events.

Project Objectives and Goals

The primary objective of the project is to provide high-quality facilities to meet institutional needs and help student-athletes succeed in both venues and advance the institution's winning spirit and drive. The goal of the project is to improve facilities for intercollegiate competition to be comparable to others in the prestigious Big Kahuna Conference.

Anticipated Benefits

- Increased revenue from sporting events.
- Increased interest by student athletes.
- Increased revenue to the local community.
- Improve students' quality of life.
- Create a living and learning environment outside of the classroom.
- Increase the university's ability to compete with other programs in the Big Kahuna Conference.

Project Alternatives

This project provides three cost alternatives:

- GOLD alternative. The GOLD alternative requires the construction of the ABU Indoor Athletic Complex and will provide each sport with a separate facility. Within each facility, each sport team is provided competition areas, which will be capable of seating 15,000 and include sports lounges. In addition, each sport team will have separate practice areas, training rooms, and locker rooms.
- SILVER alternative. The SILVER alternative provides each sport (tennis and volleyball) its own facility to practice and compete, but it requires the sport program to be shared by the men and women. Lounges, training areas, and locker rooms will be provided separately for the men and women.
- BRONZE alternative. The BRONZE alternative consolidates both sports programs within the same complex. The men's volleyball and tennis teams would be required to share the same sports lounge, training area, and locker room. The same is true for the women's teams. Each sport would have courts that would be used for both practice and competition.

Deliverable Work Breakdown Structure

The product of the project will result in the new construction of the university's Indoor Athletic Complex (100,000 square feet). The complex will consist of competition and training facilities for athletes, athlete lounges, and training rooms. It will seat 15,000 spectators and contain a concession area with a food court. The complete WBS is illustrated in Figure 6A.2.

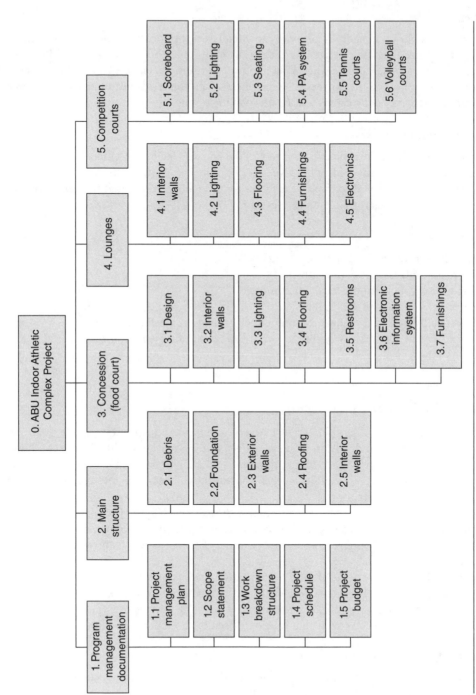

Figure 6A.2 ABU indoor athletic complex deliverable work breakdown structure

Cost Estimates

Cost estimates were derived using a parametric cost estimation technique with final estimates subjected to expert review. As the data used to develop these estimates is limited for similar projects, these estimates were based on generic cost estimating relationships and then followed by cost plus contractor responses to request for proposals. As a result, these estimates are rough order of magnitude estimates with an accuracy of ±35%. Cost estimates by alternative are provided in the Screening Criteria Overview.

Resource Estimates

As a result of the severe winter conditions in the region, major construction projects are scheduled mainly during the spring through fall period. Accordingly, this project will be competing for resources with other major construction projects in the area. Specific resources have been identified that are expected to be scarce or have a limited availability during project execution.

People
- Crane operators. There is an existing short supply of crane operators that will be required for the renovation of the main building exterior as well as the library addition.

Equipment
- 20-ton cranes. Due to the expense required to operate and maintain these cranes, only two are available locally. This crane is required for work on the exterior section of the main building.

Material
- Steel. Steel has been in short supply recently due to world demand. Steel beams are required for the construction of the complex.

Risks and Mitigation Strategies

Primary risks to the ABU Indoor Athletic Complex have been identified and a mitigation strategy has been developed. Risks affecting this project include:
- Schedule delays. Delays in completing the project may impact the fall semester and disrupt the campus as students return and fall classes commence. This risk will be mitigated by preparing a plan to delay the start of the volleyball and tennis programs, if necessary. Since there will be no scholarship students during the first year, the cost of delay, if necessary, is minimal.
- Cost increases. Recently raw material prices for steel and concrete have increased significantly due to world demand. These increases have the potential to exceed early estimates. This risk will be mitigated by hedging steel and concrete at current prices. This will ensure a stable price regardless of future price trends.
- Environmental. Because the complex is being developed on previously undeveloped land, the possibility exists that construction may be impacted by endangered species. The red-haired woodpecker is a local species protected under the Endangered Species Act and has been identified in various spots around the local area. This risk has been mitigated through the selection of the building site. The proposed site is not conducive to vegetation preferred by the species, and initial studies and surveys have not identified any active nesting on or near the building site.

Constraints

The primary constraints with regard to the renovation of the ABU Indoor Athletic Complex are:

- Work must be completed prior to the start of fall semester 2012.
- Key decision makers may be difficult to contact during project period (summer session).
- The project is required to be conducted in accordance with environmental approvals.
- Vehicles weighing more than 5-gross vehicle tons require advance approval to enter campus grounds.

Assumptions

The following assumptions are germane:
- Approval will be received for all environmental and building permits.
- Prior project can be completed prior to fall semester 2012.

6.13 APPENDIX 6B—CHOICE MODEL ALTERNATIVES FOR STUDENT SERVICES CENTER

Project 2 to Renovate & Expand Davidson Student Services Center is aligned with the objective: "Improve existing facilities for administrative and student services staff." As with many projects, there are multiple ways it can be performed. Here we present an analysis of the alternative approaches considered and demonstrate that AHP and software tools can be used to evaluate project alternatives when the group owning the project wishes to reach a decision internally and then carry forward only one alternative. This appendix shows how we arrived at the suggested renovation and expansion project put forth as a candidate for the project portfolio for the ABU Campus Revitalization Program.

As should be the case, after the ABU strategic plan was published each subordinate organization refined the university's goals and objectives specific to its own work. In this example, the Office of Services and Administration (OSA) defined its goal with respect to student services facilities as "Meet current and future student demands for convenient and efficient service." The supporting objectives identified are listed nominally:

- Consolidate and co-locate student-facing services in one facility.
- Relocate student services from the partially converted residence hall.
- Provide sufficient space for student services to meet current and future space needs.
- Provide state-of-the-art utilities and technology for student services facilities.

Student services are currently delivered at multiple locations on campus. Although many of the high-touch student services are located in Davidson, they are stove-piped, causing students to stand in multiple lines for different services such as registration and financial aid. Davidson is overcrowded with a 22% shortage of space. Further, the facility is aging with insufficient heating and air conditioning and a lack of current technology. Some student administrative services are located in a partially converted residence hall, a facility that is not well-suited to providing such services. At the same time, many low-touch back offices services remain in Davidson, occupying space that could otherwise be used for student-facing services.

To determine how best to resolve these problems, the sponsor and his staff, with the help of representatives from facilities, defined three alternatives and four objectives for the project. The team, after discussions with experts on campus facilities, students who receive the services, and members of OSA, identified three alternative approaches to addressing the student services facilities issues. They decided to use AHP and the Comparion and Expert Choice software tools to enter their evaluations. All evaluators will first prioritize the objectives and then will enter pairwise verbal comparisons of the alternatives.

Table 6B.1 Evaluators for Davidson Student Services Center alternatives

Name	Title	Representing	Email
Mr. Jordan King	Facilities Director	University Facilities	king@abu.edu
Mr. Samuel Prince	Facilities Manager	University Facilities	prince@abu.edu
Ms. Cynthia Queen	Director	Office of Student Affairs	queen@abu.edu
Mr. Kensuke Ace	Student Member	Steering Committee	ace@abu.edu

Evaluators include the project sponsor from OSA (responsible for student services), representatives from University Facilities, and an officer from student government. The team members are listed in Table 6B.1.

The goal is to "Meet current and future student demands for convenient and efficient service." The supporting objectives identified by the team are listed nominally:

- Consolidate and co-locate student-facing services in one facility.
- Provide state-of-the-art utilities and technology for student services facilities.
- Provide sufficient space for student services to meet current and future space needs.
- Minimize cost for the student services facility.

The evaluation team also defined three potential approaches for the Davidson Student Services Facility project. The alternatives identified and their benefits, risks, and costs are:

1. Demolish and build a larger new Davidson Student Services Center (most costly).

   Benefit: Accomplishes all objectives with a clean start and a known vertical expansion
   Risk: Longer disruption of student services
   Cost: $30M

2. Renovate Davidson with expansion by 20,000 square feet.

   Benefit: Accomplishes all objectives in a shorter period of time
   Risk: Expansion must be vertical so original structure must support additional floors
   Cost: $10.5M

3. Renovate Davidson at the current size and relocate back office services to an off-campus location

   Benefit: Least costly and lengthy
   Risk: Does not provide co-location of all services functions, introducing staff inconvenience
   Cost: $5.2M

From the Expert Choice Comparion model, the objectives that the evaluation team identified and the group's prioritization results (global priorities of the objectives) are shown in Figure 6B.1.

The result of the synthesis and thus the group's recommendation is to choose Alternative 2—Renovate Davidson with an expansion by 20,000 square feet, pending architectural analysis to determine whether the current structure can accommodate an additional floor. The synthesis results are shown in Figure 6B.2. As can be seen, the group chose a larger Davidson facility, whether through renovation with expansion (51.07%) or demolition and rebuilding a larger facility (42.09%), over renovating at the current size with relocation of back office services (6.84%).

Evaluators performed a sensitivity analysis on the results to determine whether a change in the priority of an objective would cause the recommendation to be different. The before and after dynamic sensitivity graphs from Comparion are shown in Figures 6B.3 and 6B.4, respectively.

When the priority of the objective to provide state-of-the-art utilities and technology was increased from just over 14% to about 45%, the alternative to demolish and build a new, larger Davidson

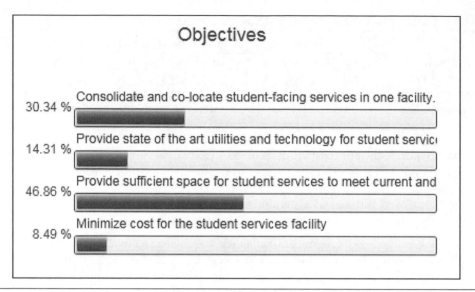

Figure 6B.1   Objectives and evaluation team priorities for services facilities goal

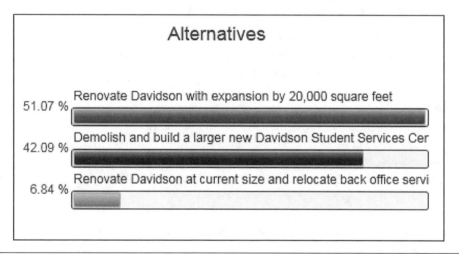

Figure 6B.2   Davidson Student Center alternatives evaluation results

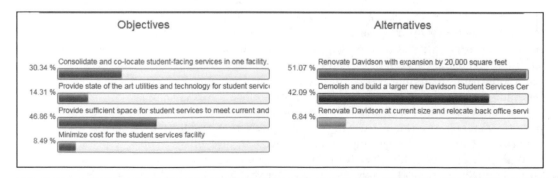

Figure 6B.3   Dynamic sensitivity graph with original priorities

Student Services Center became the preferred alternative (see Figure 6B.4). Since it took such a large change in the priority of an objective to change the preferred alternative, we can draw the conclusion from this particular dynamic sensitivity analysis that the choice is not sensitive to small changes in the priority of the technology objective.

However, it can be seen from the performance sensitivity graph in Figure 6B.5 that the alternative to renovate with an expansion is preferred for the two most important objectives concerned with consolidation and sufficient space. The alternative to demolish and build a new center was preferred for the technology objective and the alternative to renovate at the current size while relocating back office services was considered best in supporting the objective to minimize cost. Overall, the group chose the renovation and expansion alternative and submitted only that alternative as a candidate for the project portfolio.

The process of entering and prioritizing objectives for this evaluation is exactly the same as that described in Chapter 4. However, we have not yet described in detail the processes of entering alternatives, synthesizing the evaluation results, and performing sensitivity analysis. These are addressed in Chapter 7 where the project portfolio is prioritized and sensitivity analysis is performed to test the sense of rightness of the results. For purposes of this chapter, however, we simply wish to show

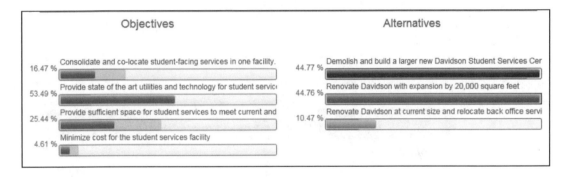

Figure 6B.4   Change in preferred alternative with large change in priority of technology objective

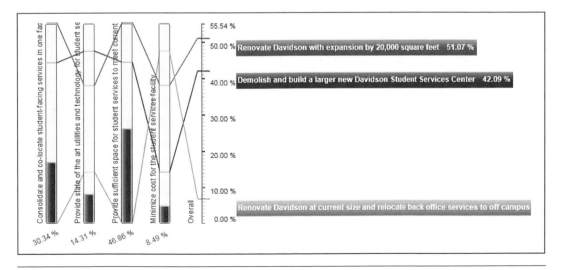

Figure 6B.5   Performance sensitivity graph

that the same process and software can be used to decide among alternatives. The main difference between choosing a portfolio and choosing the best alternative is that for the portfolio, multiple alternatives that together represent the portfolio are selected, while for making a choice among alternatives, only one is chosen.

6.14 APPENDIX 6C—AACE ESTIMATE CLASSIFICATIONS

AACE International has created a cost estimate classification system as Recommended Practice Number 17R-97. This system was designed to provide cost estimating guidelines that are generic enough to be used in a variety of industries (AACE, 1997). AACE defines five classes of estimates, with Class 5 as the highest level and Class 1 as the most detailed. The five characteristics used to distinguish among the levels are:

1. Degree of project definition
2. End usage of the estimate
3. Estimating methodology
4. Estimating accuracy
5. Effort required to produce the estimate (AACE, 1997)

Table 6C.1 describes the generic classifications recommended and describes Class 1 through Class 5 for each of the characteristics.

Table 6C.1 Generic cost estimate classification matrix (AACE, 1997)

ESTIMATE CLASS	Primary Characteristic	Secondary Characteristic			
	LEVEL OF PROJECT DEFINITION Expressed as % of complete definition	END USAGE Typical purpose of estimate	METHODOLOGY Typical estimating method	EXPECTED ACCURACY RANGE Typical +/- range relative to best index of 1 [a]	PREPARATION EFFORT Typical degree of effort relative to least cost index of 1 [b]
Class 5	0% to 2%	Screening or Feasibility	Stochastic or Judgment	4 to 20	1
Class 4	1% to 15%	Concept Study or Feasibility	Primarily Stochastic	3 to 12	2 to 4
Class 3	10% to 40%	Budget, Authorization, or Control	Mixed, but Primarily Stochastic	2 to 6	3 to 10
Class 2	30% to 70%	Control or Bid/ Tender	Primarily Deterministic	1 to 3	5 to 20
Class 1	50% to 100%	Check Estimate or Bid/Tender	Deterministic	1	10 to 100

6.15 REFERENCES

AACE International (1997). *Recommended Practice for Cost Estimate Classification*. 17-R-97. Morgantown, WV.

Apple (2007). Annual Report. http://emi.compustat.com/cgi-irwinus-doc/docserver.cgi?keytype=ID&keyval =5548885&doctype=ED%3A10%2DK&docformat=html&gv=0&date=20071115&action=STREAM&i e=.html (retrieved April 18, 2008).

Chao, R. and S. Kavadias (2008). "A Framework for Managing the NPD Portfolio: When and How to Use Strategic Buckets. *Management Science*, 54:5, 907-921.

Christensen, P. et al. (1997). Cost Estimate Classification System, *AACE International Recommended Practice 17R-97*. TCM Framework: 7.3—Cost Estimating and Budgeting. http://www.aacei.org/technical/rps/17r-97.pdf (retrieved April 24, 2010).

Gallos, Joan, ed. (2008). *Business Leadership: A Jossey-Bass Reader*, 2nd ed. San Francisco, CA: John Wiley & Sons.

Higgins, R. C. (2007). *Analysis for Financial Management*. New York, NY: McGraw-Hill/Irwin.

Levine, Harvey A. (2005). *Project Portfolio Management: A Practical Guide to Selecting Projects, Managing Portfolios, and Maximizing Benefits*. San Francisco, CA: Jossey-Bass Business and Management Series.

Morris, Peter W. and Jeffrey K. Pinto, eds. (2007). "Project Portfolio Selection and Management" (Chapter 5). *The Wiley Guide to Project, Program and Portfolio Management*. John Wiley & Sons. http://common .books24x7.com/book/id_23408/book.asp (retrieved April 1, 2010).

Ross, S. A. (1995). Uses, Abuses and Alternatives to the Net-present Value Rule. *Financial Management*, 24:3, 96-102.

Shenhar, Aaron, Dragan Milošević, Dov Dvir, and Hans Thamhain (2007). *Linking Project Management to Business Strategy*. Newton Square, PA: Project Management Institute.

ThinkQuest (2010). Oracle Education Foundation. Not for Commercial Purposes. http://library.thinkquest .org/3096/42analy2.htm (retrieved May 21, 2010).

VentureChoice (2010). http://www.venturechoice.com/articles/average_rate_of_return.htm (retrieved May 21, 2010).

Weaver, Samuel and John Weston (2001). *Finance and Accounting for Nonfinancial Managers*. New York, NY: McGraw-Hill.

Whetten, David A. and Kim S. Cameron (2007). *Developing Management Skills*, 7th ed. PHI Learning. Upper Saddle River, NJ: Prentice-Hall

7

Prioritizing Candidate Projects

"Nothing is more difficult, and therefore more precious, than being able to decide."
—Napoleon Bonaparte

Selecting projects for a portfolio from a long list of candidates can often be very difficult. Even though we've reduced the number of project possibilities to a manageable number through the pre-screening and screening process, difficult decisions still need to be made to evaluate anticipated benefits of each candidate project and begin the portfolio selection process. In this chapter, the candidate projects are prioritized by transferring the approved candidate project alignment matrix into the project portfolio evaluation model, identifying personnel to evaluate the projects' relative contribution to achieving organizational objectives, and performing sensitivity analysis to determine the sense of rightness of the evaluation results. As shown in Figure 7.1, during this part of the selection phase, we determine the relative benefit of each of the candidate projects in terms of achieving organizational strategy.

At the end of this process, the list of candidate projects is prioritized in terms of anticipated contribution to achieving the organization's goals. This doesn't mean that the projects with the highest priorities should be selected in order until funds run out. We will discover that there are other important considerations. However, when the proper tools are used, the prioritized list of candidate projects contains the ratio-scale relative anticipated contribution of each project to the achievement of organizational strategy and provides the foundation for the eventual selection of the optimal portfolio.

7.1 PPM ROLE IN PRIORITIZING ALTERNATIVES

Project portfolio management (PPM) personnel play an active and facilitative role in the process of prioritizing the alternatives, or candidate projects. They oversee the process of preparing the evaluation model, identifying and selecting the participants, and analyzing the results. The portfolio management board (PMB) is responsible for conducting the evaluation and any necessary iteration. Additionally, they review the outcome with the Executive Review Board (ERB) and, where appropriate for the organization, with senior executives. It is incumbent on the PMB to establish a process for prioritizing the alternatives that best fits within the organization's existing governance. After obtaining the relative priorities of the alternatives, the PMB and ERB manage the optimization and selection process described in the subsequent two chapters.

The PMB, as the group responsible for leading PPM, assigns a facilitator (project manager) who enters the alternatives information into the model, including any descriptive information. In addition, the PMB specifies the standard, consistent information to be entered for each project. For

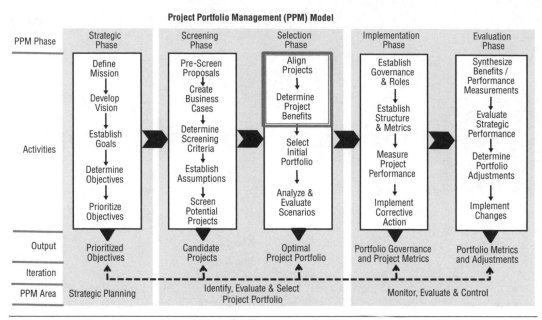

Figure 7.1   Align projects, determine benefits, and portfolio evaluation considerations

example, the entry could be "to maintain consistency and traceability, use the project description from the business case." If the organization requires a project code or number for tracking purposes, then this should also be entered to maintain traceability. Once all alternatives are entered, each project is aligned with the objective(s) it supports.

7.2 PRIORITIZING CANDIDATE PROJECTS OVERVIEW

One might be tempted to simply assume that all projects making it through the screening process and into the candidate project list are of equal importance in achieving objectives. This assumption of equality is mistaken; some candidate projects make greater contributions to achievement of their respective objectives than others, just as some objectives contribute more to achieving the goal than others. In prioritizing the objectives in Chapter 4, the evaluators made difficult but informed and reasoned judgments about the relative importance of the objectives in achieving the goal. More importantly, they established ratio-scale priorities for how much each objective contributes. By transferring the approved candidate project alignment matrix into the project portfolio evaluation model tools, we begin to extend our previous evaluation model from Chapter 4 and follow a similar process for determining the candidate projects' relative contributions to the objectives they support, and to the goal.

The objectives hierarchy in the evaluation model is a direct representation of the strategic plan, or at least the portion of the strategic plan that covers the portfolio to be selected. The alignment matrix shows which candidate projects support which objectives from the strategic plan, but not how much or how well they support the objectives. Thus, the evaluation model provides direct traceability of each candidate project back to the objective(s) it supports in the strategic plan. By identifying candidate projects, and aligning these projects to specific objectives, the alignment matrix provides the structural foundation for determining the relative importance (benefits) of each candidate project.

With the model updated to include candidate projects, participants are selected to evaluate the anticipated relative contribution of each project. Identifying the right people to participate in the project prioritization process and tailoring their respective roles and responsibilities are important to deliver the most accurate outcome for the organization. Once identified, participants evaluate each project against each other project in terms of its effectiveness in supporting a given objective, or they rate its anticipated contribution to achievement of the objective. The combined evaluators' judgments produce a local priority (its anticipated contribution relative to a particular objective) and a global priority (its anticipated contribution relative to the goal). With all judgments provided, evaluators and the facilitator determine whether the derived results make sense and whether iteration is required. Sensitivity analysis is performed to answer *what if* questions, such as how the priorities change if the priority of an objective were to change. The final output of this process is the priority for each project, representing the project's total anticipated benefit or relative contribution to the goal as well as its anticipated relative contribution to each objective.

7.3 STRUCTURE THE MODEL

Structuring the model includes creating the objectives hierarchy, adding the alternatives to be considered, and mapping the alternatives to the objectives or sub-objectives they support at the lowest level in the hierarchy. The lowest level of objective or sub-objective supported by an alternative is sometimes called a covering objective. During the analytic hierarchy process (AHP) evaluation process described in Chapter 4, the objectives hierarchy was created and the ratio-scale relative priorities of the objectives were determined. To conclude the structuring process, evaluators and their roles were specified and the objectives were evaluated. To complete the structuring of the model in this chapter, then, it is necessary to add the list of candidate projects as the alternatives to be considered and to identify the covering objective(s) for each alternative.

7.3.1 Adding Alternatives to the Model

The project candidate list was identified during the screening process, and an alignment matrix was created thus serving as the source material for completing the structuring of the model. In addition, the evaluators for the alternatives and their specific roles in terms of who will evaluate what are determined to complete the structuring.

To produce accurate priorities for the alternatives, evaluators must not only understand the organizational objectives, but must have as much information as necessary to have a common understanding of the alternatives they will evaluate. As such, descriptive information about each alternative, usually from the business cases prepared during screening, can be provided along with the model, or orientation sessions can be conducted by PMB personnel to review the alternatives. The level of information needed is dependent on the nature of the organization and its evaluators and the degree to which they are intimately familiar with the objectives and the alternatives to be considered.

7.3.2 Map Alternatives to Objectives to Establish Contribution

With the evaluation model updated to include the alternatives and descriptions, alternatives can be mapped to the objectives they support as shown in the alignment matrix in Table 7.1. This mapping is derived from the candidate project alignment matrix.

As previously stated, the alignment matrix is a hierarchical representation of the strategic plan showing which alternatives support which objectives. Thus, we continue to maintain a structure consistent with the strategic plan as we progress through the prioritization process. When mapping alternatives to objectives, it must be applied to each of the lowest-level sub-objectives of a multi-level hierarchy and not to a parent level. These lowest-level sub-objectives are also known as covering

Table 7.1 Sample alignment matrix

Candidate Projects (Alternatives)	Objectives				
	Objective 1	Objective 2	Objective 3	Objective 4	Objective 5
Project Candidate 1					x
Project Candidate 2		x			
Project Candidate 3					x
Project Candidate 4	x				
Project Candidate 5	x				
Project Candidate 6	x				
Project Candidate 7			x	x	
Project Candidate 8	x				
Project Candidate 9		x			
Project Candidate 10	x	x	x	x	x
Project Candidate 11		x			
Project Candidate 12				x	x
Project Candidate 13			x		
Project Candidate 14			x		
Project Candidate 15			x		
Project Candidate 16	x				
Project Candidate 17		x		x	x
Project Candidate 18				x	
Project Candidate 19	x				

objectives or terminal nodes. The terminal nodes are used for mapping because the priorities for each sub-objective are applied at the lowest level of the hierarchy; they are aggregated upward to each parent level as described in Chapter 4 in Section 4.5.1 describing local and global priorities. Not all alternatives support all objectives, in fact, quite the contrary. Many project alternatives support only one of the objectives.

7.3.3 Specify Evaluators and Their Roles

With the evaluation model updated to include the alignment of candidate projects' contributions to covering objectives, the PMB coordinates with the ERB to identify appropriate personnel to perform the evaluation of alternatives. Remember that the personnel are not just anyone. They are people who understand both organizational goals and objectives and the candidate projects. The purpose of the alternatives evaluation is to obtain accurate and consistent relative priorities for the project candidates. The relative priorities represent the anticipated benefit of each alternative in achieving the organization's goal. Using carefully selected people with strategic perspective to evaluate projects within their areas of expertise or domains increases the accuracy of the priorities. In turn, accurate and consistent priorities better inform the organization about which projects are most important and which are least important.

Participants can be assigned to evaluate all projects supporting all objectives or to evaluate only projects supporting particular objectives—a distinct advantage of using appropriate decision support software tools. People selected to evaluate all projects are those with a macro view of the organization, intimately familiar with the strategic plan, and occupy executive or senior positions within the organization. These individuals have the organizational perspective and knowledge to provide informed judgments regarding the value or importance of projects supporting their respective objectives. Assignment of individuals to specific projects and objectives can also be tailored to their particular fields of expertise or functional areas.

An organization attempting to evaluate different types of projects, such as building construction and IT projects, may want to assign executives from the construction division to evaluate construction projects and IT executives to evaluate IT projects. The IT executives may not feel comfortable evaluating construction projects because these projects are outside their field of expertise. In some large organizations these projects might even be in separate portfolios with different teams of evaluators. The point is to identify and select personnel to evaluate projects within their domain to obtain accurate and consistent priorities. It is also advisable that multiple evaluators be assigned to evaluate alternatives within their areas of expertise to avoid giving responsibility to only one expert who may be biased or have an incomplete perspective.

However, in a mature organization, in which all evaluators understand the value of all candidate projects, we recommend that all evaluators judge all projects. Specialization can be applied in exceptional circumstances, such as choices to be made among highly complex technological alternatives.

Just as it would not be wise to invite personnel to assist in prioritizing projects who were not familiar with the goals and objectives in the strategic plan, inviting recently hired personnel who are unfamiliar with the candidate projects might also be an unwise choice. A recently hired key executive must be thoroughly briefed prior to participating in an evaluation. Consideration of each person's respective area of expertise and position are critical to identifying the right participants and assigning evaluation roles and responsibilities consistent with their knowledge.

7.4 MEASURE BY CONDUCTING THE EVALUATION

Prior to conducting the evaluation of the alternatives, the PMB determines the measurement methods to be used, specifies how the evaluation will be conducted, and prepares appropriate orientation materials and sessions for participants.

7.4.1 Select Measurement Methods

Recall that only two measurement methods were available for prioritizing objectives, pairwise comparison and direct priority input; these are also available as measurement methods for prioritizing alternatives along with absolute measurement methods, including rating scales, utility curves, and step functions. Although the pairwise comparison method was used to evaluate the objectives, in project portfolio selection the number of alternatives can be large, thus requiring an excessive number of comparisons. Recall the formula for calculating the number of pairwise comparisons required is $(n \times (n - 1))/2$. With 100 project candidates, for example, the number of comparisons required is $(100 \times 99)/2 = 4950$.

To reduce the number of pairwise comparisons, if feasible, project portfolio management might ask evaluators to assess only small subsets of the projects. More often they choose to apply absolute measurement methods to prioritize alternatives, including rating scales, simple utility curves, and step functions. Rating scales are most often used to prioritize alternatives for project portfolio selection, but all three absolute measurement methods are described. A different measurement method can be chosen for each covering objective; all alternatives supporting that covering objective are evaluated using the chosen measurement method.

Rating Scales

Rating scales are used to compare alternatives to a defined scale rather than comparing them to each other (Forman, 2001). When the number of alternatives is manageable, pairwise comparison can produce more accurate decisions. However, when the number of alternatives is large, making the number of pairwise comparisons cumbersome and the judgments perhaps less consistent because of their sheer number, consider using a rating scale.

With a rating scale, evaluators rate the alternatives with regard to how well each one supports its covering objectives. Words are used to represent corresponding priorities, and in this context, are called intensities such as Outstanding, Excellent, Very Good, and so on to None or Not at All. A typical rating scale is shown in Figure 7.2.

Note that the sample rating scale contains nine intensity levels, each of which has an associated priority value. The priority values are derived through pairwise comparison rather than by arbitrary assignment and are then normalized so that the intensity with the highest priority is equal to 1.000. Default rating scales supplied with some decision support software have already been evaluated in this manner. We encourage the use of properly constructed rating scales as surrogates for pairwise comparisons when the number of alternatives is large, as is often the case in project portfolio prioritization.

Step Functions and Utility Curves

While rating scales are an effective substitute for pairwise comparisons, step functions and utility curves translate known information about the alternatives with respect to an objective into ratio-scale priorities. The translation formulas are developed by expert judgment or by those with considerable experience. The translations are derived using pairwise comparisons of the value or priority to be assigned at different values of the known information.

Test grades represent an opportunity for a common misuse of a step function, for example, 90-100 receiving an A, and so on until 60-69 represents a D, and anything below 60 receives an F. The common misuse comes about because the test scores are not ratio-scale numbers—is a score of 90 twice as good as a score of 45? We think most would say that a score of 45 is unacceptable, making

Name	Value		Actions
Outstanding	1		Delete
Excellent	0.92		Delete
Very Good	0.865		Delete
Good to Very Good	0.621		Delete
Good	0.555		Delete
Moderate to Good	0.423		Delete
Moderate	0.25		Delete
A Tad	0.04		Delete
None	0		Delete

Figure 7.2   Sample rating scale with intensities and priorities (Expert Choice, 2011)

a score of 90 much more than twice as good as a score of 45. Perhaps a utility curve or a ratio-scale step function could better represent test scores, with no value received for any score less than 60 and with exponentially increasing value calculated for the highest scores. To be meaningful the priorities, or values, assigned must be derived using pairwise comparisons of the relative values or utility assigned.

7.4.2 Establish Measurement Options

After the measurement methods are established for each objective, it is necessary to establish the options for evaluation, navigation, and the display of information during the evaluation. Selecting evaluation options is a function of the PMB. Ultimately, the options selected depend on the preferences of the PMB with consideration given to the personnel conducting the evaluation. The options selected address the evaluation itself, navigation through the evaluation, and the manner of displaying information to participants.

7.4.3 Prepare the Participants

To perform measurements and determine the relative priorities of the objectives, the facilitator notifies the selected participants and prepares them by conducting an orientation to familiarize them with the process and the use of any software tools, making them aware of their roles and responsibilities and ensuring a common understanding of the alternatives they are evaluating as well as the objectives against which they are evaluating them. The facilitator also communicates the logistics of the evaluation and the deadline or timeframe by which all evaluations are to be completed.

Once that has been done, the evaluation can be conducted by gathering judgments from the participants either synchronously or asynchronously. Synchronous evaluation meetings enable discussions and clarifications to take place but, of course, require that all participants be available at the same time regardless of location or time zone. They are useful vehicles for conducting orientations, reviewing roles and responsibilities, and ensuring common understanding of the items to be evaluated. Asynchronous evaluation allows participants to conduct evaluations at a time and place that is convenient for them. It is now time to conduct the evaluation and obtain the individual judgments.

7.5 SYNTHESIZE TO DERIVE PRIORITIES FOR THE ALTERNATIVES

When all evaluators have completed their input, the results are synthesized to produce the ratio-scale relative priorities for each alternative with respect to the goal.

7.5.1 Local and Global Priorities for Alternatives

Recall the discussion in Chapter 4 of local and global priorities describing how they are derived for elements in the objectives hierarchy. The global priority of a covering objective is multiplied by the value of the combined evaluator responses to yield the priority of the alternative with respect to the covering objective. The priority of the alternative with respect to the goal is then derived by summing the priorities of the alternative with respect to all of its covering objectives. Figure 7.3 shows a sample data grid after both objectives and alternatives have been evaluated.

The black cells indicate that an alternative does not support an objective. In this simple hierarchy, it can be seen that the alternatives supporting all objectives were evaluated using rating scales and that the combined evaluator result for the Project 1—Renovate Existing Student Dormitories—has a value of 0.851. In this case, the rating scale used is shown in Figure 7.4.

Ideal mode			RATINGS	RATINGS	RATINGS	RATINGS	RATINGS
Alternative	Total	Costs	Academic Land Use and Facilities (L: .315 G: .315)	Services and Administration Facilities (L: .281 G: .281)	Intercollegiate Athletics Facilities (L: .204 G: .204)	Recreation Services Facilities (L: .118 G: .118)	Residential and Conference Facilities (L: .081 G: .081)
1. Renovate Existing Student Dormitories	.069	22.1					.851
2. Renovate & Expand Davidson Student	.252	10.5		.897			
3. Construct Dr. Mary Haven Student	.074	8.7					.908
4a. (GOLD) Renovate & Expand C.W.	.301	8.6	.954				
4b. (SILVER) Renovate & Expand C.W.	.203	6.5	.645				
4c. (BRONZE) Renovate & Expand C.W.	.125	4.2	.396				
5. Renovate Benjamin Stadium & Field	.184	44.5			.673	.396	
6. Renovate Mason Hall Research	.145	7.4	.461				
7. Construct ABU Medical Clinic	.239	16.4		.851			
8. ABU Revitalization Program	.382	2	.634	.360	.360	.040	.040
9. Construct Paisley Hall Student	.210	8.7		.747			
10. Renovate Deluth Hall Dining Facility	.017	8.5				.113	.040
11a. (GOLD) Construct ABU Indoor	.204	45.2			1.000		
11b. (SILVER) Construct ABU Indoor	.132	35.5			.645		
11c. (BRONZE) Construct ABU Indoor	.081	24.2			.398		
12. Construct ABU Distance Learning	.272	9.3	.862				
13. Expand Campus Share Ride Services	.226	3.6		.776		.040	.040
14. Construct Campus Theatre	.102	7.4				.862	
15. Construct ABU Faculty Technology &	.227	12.6	.719				

Figure 7.3   Sample data grid after synthesizing results

Outstanding	Excellent	Very Good	Good to Very Good	Good	Moderate to Good	Moderate	A Tad	None
1 (1.000)	2 (.862)	3 (.690)	4 (.556)	5 (.467)	6 (.360)	7 (.259)	8 (.040)	9 (.000)

Figure 7.4   Rating scale used to evaluate how well alternatives support covering objectives

The three evaluators in this case evaluated Project 1 as Excellent, Very Good, and Outstanding, respectively, yielding individual ratings of 0.862, 0.690, and 1.000. Assuming that the participant input was weighted equally, the average value of their responses was 0.851. The relative priority of the only covering objective for this alternative is 0.081, yielding an overall total benefit or relative priority of 0.851 × 0.081 = 0.069. In the case of Project 13—Expand Campus Share Ride Services—that has three covering objectives, we can follow the same process to yield 0.776 × 0.281 + 0.040 × 0.118 + 0.040 × 0.081 = 0.226.

What has been shown is a simple objectives hierarchy using pairwise comparisons to evaluate the relative importance of the objectives and ratings scales to evaluate how well the alternatives support them. Forman and Peniwati (1998) noted that there are many ways to synthesize information, and the reader is encouraged to review their work for a detailed discussion of synthesizing results.

7.5.2 Ideal versus Distributive Mode

Using AHP, synthesis can be performed in two modes, ideal or distributive. When prioritizing objectives, either mode is appropriate since pairwise comparisons yield the same results in either mode. However, if ratings scales or other absolute measures are used when evaluating alternatives, the choice of mode can matter when prioritizing alternatives or candidate projects.

In general the ideal mode is used in PPM. When alternatives are compared pairwise, they all have priorities that are related to, or dependent on, the priorities of all the other alternatives. When using rating scales or other absolute measurement methods, in ideal mode it is possible to add an alternative and apply the rating scale(s) to determine the benefit without changing the data grid total benefit of the other alternatives. Thus, Forman (2010) recommends that the ideal mode be used with PPM; when projects are added to or removed from the portfolio, the ratio-scale relative anticipated benefits of the existing or remaining alternatives do not change with respect to each other and their rank remains the same even though the absolute global priorities when normalized to sum to 1.000 would change. So if Project A is originally evaluated as having twice the anticipated benefit of Project B, that ratio remains the same even with additions to or deletions from the portfolio, presuming that their status as members of the portfolio remains the same and no reevaluation has been performed.

On the other hand, with distributive mode, if a new alternative is added, it will change the total benefit for the original alternatives because the size of their slice of pie has become smaller. As it should, it can also change the order of their ranking. For example, in an election with two seats and only two candidates, A and B, a poll might reflect that A leads over B 55% to 45%, meaning Candidate A is ranked first, but both can be elected. However, if Candidate C enters the race who is ideologically similar to Candidate A, Candidate C can take a share of Candidate A's supporters. Then, if Candidate B holds on to 45% and Candidates A and C have only 35% and 20%, respectively, that means that Candidate B has taken the lead and Candidates B and A will be elected (run-offs ignored). This phenomenon is known as rank reversal. Since the poll percentage (or pairwise) comparison of the available candidates is dependent on who is in the race, this rank reversal should be allowed.

Because with PPM we may wish to add or delete alternatives without disturbing the relative anticipated benefit of the other candidates, we recommend the ideal mode for synthesizing results.

7.5.3 Consistency

As described in Chapter 4, evaluators may be more or less consistent in their judgments. Accurate decisions are usually based on consistent judgments, but some degree of inconsistency is tolerable. Being entirely consistent means that when an evaluator enters a judgment, for example, that Project A supports Objective 1 better than Project B does, and Project B supports Objective 1 better than Project C does, the same evaluator would judge that Project A supports Objective 1 better than Project C does. An inconsistency ratio of 0.00 would represent perfectly consistent choices. An inconsistency ratio of 1.00 represents what would be expected with judgments made at random rather than intelligently.

AHP allows some degree of inconsistency. An inconsistency ratio of 0.10 or less for the combined evaluator results is considered acceptable. With the right tools, the facilitator can easily review inconsistencies for each evaluator as well as for the combined results.

Forman and Selly (2001) note several reasons for inconsistency:

- Clerical error
- Lack of information or understanding
- Lack of concentration on the part of the evaluator
- Inconsistency that exists in the real world
- Inadequate model structure

Of particular concern during the selection of evaluators is lack of knowledge. Forman and Selly (2001) note "If one has little or no information about the factors being compared, then judgments will appear to be random and a high inconsistency ratio will result."

High rates of inconsistency may indicate that either particular individuals, or the group, may have different interpretations of the meaning of the elements in the objectives hierarchy. Clarification may be necessary. The facilitator reviews the inconsistencies and identifies solutions to discuss with the evaluators in a follow-up session. We recommend that the evaluators are asked to make any changes with the guidance of the facilitator or evaluation model project manager.

7.5.4 Sensitivity Analysis

Sensitivity analysis is used to determine how the alternatives performed against the objectives and to understand how sensitive the alternatives are to changes in the relative priority of objectives (Forman, 2001). Sensitivity analysis lets us consider the sense of rightness of the evaluation results and can also signify the need to iterate (Forman, 2010). This could be the case if a small change in the relative importance of one or more objectives results in changes in the selection of alternatives, or even when the evaluators have misunderstood an objective; for example, evaluating alternatives with high risk as preferable rather than evaluating low risk as preferable. Three types of sensitivity analysis are discussed: (1) dynamic, (2) performance, and (3) gradient. These can be produced by software tools with appropriate features and are described in the American Business University (ABU) Campus Revitalization Program example later in the chapter.

Dynamic sensitivity analysis enables us to see the immediate impact on the priority of alternatives by changing the priorities of objectives. When the priority of one objective is increased, the priorities of the remaining objectives are decreased accordingly. Dynamic sensitivity can also be used to illustrate changes in the priorities of sub-objectives, if any. Performance sensitivity analysis allows us to adjust the priority of one or more objectives to see how the priorities of the alternatives change given the adjustment. Gradient sensitivity analysis shows how sensitive the alternatives are to changes in the priority of a single objective by displaying each alternative as a gradient plotted against a single objective as its importance changes from 0 to 100%.

7.6 ITERATE AS NECESSARY

After synthesis of evaluator input, the project manager or other members of the PMB review the output or meet with evaluators to discuss the validity of the results and to raise any questions, such as whether alternatives with the highest priority seem to be the right choice and whether any objectives might be missing from the model (Forman, 2010). This could be the case if an alternative is best on every objective, which might indicate a missing objective. A missing objective might require a decision by the ERB to revisit or revise the strategic plan.

Another reason to iterate might arise when the objectives are evaluated prior to the alternatives (Forman, 2010). In many cases, evaluation of the alternatives can influence the priorities of the objectives because of what is learned during alternatives evaluation, a phenomenon known as feedback (Forman, 2010). This is why, when the same participants evaluate alternatives and objectives, we recommend evaluating alternatives first such that the feedback from prioritizing alternatives influences the prioritization of objectives. In the case of the ABU example in this book, however, the evaluators were assigned specific roles, either to evaluate objectives or to evaluate alternatives, so such feedback does not apply. Forman (2010) states that, "With adequate iteration, the results of an AHP model will be intuitive." Forman goes on to explain that the results agree with intuition after the evaluation and any necessary iteration, but do not necessarily agree with intuition as it was before the evaluation, that is, intuition can change during the experience.

7.7 PRESENT RESULTS AND MAINTAIN GOVERNANCE OF THE PROCESS

Once the results have been obtained, analyses performed and reviewed with the evaluators, and any necessary adjustments made, including iteration based on participant perceptions, the PMB presents the ERB with the evaluation outcome that includes sensitivity analysis. In doing so, the PMB's purpose is to communicate the results and obtain ERB approval for the path forward. The most important results are the ratio-scale priorities for the alternatives; they are proportional measures of the anticipated benefits of the projects toward achieving the organization's objectives. These measures form the foundation for the eventual selection of the optimal portfolio. The PMB conveys that the next steps include identifying organizational constraints, assumptions that must be made about resources, the assignment of risk to alternatives, and the development of multiple scenarios. During these sessions the ERB approves the prioritization of the alternatives, given that constraints have not yet been imposed, and assigns action items to be resolved. The ERB also approves the recommended path forward and provides guidance to the PMB about organizational risk assumptions, resources, and the distribution of projects across objectives, project categories, or strategic buckets. Also addressed are any other constraints that may be necessary to define the boundaries in developing the portfolio scenarios.

7.8 ABU CAMPUS REVITALIZATION PROGRAM EXAMPLE

The output of the screening process in Chapter 6 resulted in a list of portfolio candidate projects and a candidate alignment matrix that has been reviewed and approved by the ABU Board of Trustees. This alignment matrix provides the necessary input for the ABU Steering Committee to extend the project portfolio evaluation model from Chapter 4. Using a project portfolio decision support software product such as Expert Choice's Comparion allows the organization to apply a compensatory decision making process to evaluate the priority, or anticipated contribution, of each project by performing pairwise comparisons or other measurement methods. The steps to perform these actions are discussed and illustrated in this section.

To transition the candidate alignment matrix into the project portfolio evaluation model, the projects must be added as alternatives to the software evaluation model created in Chapter 4.

7.8.1 ABU Campus Revitalization Program Alignment Matrix

During the screening process, the alignment matrix shown in Table 7.2 was refined by further clarifying the objectives. In this case refining the definition of the objectives provided more clarity and differentiation for the project sponsors, and now, with a common understanding, the Steering Committee can be more specific about the alignment between alternatives and objectives, thus improving the quality of the evaluation. Recall from the discussion in Chapter 6 that an X in the matrix denotes that a project is aligned with an objective, an O denotes that the project was no longer aligned after clarification of the objectives, and a blank indicates that the project was never considered to be, and is not, aligned with an objective. When an alternative does not contribute to the achievement of an objective, it can be omitted from consideration against that objective (less work for the evaluators); alternatively, it can be evaluated as providing no contribution (more work for the evaluators).

7.8.2 Prepare to Evaluate the Alternatives Using AHP and Comparion

In this section the evaluation model for the ABU alternatives is prepared in Comparion by adding to the model created in Chapter 4 to prioritize the objectives. In this and the next several chapters, screen shots with explanations are used to demonstrate how the software tool supports the prioritization of candidate projects with respect to the objectives they support. It applies the priorities established for the objectives earlier to correctly calculate the relative anticipated contribution of each alternative toward achieving the goal. Once again, the illustrations are intended to make it easy to move comfortably through the software while focusing on the process of making portfolio decisions.

Table 7.2 Alignment matrix of candidate projects to objectives

Candidate Projects	Objectives				
	Academic Land Use and Facilities	Services and Administration Facilities	Intercollegiate Athletics Facilities	Recreation Services Facilities	Residential and Conference Facilities
1. Renovate Existing Student Dormitories (Jarvis, Davis, and Sewall Halls)	O				x
2. Renovate & Expand Davidson Student Services Center	O	x		O	O
3. Construct Dr. Mary Haven Student Housing Center (Off-Campus Facility)	O	O			x
4a. (GOLD) Renovate & Expand C.W. Benson Campus Library	x	O			O
4b. (SILVER) Renovate & Expand C.W. Benson Campus Library	x	O			O
4c. (BRONZE) Renovate & Expand C.W. Benson Campus Library	x	O			O
5. Renovate Benjamin Stadium & Field house	O		x	x	
6. Renovate Mason Hall Research Center	x				O
7. Construct ABU Medical Clinic	O	x			
8. ABU Revitalization Program Regulatory & Environmental Approval Project (**Enabling Project**)	x	x	x	x	x
9. Construct Paisley Hall Student Services Center	O	x		O	O
10. Renovate Deluth Hall Dining Facility	O			x	x
11a. (GOLD) Construct ABU Indoor Athletic Complex	O		x	O	O
11b. (SILVER) Construct ABU Indoor Athletic Complex	O		x	O	O
11c. (BRONZE) Construct ABU Indoor Athletic Complex	O		x	O	O
12. Construct ABU Distance Learning Center	x				O
13. Expand Campus Share Ride Services		x		x	x
14. Construct Campus Theatre	O			x	
15. Construct ABU Faculty Technology & Research Center	x	O			O

To reinforce the learning experience, we encourage you to log on to the software provided with this book and perform each of the steps while reading the material. The material to be entered can be copied and pasted from the Word document ABU_Extracts.docx on the publisher's website or can be entered by hand using the candidate projects from Table 7.2; alternatively, you may wish to use your own actual or hypothetical portfolio candidates.

7.8.3 Structure the Model

To begin the process of establishing the alternatives in Comparion, go to the Comparion site at the link provided with the book or by your instructor, enter your e-mail address and password, and select the "Log In" button as described in Chapter 4. If necessary, select the appropriate work-group by clicking on its name. Select the project in which the evaluators prioritized the objectives in Chapter 4.

Recall that in Chapter 4 we entered the ABU facilities objectives into the model, established the objectives evaluators and their roles, and prepared the evaluators for the process. The evaluators prioritized the objectives individually, and the results were synthesized, yielding the combined judg-ments for prioritized objectives. At this point, the alternatives, or candidate project list, must be added to the model. In addition, as a part of structuring the decision, it is necessary to identify which objectives are supported by each of these alternatives as well as add participants who will evaluate the alternatives, and then establish their roles.

Add Alternatives

To input the alternatives, select the "Structure" tab, and then "Alternatives" to obtain the view shown in Figure 7.5.

Although the alternatives can be keyed one at a time just as we entered the objectives in Chapter 4, the simplest way to enter all the alternatives at once is to prepare a list in a text or Word document and copy and paste it into Comparion. In this case we have taken the list of candidate projects from Table 7.2 and placed them in a Word document shown in Table 7.3. Note that Projects 4 and 11 include alter-natives for each of three approaches, since each approach is evaluated separately. Although it is possible for projects with alternative approaches to support different objectives, in this example, as is usually the case, each of the three approaches is aligned with the same objective(s). The degree to which each sup-ports its objectives is different, which is why each approach is considered a separate alternative.

To enter the alternatives, simply copy this list from the Microsoft Word document found in the WAV material, click on "Add" and select "Paste from clipboard" as shown in Figure 7.6. By selecting the option to paste the alternatives from the clipboard, the list is displayed in a Comparion dialogue box shown in Figure 7.7 that allows new alternatives to be typed in or simply accept the list we copied by selecting "OK."

By selecting "OK," the alternatives (list of candidate projects) are added to the model with a par-tial list as shown in Figure 7.8. The entire list can be seen by using the scroll bar at the right of the

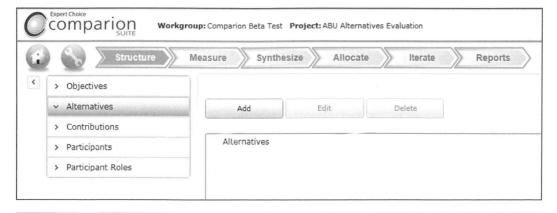

Figure 7.5   Structure decision and identify alternatives screen

Table 7.3 List of candidate projects for ABU facilities portfolio

1. Renovate Existing Student Dormitories (*Jarvis, Davis, and Sewall Halls*)
2. Renovate & Expand Davidson Student Services Center
3. Construct Dr. Mary Haven Student Housing Center (*Off-Campus Facility*)
4a. (GOLD) Renovate & Expand C.W. Benson Campus Library (*Alternatives Project*)
4b. (SILVER) Renovate & Expand C.W. Benson Campus Library (*Alternatives Project*)
4c. (BRONZE) Renovate & Expand C.W. Benson Campus Library (*Alternatives Project*)
5. Renovate Benjamin Stadium & Field house
6. Renovate Mason Hall Research Center
7. Construct ABU Medical Clinic
8. ABU Revitalization Program Regulatory & Environmental Approval (*Enabling Project*)
9. Construct Paisley Hall Student Services Center
10. Renovate Deluth Hall Dining Facility
11a. (GOLD) Construct ABU Indoor Athletic Complex (*Alternatives Project*)
11b. (SILVER) Construct ABU Indoor Athletic Complex (*Alternatives Project*)
11c. (BRONZE) Construct ABU Indoor Athletic Complex (*Alternatives Project*)
12. Construct ABU Distance Learning Center
13. Expand Campus Share Ride Services

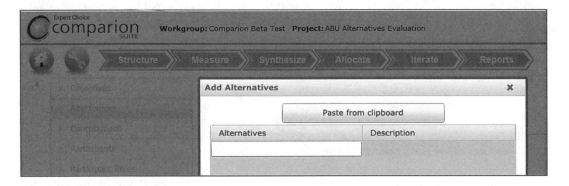

Figure 7.6   Options for adding alternatives

window. With all the alternatives transferred into the model, the descriptions for each alternative (candidate project) are added.

Note that if the alternatives, or the objectives hierarchy, have not already been structured using other means, the facilitator can invite participants to join a TeamTime group session to brainstorm either alternatives, the objectives hierarchy, or both, by selecting the "TeamTime Brainstorming" buttons at the upper right of the window shown in Figure 7.8. In this case the objectives were added as output from the ABU facilities strategic plan, and the alternatives were defined by the pre-screening and screening processes. However, during strategic planning, this tool provides the capability to brainstorm the objectives hierarchy and to add alternatives the group wishes to include in the evaluation.

Add Descriptions for Alternatives

To promote consistent understanding of each alternative among evaluators and to assist in traceability to the business case, Comparion allows a description to be entered for each alternative. To do this

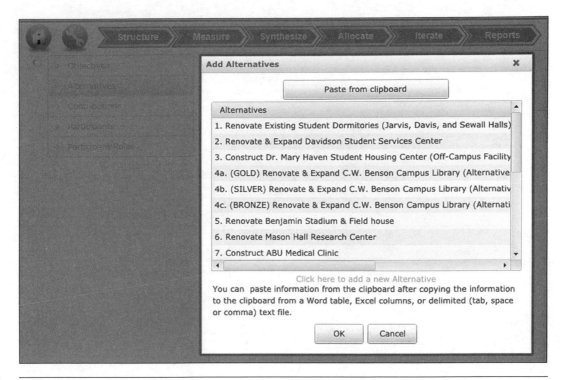

Figure 7.7   Decision alternatives from clipboard to "Edit" or "Accept"

Figure 7.8   Portfolio candidate list as alternatives in model

select each alternative and then select "Edit Information Document" on the right side of the screen (see Figure 7.9).

When the edit window opens, type the description of the project or copy and paste it from the business case. Copy and paste ensures consistency and provides a more productive way to enter the information. In the example shown in Figure 7.10, the Background, Project Rationale, Project Objectives and Goals, Anticipated Benefits and, because this is one of three alternative approaches

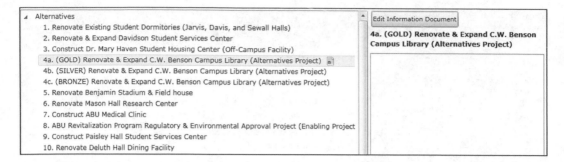

Figure 7.9   Select "Edit Information Document" to add the description of an alternative

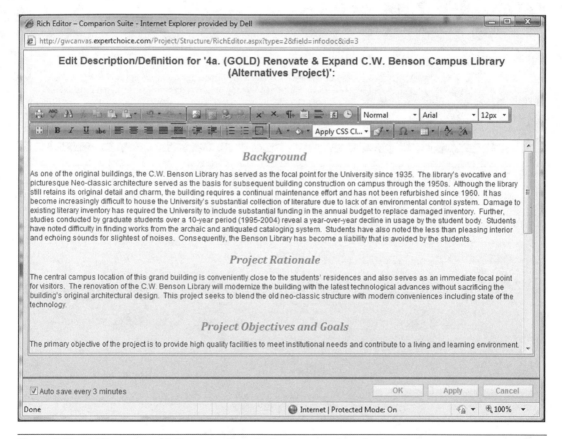

Figure 7.10   Adding selected information from the business case into the description

to the C. W. Benson Campus Library project, the Project Alternatives sections of the business case are added to the description of this alternative so evaluators not intimately familiar with the project obtain a good understanding of its purpose.

The information provided in the description should be consistent across all alternatives and should include business case fields as specified by the Steering Committee (PMB). When the information has been pasted, click "Apply" and then "OK" to close the edit window. The information will appear in the "Description/Definition" pane on the right side of the screen (see Figure 7.11).

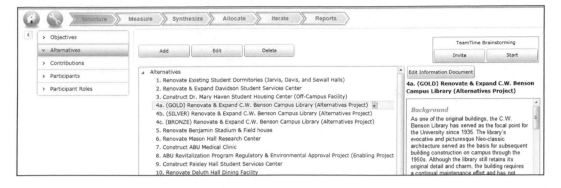

Figure 7.11   Description/definition pane after entry or paste

When all alternatives have been entered and the descriptive information supplied, the information from the business cases pertaining to which objectives are supported by each alternative can be used to map the alternatives to the objectives.

Map Alternatives to Objectives to Establish Contribution

With the evaluation model updated to include the alternatives and descriptions, alternatives can be mapped to the objectives they support as shown in the alignment matrix in Table 7.2. Not all alternatives support all objectives; in fact, here most of the project alternatives support only one of the objectives, as is often the case with real portfolio candidates. To establish the proper alignment of alternatives with objectives in the Comparion model, select "Contributions" (see Figure 7.12).

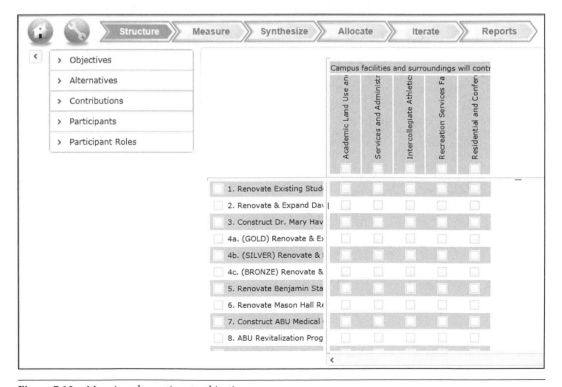

Figure 7.12   Mapping alternatives to objectives

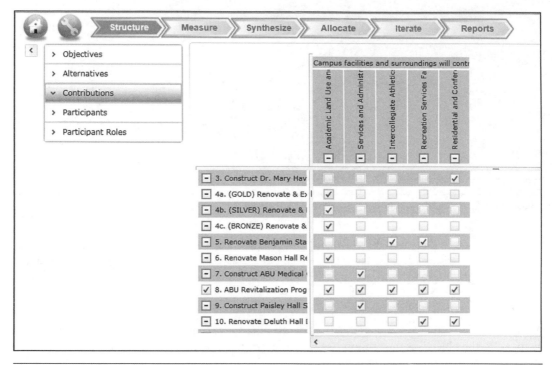

Figure 7.13   Define contributions by mapping alternatives to objectives

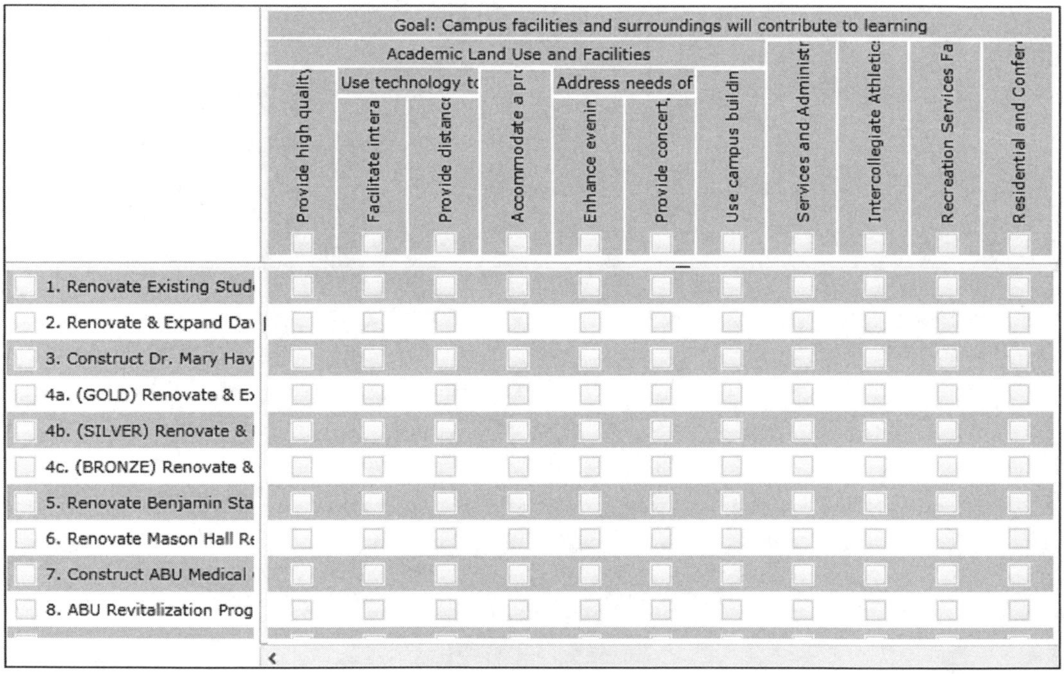

Figure 7.14   Mapping alternatives to covering objectives (terminal nodes as sub-objectives)

Select the Covering Objectives

As shown in Figure 7.13, select the covering objectives supported by each alternative by checking the appropriate boxes in the matrix. To select all objectives for an alternative, meaning that the alternative supports all objectives, check the box to the left of the alternative; for example, Project 8 supports all five objectives as can be seen in Figure 7.13. To select all alternatives for an objective, meaning that all alternatives support that objective, check the box under the objective. Use the Comparion help functions for explanations of these options. Regardless, the mapping of alternatives should match that presented in the approved candidate alignment matrix. Scroll down and to the right as necessary to complete the matrix.

Select the Covering Objectives with Sub-objectives

In the ABU example, the objectives hierarchy contains only one level rather than sub-objectives, sub-sub-objectives, and so on. In many real-world instances, the objectives hierarchy contains multiple levels, and alternatives are mapped to each of the lowest-level sub-objectives that they support. The matrix shows the covering objectives, or terminal nodes, as vertical text. Like the Goal, when there are sub-objectives, the parent objectives are shown horizontally above the vertical text for the terminal node, as shown in Figure 7.14 that displays the following objectives hierarchy:

- Goal: Campus facilities and surroundings will contribute
  - ▶ Academic Land Use and Facilities
    - ▪ Provide high-quality facilities to meet institutional needs by renovating or replacing obsolete facilities
    - ▪ Use technology to improve learning, teaching, and research
      - ▪ Facilitate interactive, participative, and project-based learning
      - ▪ Provide distance learning technology capability
    - ▪ Accommodate a projected enrollment growth
    - ▪ Address needs of nontraditional and community audiences
      - ▪ Enhance evening class facilities
      - ▪ Provide concert, presentation, and conference facilities
    - ▪ Use campus buildings for continuing and distance education
  - ▶ Services and Administration Facilities
  - ▶ Intercollegiate Athletics Facilities
  - ▶ Recreation Services Facilities
  - ▶ Residential and Conference Facilities

To see the entire text of an objective or sub-objective, hover above its abbreviation in the box.

Specify Evaluators and Their Roles

In reviewing the objectives, or project categories, in Table 7.2, ABU might consider selected members of the Board of Trustees to evaluate all projects while assigning the Director of the Office of Administration and direct reports to evaluate only those projects listed under the Services and Administration Facilities category. Once again, the point is to select participants to evaluate projects who understand their value in the context of organizational objectives.

Select ABU Personnel to Participate in Prioritizing Projects

In Chapter 4 the objectives were prioritized with respect to the goal of the ABU Campus Revitalization Program. In this chapter a different set of evaluators is nominated to evaluate the alternatives with respect to the objectives they support. The ABU Steering Committee selected and reviewed with

Table 7.4 Selected project evaluators

Name	Title	Representing	email
Mr. Bryan Parker	Vice Chairman	Steering Committee	parker@gwu.edu
Ms. Sharon Davis	Program Manager	PMO	davis@gwu.edu
Ms. Kathryn Stevens	Director of Facilities	University Facilities	stevens@gwu.edu

the Board of Trustees three evaluators representing the Steering Committee, the Project Management Office (PMO), and the university facilities.

The Steering Committee believed that one appropriate high-level representative from each of the three groups was sufficient to evaluate how well each candidate project (alternative) contributes to each objective. The selected evaluators are identified in Table 7.4.

To add and invite the participants who will evaluate only the alternatives, select the "Participants" step under the "Structure" tab and then "Add Participants." Select "Enter or Paste from Clipboard" and, as shown in Figure 7.15, type the new evaluators' e-mail addresses and names, then select "OK." In this case the added participants do not have project manager privileges for the evaluation model and we do not generate a password and send it via e-mail. Because these are fictitious evaluators, leave the boxes unchecked. In an actual situation, these boxes can be checked to have the system provide a randomly generated password for each participant and send a registration notification that you, as the project manager, can tailor.

As shown in Figure 7.16, three participants have been added who will evaluate the alternatives, but who have not provided any input. With the alternatives evaluators entered, it is necessary to establish their roles in the evaluation. This functionality allows for the PMB and ERB to be specific not only about who will participate in the candidate project evaluation process, but also what each will

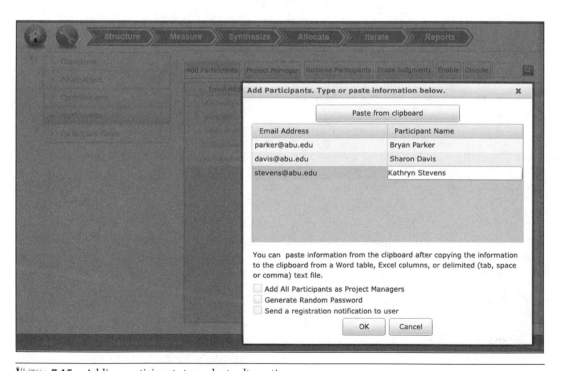

Figure 7.15   Adding participants to evaluate alternatives

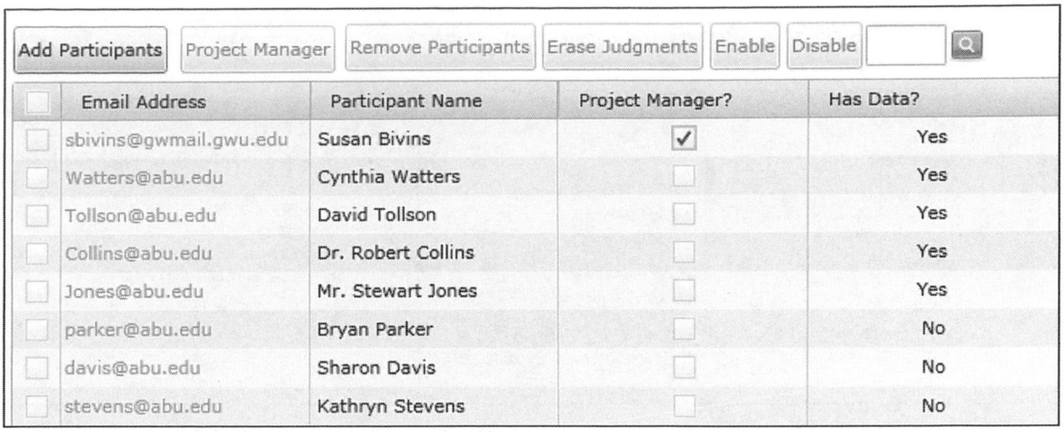

Email Address	Participant Name	Project Manager?	Has Data?
sbivins@gwmail.gwu.edu	Susan Bivins	✓	Yes
Watters@abu.edu	Cynthia Watters		Yes
Tollson@abu.edu	David Tollson		Yes
Collins@abu.edu	Dr. Robert Collins		Yes
Jones@abu.edu	Mr. Stewart Jones		Yes
parker@abu.edu	Bryan Parker		No
davis@abu.edu	Sharon Davis		No
stevens@abu.edu	Kathryn Stevens		No

Figure 7.16 Alternatives evaluators added showing no input yet

evaluate. This is an important benefit of using project portfolio decision tools such as Expert Choice. Having the capability to tailor the specific inputs from selected evaluators allows the organization to leverage the experience and expertise of specific individuals for only that part of the evaluation for which they are qualified. Naturally, this also prevents personnel from evaluating areas for which they are not qualified.

The team that evaluated the relative importance of the objectives with respect to the goal in Chapter 4 included two members of the Board of Trustees, the Chairman of the Steering Committee, and the Faculty Director of the PMO—people with a high-level perspective of the organization, its goal, and objectives. For the purpose of evaluating how well the project alternatives contribute to achievement of the objectives they support, a different team of individuals closer to the action has been chosen; a group that has a more detailed perspective of the projects and a thorough understanding of the meaning of the objectives.

The Comparion software allows the roles of evaluators to be tailored to evaluate only objectives, only alternatives, or both alternatives and objectives. In addition, participants can be assigned to evaluate only specific objectives or only specific alternatives. For example, to choose among the three approaches to the ABU library renovation project, the Steering Committee might choose only specific people with expertise in library management and construction. In addition, those chosen just for the purpose of evaluating the three library alternatives might be excluded from evaluating any other alternatives.

Establish ABU Participant Roles

With ABU evaluators for the alternatives added, it is necessary to specify their roles. To do so, navigate to the "Structure" tab, "Participant Roles" and select each of the alternatives evaluators in turn by highlighting the evaluator's name. To assign roles simultaneously, hold down the CTRL key and select each of the alternatives evaluators in turn so all three are highlighted (see Figure 7.17).

The default setting is for all evaluators to evaluate all alternatives against all objectives and to evaluate all the objectives with respect to each other. In this case, all three of the evaluators are to evaluate only all the alternatives with respect to the objectives.

Note that we can specify roles "For Objectives" or "For Alternatives." In this case, all three evaluators have exactly the same role, that is, to evaluate all alternatives against their covering objectives. When "For Objectives" is selected under "Participant Roles," as is the case in Figure 7.18, uncheck the

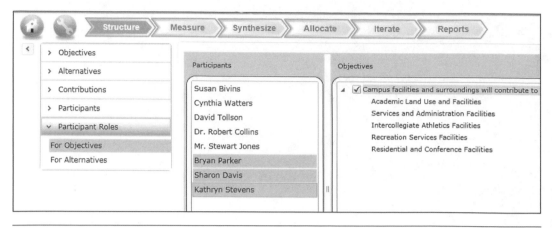

Figure 7.17   Setting evaluator roles for objectives for three evaluators

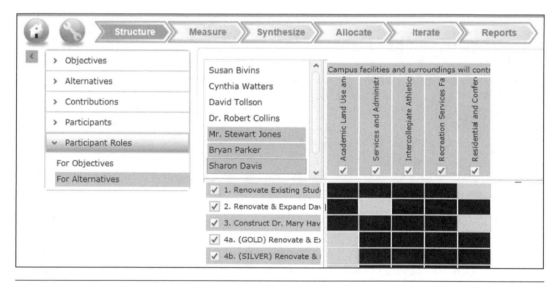

Figure 7.18   Assign participant roles for alternatives

box next to the goal "Campus facilities and surroundings will contribute to . . ." By unchecking this box, these participants will not evaluate the objectives listed under the goal, thus, they will not see any of the objectives evaluation steps. Select "For Alternatives" as shown in Figure 7.18 to establish participant role assignments for the alternatives.

The rows in the matrix in Figure 7.18 represent the alternatives, while the columns represent the covering objectives. The shaded rectangles in the matrix on the screen indicate whether an alternative supports (is mapped to) a covering objective and whether the selected evaluator(s) will evaluate the alternative (row) against the particular objective. Black indicates no relationship between the alternative and the objective; the alternative does not contribute to achieving the objective. Gray cells on the screen indicate that although the alternative contributes to the objective, the selected participant(s) will not be asked to evaluate the degree to which it contributes. Light-shaded cells in Figure 7.18, which appear green on the actual Comparion screen indicate that the alternative contributes to the objective and that the participant(s) will evaluate the relative contribution.

Because all three of the new evaluators are assigned to evaluate all alternatives against their covering objectives, accept the default of evaluating all alternatives against all covering objectives. Of course, if some evaluators are only assigned to evaluate some of the alternatives, or evaluate alternatives for only some of the objectives, tailor this process for the individual roles. It is also possible, and perhaps desirable while learning, to assign roles to an evaluator one objective at a time and one alternative at a time.

7.8.4 Measure—Establish the Evaluation Approach

With alternatives entered and roles assigned, it is necessary to define the measurement methods to be used, select options for presenting the material to participants, and conduct the actual evaluation.

Select Measurement Methods

Originally all measurements using AHP were performed using pairwise relative comparisons of the elements in the hierarchy. AHP and the Expert Choice products were subsequently modified to allow absolute as well as relative measurement to derive the priorities of the alternatives with respect to the objectives.

Thus, although the objectives must be evaluated using pairwise comparisons or direct entry of priorities obtained by other valid means, alternatives can now be evaluated using the default pairwise comparisons, or by using absolute measurement scales, including rating scales, utility curves, and step functions as well as direct priority input. The definitions of each of these can be found in Comparion help. Regardless of the measurement method chosen, all measurements with Expert Choice possess the ratio-scale property, as described in Chapter 3. This prevents mathematically meaningless results that are often generated using weights and scores in spreadsheets and other decision methods and tools. As described, for organizations with a large number of alternatives to consider, pairwise comparison can be cumbersome and time-consuming, therefore, consider using other measurement methods for evaluating alternatives, as in this example.

To establish measurement methods for the alternatives, select the "Measure" tab, "Measurement Methods" step, and "For Alternatives" as shown in Figure 7.19.

Next, select the first objective, Academic Land Use and Facilities and select the arrow on the drop-down menu under "Measurement Type" to see the choices shown in Figure 7.20. These choices indicate how the alternatives for the selected objective will be evaluated.

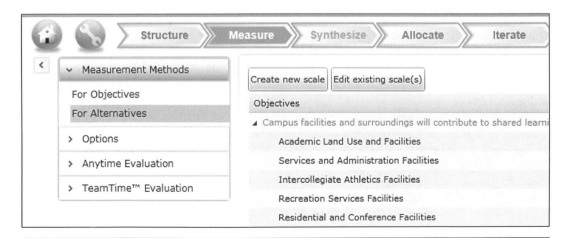

Figure 7.19 Preparing to select measurement methods for alternatives

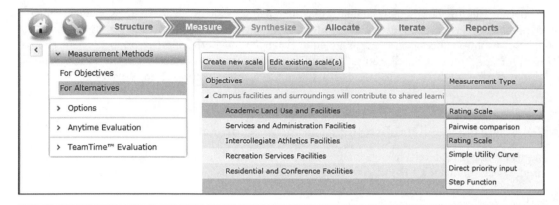

Figure 7.20   Choosing the measurement type for alternatives with respect to an objective

Pairwise Comparison

When "Pairwise comparison" is chosen, a pairwise comparison of each supporting alternative with each other supporting alternative is presented to each assigned evaluator until all pairwise comparisons for that objective have been displayed; if pairwise comparison is used for all objectives, then the same is presented for each subsequent objective until all comparisons of the supporting alternatives for all objectives have been presented. When the number of alternatives is manageable, as in the 19 projects for the ABU example, pairwise comparison can produce more accurate decisions. However, when the number of alternatives is large, making the number of pairwise comparisons cumbersome and the judgments perhaps less consistent because of their sheer number, consider using a rating scale or other measurement type. Many organizations have a larger candidate list for portfolio selection and, for most, we recommend the use of other measurement methods.

Ratings Scales

Ratings scales are useful substitutes for pairwise comparisons when the number of alternatives is large. With a rating scale, evaluators rate each alternative with regard to how well it supports its covering objectives. Here we examine how to create a rating scale.

ABU Rating Scale Example

Let's suppose we want to use a rating scale for one of the objectives, Services and Administration Facilities. Select the "Services and Administration Facilities" objective and "Rating Scale." The "Default Rating Scale" will automatically be selected as shown in Figure 7.21.

You may use the default rating scale, modify an existing scale, or create a new one. Use "Create a new scale or Edit existing scale(s)" by selecting the appropriate tab above the objectives, as shown in Figure 7.22.

The default rating scale shows a nine-point scale with the assigned intensity levels for each of the nine points. Users can reduce or increase the number of points, edit the intensity value for each, and change the name of each point to be more meaningful for the particular organization or evaluators. When changing intensity values, derive them by performing pairwise comparisons and then perform an eigenvector calculation to ensure that they maintain their ratio-scale properties; the default rating scales provided with Comparion have already been calculated in this manner. (Eigenvectors are mathematically defined in linear algebra and their calculation is beyond the scope of this book; users should simply avoid changing intensity values in rating scales without applying this concept.) Changes can be saved as new rating scales with unique names by saving a copy and renaming it after editing the values.

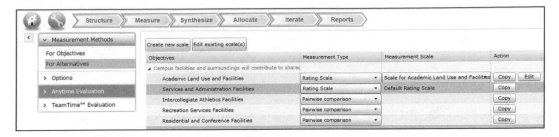

Figure 7.21   Using a rating scale as the measurement type

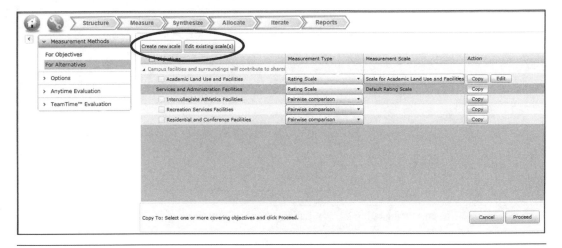

Figure 7.22   Create a new rating scale or edit an existing rating scale

In this example we are changing the names of the points in Figure 7.23 to more closely relate to what we are asking the ABU evaluators, that is, how well a given project meets the associate objective, from Perfectly to Extremely Well, and so on, to perhaps Not at All instead of None. To edit the rating scale, select the "Name" or "Value" and make the desired modifications as shown in Figure 7.23. The values are also known as the intensities. To add a new intensity, name it and assign a value for it, select "Add a new rating intensity to this scale." Type a descriptive name for the new rating scale, in this case, Rating Scale for ABU Alternatives. When finished preparing the rating scale, click on "Save" at the bottom of the window to apply it to evaluation of the alternatives for the selected objectives.

In this example we did not change the number of intensities, which can be accomplished by selecting the "Delete" button under "Actions" or by selecting "Add new rating intensity to this scale." When a new rating intensity is added, it is automatically placed in the correct numerical position, that is, if we were to add an intensity level called Really Great and give it a value of 0.95, it would automatically be placed between Excellent and Outstanding. In this case the values of the intensities are unchanged, leaving them the same as the default rating scale values. Values can be changed by keying a new value into the selected row in the Value column. Note the caution to ensure ratio-scale properties for modified or added intensities.

Because in this example we have elected to use a rating scale for all the alternatives supporting the Academic Land Use and Facilities objective, the evaluators are asked to rate each alternative with respect to this objective; they will see screens similar to the one shown in Figure 7.24.

Let's use the rating scale we just created to evaluate the first three objectives by selecting "Rating Scale" from the "Measurement Type" drop-down list and "Rating Scale for ABU Alternatives" from the

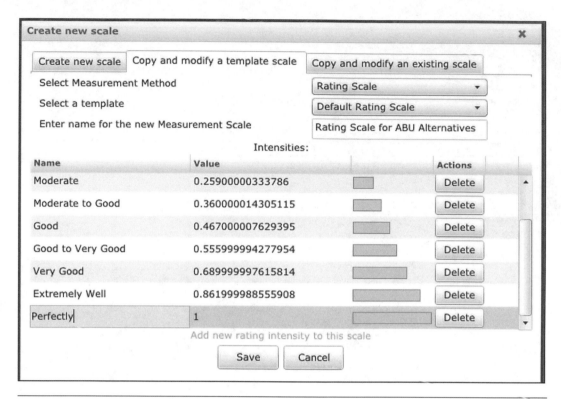

Figure 7.23   Editing an existing rating scale and giving the new scale a name

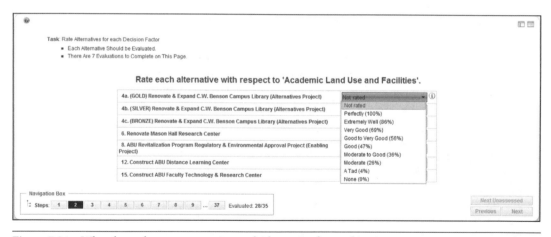

Figure 7.24   What the evaluator sees—rating each alternative for an objective

"Measurement Scale" drop-down list, as shown in Figure 7.25. To explore some other measurement methods, let's select "Simple Utility Curve" for the Recreation Services Facilities objective and "Direct priority input" for the Residential and Conference Facilities objective, also as shown in Figure 7.25.

Step Functions and Utility Curves
Recall that while rating scales are an effective substitute for pairwise comparisons, step functions and utility curves translate known information about the alternatives with respect to an objective into

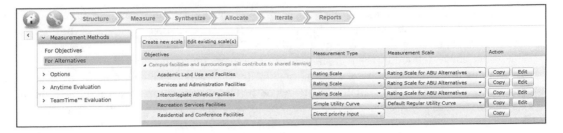

Figure 7.25 Select measurement methods for the alternatives for each covering objective

ratio-scale priorities. The translation formulas are developed by expert judgment or by those with considerable experience. The translations are derived using pairwise comparisons of the value or priority to be assigned at different values of the known information. More explanation of step functions and utility curves can be found in the contextual Comparion help screens.

ABU Utility Curve Example

Using a utility curve for the Recreation Services Facilities objective, we will demonstrate how to specify the curve. Assume that the curve is nonlinear and that it has been derived by performing pairwise comparisons of the perceived value or priority of several points on the curve. After selecting "Simple Utility Curve" for the objective, select "Create new scale" or "Copy and modify an existing scale" at the top of the screen and then select "Simple Utility Curve" as shown in Figure 7.26.

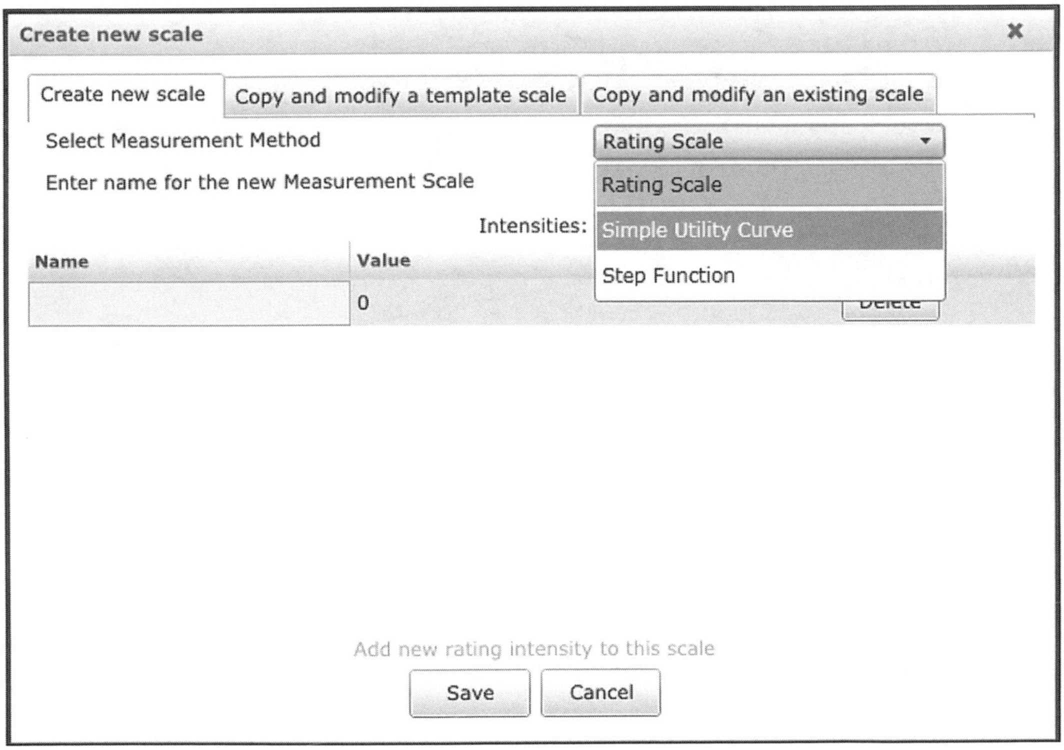

Create new scale   ✕

| Create new scale | Copy and modify a template scale | Copy and modify an existing scale |

Select Measurement Method

    Rating Scale   ▼

Enter name for the new Measurement Scale

    Rating Scale

                        Intensities: Simple Utility Curve

| Name | Value |

                                          Step Function

              0   Delete

Add new rating intensity to this scale

             Save   Cancel

Figure 7.26 Create a new simple utility curve

Modify the shape of the curve by selecting or deselecting "Linear" and using the up and down arrows (or typing a value directly) to define the shape of the curve. Change the name of the curve to the desired name and then save it, as denoted in Figure 7.27.

The utility curve defined by the recreation facilities experts illustrates that, in the ABU example provided in Figure 7.28, the utility of a recreational facility—shown as Contribution on the *x*-axis—increases slowly when it serves small percentages of the target population—shown in units on the *y*-axis, but increases rapidly when it is expected to serve larger percentages of the target population. The shape of the curve was created by unchecking the box next to Linear and by using the down arrow to create a concave curve of the desired degree. Using the up arrow will create a convex curve.

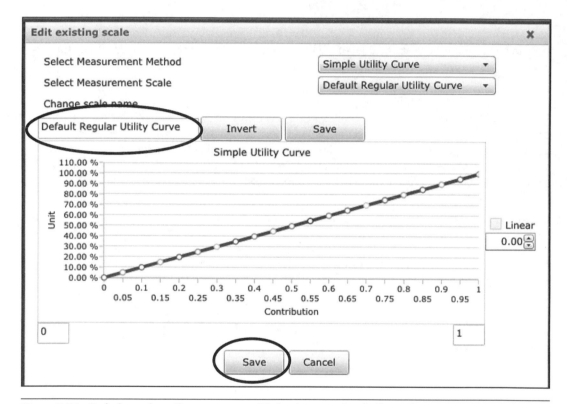

Figure 7.27   Default regular utility curve to modify for the recreation facilities objective

Direct Priority Input

Finally, select "Direct Priority Input" for the Residential and Conference Facilities objective. This option is used when ratio-scale priorities have already been established, such as when the alternatives have already been evaluated by an appropriate group and are being used directly as input to the overall evaluation. In this case direct priority input is used only as an example. It is unlikely that multiple evaluators would be allowed to input their own priorities; rather, one representative, or the evaluation model project manager is assigned as the only evaluator for this objective and inputs the ratio-scale priorities derived by the earlier process.

The results of establishing the measurement methods should look like Figure 7.29, and we are ready to establish options for the evaluation.

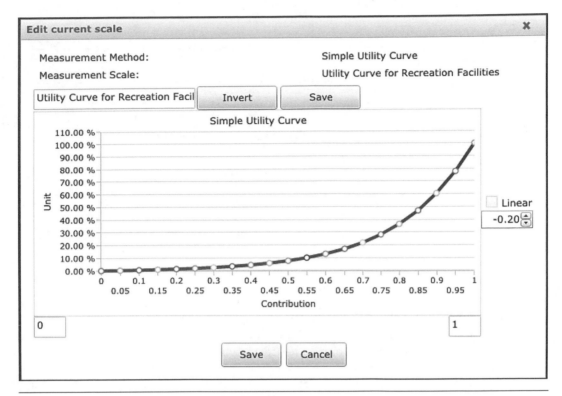

Figure 7.28   Utility curve for recreation facilities objective

Figure 7.29   Comparion screen after all measurement methods have been established

Establish Measurement Options

With the decision structured, it is necessary to establish the options for evaluation, navigation, and the display of information during the evaluation.

Evaluation Options ABU Example

Navigate to the "Measure" tab, select "Options" and then "Evaluation" as shown in Figure 7.30. The evaluation options identify what we want to evaluate, the order of evaluation, how we wish to evaluate alternatives that have rating scales, trade-off accuracy versus number of comparisons for pairwise comparisons, and select either graphical or verbal for pairwise comparisons.

For "What do you want to evaluate," choose both "Objectives" and "Alternatives," although the evaluation of objectives has already been completed by a different team of evaluators. When some

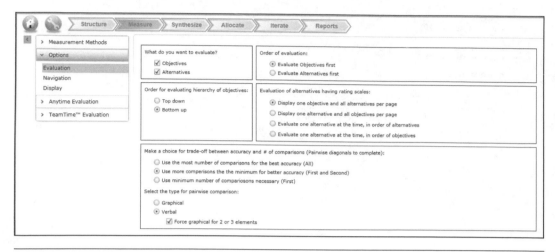

Figure 7.30   Establish evaluation options

participants evaluate both objectives and alternatives, and the PMB wants to perform them in separate phases, such as all objectives first and then later all alternatives, only one of these can be checked. "Order of Evaluation" applies to evaluators who will evaluate both objectives and alternatives and thus does not apply in this example. However, see Comparion help for rationale.

Although we are not evaluating objectives at this time, the "Order for evaluating hierarchy of objectives" applies to whether the relative importance of the sub-objectives should be determined first before evaluating the relative importance of the higher-level objectives, bottom up or the reverse, top down. Expert Choice recommends bottom-up evaluation of the objectives hierarchy to give participants a better appreciation of the significance of the elements that contribute to the higher-level objectives when they are evaluated.

For "Evaluation of alternatives having rating scales," choose "Display one objective and all the alternatives to evaluate per page." This means that the evaluator will be shown one objective at a time and asked to evaluate how well each alternative mapped to the objective supports the objective shown. This allows a participant to see the ratings for all alternatives for a covering objective on the same page and thus to make better comparisons. As can be seen in Figure 7.30, there are three other ways to present the alternative evaluations to the evaluators. Use Comparion help to learn more about these methods.

Although pairwise comparisons are not used in this example to determine the relative expected contributions of alternatives to their covering objectives, it is important to understand the meaning of "Make a choice for trade-off between accuracy and number of comparisons (pairwise diagonals to complete)" in cases where pairwise comparisons are used. Choosing "Use more comparisons than the minimum for better accuracy (first and second)" is a compromise between the maximum number and the minimum number. Using this option generates for each objective, $(n - 1) + (n - 2)$ comparisons, where n is the number of alternatives mapped to the objective. Thus, if pairwise comparisons were used for the alternatives contributing to the first objective, which has 7 alternatives associated with it, this would result in $(7 - 1) + (7 - 2) = 11$ pairwise comparisons. The number of comparisons for the alternatives for each subsequent objective can be calculated in the same manner. The maximum number of comparisons are calculated as $(n \times (n - 1)/2)$. Choosing this option provides greater redundancy and thus produces the most accurate results, but it takes more time. The minimum number of comparisons is $(n - 1)$ and should rarely be used—perhaps only when accurate pairwise graphical judgments can be made with confidence.

The "Select the type for pairwise comparison" is used to select whether pairwise comparisons are presented graphically (Graphical) or verbally (Verbal). An example of a verbal pairwise comparison is shown in Figure 7.31. Although graphical comparisons are more accurate, verbal comparisons make more sense when judging qualitative factors; as described in Chapter 4, this is because graphical comparisons can yield values that convey a false sense of accuracy, whereas verbal comparisons yield specific values for a single judgment on a 9-point scale. As discussed in Chapter 3, distinguishing among nine points is perhaps as accurate as a human being making a qualitative comparison can be. It falls within the seven plus or minus two cognitive limitation and represents approximately one order of magnitude.

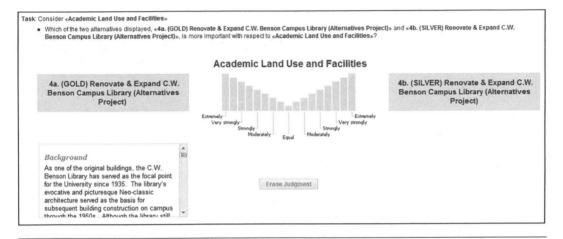

Figure 7.31 What the evaluator sees—example of verbal pairwise comparison

ABU Navigation Options Example

Navigation options direct how participants proceed through the evaluation steps. To see the navigation options shown in Figure 7.32, select "Navigation" under "Options." Unless the option to "Hide navigation box" is selected where shown in Figure 7.32, the evaluator will see the navigation box shown at the lower left of Figure 7.33 that enables him to navigate forward and backward through the evaluation. By selecting "Show next unassessed" in Figure 7.30, the evaluator is able to jump directly to the next uncompleted step, which is helpful when not all steps can be completed in one session. Selecting "Auto advance" in Figure 7.32 automatically advances the participant to the next evaluation step when the current step is completed. To force the evaluator to complete a step before going to the next, and not allow any steps to be skipped, check the "Don't allow leaving an evaluation step

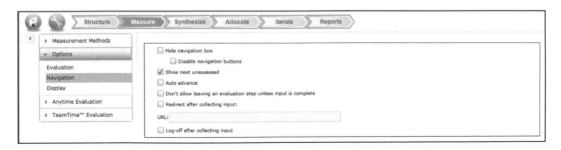

Figure 7.32 Setting navigation options

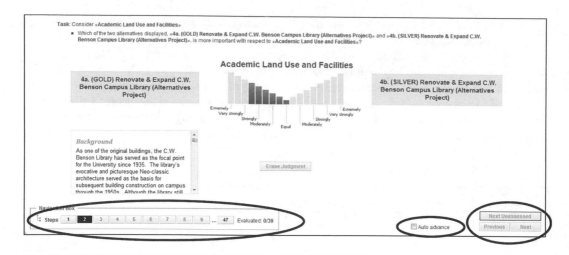

Figure 7.33   What the evaluator sees—navigation box, auto advance, and next unassessed

unless input is complete" box shown in Figure 7.32. This option can frustrate evaluators who may wish to give more thought to a particular step even though they are ready to proceed to subsequent steps. A participant can be directed to a particular URL after the evaluation is complete by checking the "Redirect after collecting input" box shown in Figure 7.32 and supplying a URL address in the box. It can be automatically logged off after the evaluation is complete by checking the "Log-off after collecting input" box. These options provide more or less control of the evaluators' navigation. For inexperienced evaluators, check "Don't allow leaving an evaluation step unless input is complete, Auto advance" and "Log-off after collecting input."

ABU Display Options Example

The display options allow for selecting which results to show the evaluators. Navigate to the display options by selecting "Display" under "Options" as shown in Figure 7.34. On this screen, select what to show participants during the evaluation for intermediate and overall results. You need to decide whether to display sensitivity analysis graphs and, if so, if you want them displayed for the individual or combined results. Additionally, decide whether or not to show the welcome page, thank you page, inconsistency ratio, information documents associated with objectives and alternatives, and the full path of the objectives. Also, participants can be allowed to enter comments during the evaluation such as those that might explain or support a certain choice for later discussion or clarification.

Showing individual intermediate and overall results is recommended as well as the individual's inconsistency ratio to allow reevaluation of elements that do not seem appropriate, or to examine results that are highly inconsistent. Showing combined results should usually be left unchecked to avoid unduly influencing the participant. It is recommended that the welcome page and thank you pages be shown as well as supporting information documents. These pages can be customized by selecting the edit button next to each of these two options. The full objective path normally should not be selected unless necessary to distinguish similar sub-objectives for multiple different objectives. Select "Allow comments" to enable evaluators to document the reasons for their selections or to indicate confusion about decision elements; if comments are allowed, ensure that they will subsequently be read and used for productive discussion, particularly with new groups of evaluators.

The example in Figure 7.35 contains one of the intermediate results screens that is shown when, for example, a cluster or meaningful subset of the evaluation is finished, such as the completion of

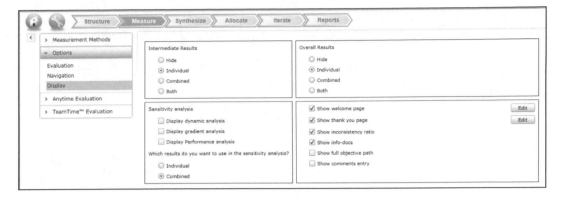

Figure 7.34 Setting display options

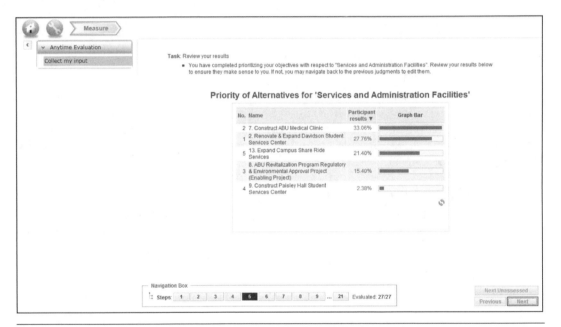

Figure 7.35 What the evaluator sees—individual intermediate results for one objective

the ratings for all the supporting alternatives for a given objective. Figure 7.35 specifically shows what an evaluator sees after completing all the ratings for the Services and Administration Facilities objective.

Check the Progress of the ABU Evaluation

Once the invitations have been sent, use the "Manage Project" wrench symbol, "Project Status" menu, and select "Evaluation Progress" (see Figure 7.36).

As seen in this example, the four evaluators of the objectives have each completed all ten of their comparisons, while, as expected, the three evaluators of the alternatives have not yet begun. As expected, the Project Managers (Professor Forman, Susan Bivins, and Michael Bible) and the Administrator will not be contributing judgments for the evaluation. In some cases the project manager or

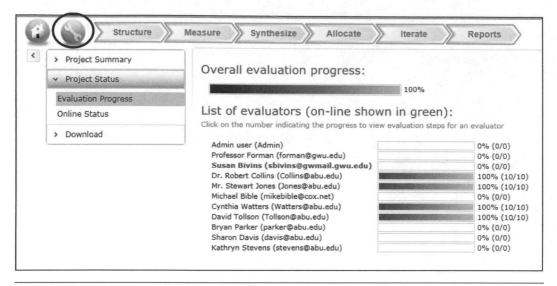

Figure 7.36   Showing the progress of the evaluations

person managing the evaluation process may also be one of the active contributors, but here that is not the case. If an evaluator has partially completed judgments, the percent of judgments completed will be shown. One advantage of the asynchronous evaluation capability in Comparion is that evaluators can not only log on at a convenient time, but they can also interrupt their evaluations if necessary and resume them later.

Verify the ABU Alternatives Evaluation Steps

Use the "Evaluation Progress" screen shown in Figure 7.36 to view the evaluation steps and to verify that what the participants see corresponds with your intent. Click on the numbers to the right of the participant whose steps you want to verify; in this case, to check the path for Bryan Parker, click on the 0% (0/27) to be taken directly to the first screen that he will see when he begins his evaluation, as shown in Figure 7.37.

The first step, shown in Figure 7.37, is the welcome screen. Note the message in the upper left corner when viewing the evaluation steps. It indicates that, although judgments may be entered, they will not be saved. In addition, it indicates which evaluator's path is being viewed. At the lower left, the "Navigation Box" shows how many steps the evaluator will see, and it can be used to move forward or backward through the steps or to jump to any particular step. At the lower right, select "Next Unassessed" item or the "Next" item to progress forward. The "Previous" button allows the evaluator to return to the last step.

Move through the screens to ensure that the evaluator will see all of the elements and only the elements assigned, in this case each objective, with the evaluation of each mapped alternative. Note that after the first "Welcome" screen, an "Auto advance" box appears at the bottom of the screen if the evaluation model project manager selected that option during structure. If the box is checked, then when a judgment is entered the next screen will automatically be presented without using the navigation buttons. Figure 7.38 shows the second screen that is the first actual request for input that Bryan Parker will see.

Note the first objective, in this case abbreviated Academic Land Use and Facilities, is presented along with the opportunity to rate each of the alternatives supporting it (for which it is a covering objective). So, for the first objective, the seven alternatives that support the objective should be seen

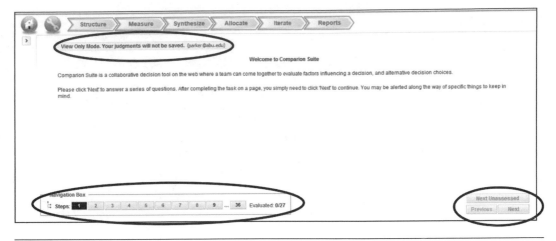

Figure 7.37   View evaluation steps for Bryan Parker—welcome screen and navigation

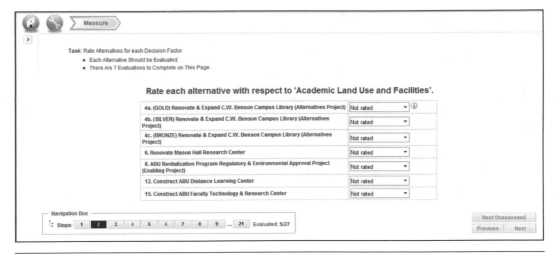

Figure 7.38   Viewing evaluation steps—first objective using the selected rating scale

with a ratings drop-down box for each. The next step, Step 3, shows the individual's results for the relative importance of the supporting alternatives for the objective, as shown in Figure 7.39, because of the options chosen previously.

Because the evaluation model project manager is merely viewing the steps, there are no results to show; thus, the "Note: There is insufficient information to calculate local results" message. However, when the evaluator is performing the evaluation, he will see his own individual intermediate and overall results in accordance with the options selected by the facilitator. The final step shows the "Thank You" screen. If the evaluation steps presented to an evaluator are not correct, return to the "Structure, Participant Roles" step and correct the role assignments.

Asynchronous Anytime Evaluation

This form of evaluation allows the evaluation model project manager to invite selected participants who can then individually complete the evaluations online at any convenient time within the

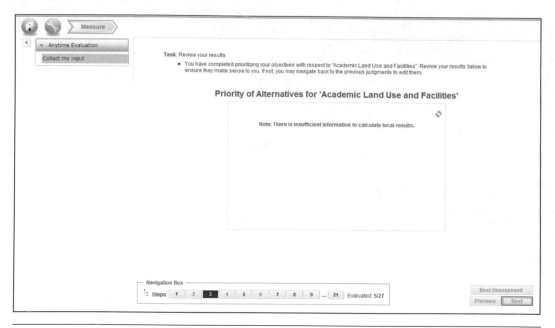

Figure 7.39   Viewing evaluation steps—showing individual intermediate results

scheduled availability of the evaluation. This capability is recommended for use in any evaluation when the participants have a common understanding of the items to be evaluated or are so geographically or time-zone disbursed as to make a synchronous meeting impracticable.

Prepare for ABU Anytime Evaluation

As shown in Figure 7.40, under "Anytime Evaluation," select "Invite Participants," and then select the e-mail addresses for the appropriate participants, in this case the three alternatives evaluators. Select "Send e-mail invitations." Note that the invitation can be edited by selecting "Edit Invite" on the right side of the window, making the necessary changes, and then selecting "Save Invite." By default, all evaluators are selected so uncheck those who should not receive this invitation.

In the sample e-mail invitation in Figure 7.41, Comparion automatically fills in the parameters that begin and end with %% with the project name, user name, access code if there is one, and the project manager name, and uses any edited information supplied. The "From" address can be selected as is or sent from the e-mail address of anyone on the project who has project manager privileges. Participants who receive this e-mail must click on the provided link to be taken directly to the first screen of their evaluations. Otherwise they must login and select the project.

After the invitations are sent, if the signed-in evaluation model project manager selects "Collect my input" as shown on the left side of the screen underneath "Anytime Evaluation, Invite Participants," she will be taken to the navigation for her own evaluation role. In this case, we have not asked the project manager to evaluate anything, so if this option is chosen, the project manager will see only the welcome, the results, and the thank you screens. When the project manager is also an evaluator, she can use the link provided in the invitation e-mail or the direct access provided with "Collect my input."

Synchronous TeamTime Evaluation

Sometimes it makes sense to conduct a real time decision meeting with all participants. This might be the case when an evaluation needs to be completed urgently, when further clarification and

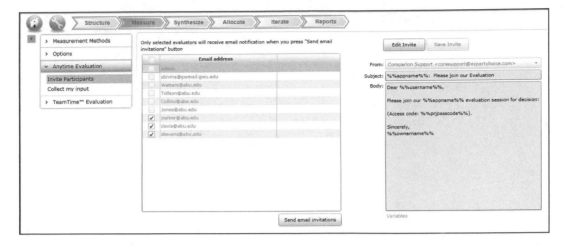

Figure 7.40   Inviting the alternatives evaluators via e-mail

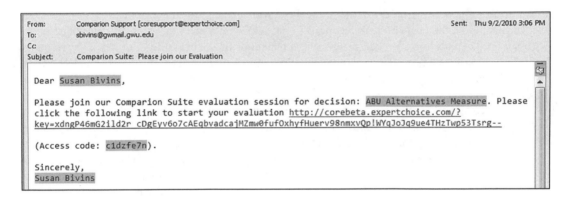

Figure 7.41   E-mail invitation to evaluators with highlighted parameters automatically filled in

discussion might be necessary, or simply when the participants can be together in the same room or online at the same time.

Prepare for ABU Synchronous Evaluation

With TeamTime, multiple participants are able to perform evaluations concurrently using keypads or by logging on to Comparion with a meeting ID or direct link. Let's suppose that the alternatives evaluators are all in different locations. As with a scheduled webinar, the participants should be aware of the plan for an impending meeting, which can be accomplished by sending an invitation. The project manager, or facilitator, selects and invites the participants and conducts the meeting. To select the participants, click on "Select participants" under "TeamTime Evaluation," as shown in Figure 7.42.

Note that the three alternatives evaluators are selected, with a mode of "On-line" and they will be full participants during the meeting. However, in this case, Dr. Robert Collins, Chairman of the ABU facilities Steering Committee, introduced during the objectives evaluation, wishes to participate in the meeting as an observer. The project manager selects "View Only" under mode for that purpose. A third alternative mode of participation in addition to "On-line" and "View Only" is "Keypad" that

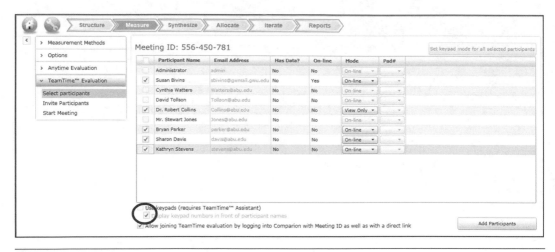

Figure 7.42   Inviting participants to a TeamTime meeting

is available in the mode drop-down menu for those with a license for the TeamTime Assistant module. In this mode, the evaluators use keypads to participate in a meeting room that has been set up with special keypads and a keypad receiver. The facilitator must check the "Use keypads" (requires TeamTime Assistant") box on the screen shown in Figure 7.42 as well as "Display keypad numbers" in front of participant names. Participants in the same meeting can be online from any location or in the meeting room.

The "Meeting ID" is displayed at the top of the "Select participants" page; check the box at the bottom of the page to "Allow joining TeamTime evaluation by logging into Comparion with Meeting ID as well as with a direct link." The facilitator can add participants to the meeting by selecting the "Add Participants" button at the lower right of the screen. Even participants who have not yet been registered to use Comparion can use the meeting ID to login, where they will provide their e-mail address and name. When they do this, participants will automatically be registered in the Comparion workgroup that contains the project.

As can be seen in Figure 7.43, if "Invite by e-mail" is selected, participants can be notified of when the meeting is to be conducted, and given the link to the URL for the meeting. The facilitator can tailor the variables, if needed, and must specify the date and time by keying it in. Clicking on the "Send E-mail" button will send the e-mail to all checked participants on the "Select participants" screen in Figure 7.42.

Participants in a TeamTime session can also be invited by phone. "Select Invite by phone" and a script will be displayed with the appropriate information for the facilitator to communicate, as shown in Figure 7.44.

Selecting "Copy and paste" will display the same information shown in Figure 7.44, along with a "Copy" button. Selecting it copies the information to the clipboard, from which it can be pasted and provided to the participants.

The project manager or facilitator selects the desired options, including whether participants will be able to see their colleagues' judgments during the meeting, and selects "Start Meeting" when ready to start the group meeting, as shown in Figure 7.45. Viewing the individual inputs of others may unduly influence some participants. This can be prevented by selecting "Start in anonymous mode (hide judgments)."

After the options have been chosen, select the "Start Session" button to make the meeting available to invited participants. The participants then login by selecting "Join Evaluation Meeting" and providing the e-mail and meeting ID as shown in Figure 7.46.

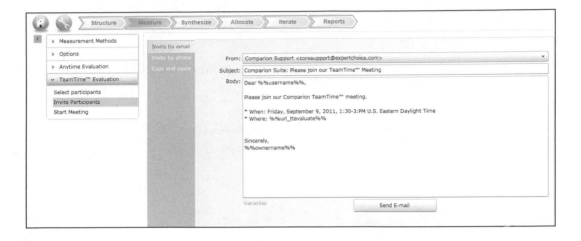

Figure 7.43   E-mail invitation for TeamTime session

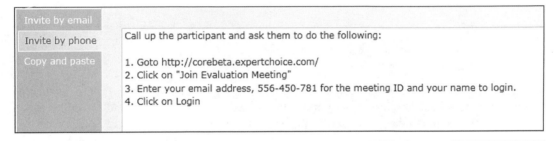

Figure 7.44   Script for inviting TeamTime participants by phone

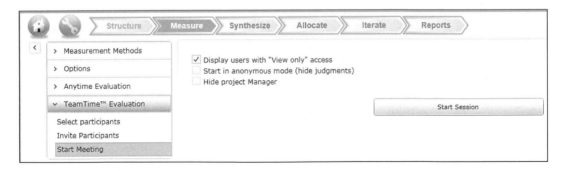

Figure 7.45   Start the TeamTime meeting options

As described in Chapter 4, the "Join Structuring Meeting" button is used by participants to join a meeting during which the objectives hierarchy is structured or alternatives added or deleted.

7.8.5 Perform the Evaluation—Collect Data and Prioritize Candidate Projects

To perform measurements and determine project priorities, the PMB (in this case the ABU Steering Committee) must establish a means to prepare the evaluators after they have been identified

Figure 7.46   TeamTime participant login

and determine a method for collecting data and synthesizing results. In preparation for evaluating the alternatives, selected evaluators are notified of the data collection process and assembled for an orientation period to familiarize them with the process and ensure they are aware of their roles and responsibilities. By performing their evaluation roles, the participants establish the relative expected contribution of each alternative to the goal.

Collect and Synthesize Data

The evaluation model project manager, with guidance from the PMB, prescribes a method for each individual to login to the evaluation model and provide their judgments without the rest of the group present, or has prescribed that the entire team be present to provide a consensus judgment after deliberating, or some combination of these. As seen, Expert Choice's Comparion software provides a TeamTime function for local or distributed groups or teams to perform real time collaboration to structure decisions or perform evaluations. For these meetings, the Comparion project manager, or another designee of the PMB, acts as the facilitator to guide the group during the meeting. With the planning complete, it is now time to obtain the actual judgments.

Forman and Peniwati (1998) noted that synthesis can be performed in several ways when multiple individuals are involved in making a decision, "including: (1) aggregating the individual judgments for each set of pairwise comparisons into an aggregate hierarchy; (2) synthesizing each of the individual hierarchies and aggregating the resulting priorities; and (3) aggregating the individual's derived priorities in each node in the hierarchy." Recall that in the case of the example ABU evaluation, the results for each individual are aggregated and shown to that individual; when all evaluations are complete, the results for the individuals are synthesized to produce an overall result.

The synthesis, using the appropriate tools, results in mathematically sound priorities for the objectives as well as for the alternatives. The team then examines whether the output seems intuitively right and uses sensitivity analysis and other instruments to help confirm the results or determine where iteration is necessary.

Collect Data

The ABU Steering Committee has now obtained ERB or Board of Trustee representative approval of personnel to participate in data collection and prioritization, notified evaluators of their selection, conducted preevaluation orientation to assign individual or group roles and responsibilities, provided preliminary training on how the prioritization process will be performed, communicated the access code, if any, and the deadline or timeframe by which all evaluations are to be completed, and encouraged a common understanding of the objectives and alternatives. TeamTime and other collaboration tools are useful vehicles for conducting orientations, reviewing roles and responsibilities, and ensuring common understanding of the items to be evaluated.

Collecting ABU Data and Prioritizing Candidate Projects

With evaluators notified and orientation complete, each evaluator logs in to Comparion using the e-mail address established in the model; for example, Bryan Parker will login as parker@abu.edu and will click on "I have and would like to use an Access Code" that will open the access code window, as shown in Figure 7.47. Recall that the access code established in this version of the model is ABU Alternatives. Participants who do not specify an access code are shown all the projects in the workspace in which they are specified evaluators and can choose the project by selecting the "Evaluate" indicator next to the one for which they will now enter judgments.

As Bryan Parker, complete all steps of the evaluation using the navigation boxes or auto advance, whichever is comfortable. The evaluator is taken through the steps the facilitator reviewed during "View Evaluation Steps," but now judgments are recorded. During the evaluation, after judgments have been entered for all the alternatives associated with a given objective, the evaluator will see an interim review screen that shows the priorities calculated as a result of his responses for each alternative associated with the objective. The review screen asks the evaluator to either confirm that the priorities make sense or to navigate back to the previous judgments and edit them, as shown in Figure 7.48.

Note that on these review screens the evaluator sees the individual local priorities derived for the alternatives for the given objective based on the judgments entered. After the evaluations are

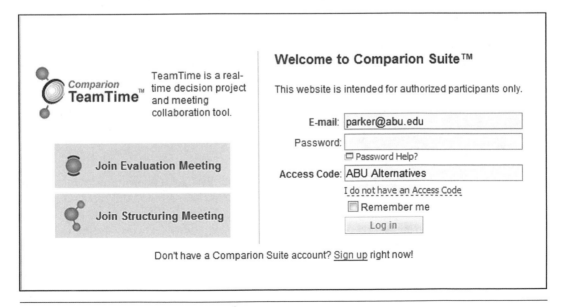

Figure 7.47 Login to Comparion as an evaluator

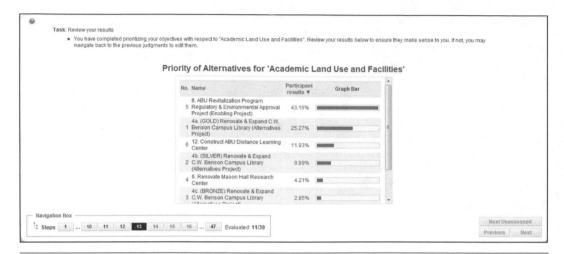

Figure 7.48   Review screen after prioritizing the alternatives for an objective

complete, his results are synthesized with those of the objectives evaluators, as well as the other alternatives evaluators, to determine the global priorities for each alternative.

When the evaluator is satisfied with the relative priorities established for the alternatives supporting the particular objective, he can move on to the next unassessed items that address the set of alternatives for the second objective, and so on until all items have been evaluated. After the alternatives for each objective have been completed, a review screen similar to that in Figure 7.48 is presented. After all judgments have been entered, a thank you message is displayed to the evaluator, if that option was chosen. The evaluator may then log out.

7.8.6 Synthesize the Results

Synthesis combines the evaluation results from all participants in a mathematically sound manner (when using tools that produce them), including ratio-scale priorities for both the objectives and the alternatives with respect to the covering objectives.

The status of the evaluations can be determined by logging in, selecting the desired project, then the "Manage Project" wrench symbol. Select "Project Status" and "Evaluation Progress" as discussed earlier. This is found under "Checking the Progress of the ABU Evaluation" and shown in Figure 7.36. To complete the example ABU evaluation, login as each participant in turn and complete the judgments on behalf of the fictitious participants. In a real situation, once the project owner has ensured that all participants have completed their evaluations, the project owner views the results.

Review the ABU Alternatives Evaluation Results

In this example, select the "Synthesize" tab and select "Overall Results" to view the display shown in Figure 7.46. Overall results by default shows the objectives in the left pane and the alternatives in the right pane with their global priorities that are calculated as described in Chapter 4 with regard to the objectives only. By selecting "Normalized (Priority)" in the drop down "Normalize options" menu, the global priorities of the alternatives sum to 1.000, or, as in Figure 7.46, to 100% with respect to the goal, which is highlighted in Figure 7.49. No matter which normalization option is selected, the priorities with respect to one another, and with respect to the goal, are ratio-scale numbers.

Select one of the objectives, such as Academic Land Use and Facilities shown in Figure 7.50, to see the local priorities of the projects that support it. Projects that are not mapped to (do not support)

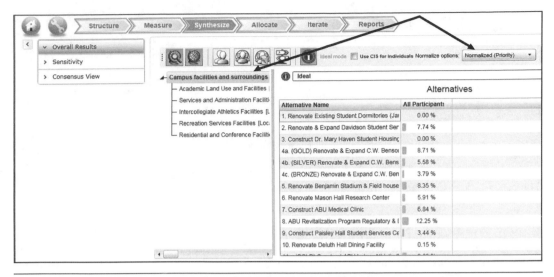

Figure 7.49 Combined evaluator results with global priorities of all alternatives

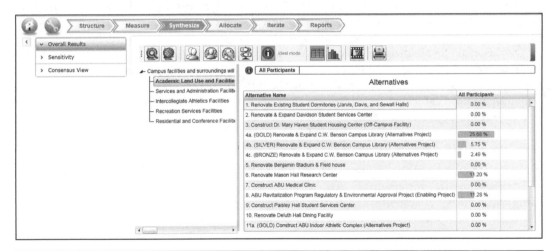

Figure 7.50 Local priorities of alternatives supporting academic land use and facilities

a given objective have local priorities of 0.00%, while those that are mapped to the objective show a local priority, which is the relative importance, based on combined evaluation results, of that supporting project, compared to other projects also supporting the same objective. Note that the local priority of Alternative 4a is 25.68%. This is a ratio-scale number that can be compared to the local priority of Alternative 4b of 5.75%. This means that the evaluators believe that Alternative 4a contributes over four times as much to the achievement of the Academic Land Use and Facilities objective as Alternative 4b (25.68/5.75 ≈ 4.47).

Local priorities of the children of a node at any given level of the hierarchy sum to 100%, so in this case, the local priorities for projects supporting Academic Land Use and Facilities add to 100%. Global priorities are the product of the local priority of the node and its parent node's global priority. The global priorities of sibling child nodes sum to the global priority of the parent node. To show the local and global priorities of the objectives, click on each of the two leftmost symbols that look like globes, as shown in Figure 7.51.

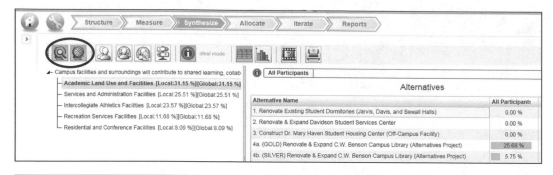

Figure 7.51   Show local and global priorities for objectives

To remove the menu and make more of the screen available for the model information, select the left-pointing arrow under the home button. To bring the menu back, select the right-pointing arrow in the same position. Hide the Comparion navigation bar and menus by selecting the magnifying glass icon at the upper right of the window. Hide the browser navigation and toolbars by using F11 (Function Key 11). Use F11 again to return to the normal view.

To see the results for one or more specific evaluators, select the two-headed symbol and check the name of the evaluator(s) whose results you want to see. In the case of Figure 7.52, Sharon Davis has been selected and her individual evaluation results are shown next to "All Participants."

On this menu (synthesize tab, overall results step), it is possible to see combined results for all of the evaluators, for individuals, and for multiple selected individuals. By creating result groups and adding people to these groups, results for groups can be seen. Please note that your specific results will likely be different from those shown because you have entered different judgment values while performing in lieu of the evaluators.

Ideal versus Distributive Mode

Using AHP, synthesis can be performed in two modes, ideal or distributive. When prioritizing objectives, either mode is appropriate since pairwise comparisons yield the same results in either mode. If ratings scales or other absolute measures are used when evaluating alternatives, the choice of mode can matter when prioritizing alternatives or candidate projects. For the ABU project, choose the ideal mode for synthesizing the alternatives evaluation for reasons described earlier by selecting the "Ideal mode" while in the "Synthesize" tab, as shown in Figure 7.53. By toggling between the two modes, observe the differences between ideal mode and distributive mode when absolute measurement methods are used.

7.8.7 Perform Sensitivity Analysis of Synthesized Results

Sensitivity analysis is used to determine how the alternatives performed against the objectives and to understand how sensitive the alternatives are to changes in the relative priority of objectives (Forman, 2001). Sensitivity analysis lets us consider the sense of rightness of the evaluation results and can also signify the need to iterate (Forman, 2010). This could be the case if a small change in the relative importance of one or more objectives results in changes in the selection of alternatives, or even when the evaluators have misunderstood an objective; for example, evaluating alternatives with high risk as preferable rather than evaluating low risk as preferable. Three types of sensitivity analysis are discussed: (1) dynamic, (2) performance, and (3) gradient. All of these can be accessed in Comparion using the "Synthesize" tab, "Sensitivity" step.

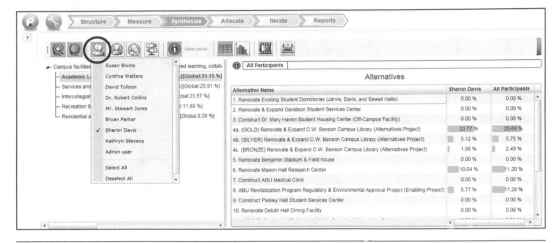

Figure 7.52 Show results for individual evaluators

Figure 7.53 Use ideal mode for PPM—toggle between modes in "Synthesize"

ABU Dynamic Sensitivity Analysis Example

Dynamic sensitivity analysis enables us to see the immediate impact on the priority of alternatives by changing the priorities of objectives. This powerful display can be used to drag the priority of an objective and immediately show the impact on the priorities of the alternatives.

By selecting the "Synthesize" tab, "Sensitivity" step, and "Dynamic Sensitivity," the objectives can be seen on the left sorted in order of decreasing priority, and the alternatives on the right are sorted in order of original entry, as shown in Figure 7.54.

However, to make the display meaningful, it is necessary to check the "Keep sorted" box to show the alternatives in descending priority. To make the results more readily comparable, check the "Normalize" box to show the highest priority alternative as 100% priority, with the other alternatives expressed as a proportion of 100%, as shown in Figure 7.55. When these boxes are checked, changes in the order of alternatives can be seen immediately when the priority of an objective is increased or decreased.

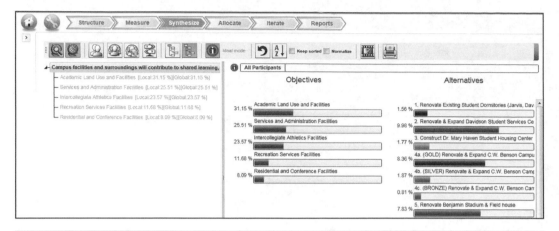

Figure 7.54   Dynamic sensitivity analysis graph without sorting and normalizing

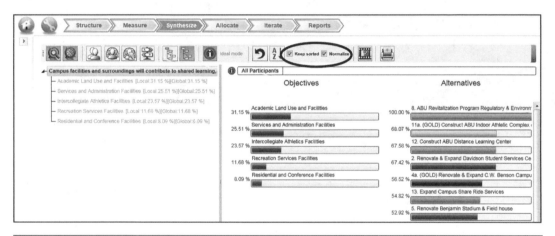

Figure 7.55   Dynamic sensitivity analysis graph sorted and normalized

As shown in Figure 7.56, when the importance of services and administration facilities is increased from 25.51% to about 65%, Projects 2 and 7, the Davidson Student Services Center and the ABU Medical Clinic alternatives jump to the top, replacing some projects that support the academic facilities objective.

When the priority of one objective is increased, the priorities of the remaining objectives are decreased accordingly. Dynamic sensitivity is also used to illustrate changes in the priorities of sub-objectives, if any, by selecting an objective rather than the goal at the far left of the screen, and then manipulating the priorities of the sub-objectives, and so on down the hierarchy.

ABU Performance Sensitivity Analysis Example

Performance sensitivity analysis allows us to adjust the priority of one or more objectives to see what the alternative priorities would be given the adjustment. It shows the relative importance of the objectives as vertical bars and draws a line (curve) for each alternative that intersects with the column for each objective. The point or height at which the line for an alternative crosses the column for an objective can be compared to the position of the intersection for other alternatives that contribute to

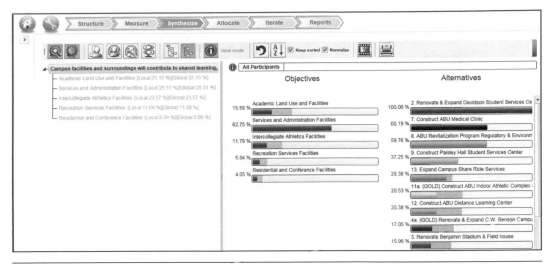

Figure 7.56 Top alternatives after increasing services and administration objective priority

the objective. When an alternative does not contribute to (is not mapped to) an objective, the intersection point is at the bottom, or 0.00%, as expected.

In Figure 7.57, select the "Synthesize" tab, "Sensitivity," and "Performance Sensitivity." The results of the evaluation show the top five projects and their priorities:

1. 8. ABU Revitalization Program Regulatory and Environmental Approval Project (14.80%)
2. 11a. (GOLD) Construct ABU Indoor Athletic Complex (10.07%)
3. 12. Construct ABU Distance Learning Center (10.00%)
4. 2. Renovate and Expand Davidson Student Services Center (9.98%)
5. 4a. (GOLD) Renovate & Expand C. W. Benson Campus Library (8.36%)

When the priority of Intercollegiate Athletics Facilities is increased by dragging the objective bar up to about 43%, the top projects change dramatically, making 11a. (GOLD) Construct ABU Indoor Athletic Complex the highest priority project, as shown in Figure 7.58. The priorities of the

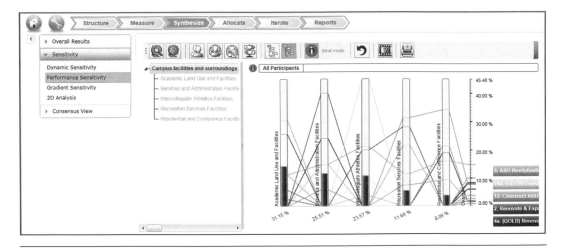

Figure 7.57 Performance sensitivity as a result of the evaluation

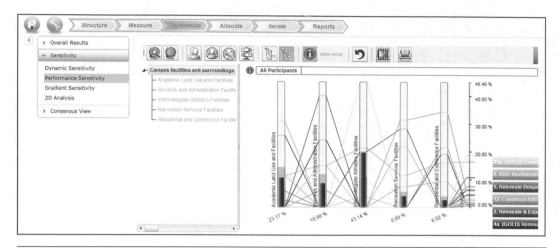

Figure 7.58   Performance sensitivity with intercollegiate athletics facilities priority increase

alternatives can be dramatically modified by adjusting the priorities of an objective. By increasing the priority of one objective, the priorities for the other objectives are reduced. In this case, with the reduction of Academic Land Use and Facilities from 31.15% to 23.17%, the library renovation project has dropped out of the top five projects.

This is another way that AHP and Comparion allow us to play what if. In this case, if Intercollegiate Athletics were to become more important than Academic Land Use and Facilities, fewer academic facilities projects and more intercollegiate athletics projects rise to the top.

ABU Gradient Sensitivity Analysis Example

Gradient sensitivity analysis shows how sensitive the alternatives are to changes in the priority of a single objective by displaying each alternative as a gradient plotted against a single objective as its importance changes from 0% to 100%. Select the "Synthesize" tab, then "Sensitivity" and then "Gradient Sensitivity." A vertical line through the horizontal axis defines the synthesized priority of the objective. The gradients are lines representing each alternative, showing how the relative priority of the alternative changes as the importance of the objective changes. As the objective line is dragged to the right or left, the relative priorities of the alternatives can change. Gradient sensitivity analysis, in particular, enables us to see the point at which the priorities of alternatives change because of a dynamic change in the priorities of a single objective. Figure 7.59 shows the gradient sensitivity for the residential and conference facilities objective that was selected from the drop-down box listing each objective.

If the importance of the Residential and Conference Facilities objective were increased from 8.09% to about 40%, the residential facilities projects become more important than many of the other projects, including academic facilities projects. Figure 7.60 shows that Project 1, Renovate Existing Student Dormitories would become more important than, for example, Project 12, Construct ABU Distance Learning Center.

In this case, the analysis required a considerable increase in the priority of the Residential and Conference Facilities objective to dramatically change the priorities of the alternatives. However, if a slight increase in the priority of an objective significantly changes the priorities of the alternatives, a closer look at the evaluation is warranted to ensure that the results are still acceptable and *right*.

In all three types of sensitivity analysis, the results can be reset to the original priorities of the objectives by selecting the curved arrow symbol on the options icons bar. Sensitivity analysis is

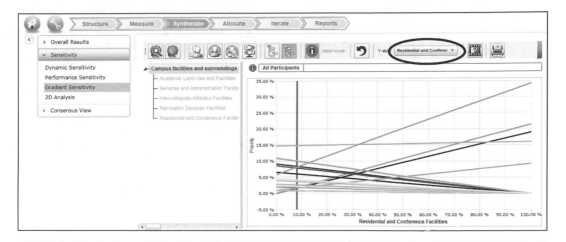

Figure 7.59   Gradient sensitivity for residential and conference facilities

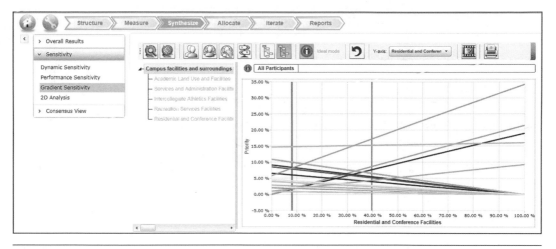

Figure 7.60   Gradient sensitivity of residential and conference facilities increased to ≈ 40%

conducted by the project owner and reviewed with the participants, or performed in a joint session with the evaluators and possibly other interested parties. These analysis techniques provide a means to help confirm the evaluation results or to identify issues that need to be addressed.

ABU 2D Analysis Example

Select "2D Analysis" to see a graph that shows how well the alternatives perform with respect to any two objectives, as shown in Figure 7.61. Select the objective to be represented by the *y*-axis and the objective to be represented by the *x*-axis from the drop-down choices at the top of the screen. The position of an alternative represented by a circle on the plot shows its performance against both selected objectives. In the case of ABU, most alternatives support only one of the objectives, so the plot in Figure 7.57 is not dramatically revealing. However, in an evaluation in which most alternatives support multiple objectives, the alternatives with the most value with respect to the two objectives shown are found in the upper right quadrant (high *y*-axis and high *x*-axis values), while those with

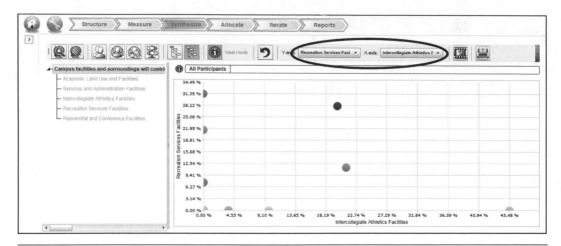

Figure 7.61   Relative performance of alternatives against two selected objectives

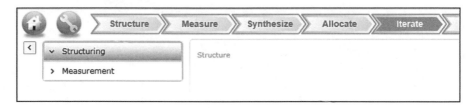

Figure 7.62   Using the "Iterate" tab to transfer back to structuring or measuring

the least value with respect to the two objectives are found in the lower left quadrant (low *y*-axis and low *x*-axis values).

7.8.8 The Need to Iterate

To support ease of iteration, Comparion offers an "Iteration" tab that provides a means to navigate directly back to "Structure" or "Measure," as shown in Figure 7.62. In this case the ABU evaluators believe that the relative priorities of the alternatives are consistent with their intuition and they are comfortable with moving forward with the results as presented.

7.8.9 Review and Present Results and Next Steps

Once the results have been reviewed with the ABU evaluators, the facilitator presents them to the Steering Committee and the ABU facilities department management. The review at this point is merely of the prioritized alternatives and their relative priorities with respect to the facilities goal. The results of prioritizing alternatives are one of the major inputs to the selection of the ABU facilities portfolio. The Steering Committee must approve the prioritization and the suggested next steps to select the optimal portfolio. As will be seen, much remains to be done.

7.9 PRIORITIZED PROJECTS—A MAJOR STEP

Synthesized results of the evaluation provide the relative priorities of the candidate projects with respect to achieving the goal. In essence, these priorities represent anticipated project benefits. By themselves, these priorities, or relative anticipated benefits, are insufficient to select an optimal portfolio because they fail to account for costs as well as other factors, including dependencies between projects and organizational constraints such as funding, critical skills, and resources. However, project prioritization provides an important function by establishing the relative anticipated benefits for each project in terms of achieving the goal and objectives, and it forms the foundation for analyzing the possible project portfolios.

In Chapter 8 we use the project priorities derived in this chapter to develop the initial project portfolio; in Chapter 9 we apply additional organizational constraints and analyze project portfolio scenarios to identify the optimal portfolio of projects given those constraints.

7.10 SUMMARY

In this chapter we demonstrated an important step in the project portfolio selection decision making process; prioritizing alternatives to derive anticipated benefits. The process used to derive these priorities is neither random nor ad hoc. It is instead methodical and disciplined, involving the most appropriate people and using well-established methods and advanced software tools. Using this process, alternatives were transferred into the AHP model and mapped to objectives, the right people were identified and selected to provide judgments to determine anticipated relative project benefits, and sensitivity analysis techniques were used to ensure sense of rightness of the outcome. Throughout, this process maintained focus on and traceability to the organization's strategic plan and resulted in a ratio-scale prioritized list of alternatives. In Chapter 8 we discuss the development of portfolio scenarios and factors to consider in establishing the boundaries of the scenarios with the ultimate intent of deriving the optimal project portfolio.

7.11 REFERENCES

Expert Choice (2011). Comparion Help Screen. http://gwcomparion.expertchoice.com/DocMedia/Help_Silverlight/Measure/Measure_Methods_for_Alternatives.html (retrieved February 24, 2011).

Forman, E. and K. Peniwati (1998). "Aggregating Individual Judgments and Priorities with the Analytic Hierarchy Process." *European Journal of Operational Research*, 108:1 (July) 165-169.

Forman, E. H. and M. A. Selly (2001). *Decision by Objectives*. River Edge, NJ: World Scientific. (Reproduced with permission from World Scientific.)

8

Considerations for Selecting the Initial Portfolio

As discovered in the previous chapter, prioritizing projects is necessary to determine the relative anticipated benefit of each project with respect to the goal, thus establishing the priorities of all candidate projects under consideration for the portfolio. Establishing relative priorities is a key step in the process; yet organizations cannot rely solely on a list of prioritized projects to derive project portfolios by selecting from the top down until funds run out. As will be seen, there are other considerations. However, the prioritized list is the primary input to the next step in the PPM selection phase, selecting an initial portfolio, which is the topic of this chapter, as shown in Figure 8.1.

Selecting project portfolios that provide the greatest opportunity to achieve strategic goals and objectives requires the application of constraints that incorporate organizational realities and limitations. Applying both prioritized projects and organizational constraints yields a portfolio that

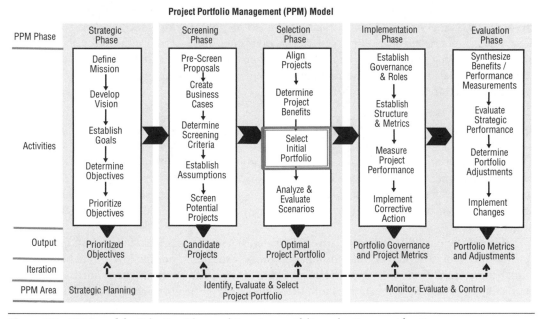

Figure 8.1   PPM model—Selection Phase—determine portfolio evaluation considerations

delivers the greatest anticipated benefit under constraints; this is the optimal portfolio that the organization can undertake given its assumptions and limitations. This chapter introduces the application of funding levels and some types of constraints; including establishing groups to ensure that no more than one alternative is funded for a project with multiple proposed approaches. The Efficient Frontier is introduced as a tool and technique to analyze a range of portfolio options at different levels of funding. In addition, the American Business University (ABU) example is used to produce portfolio scenarios at three different funding levels that are analyzed to produce an initial recommended portfolio. Chapter 9 builds on the portfolio selection concepts described in this chapter and introduces additional organizational constraints and the application of risk to derive the optimal project portfolio under constraints.

8.1 FUNDING LEVELS

Inevitably every organization has limits-constraints—on resources, funding, and critical personnel skills. These constraints directly impact project portfolio selection as well as project success during the execution of the portfolio. They must be considered during portfolio selection to account for limitations of organizational resources. It makes little sense to select a project portfolio that the organization cannot adequately fund or for which it cannot provide sufficient resource either internally or through external sources. In project management terms, organizations strive for projects that are completed on time, within budget, and to customer specifications. Similarly, organizations must expect to undertake project portfolios with a reasonable chance of success. Portfolio success is defined as maximal achievement of organizational goals and objectives under constraints.

Funding for project portfolios is an important consideration for selecting projects for the portfolio and analysis of several funding levels can be of great benefit to the portfolio selection process. There are many reasons an organization may choose to pursue multiple funding scenarios, including changes in access to capital, short term uncertainty regarding the organization's financial status, organizational budgets in process but not yet finalized, or sudden changes in the operating environment. Analyzing scenarios with varying funding levels allows the organization to evaluate which scenario provides the best relative value based on the funding conditions or other assumptions underlying the scenario. Using project portfolio management (PPM) software tools such as the Expert Choice Resource Aligner makes developing scenarios based on varying levels of funding easy. Each funding scenario, including its respective assumptions and constraints, can be saved within the software and revised or deleted as conditions and assumptions change, for example, as uncertain budgetary conditions become clearer with more information.

8.2 SELECTING THE INITIAL PROJECT PORTFOLIO

Once the organization has determined anticipated project benefits through the evaluation process, established a funding level, and defined initial constraints, the initial project portfolio can be selected. Described and demonstrated in the ABU example, an organization's portfolio managers may wish to investigate more than one portfolio that is easily accomplished with the appropriate portfolio selection software.

Selection of a portfolio uses the relative anticipated benefit of the prioritized projects as input, the estimated cost of each project from the business cases, a specified funding level (total budget), and initial constraints. These values, or parameters, are entered into an appropriate portfolio decision modeling tool and used to maximize the anticipated benefit of the portfolio at a given funding level, subject to constraints. Such a set of parameters is called a portfolio scenario. With the right tools an organization can easily evaluate more than one such scenario before selecting an initial portfolio. The

PMB's role in this process is to identify initial portfolios based on previous coordination and guidance from the executive review board and present them to it for review and approval or additional guidance. To make an informed portfolio selection decision, executives need detailed information on each portfolio, including information about the list of projects contained within each suggested portfolio, comparative advantages and disadvantages, the anticipated benefit achieved, and other considerations.

8.3 EFFICIENT FRONTIER

Selecting a project portfolio from a set list of candidate projects requires organizations to evaluate the set of candidates in its entirety, in terms of what the portfolio is expected to cost and to generate in terms of benefits. Mike Gruia (2003) appropriately noted ". . . only using the net present value approach to make investment selections is not sufficient or plausible for portfolio level decisions. This understanding leads us to modern portfolio economics and the adaptation of a powerful investment theory tool—the Efficient Frontier."

Developing individual portfolio scenarios is useful if the organization wants to assess relatively few funding or constraint-based scenarios or conduct preliminary contingency planning. However, we need a more efficient method to analyze a range of options. Developed by Nobel laureate Harry Markowitz and others, the Efficient Frontier is a graphically displayed curve, derived from a portfolio optimization model, illustrating the best possible combinations of project portfolios. It reveals the value (benefits) expected to be created at various levels of available funding while accounting for other resource constraints and organizational considerations.

In 1952, Markowitz published an article "Portfolio Selection" in which he defined modern portfolio theory (MPT). According to MPT, an optimal portfolio is the portfolio that delivers the maximum expected return for a given level of risk (Markowitz, 1952). He further defined risk as the standard deviation of return and sought to diversify assets in a portfolio to minimize the variance of the return. Since then, Markowitz and other researchers in MPT have won the Nobel Prize for Economics; the theory has been widely adopted in finance, and, more recently, has been applied to project portfolio investments. The concept of multiple portfolios, each optimized at a given level of risk, became known as the Efficient Frontier, a model applied later in this chapter to show optimal anticipated or expected benefit at various levels of funding in the project portfolio. The adaptation of MPT to project portfolio selection substitutes the anticipated or expected benefits for risk on the y-axis while maintaining cost on the x-axis. Anticipated benefits are the synthesized relative benefits derived from the evaluation. Expected benefits, as described in the next chapter, factor risk against the anticipated benefits derived from the evaluation results.

Viewing the Efficient Frontier derived from a portfolio optimization model simplifies a complex problem by graphically illustrating the value (benefits) of a range of efficient portfolio outcomes along a curve to help the organization make trade-offs between portfolio value and cost. In addition to examining the curve, more understanding of the trade-offs is obtained by assessing the actual anticipated cost and the list of funded projects at that total cost. More importantly, the Efficient Frontier displays the maximum benefit achievable for each level of funding and shows the incremental benefit obtained for each increment of cost.

In the Efficient Frontier graph, portfolios falling along the curve are efficient because the organization is receiving maximum benefit for the associated portfolio cost. Portfolios can be selected on or below the curve but not above the curve. In a portfolio optimizer such as Expert Choice's Resource Aligner, the combination of projects selected provides the greatest benefit for each budget level considered given the specified constraints. There are many other possible combinations of projects that could be selected at a given budget level under the same constraints, but they would provide less total benefit than the combination selected by the optimizer; in other words, they would fall below the curve. Many organizations order their projects by priority and then select them one by one until they run out of budget. This practice nearly always results in portfolios that provide less than optimal benefits, yielding combinations of funded projects that fall below the curve. Mike Gruia (Levine, 2005) provides a few reasons to account for why portfolios fall under the curve, including too many low value projects and significant mismatch between supply and demand of skill competencies. These result in portfolios with less benefit than could be the case at a given level of funding. Factors contributing to the selection of portfolios below the curve should be further analyzed.

A sample Efficient Frontier is illustrated in Figure 8.2. Each new entrant selected for a portfolio is displayed along the curve by a dot. Portfolio cost is plotted along the x-axis while the percentage of total anticipated benefit obtained by the portfolio is plotted on the y-axis at each point. Cost increases as we move from left to right on the x-axis while the percentage of benefits received increases as we move from the bottom to the top on the y-axis. The points plotted along the curve represent the Efficient Frontier or optimal combination of alternatives in terms of benefits for a given portfolio cost. Graphically illustrating various portfolios with increasing costs and value allows the organization to evaluate at what point it is receiving the best value for its investment.

In analyzing the Efficient Frontier curve in Figure 8.2, a positive relationship between cost and benefits is observed. As cost increases, so does the anticipated benefit. However, as the shape of the curve is convex, the relationship between cost and benefits is not equal as we move along the curve from the 0, 0 point. Instead, greater increase in the value per unit of increase in cost is being provided

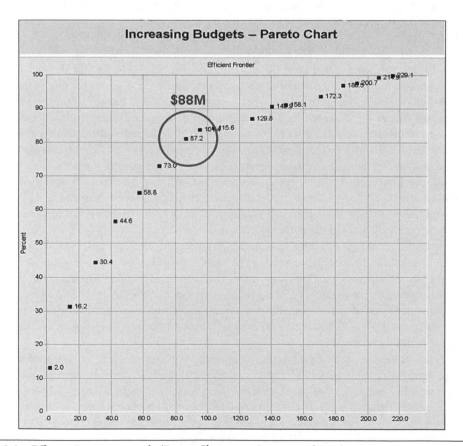

Figure 8.2   Efficient Frontier example (Expert Choice 11.5 Resource Aligner)

in lower parts of the curve with 0-80% of anticipated benefits, as indicated by the steep slope of the curve; and less increase in value per unit of increase in cost shown on the flatter part of the curve with between 80-100% of anticipated benefits. The shape of this curve presents a quandary for the organization, which is to determine at which point the best value is being received for the funding invested. While the organization may have $100M to allocate for a portfolio of projects, does that mean that all $100M should be allocated? Would the decision be different if better value could be achieved at a lower funding level? In this case, better means a greater increment in the total benefit for each unit of increment in cost.

In Figure 8.2, observe that by allocating about $88M the organization can receive ≈ 81% of total benefits. Yet, for an additional ≈ $132M, the organization only receives an additional ≈ 19% of benefits. Is the additional investment of ≈ $132M worth another ≈ 19% of benefits? Again, the graphical illustration presented by the Efficient Frontier provides a useful view of a range of portfolios at different budget levels and allows informed and reasoned trade-offs between cost and value while realizing maximum benefit for the capital being invested for the selected portfolio.

The Efficient Frontier can lead to a clear portfolio choice based on analysis of benefits versus costs with all constraints addressed by the portfolio optimization model. However, analysis of the Efficient Frontier may also reveal multiple combinations of portfolios suitable for selection as the portfolio and the choice may not be as obvious as illustrated in our Figure 8.2 example. Instead, the Efficient Frontier analysis may result in more than one portfolio scenario capable of meeting the organization's definition of optimal. For instance, using a portfolio budget of $88M would lead to obtaining approximately 81% of benefits for our example in Figure 8.2. The obvious disadvantage of the $88M portfolio is that it does not achieve 100% of the benefits. The organization may be willing to increase capital investment in the portfolio to gain added benefits even when there are diminishing returns. The added benefit created by a $105M portfolio, although only minimal, may be perceived as worth the added investment.

8.4 CONSTRAINT FOR THE INITIAL PORTFOLIO—GROUPS

As discussed previously in this book, it is common for sponsors to submit proposals with multiple versions of the same project, for instance, a project proposal that specifies three levels of scope and budget requirements: GOLD, SILVER, and BRONZE. The GOLD option might represent the most preferred option while BRONZE would represent a scaled-down and least-preferred option. The SILVER option would be somewhere between in terms of scope and budget. In a mutually exclusive relationship, only one of these options can be selected. When one of these projects is selected, the other options are excluded. To select the portfolio, we must disallow the selection of more than one of these options.

Establishing groups that are collections of alternatives that are related in some way, such as the ABU projects that have multiple approaches, is one a technique used to represent relationships among portfolio candidates. Grouped alternatives (candidate projects) are subject to one of three group constraints in terms of how many of the group can be funded during portfolio selection, including ≤ 1, = 1, and ≥ 1. The ≤ 1 constraint allows for no more than one alternative to be selected but provides flexibility to select none if appropriate. The = 1 constraint mandates that one and only one alternative from the group must be selected for the scenario. Finally, the ≥ 1 constraint specifies that at least one alternative must be selected but provides the flexibility to select every project in the group if appropriate.

Thus, assigning the ≤ 1 constraint to this group ensures that no more than one of the project approaches will be funded. As the scenario parameters change, it is expected that different options will be selected. Although the GOLD option may provide the most benefit of the group of three approaches, when considered in the context of the entire portfolio scenario, the BRONZE option may enable a portfolio with greater total benefit.

Having explored many of the basic portfolio selection concepts, we will use the ABU Campus Revitalization example to illustrate how to implement these concepts with Expert Choice decision support software tools.

8.5 ABU INITIAL PORTFOLIO SELECTION EXAMPLE

The ABU Campus Revitalization Program was initiated as the result of an unexpected $200M endowment from prominent alumni. The Board of Trustees initially envisioned utilizing the endowment to start all projects at the same time or as soon as possible. However, concerns were raised from the student body and local community that this strategy would create significant disruption on campus and negatively impact the local community. Further, the students wanted assurances that projects would be distributed to provide maximum benefit to all educational interests. As a result of stakeholder concerns and new information, the Steering Committee was directed to evaluate and select an initial project portfolio based on specified funding levels and known constraints that included establishing project groups to ensure no more than one of multiple approaches to the same project is funded.

8.5.1 ABU Initial Project Portfolios

Accordingly, the initial project portfolio evaluation is based on funding levels for each of the following portfolio scenarios—$200M (base), $50M, and an alternate portfolio scenario that provides the most benefit while limiting negative impact to the campus and the local community and ensuring appropriate project oversight by campus facilities management. No dollar amount was specified for this portfolio. The $200M scenario represents the total portfolio of projects that can be undertaken with the $200M endowment. The $50M scenario is a funding limit established by the Board of Trustees at the request of the local community and represents community leadership's view of how much of the endowment could be spent without disruption to the local community. Finally, the Steering Committee has been tasked with determining the optimal combination of projects that can be completed to provide the most benefit, while limiting disruption on campus and in the local community. For this third scenario the Steering Committee agreed to use the Efficient Frontier to determine the portfolio with the greatest benefit for the funding required. The resulting recommendations are intended to be used by the Board of Trustees to reach a consensus on a reasonable portfolio solution for all stakeholders at the next quarterly meeting with community leaders and campus representatives.

In considering projects for the portfolio, the Board of Trustees provided the following guidance in selecting projects for each scenario. The Steering Committee must be cognizant of which area of campus each project will affect to avoid consolidating all projects in one localized area. The Steering Committee should also be aware that new construction projects on heretofore undeveloped ABU property will be less disruptive to the community and the campus than changes to existing facilities.

To analyze various portfolio scenarios, the Expert Choice Resource Aligner module or its equivalent is required. The Resource Aligner allows organizations to select an optimal project portfolio subject to constraints such as budget, resources, balance and coverage, and dependencies among projects.

8.5.2 Preparing the Model

To reinforce the concepts presented, the reader should access the ABU file containing the prioritized objectives and candidate projects prepared in Chapters 4 and 7, and then follow the steps in this chapter to learn how to select the initial portfolio, create portfolio scenarios, and analyze the Efficient Frontier. If your example model was created in Expert Choice Desktop rather than Comparion, simply open it on your workstation with Expert Choice Desktop. If the evaluation model you have completed thus far was prepared in Comparion, it must first be downloaded to the Expert Choice Desktop Resource Aligner. To do so, simply open the project in Comparion, select the "Allocate" tab, "Resource Allocation and Alignment" step, and then select "Download Comparion project to Expert Choice Desktop and use Resource Allocation feature" area as shown in Figure 8.3.

The "File Download" window opens as shown as in Figure 8.4. Select "Save" to save the file in a location of your choice. Click on "Save" and complete the download process to your workstation. Alternatively, simply open the file in Expert Choice Desktop without saving and begin work immediately by selecting "Open".

If saved, the file can be opened directly in Expert Choice Desktop as described in Chapter 4, Appendix 4A. Open the file just downloaded from Comparion or the one that you prepared earlier in Expert Choice Desktop. When the model is downloaded from Comparion, it is necessary to recalculate the results in Expert Choice, in which case simply select "Yes" when presented with the opportunity as shown in Figure 8.5. If the model was prepared directly in Expert Choice Desktop, this choice is not presented. Select "Yes" again when asked "Recalculate for all participants?"

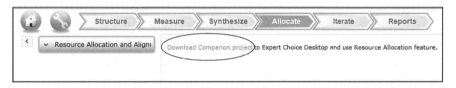

Figure 8.3   Prepare to download model from Comparion to Expert Choice

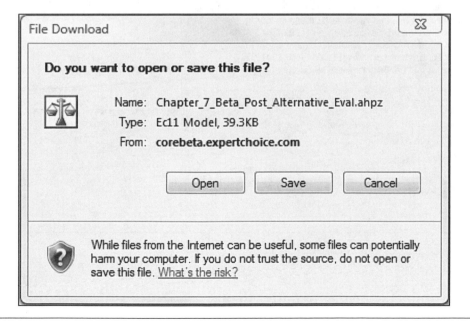

Figure 8.4   Select Expert Choice "File" format and "Save" to workstation

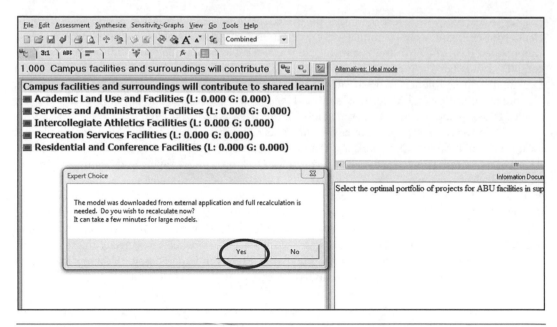

Figure 8.5   Recalculate the results in Expert Choice after download from Comparion

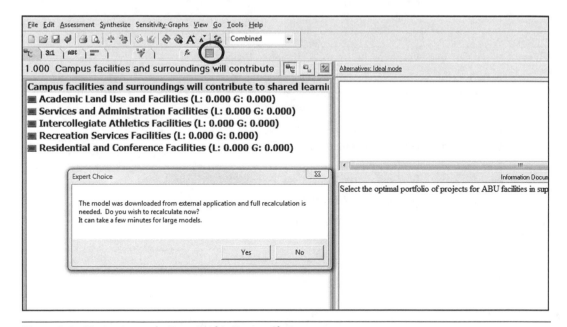

Figure 8.6   Navigating to the Data Grid in Expert Choice

8.5.3 Introduction to the Resource Aligner

Now that the evaluation model has been downloaded, cost and constraint information is entered using the Resource Aligner to prepare the three portfolio scenarios and determine the recommended initial portfolio. To navigate to the Resource Aligner, first select the "Data Grid" icon as shown in Figure 8.6.

Expert Choice shows the grid view of alternatives and objectives displayed in Figure 8.7 with the normalized local priorities of each alternative shown in the grid for each objective the alternative supports. Black elements in the grid indicate objectives to which an alternative does not contribute. Note that the default view shows the combined results. Navigate among the menus and use the help menu to learn the functions performed in this view.

Select "View" and "Totals Column" and note that the "Total" column in Figure 8.8 shows the relative benefit contribution of each alternative to the goal as derived from the evaluation model. The

AID	Alternative	RATINGS Academic Land Use and Facilities (L: .311 G: .311)	RATINGS Services and Administration Facilities (L: .255 G: .255)	RATINGS Intercollegiate Athletics Facilities (L: .236 G: .236)	INCR Recreation Services Facilities (L: .117 G: .117)	DIRECT Residential and Conference Facilities (L: .081 G: .081)
A1	1. Renovate Existing Student Dormitories					.555
A2	2. Renovate & Expand Davidson Student		1.000			
A3	3. Construct Dr. Mary Haven Student Housing					.627
A4	4a. (GOLD) Renovate & Expand C.W. Benson	.836				
A5	4b. (SILVER) Renovate & Expand C.W. Benson	.187				
A6	4c. (BRONZE) Renovate & Expand C.W.	.081				
A7	5. Renovate Benjamin Stadium & Field house			.438	.897	
A8	6. Renovate Mason Hall Research Center	.365				
A9	7. Construct ABU Medical Clinic		.602			
A10	8. ABU Revitalization Program Regulatory &	.367	.372	.466	.367	.469
A11	9. Construct Paisley Hall Student Services		.372			
A12	10. Renovate Deluth Hall Dining Facility				.238	.271
A13	11a. (GOLD) Construct ABU Indoor Athletic			1.000		
A14	11b. (SILVER) Construct ABU Indoor Athletic			.212		
A15	11c. (BRONZE) Construct ABU Indoor Athletic			.082		
A16	12. Construct ABU Distance Learning Center	1.000				
A17	13. Expand Campus Share Ride Services		.149		1.000	1.000
A18	14. Construct Campus Theatre				.688	
A19	15. Construct ABU Faculty Technology &	.420				

Figure 8.7   Grid of alternatives and objectives with priorities

AID	Alternative	Ideal mode Total	RATINGS Academic Land Use and Facilities (L: .311 G: .311)	RATINGS Services and Administration Facilities (L: .255 G: .255)	RATINGS Intercollegiate Athletics Facilities (L: .236 G: .236)	INCR Recreation Services Facilities (L: .117 G: .117)	DIRECT Residential and Conference Facilities (L: .081 G: .081)
A1	1. Renovate Existing Student Dormitories	.045					.555
A2	2. Renovate & Expand Davidson Student	.255		1.000			
A3	3. Construct Dr. Mary Haven Student Housing	.051					.627
A4	4a. (GOLD) Renovate & Expand C.W. Benson	.260	.836				
A5	4b. (SILVER) Renovate & Expand C.W. Benson	.058	.187				
A6	4c. (BRONZE) Renovate & Expand C.W.	.025	.081				
A7	5. Renovate Benjamin Stadium & Field house	.208			.438	.897	
A8	6. Renovate Mason Hall Research Center	.114	.365				
A9	7. Construct ABU Medical Clinic	.154		.602			
A10	8. ABU Revitalization Program Regulatory &	.400	.367	.372	.466	.367	.469
A11	9. Construct Paisley Hall Student Services	.095		.372			
A12	10. Renovate Deluth Hall Dining Facility	.050				.238	.271
A13	11a. (GOLD) Construct ABU Indoor Athletic	.236			1.000		
A14	11b. (SILVER) Construct ABU Indoor Athletic	.050			.212		
A15	11c. (BRONZE) Construct ABU Indoor Athletic	.019			.082		
A16	12. Construct ABU Distance Learning Center	.311	1.000				
A17	13. Expand Campus Share Ride Services	.236		.149		1.000	1.000
A18	14. Construct Campus Theatre	.080				.688	
A19	15. Construct ABU Faculty Technology &	.131	.420				

Figure 8.8   Viewing the "Total" column showing benefit for each alternative

236

total for a project alternative is calculated by summing the global priorities of the alternative for all the objectives it supports and maintains its ratio-scale properties.

The benefit for an alternative for a given objective is the product of its local priority and the global priority of the covering (lowest level) objective or sub-objective; so, for Project 4a it is calculated as $0.836 \times 0.311 = 0.260$. For Project 5, it is calculated as $(0.438 \times 0.236) + (0.897 \times 0.117) = 0.208$, since Project 5 supports two objectives.

The value in the "Total" column is the same value shown in the Resource Aligner "Benefit" column for the alternative as seen in Figure 8.9. "Total" and "Benefit" are just two different names for the same information. Next, select the Resource Aligner icon circled in Figure 8.8 to move to the Resource Aligner module.

Figure 8.9 shows the ABU Campus Revitalization Program candidate projects, including, in the "Benefit" column, the calculated benefit for each shown in the "Total" column in the grid in Figure 8.8. The sum of the candidate project (or alternative) benefits is 2.778 in this case, the total of the individual calculated benefits for the alternatives; it represents the maximum achievable benefit to be obtained if all candidate projects could be selected for the project portfolio.

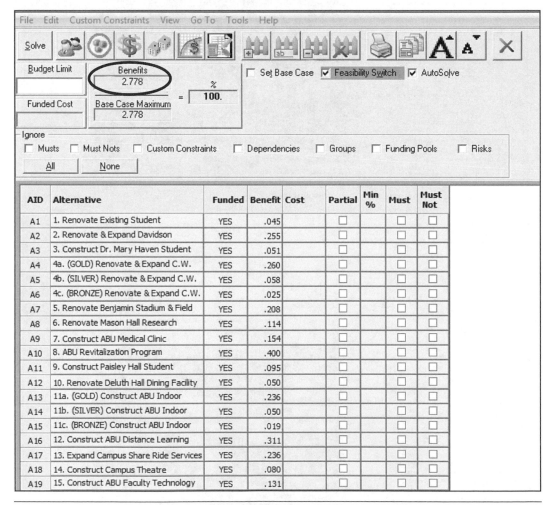

Figure 8.9 Resource Aligner showing project benefits and total benefit with "All" selected

In this example not all projects can be selected regardless of the available budget. For example, only one of the alternatives for Project 4 and only one of the alternatives for Project 11 can be selected because Projects 4 and 11 have GOLD, SILVER, and BRONZE alternative approaches; only one at most can be selected for each of the two projects. Therefore, the total benefit is not truly realistic because it contains the costs for all three alternatives for each of the two projects. During the discussion of groups later in this chapter, you will learn how to ensure that the correct benefits and costs are reflected in the model.

The benefits displayed by default are the actual ratio-scale numbers calculated in the decision model. It is easier for many people to understand the relative benefits to be obtained by alternatives if the benefits are normalized, with the alternative having the highest benefit receiving a normalized benefit of 1.000 and all others calculated as a relative percentage of 1.000. Thus, Project 8, ABU Revitalization Program, with an un-normalized benefit of 0.400, will receive a normalized value of 1.000, while the benefit for all others is divided by 0.400 to yield the normalized benefit. For example, Project 11b that has an un-normalized value of 0.050 will have a normalized value of 0.050/0.400 = 0.125. To use the normalized benefits, close the Resource Aligner and, in the Data Grid, use the "Totals" menu "Normalize" and select "% of Maximum" as shown in Figure 8.10. Other choices are "Priority" that calculates the relative values as a percent of the total and the value of all alternatives sums to 1.000 or "Multiple of Minimum" that sets the value of the alternative with the lowest benefit to 1.000. In this case that value is assigned to Project 11c, and all other benefits are recalculated as a ratio of their values to 1.000. For now, proceed through the example leaving the benefits un-normalized.

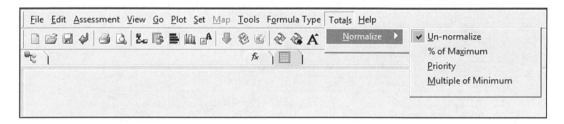

Figure 8.10   Normalizing the benefits

Before any constraints are entered, Resource Aligner shows "YES" in the "Funded" column for all alternatives. Costs for each alternative are entered from the information provided in the business cases accompanying each project, as shown in Figure 8.11. When cost is entered for an alternative, the former "YES" in the "Funded" column becomes "NO" because a "Budget Limit" has not yet been specified, and thus, any cost exceeds it.

The costs can be typed in one at a time, but a simpler way is to copy the cost column from an Excel spreadsheet and paste it into the "Cost" column in the Resource Aligner. To format the number, such as for the number of decimal places to show, use the "View" menu, then "Format."

To see any column added to the Resource Aligner in the Data Grid, use the "Edit" menu and then "Export columns to Data Grid" as shown in Figure 8.12. Select which columns from Resource Aligner to view in the Data Grid. This function inserts Resource Aligner columns into the Data Grid, along with the ability to insert user-defined columns. The columns in the Data Grid can be exported to Excel later or mapped to external databases, thus supporting import and export of data to and from the Data Grid; note that this function works with the Data Grid rather than directly with the Resource Aligner module.

Let's add the "Funded" column to the Data Grid. Select "Funded" under "Available RA columns:" in Figure 8.12 and click on the arrow pointing to the right. This places "Funded" in the "Columns to export"; click on "Export" at the lower right to export the selected columns. After Resource Aligner is

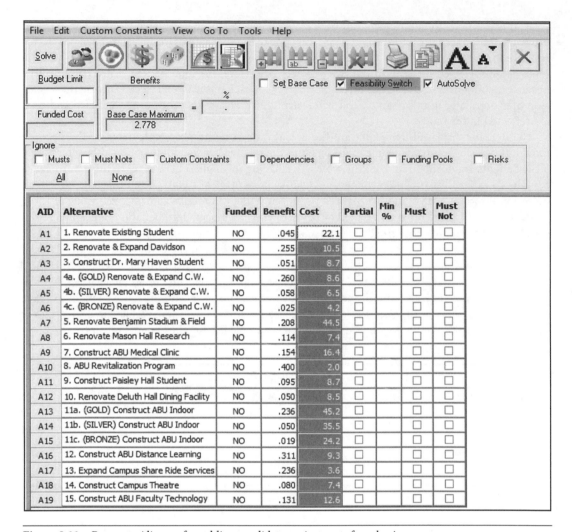

Figure 8.11   Resource Aligner after adding candidate project costs from business cases

closed, you will see the "Funded" column in the Data Grid as shown in Figure 8.13. Of course, since no projects are selected for the portfolio yet, all the entries in the "Funded" column at this point are "NO," indicating they are not funded.

The "Cost" and "Total" columns are automatically synchronized between the Resource Aligner and the Data Grid, so it is not necessary to explicitly export them. However, to actually view them in the Data Grid, go to the Data Grid "View" menu and select the column types to be displayed. Remember, the "Total" column in the Data Grid is called "Benefit" in the Resource Aligner.

To close the Resource Aligner window, select the "x" in the upper right corner of the window. When prompted whether to save the designated Resource Aligner specifications, as shown in Figure 8.14, select "Yes." This preserves the information and parameters established; by failing to select "Yes", the specifications will not be saved in the model and will need to be reentered. For example, unless you respond "Yes," the cost data just entered will not be preserved and will be blank the next time you open the Resource Aligner. Once a set of information is saved, the information remains saved even if you respond "No" when asked whether you want to save, thus, it is only necessary to respond "Yes" after you have added or modified any data or constraints.

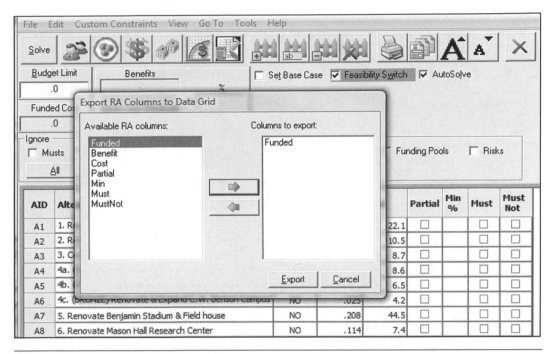

Figure 8.12   Export columns to Data Grid

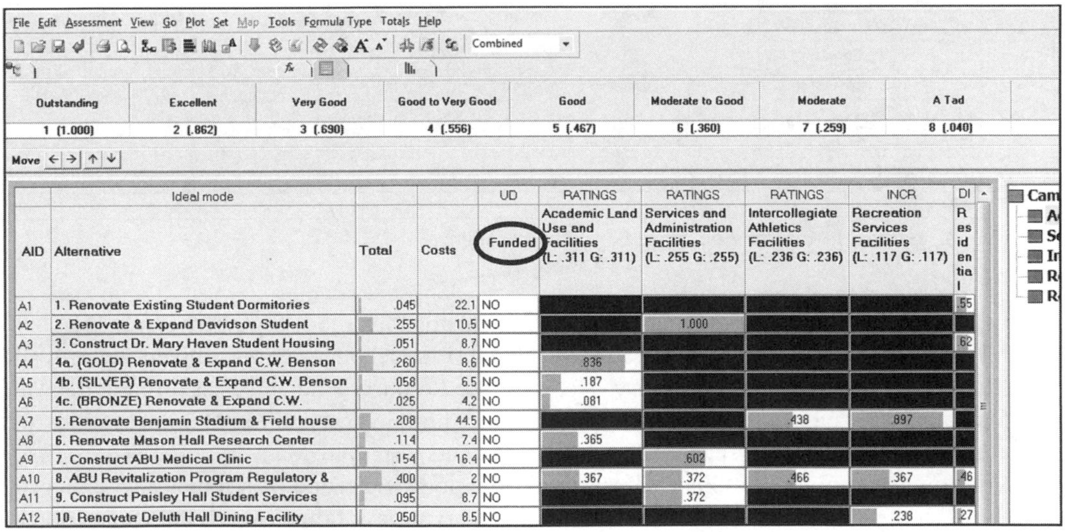

Figure 8.13   Funded column in Data Grid after export from Resource Aligner

After the Resource Aligner window is closed, changes to the model are preserved by saving the file using the "File" menu and "Save". To change the file name in order to maintain a copy of the model after each major step, use "File," "Save As" and type a new meaningful file name as shown in Figure 8.15. Doing so will enable you to restart at any major step of the analysis without having to repeat all the steps.

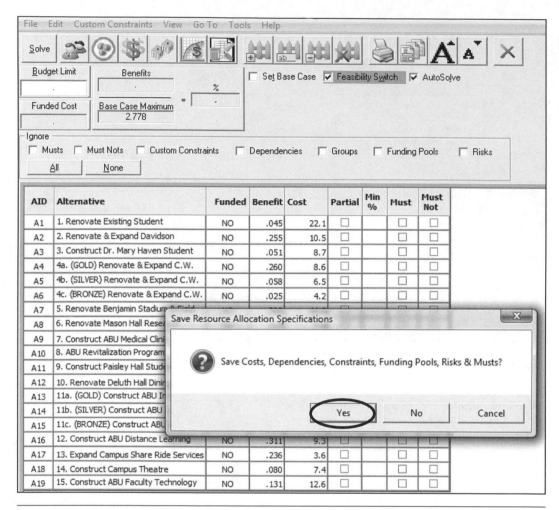

Figure 8.14   Saving the information created in Resource Aligner

The Resource Aligner provides an extremely powerful portfolio modeling capability. In this chapter and the next, several of its capabilities are explained. However, many of the inherent features and subtleties are not described. The objective is to introduce Resource Aligner basics through the ABU portfolio analysis examples. For more information, use the "Help" menu to obtain definitions and explanations of parameters, menu items, and other elements displayed. Many important concepts are explained quite well in the "Resource Aligner-Main Window" topic, and we strongly advise that you read it. Select the "Search" tab in Expert Choice Help and type any of the items on the screen into the keyword box, for example "Feasibility Switch," to bring up the topic.

8.5.4 Preparing for ABU Initial Portfolio Selection

Before proceeding with the initial selection of the ABU Campus Revitalization Program portfolio, recall that some projects have multiple approaches, each requiring a different level of funding. One project, Project 2, was discussed in Appendix 6B of Chapter 6. Its sponsors defined three approaches with three different funding requirements, and they wanted to select only one of them for further consideration in the list of candidates, therefore, they conducted a separate evaluation. Two other

Figure 8.15   Saving the file with a new name

project sponsors, for Project 4 and Project 11, each also having three approaches with different funding requirements, decided to submit all three as candidates; the sponsors are willing to accept any of the three approaches as members of the portfolio. Of course, the total cost for the ABU facilities candidate projects is dependent on which of the three alternatives is selected for each of Projects 4 and 11. In addition, it makes sense that only one of the three approaches for each project is selected. Also, the cost for Project 2 must be determined.

Project 2, Renovate and Expand Davidson Student Services Center, as discussed in Appendix B of Chapter 6, had three approaches with three different costs. Only the cost of the approach selected during the Davidson evaluation is relevant:

1. Demolish and build a larger new Davidson Student Services Center (most costly)

   Benefit: Will accomplish all objectives with a clean start and a known vertical expansion
   Risk: Longer disruption of student services
   Cost: $30M

2. Renovate Davidson with an expansion by 20,000 square feet

   Benefit: Will accomplish all objectives in a shorter period of time
   Risk: Expansion must be vertical so original structure must support additional floors
   Cost: $10.5M

3. Renovate Davidson at current size and relocate back office services to off-campus location

   Benefit: Least costly and lengthy
   Risk: Does not provide co-location of all services functions, introducing staff inconvenience
   Cost: $5.2M

Using Comparion, the Davidson Choice evaluation team selected the second option; thus, $10.5M was entered as the cost for Project 2.

ABU Groups for Projects with Multiple Alternatives

Prior to solving for the best portfolio of projects at a given budget level according to the three scenarios prescribed to the Steering Committee by the Board of Trustees, it is necessary to ensure that for the two projects that have GOLD, SILVER, and BRONZE alternatives, no more than one of the three alternatives is selected for each of them. This applies to Project 4 (Renovate & Expand C. W. Benson Library) and Project 11 (Construct ABU Indoor Athletic Complex). To ensure that this is the case, we will establish groups for the three projects for both Projects 4 and 11 and specify a constraint to select no more than one project from each group.

To get started, reopen the model if closed, go to the "Data Grid" and then select the "Resource Aligner" icon as shown in Figure 8.8. To manage the two projects with multiple approaches, use the "Groups" function in the Resource Aligner. Note the row of icons across the top of the Resource Aligner window directly under the menu bar. Hover over each icon to discover the functions it provides. Select the icon for "Groups" as shown in Figure 8.16.

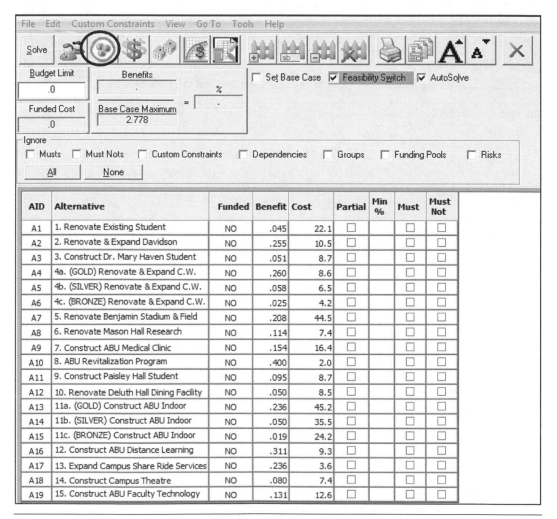

Figure 8.16   Select the groups icon to establish a group

Selecting "Groups" opens a new window as shown in Figure 8.17. The functions in this window allow you to add, edit, or remove a group, remove all groups, and add and remove alternatives from groups. It also displays possible rules that can be applied to a group under the "Group ID Legend," specifying how many alternatives can be chosen from a specific group.

In this case we want to create a group for Alternatives 4a, 4b, and 4c and another group for Alternatives 11a, 11b, and 11c. In each case allow the number of alternatives that can be selected from the group to be ≤ 1. Choosing this option means that, at most, only one project may be chosen for each group, and it allows for the possibility that none of the three alternatives in each group need be selected. Groups provide a means to impose constraints for multiple approaches to the same project. Other types of dependencies among projects are introduced in Chapter 9. Choose the "Add Group" icon and specify the group name and group type for the Project 4 alternatives as shown in Figure 8.18.

Once the group has been created, select it by clicking on its name on the right side of the window, and then highlight each of the three alternatives on the left side of the window and select the "Add Alternative" icon in turn, as shown in Figure 8.19, or hold down the CTRL key and select multiple alternatives until all three are shown on the right side of the window. Respond "Yes" when asked whether to add each alternative to the group. Note the manner in which Expert Choice identifies the alternatives under the "AID" column as shorthand used throughout the model for alternative IDs. These are permanent identifiers for the alternatives that are automatically generated when the model is created.

When the group is complete, the same procedure can be followed to add the second group for the Indoor Athletic Complex Alternatives.

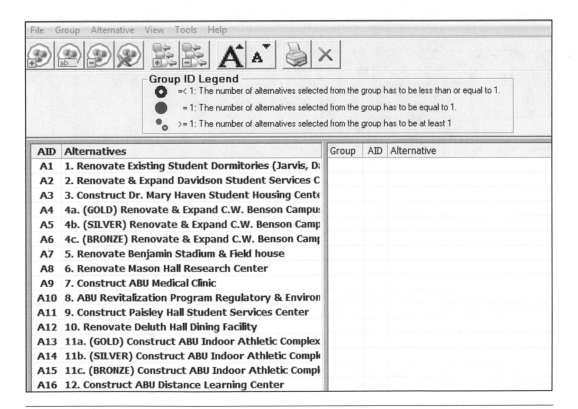

Figure 8.17 Groups Window functions

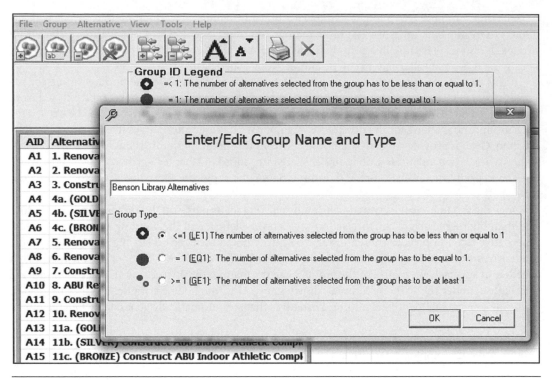

Figure 8.18 Create group for Benson Library project alternatives

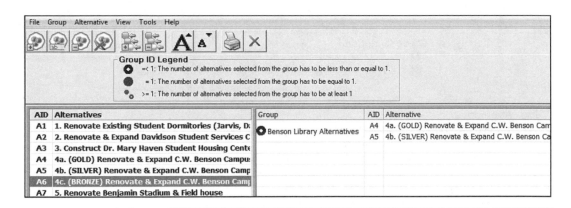

Figure 8.19 Adding the alternatives to the Benson Library group

In our earlier work, remember that the maximum benefit of 2.778 represented the total benefit for all projects, as shown in Figure 8.20. However, that total included the benefits for all three alternatives for Project 4 and all three alternatives for Project 11, so it is an overstated maximum benefit. It is not possible to achieve 100% of the stated benefits using this number, so the portfolio would always fall short even if the budget provided were large enough to accommodate all projects. It is more realistic to direct the Resource Aligner to consider constraints such as those imposed by groups when calculating the percent of maximum benefit attained for any budget level. To accomplish that, check the "Set Base Case" as shown in Figure 8.20 and select the box next to "Groups." Notice that the "Base Case Maximum" achievable benefit when constraints are considered is now 2.626 rather than

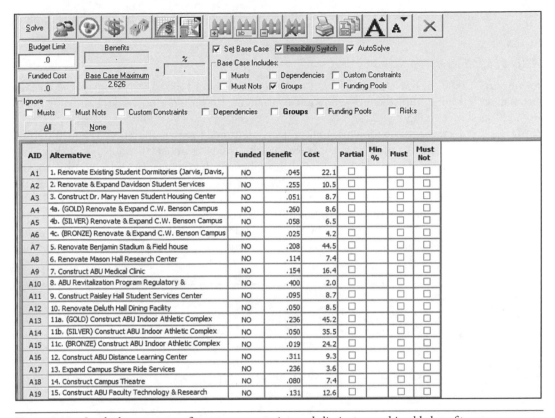

Figure 8.20   Set the base case to reflect group constraints and eliminate unachievable benefits

2.778. The reduction represents the elimination of consideration of the benefits for the SILVER and BRONZE alternatives for Projects 4 and 11 in the possible total, since the maximum benefits for each of these projects can only be achieved through the selection of the GOLD alternative.

Note also the "Feasibility Switch" option shown in Figure 8.20; if checked it will have a green background on the screen when there is a feasible portfolio solution and will turn red when a constraint or budget option is entered that results in an infeasible solution, such as establishing a constraint that cannot be satisfied. Also, it is possible to ignore any type of constraint specified by checking its "Ignore" box to show the scenario results as though these constraints were not imposed. In this case the "AutoSolve" box is checked to show the results of any changes immediately. If unchecked the "Solve" button at the upper left is used to recalculate the results.

Assuming the GOLD alternatives are chosen for each of Projects 4 and 11, the costs of all projects can be added and will sum to $215.5M, which is more than the endowment of $200M. Having completed the necessary preparations, the initial ABU facilities portfolios requested by the Board of Trustees can be selected. Although we could have pursued a number of other Resource Aligner capabilities in this preparation such as establishing funding pools, we did not include them all in this example. The reader may wish to experiment with such capabilities by using the Resource Aligner "Help" menu.

8.5.5 ABU Initial Portfolio Selection Scenarios

Recall that the Board of Trustees asked the Steering Committee to provide three portfolio scenarios, one with a budget of $200M, another with a budget of $50M, and an alternate recommended portfolio scenario based on the Efficient Frontier concept that provides the most benefit per unit of investment.

ABU $200M Portfolio Scenario

By entering "200.0" in the "Budget Limit," the Resource Analyzer immediately displays the selected alternatives by highlighting them in yellow and by changing the designation in the "Funded" column to "YES," as shown in Figure 8.21.

As seen, with the entire endowment all projects are funded except the SILVER and BRONZE alternatives for Projects 4 and 11, in accordance with the groups established and Project 1 (Renovate Existing Student Dormitories). Project 1 has a lower benefit than any of the selected projects and costs more than the remaining $6.6M of the $200M available. The "Funded Cost" result shows the total cost of alternatives funded is $193.4M, the total benefits achieved is 2.581 of 2.626, yielding a 98.29% of possible benefits achieved with this portfolio scenario.

A closer analysis of the projects within this portfolio reveals that project locations are widely dispersed across the campus rather than concentrated in a single area. Unfortunately, this portfolio

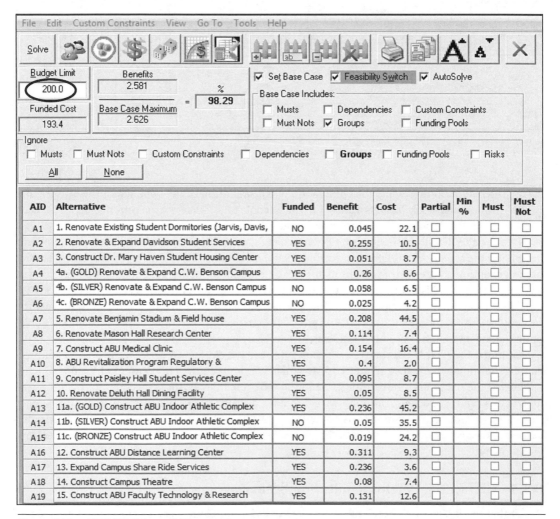

Figure 8.21   ABU $200M portfolio scenario

conflicts with the Board of Trustees' desire to limit the amount of disruption on campus and to the local community due to the volume of concurrent projects.

To save this scenario, use the Resource Aligner "Portfolio Scenarios" icon or "Go To" menu, select "Portfolio Scenarios" and select "New Scenario." Key in the scenario name, in this case "ABU $200 Million" as shown in Figure 8.22, then click "OK."

When asked whether to "Copy existing scenario settings to new scenario," select "Yes" in order to retain constraints, grouping, and other options in the saved scenario.

ABU $50M Portfolio Scenario

The $50M scenario reflects the recommendation community leaders specified as an amount intuitively believed to limit negative impact on the community. As shown in Figure 8.23, this scenario selects Projects 2, 4a, 6, 12, 13, and 14 at a funded cost of $48.8M and provides 63.06% of the program's benefits. The portfolio also seems intuitively to consist of a good mix of renovation versus construction projects that limits the impact on the university and the local community.

Notable in this portfolio selection is that many projects with a higher benefit than Project 14 (Construct Campus Theatre) were not selected. This is because they were not affordable at the $50M budget level, once the first six alternatives with even higher total benefits and affordable costs were funded. In fact, selecting Project 9 (Construct Paisley Hall Student Services Center) would have resulted in a greater benefit than Project 14 with a resulting cost of only $50.1M. The Steering Committee might wish to perform further scenario analysis and present this to the Board of Trustees as a slightly modified alternate scenario for slightly increased cost.

However, in assessing this portfolio against the program's objectives, this portfolio does not provide representation across all objectives. Intercollegiate Athletic Facilities, Recreation Services

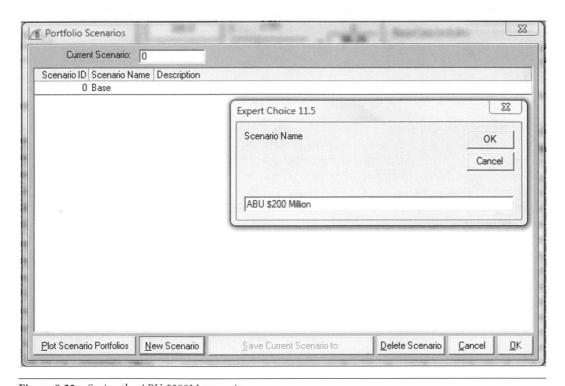

Figure 8.22   Saving the ABU $200M scenario

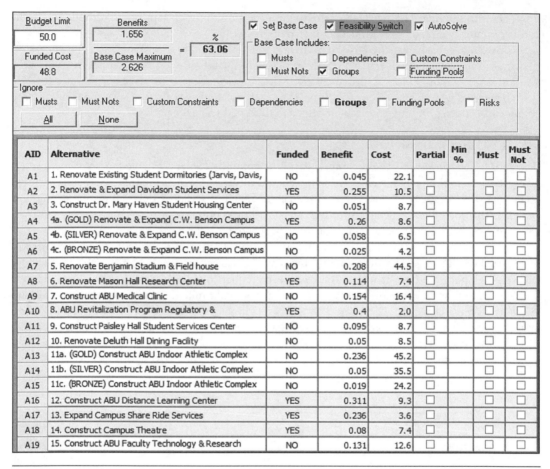

Figure 8.23 ABU $50M portfolio scenario

Facilities, and Residential and Conference Facilities are sparsely represented as compared to Academic Land Use and Services and Administration objectives. Thus, the members of the Steering Committee are concerned that this portfolio does not have a broad enough impact on achieving the objectives across the population of students or the university.

To retain this as a saved scenario, in this case as the ABU $50M scenario, use the Resource Aligner "Go To" menu, select "Portfolio Scenarios," then select "New Scenario" and type in the name of the new scenario, in this case "ABU $50 Million," and click on "OK," then say "Yes," as shown in Figure 8.24.

When asked whether to "Copy existing scenario settings to new scenario," select "Yes." Once these scenarios are saved, they can be instantly recalled by selecting the "Go To" menu, "Portfolio Scenarios," selecting the desired scenario and clicking on "OK" as shown in Figure 8.25. In the example shown in Figure 8.25, the ABU $200 Million scenario had been the scenario most recently used, shown by the number "1" in the "Current Scenario" area. To switch to Scenario 3, "ABU $50 Million," select it and click on "OK" in Figure 8.25. Scenarios are given sequential numbers when saved by the Resource Aligner. If a scenario is saved and then deleted, its number is not reused. Thus, the scenario list skips scenario Number 2 because it had been created and then deleted.

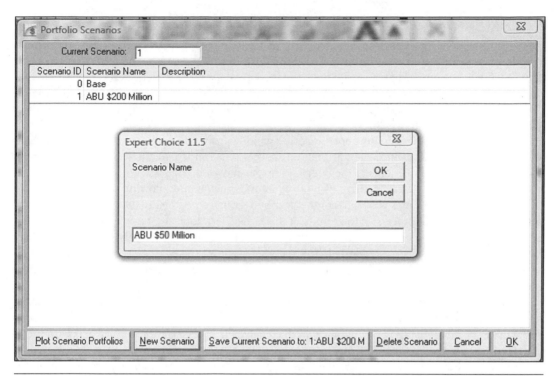

Figure 8.24   Saving the ABU $50M scenario

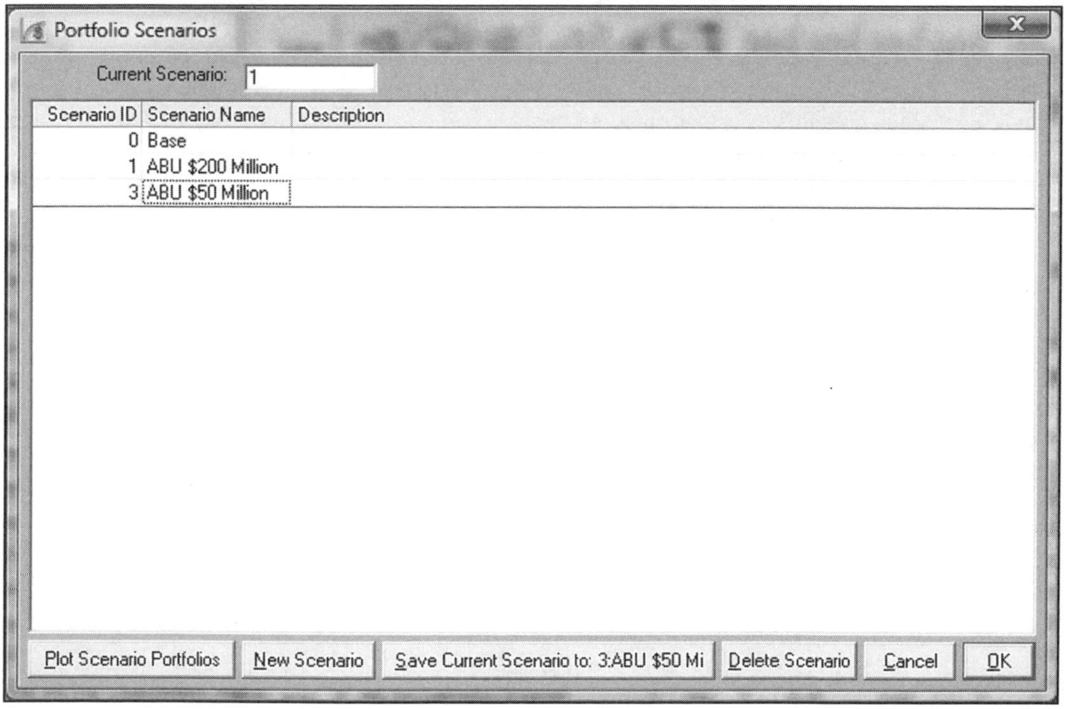

Figure 8.25   Switching to any saved scenario

ABU Alternate Initial Portfolio Using Analysis of the Efficient Frontier

The ABU Board of Trustees asked the Steering Committee to prepare a third proposed portfolio based on assessing the Efficient Frontier. To accomplish this, the Steering Committee relied on the Expert Choice Resource Aligner capability to test incrementally increasing budgets and plot the Efficient Frontier against those increments. This capability is reached in two ways, either by selecting the "Go To" menu and "Increasing Budgets" or by selecting the "Increasing Budgets" icon in Resource Aligner as shown in Figure 8.26.

Performing one of these actions opens another window from which to select parameters such as the number of increments and whether, once an alternative is funded, to allow it to be unselected in favor of one with higher benefits as the budget grows, as shown in Figure 8.27.

For now, leave the default choices of plotting 25 increments and allowing an alternative to be deselected if a different mix is optimal at the next budget increment. Note, however, that portfolio selection is an iterative process; if the results of the earlier iterations are made public, it can be disconcerting to project sponsors to see their projects among those funded, only to find with a later iteration that they have been deselected. This parameter allows the process to be performed either way. In organizations with mature portfolio management processes, such changes are understood and more readily accepted.

To see the ABU Efficient Frontier, click on "Solve" at the upper left to plot the Efficient Frontier at the bottom of the window and to generate the reports. The Efficient Frontier for ABU is shown in Figure 8.28. Note that the percent of achievable benefits is plotted on the vertical axis with increments in cost plotted on the horizontal axis.

The plot and the reports to be explained shortly are contained in three different panes within the same window. The size of the reports and the plot portions can be changed for better viewing by sliding the dividers between the panes.

Although it can be seen that there is a steep and steady increase in benefits for increments in cost until we reach $92.8M, there is a larger increase in cost between $92.8M and $104.2M to obtain an equivalent increase in benefits. The alternatives funded at the $92.8M level could represent our chosen third scenario. However, to be more precise, review the two panes in the middle of the window in Figure 8.29. Each contains information about benefits and costs at a given budget incremental level and each is scrollable independently.

The left pane, shown in Figure 8.29, contains a row for each alternative and a column for each funding level. For each budget increment in the top row, it shows the percent of benefits achieved and the cost for the funded alternatives. It also shows which alternatives are funded by placing the word "FUNDED" in the row for each selected alternative, for each budget increment column, and then leaving the unfunded alternatives at that increment blank.

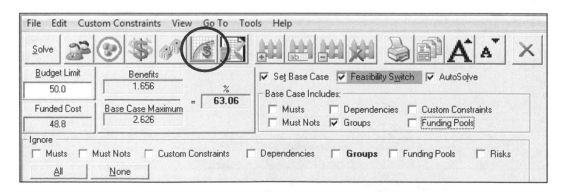

Figure 8.26   Selecting the increasing budgets icon in the Resource Aligner

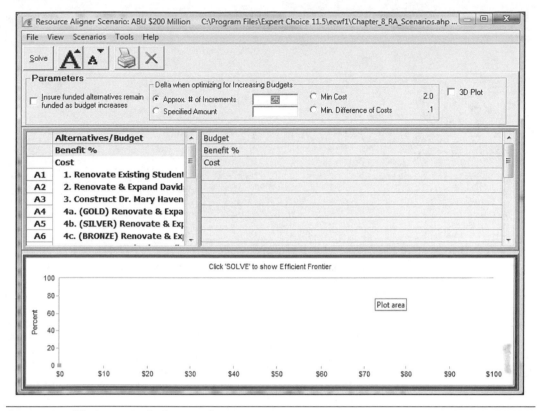

Figure 8.27   The increasing budgets window

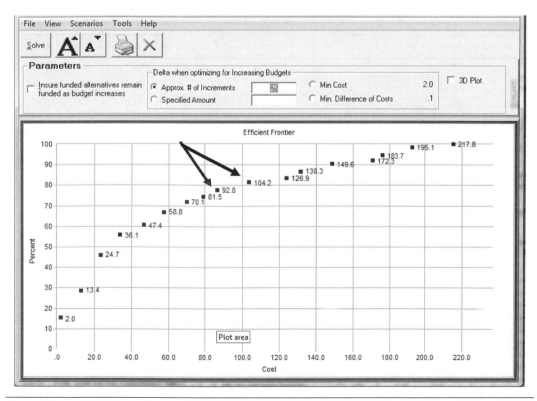

Figure 8.28   ABU Efficient Frontier

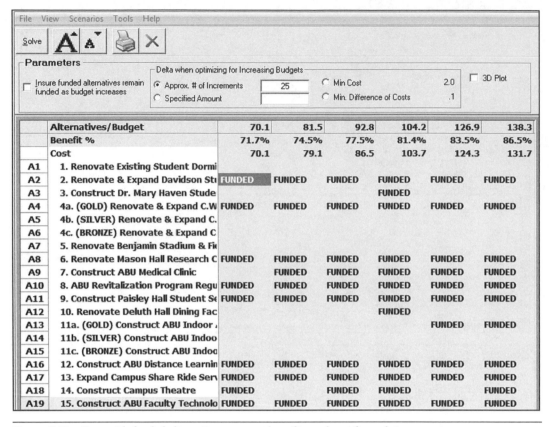

Figure 8.29   Pane with funded alternatives, percent benefits, and cost for each increment

The right pane of the screen, shown in Figure 8.30, displays the same information but with a list of only the funded alternatives instead of all funded and unfunded alternatives.

In addition, each budget increment is between $11.3 and $11.4M in Figure 8.30. Each increment shows which alternatives are funded and not funded, the percent of benefit achieved, and the total actual projected cost. This report helps to confirm that while the increase in the benefit between the $92.8M budget level and the $104.2M budget level is 3.9% (81.4% − 77.5%), the actual incremental cost is $17.2M, or about 19%, to achieve that increased benefit. At the next increment the increase in benefits is even smaller (2.1%) and the increase in cost is even more dramatic ($23.6M), suggesting that the cost of funded alternatives at $86.5M is the best portfolio scenario given the guidance imposed thus far by the Board of Trustees. The resulting portfolio is shown in Figure 8.31.

Comparing Selection by Optimization to Rank Order by Benefit Approach

Note that Figure 8.31 shows that for about 43% of the $200M grant ($86.5/$200), this portfolio achieves over 77% of the possible total benefits for the portfolio candidates. Organizations that do not use optimization such as that just shown using the Resource Aligner often choose to fund only the top-rated projects in terms of benefit until they run out of funds. Sorting ABU candidate projects by benefit results in the prioritized list shown in Table 8.1.

The shaded cells represent the groups created earlier for the three approaches and funding levels for Projects 4 and 11. Only the benefits and the cost for the GOLD level for each of the two projects

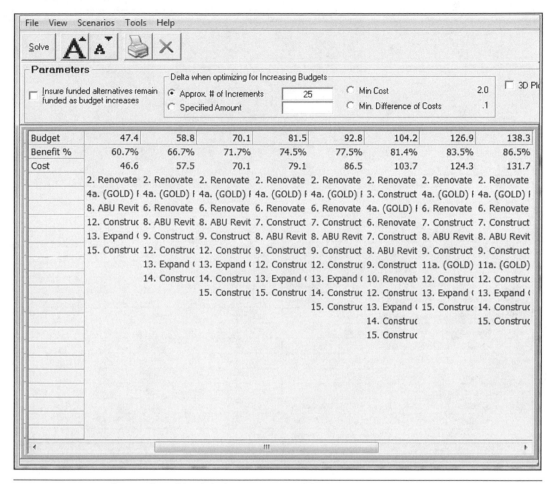

Figure 8.30   Pane showing list of funded alternatives at each budget increment

are counted in the total benefit and total cost; this is equivalent to checking "Groups" in "Base Case Includes" in the Resource Aligner.

Proceeding from the top of the list, we can force the Resource Aligner to select the project with the highest relative benefit, Project 8, followed in turn by Project 12, and so on until the $86.5M budget is exhausted. This occurs at an actual estimated cost of $79.2M, after funding Project 11a, since the project with the next highest priority, Project 5, costs $45.2M, far exceeding the budget. Even with partial funding, only $6.7M is still available given the funding level. With so little partial funding it is doubtful that sufficient progress can be made on Project 5 before the next funding cycle. Fully funding the project would require increasing the budget to $123.7M, an additional $37.2M. We can calculate the anticipated total benefits of this portfolio by hand or force the Resource Aligner to select only the highest priority projects until funds run out, as shown in Figure 8.32.

As can be seen, using the priority ranking method to select the project portfolio results in only 64.66% of the total possible benefits attained while spending about 40% of the total grant of $200M, whereas using the optimization method resulted in a total benefit of 77.53% while spending about 43% of the total grant. Even if we prorate the anticipated benefits for Project 5 using the remaining $6.7M, less than 66% of the benefits are achieved while spending the same 43% of the total grant.

| File | Edit | Custom Constraints | View | Go To | Tools | Help |

Solve

Budget Limit: 86.5
Benefits: 2.036
% = 77.53
Funded Cost: 86.5
Base Case Maximum: 2.626

☑ Set Base Case   ☑ Feasibility Switch   ☑ AutoSolve

Base Case Includes:
☐ Musts   ☐ Dependencies   ☐ Custom Constraints
☐ Must Nots   ☑ Groups   ☐ Funding Pools

Ignore
☐ Musts   ☐ Must Nots   ☐ Custom Constraints   ☐ Dependencies   ☐ **Groups**   ☐ Funding Pools   ☐ Risks

All   None

AID	Alternative	Funded	Benefit	Cost	Partial	Min %	Must	Must Not
A1	1. Renovate Existing Student Dormitories (Jarvis, Davis,	NO	.045	22.1	☐		☐	☐
A2	2. Renovate & Expand Davidson Student Services	YES	.255	10.5	☐		☐	☐
A3	3. Construct Dr. Mary Haven Student Housing Center	NO	.051	8.7	☐		☐	☐
A4	4a. (GOLD) Renovate & Expand C.W. Benson Campus	YES	.260	8.6	☐		☐	☐
A5	4b. (SILVER) Renovate & Expand C.W. Benson Campus	NO	.058	6.5	☐		☐	☐
A6	4c. (BRONZE) Renovate & Expand C.W. Benson Campus	NO	.025	4.2	☐		☐	☐
A7	5. Renovate Benjamin Stadium & Field house	NO	.208	44.5	☐		☐	☐
A8	6. Renovate Mason Hall Research Center	YES	.114	7.4	☐		☐	☐
A9	7. Construct ABU Medical Clinic	YES	.154	16.4	☐		☐	☐
A10	8. ABU Revitalization Program Regulatory &	YES	.400	2.0	☐		☐	☐
A11	9. Construct Paisley Hall Student Services Center	YES	.095	8.7	☐		☐	☐
A12	10. Renovate Deluth Hall Dining Facility	NO	.050	8.5	☐		☐	☐
A13	11a. (GOLD) Construct ABU Indoor Athletic Complex	NO	.236	45.2	☐		☐	☐
A14	11b. (SILVER) Construct ABU Indoor Athletic Complex	NO	.050	35.5	☐		☐	☐
A15	11c. (BRONZE) Construct ABU Indoor Athletic Complex	NO	.019	24.2	☐		☐	☐
A16	12. Construct ABU Distance Learning Center	YES	.311	9.3	☐		☐	☐
A17	13. Expand Campus Share Ride Services	YES	.236	3.6	☐		☐	☐
A18	14. Construct Campus Theatre	YES	.080	7.4	☐		☐	☐
A19	15. Construct ABU Faculty Technology & Research	YES	.131	12.6	☐		☐	☐

Figure 8.31   Alternate portfolio based on Efficient Frontier analysis

Table 8.1 ABU candidate projects sorted by benefit

Alternative	Benefit	Cum Benefit	Cost	Cum Cost
8. ABU Revitalization Program Regulatory & Environmental Approval Project (Enabling Project)	0.400	0.400	2.0	2.0
12. Construct ABU Distance Learning Center	0.311	0.711	9.3	11.3
4a (GOLD) Renovate & Expand C. W. Benson Campus Library (Alternatives Project)	0.260	0.971	8.6	19.9
2. Renovate & Expand Davidson Student Services Center	0.255	1.226	10.5	30.4
13. Expand Campus Share Ride Services	0.236	1.462	3.6	34.0
11a. (GOLD) Construct ABU Indoor Athletic Complex (Alternatives Project)	0.236	1.698	45.2	79.2
5. Renovate Benjamin Stadium & Field House	0.208	1.906	44.5	123.7
7. Construct ABU Medical Clinic	0.154	2.060	16.4	140.1
15. Construct ABU Faculty Technology & Research Center	0.131	2.191	12.6	152.7
6. Renovate Mason Hall Research Center	0.114	2.305	7.4	160.1
9. Construct Paisley Hall Student Services Center	0.095	2.400	8.7	168.8
14. Construct Campus Theater	0.080	2.480	7.4	176.2
4b (SILVER) Renovate & Expand C. W. Benson Campus Library (Alternatives Project)	0.058	2.480	6.5	182.7
3. Construct Dr. Mary Haven Student Housing Center (Off-Campus Facility)	0.051	2.531	8.7	191.4
11b. (SILVER) Construct ABU Indoor Athletic Complex (Alternatives Project)	0.050	2.531	35.5	226.9
10. Renovate Deluth Hall Dining Facility	0.050	2.581	8.5	235.4
1. Renovate Existing Student Dormitories (Jarvis, Davis, and Sewall Halls)	0.045	2.626	22.1	257.5
4c (BRONZE) Renovate & Expand C. W. Benson Campus Library (Alternatives Project)	0.025	2.626	4.2	261.7
11c. (BRONZE) Construct ABU Indoor Athletic Complex (Alternatives Project)	0.019	2.626	24.2	285.9
	2.626		215.5	

Total Benefits from Funded Projects   1.698
Percent Benefits Attained   64.66%

Solve

Budget Limit: 86.5
Benefits: 1.698
Funded Cost: 79.2
Base Case Maximum: 2.626
% = 64.66

☑ Set Base Case   ☑ Feasibility Switch   ☑ AutoSolve

Base Case Includes:
☐ Musts   ☐ Dependencies   ☐ Custom Constraints
☐ Must Nots   ☑ Groups   ☐ Funding Pools

Ignore
☐ **Musts**   ☐ **Must Nots**   ☐ Custom Constraints   ☐ Dependencies   ☐ **Groups**   ☐ Funding Pools   ☐ Risks
All   None

AID	Alternative	Funded	Benefit	Cost	Partial	Min %	Must	Must Not
A1	1. Renovate Existing Student Dormitories (Jarvis, Davis,	NO	.045	22.1	☐		☐	☑
A2	2. Renovate & Expand Davidson Student Services	YES	.255	10.5	☐		☑	☐
A3	3. Construct Dr. Mary Haven Student Housing Center	NO	.051	8.7	☐		☐	☑
A4	4a. (GOLD) Renovate & Expand C.W. Benson Campus	YES	.260	8.6	☐		☑	☐
A5	4b. (SILVER) Renovate & Expand C.W. Benson Campus	NO	.058	6.5	☐		☐	☑
A6	4c. (BRONZE) Renovate & Expand C.W. Benson Campus	NO	.025	4.2	☐		☐	☑
A7	5. Renovate Benjamin Stadium & Field house	NO	.208	44.5	☐		☐	☑
A8	6. Renovate Mason Hall Research Center	NO	.114	7.4	☐		☐	☑
A9	7. Construct ABU Medical Clinic	NO	.154	16.4	☐		☐	☑
A10	8. ABU Revitalization Program Regulatory &	YES	.400	2.0	☐		☑	☐
A11	9. Construct Paisley Hall Student Services Center	NO	.095	8.7	☐		☐	☑
A12	10. Renovate Deluth Hall Dining Facility	NO	.050	8.5	☐		☐	☑
A13	11a. (GOLD) Construct ABU Indoor Athletic Complex	YES	.236	45.2	☐		☑	☐
A14	11b. (SILVER) Construct ABU Indoor Athletic Complex	NO	.050	35.5	☐		☐	☑
A15	11c. (BRONZE) Construct ABU Indoor Athletic Complex	NO	.019	24.2	☐		☐	☑
A16	12. Construct ABU Distance Learning Center	YES	.311	9.3	☐		☑	☐
A17	13. Expand Campus Share Ride Services	YES	.236	3.6	☐		☑	☐
A18	14. Construct Campus Theatre	NO	.080	7.4	☐		☐	☑
A19	15. Construct ABU Faculty Technology & Research	NO	.131	12.6	☐		☐	☑

Figure 8.32   Forcing Resource Aligner to select the highest priority projects until funding is exhausted

The difference in percent of benefits achieved using optimization to select the portfolio rather than selecting projects in order of benefits until the funding runs out is dramatic. Organizations using the rank-order selection process and related approaches are sub-optimizing their project portfolio expenditures. The portfolio selected thus far and shown in Figure 8.31 remains the recommended portfolio.

8.5.6 ABU Initial Portfolio Conclusions and Recommendations

Two of the selected projects, Project 8 (Environmental and Regulatory Permitting) and Project 13 (Expand Share Ride Services), are believed to be low impact projects and will cause minimal disruption to students or the local community. Review of the portfolio against the objectives shows satisfactory representation across all objectives, except Intercollegiate Athletics Facilities. However, the two projects providing the most benefit for this objective will require two years to complete architectural drawings and contracting and thus may not be time critical projects for the initial selection. Nonetheless, the fact that the Intercollegiate Athletics objective is not addressed by any funded project in the preferred scenario must be explicitly stated during the presentation to the Board of Trustees.

Further, review of the mix of projects indicates a broad section of the student population and the university will benefit from this portfolio. Finally, given the combination of projects, the impact on the local community is intuitively not expected to be significantly greater than the impact of the projects funded under the $50M scenario while the benefit is expected to be considerably greater.

The Steering Committee recognizes that this initial portfolio, while it satisfies the constraints already imposed and is within budget guidelines, does not yet fully address the balance of project types and coverage across objectives that the Board of Trustees may wish to impose, and does not include consideration of risk and the potential impact of risk on benefits. The Steering Committee must request guidance from the Board of Trustees about the concerns it has raised and obtain consensus on additional considerations to be addressed before the final portfolio can be prepared and approved. Chapter 9 demonstrates how to impose the necessary constraints to address balance and coverage and how to account for risk in the portfolio model as well as introducing additional types of constraint.

8.6 SUMMARY

Selecting the initial project portfolio with only minimal required constraints, and reviewing different scenarios by simply changing funding levels, is an important step toward identifying and selecting the optimal portfolio. Using portfolio optimization modeling tools and techniques, scenarios can be generated to select project portfolios within the organizational constraints and assumptions specified thus far. Using optimization has been shown to be superior to selecting projects in descending order of priority until funding is exhausted. We have discussed how relationships among projects, such as alternative approaches and budget levels for the same project, can be considered during portfolio selection. In addition, we have shown how different budget scenarios can be used to generate different initial portfolios. These scenarios can represent various sets of organizational assumptions.

For organizations with new or immature PPM processes, the development of initial project portfolio scenarios is a major step beyond traditional ad hoc portfolio selection methods such as BOG-SAT. However, this is not sufficient for selecting the best portfolio for the organization. Risk and other factors must be considered as well when deriving the portfolio. In Chapter 9 we illustrate how accounting for these factors results in the selection of the optimal project portfolio under additional constraints.

8.7 REFERENCES

Gruia, Mike (2003). "The Efficient Frontier Technique for Analyzing Project Portfolio Management," A UMT White Paper (November). UMT, New York, NY.

Levine, Harvey A (2005). "Project Portfolio Management: A Practical Guide to Selecting Projects, Managing Portfolios, and Maximizing Benefits." San Francisco, CA: Jossey-Bass.

Markowitz, Harry M. (March, 1952). Portfolio Selection. *The Journal of Finance*, Volume 7, Number 1: pp. 77-91.

9

Additional Considerations for Selecting the Project Portfolio

In the previous chapter we demonstrated how to select initial project portfolios while accounting for some potential organizational constraints such as grouping alternatives that represent multiple approaches to a project. The American Business University (ABU) example illustrated how stakeholders such as the organization's customers, community, and employees influence the selection of project portfolios. As shown in Figure 9-1, in this chapter we will analyze and evaluate multiple scenarios in order to select the optimal project portfolio for the organization. The chapter introduces other kinds of constraints, including critical resource constraints and project dependencies, and presents methods to ensure portfolio balance and coverage, incorporate risk, and select the organization's optimal portfolio. The discussion of balance and coverage addresses the selection of portfolios with adequate distribution of projects across objectives, divisions, or departments to balance the interests of stakeholders and provide coverage across products lines or business areas in accord with executive direction. In addition, anticipated benefits depend on successfully completing the projects within the portfolio; these anticipated benefits must be tempered by considering risk. This chapter thus also describes how to factor risk or the likelihood of success of the candidate projects into selection of the portfolio.

9.1 ORGANIZATIONAL POWER AND POLITICAL ENVIRONMENT

While we want to select a portfolio of projects that maximizes benefits at a specified cost under certain constraints to achieve strategic goals and objectives, it is also necessary to maintain organizational morale, well-being, and cohesion. Organizations are comprised of human beings with individual behaviors and complex interactions, and it's natural for an organization to develop its own unique internal political and power environment with competing interests and attitudes. The complex dynamics of human interaction, interpersonal relationships, individual personalities and perspectives combined with individual and group responsibilities, positions, and goals all influence business decisions, including selecting project portfolios. Pinto (1998) defines power as the ability to get activities or objectives accomplished in an organization in the way one wants them done, while Cohen (2002) notes politics is defined as the study of who gets what, when, and how. To understand the true nature of the role of politics and power within an organization, Pinto (1998) offers six

Project Portfolio Management (PPM) Model

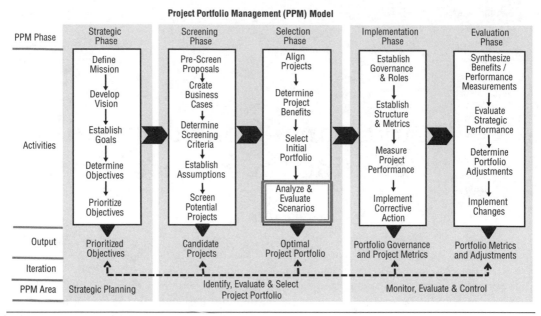

Figure 9.1   Other considerations for selecting the portfolio

propositions with which the portfolio management board (PMB) and project portfolio personnel should be familiar:

1. Most important decisions in organizations involve the allocation of scarce resources. Pinto contends that the majority of important decisions made within organizations involve the allocation or distribution of these scarce resources among a number of competing demands.
2. The decision process often involves bargaining, negotiating, and jockeying for position. Since they cannot obtain all the resources they want due to scarcity, individuals or groups resort to compromise or negotiation to obtain as much as possible at the expense of someone else, and often at the expense of the organization.
3. Organizations are coalitions composed of a variety of self-interested groups. Whether marketing versus finance or project management versus operations management, each group has its own self-interests. These interests may be related to the organization's strategic goals and objectives, but nevertheless provide the foundation for conflict and sub-optimize the organization's achievements.
4. Groups differ in terms of goals, values, attitudes, and timeframes. Pinto (1998) points to a landmark research study conducted by Paul Lawrence and Jay Lorsch (1969) that investigated the manner in which roles and attitudes differ among groups in organizations; they introduced what they called *organizational differentiation*. The concept of differentiation was used to describe the fact that as individuals enter the organization and join a functional group such as accounting or marketing, they develop a set of values and objectives in accord with that functional group as opposed to organization-wide values and objectives.
5. As a result of scarce resources and persistent differences, conflict is central to organizational life. Pinto observed that this proposition forms the underlying rationale behind the political model of organizational life. As differences and contradictions exist within organizational groups, conflict is a natural and reoccurring fact of organizational life.

6. Because conflict is inevitable, the use of power and politics becomes a mechanism for resolving conflict situations. Entities within the organization are aware of the conflicts that occur between individuals and groups and use political influence as a method to resolve this conflict. Pinto contends that political behavior is an important tool for controlling and resolving conflicts in cost-effective and useful ways. As a result, politics can be characterized as a natural consequence of the interaction between organizational entities. This natural view of politics is seen as an expected by-product of company life.

The PMB and others participating in the project portfolio selection process must recognize that conflict is inevitable, understand its source, and manage it constructively. Members of organizations undertaking project portfolio management (PPM) for the first time or increasing the maturity of the process are introducing organizational change, either transformational or incremental. Talking about the vision is not enough to achieve acceptance. Detailed tactical planning, changes in systems of measurement and reward, and frequent communication at all levels, with obvious top management support, are necessary to implement a decision process that surpasses the rule of the loudest voice or most influential person. Even when change is implemented well, conflict still arises. The PMB contributes to reducing concerns or apprehension within the organization's political environment by recognizing that Pinto's dynamic exists and by understanding how to incorporate techniques into portfolio selection to address it. PPM techniques are employed to balance the portfolio and provide coverage across competing interests of the power and political environment.

9.2 BALANCE AND COVERAGE OF PROJECTS ACROSS OBJECTIVES

Pinto's six organizational politics and power propositions illustrate the dynamic nature of an organization's political and power environment. Project portfolio selection personnel in conjunction with senior executives can account (at least partially) for this environment by incorporating constraints into the portfolio evaluation model. These constraints enable the right balance of projects across competing interests while providing project coverage across objectives. These constraints not only help mitigate conflict but also ensure that the resource requirements of organizations do not fluctuate wildly from period to period.

In assessing balance and coverage, Levine (2005) noted "the goal of seeking the right balance (of projects) flows logically from the first goal, strategic alignment. Here the principal concern is to achieve the desired balance of projects in terms of a number of parameters." Some of the parameters described included project duration, degree of risk, and type of product. Defining what balance means to the organization and devising the right considerations for the portfolio scenario are key to the effective use of these constraints—or parameters as Levine calls them. The entire PPM process is governed by senior managers who consider realistic, unique, and sometimes political constraints within their organizations without sacrificing the attainment of organizational goals and objectives.

Projects can be grouped by category such as new product development, research and development, product enhancement, manufacturing, and the like to ensure distribution of projects among types of products, lines of business, or geographies. Using project portfolio software tools, the PMB effectively translates guidance from the executive review board (ERB) into constraints, with parameters that can be varied to produce different portfolio scenarios. For instance, executives may provide guidance to ensure the selection of at least one project for each objective or for each division. In addition, executives may wish to set maximum limits on the number of projects of a certain type or the number of projects selected for each objective. Such constraints prevent satisfying a single objective, no matter how important, at the expense of others and are used to manage the distribution of projects across objectives, business areas, or product lines. Incorporating balance and coverage, in conjunction with other kinds of project portfolio constraints, offers executives powerful capabilities to select portfolios that recognize the organization's unique political and resource environments.

9.3 RESOURCE LIMITATIONS

As described in Chapter 8, every organization has limits on resources. Just as it makes little sense to select a portfolio that exceeds the organization's funding capability, selecting a portfolio that cannot be effectively resourced, either internally or through external sources, is a recipe for failure.

Resources are commonly classified as labor, equipment, and materials and nearly every—if not every—organization has a limited amount of them. The adverse effects of organizational failure to adequately address resource constraints are well-documented. Meredith and Mantel (2006) note three particularly common problems in organizations trying to manage multiple projects; (1) delays in one project disrupt other projects because of common resource needs or dependencies, (2) inefficient use of resources results in peaks and valleys of utilization, and (3) bottlenecks in resource availability or lack of required technological inputs result in delays that depend on those scarce resources or technology.

Although keeping current projects on track is a function of project management rather than a portfolio management issue, identifying and accounting for known resource constraints during the selection of the project portfolio and monitoring progress appropriately can reduce or prevent resource problems. Portfolio resource constraints can be applied within PPM software to prevent over-allocation of critical resources. Numerous studies have been conducted to determine the causes of project failure. One of the primary problems is the lack of availability of critical skills (Young, 2007). Assuming at the time of a candidate project's selection into the portfolio that a critical skill will be available during project execution without resource planning is a mistake.

Accounting for constrained personnel skills such as those noted by Young (2007) during portfolio selection can reduce future problems associated with critical skill availability by setting intelligent limits on such resources. We do not suggest including limits for every skill, rather, specify constraints for those skills determined to be critical to the portfolio. At a minimum, considering constrained critical skills during portfolio selection can identify a shortage that can be addressed without specifying a portfolio selection constraint. If it cannot be adequately managed otherwise, a portfolio constraint can be specified to prevent over-allocation. This results in portfolio scenarios that can be adequately supported during execution and provides an opportunity to remedy an unacceptable skills shortfall.

Equipment and materials can be considered portfolio-level resource constraints in some organizations, such as those that perform specialized construction, leading edge technology development, and pharmaceutical projects. For example, a pharmaceutical company using a certain chemical compound with limited supply across a portfolio of its products could specify a constraint on the number of available units of the compound across the portfolio.

The vast majority of resource constraints are better managed at the project and enterprise project management (EPM) level using EPM software, while others are truly portfolio-level critical resources. For example, a construction company may consider its own project managers to be a critical resource on which the number of concurrent projects in the portfolio depends, while it does not consider the availability of concrete mixers to be important to the portfolio even though it matters for individual projects. Since this example company does not choose to outsource project management, it might believe that the number of qualified project managers is indeed a portfolio-level constraint. On the other hand, the number of concrete mixers the company might need in a given unit of time for all concurrent projects is defined for each project and aggregated across the enterprise's projects using EPM software. The number of concrete mixers the organization owns or rents is deemed flexible, while the number of qualified project managers is not. The PMB must apply judgment to identify the resources that introduce constraints at the portfolio level, versus those at the project or aggregated enterprise project level. The former must be considered in the context of selecting the optimal portfolio(s), while the latter can be addressed by appropriate EPM planning, monitoring, and control.

9.4 OTHER TYPES OF CONSTRAINTS

Several other types of constraint can be introduced into portfolio selection models using tools capable of accommodating them, including Expert Choice's Resource Aligner.

9.4.1 Mandatory and Prohibited Projects

Earlier chapters described that some projects may be considered mandatory such as those necessary to achieve regulatory compliance. A project might also be considered mandatory due to strong feelings on the part of one or more executives, or as a negotiating position. Others may become prohibitive due to excessive cost or the discovery of environmental factors that prevent successful execution or, again, because executives choose to rule it out for any reason, including intuition. The ERB and PMB can employ *must select* and *must not select* constraints in PPM tools equipped to address these needs. As implied by its name, a must select indicates that the project is mandatory and must be funded as part of the portfolio. Conversely, the must not select indicates that, for a specific reason, the project cannot be selected. Features within the PPM tools provide executives and the portfolio management team a technique to manage mandatory projects and to prohibit specific projects.

9.4.2 Project Dependencies and Enablers

Rarely, if ever, are all the projects within a candidate project pool independent of each other, that is, they are not equally selectable in their own right without regard to any relationships among them. Project relationships within a pool of candidate projects affect portfolio selection outcomes, because any relationships can introduce constraints. Some relationships can justify the selection of a project that otherwise provides little measurable benefit except that it facilitates the execution of other dependent, benefit-generating projects (Roberts, 2007). Such projects are known as enablers or enabling projects. In addition to the special case of groups discussed in Chapter 8 that provide for, at most, selection of one activity level (e.g., GOLD, SILVER, BRONZE, or none) for a project with multiple proposed approaches, there are three basic types of relationships among candidate projects: (1) mutually dependent, (2) dependent, and (3) mutually exclusive.

In a mutually dependent relationship, multiple projects are dependent on one another. For instance, Projects A and B are dependent on each other and both must be included in the scenario if either project is selected. Mutually dependent projects require inclusion of both projects in the portfolio if either project is selected or, conversely, that both be excluded if either is excluded. The necessity of including the second project in the portfolio reduces resources and funding for other projects that might otherwise have provided more anticipated expected benefits. A new office building complex project, for example, could be dependent on an infrastructure project to develop the roads, power, water, and sewer systems. Assuming that the office complex project is the reason for the infrastructure project, and that the infrastructure project must be undertaken to support the office complex, then both must be selected or both must be rejected.

In a dependent relationship, one project is dependent on a second project, but the inverse may not be true. For instance, Project B is dependent on Project A. That is, if Project B is selected by the scenario, Project A would have to be included automatically because Project B is not possible without Project A. However, Project A could be selected without Project B because Project A is not dependent on Project B. While this relationship is less restrictive than a mutually dependent relationship, as with any constraint it decreases the flexibility in project selection during scenario development. A notable example of a dependent relationship is the completion of an enabling project (i.e., mandatory project) such as an environmental impact assessment project prior to starting a construction project in an environmentally sensitive area. In this example, if the construction project was selected in the scenario, the environmental impact assessment project would also have to be included. However, the environmental impact assessment project could be selected without requiring the selection of the specific construction project.

In a mutually exclusive relationship, designated projects are exclusive of each other. That is, if one project is included, then another (or others) must be excluded to prevent overlap or duplication between selected projects.

9.4.3 Establishing Funding Pools

In organizations with multiple sources of funding, certain projects within a portfolio might be limited to specific funding pools such as different organizational budget accounts, government grants, and specific customer accounts, to name a few. Funding pools are established based on source or type of funding by aligning projects to their respective funding streams, for example, an airport enhancement project funded in part by the FAA and in part by the city or county in which the airport is located. By defining funding pools, the project owner, with executive guidance, specifies limits on each funding source for each alternative and for the portfolio and can easily limit, for each portfolio scenario, how much is actually allocated to each alternative and to the selected portfolio. Application of funding pool spending limits introduces another constraint when selecting the optimal portfolio, but one that is often necessary.

9.5 ACCOUNTING FOR PROJECT RISK IN PORTFOLIO SELECTION

In the course of selecting and managing project portfolios, organizations encounter, measure, and manage both portfolio and project risks. This section describes both, but we focus on assessing project risk as it affects selecting the optimal project portfolio.

9.5.1 Portfolio Risk

Managing portfolio risk is often about ensuring diversification such that the realization of one type of risk only affects some of the projects in the portfolio. The organization strives to balance its portfolio by obtaining a mix of both high- and low-risk projects, including product lines, project types such as new technology versus simpler product enhancements. Furthermore, they balance the portfolio by kinds of risk such as labor, weather, and environmental.

Accounting for portfolio risk incorporates uncertainty about how well a project delivers the anticipated benefits for the proposed cost. Project portfolios are selected to maximize benefits at specific budgets while accounting for constrained resources. However, what are the chances of achieving strategic objectives if all of the projects are high risk, over budget, behind schedule, not to customer specification, or cannot be completed at all? Would an organization undertake a portfolio of projects with a good chance of failing? Would it be better to select a portfolio providing fewer or less benefits but a higher probability of success in actual achievement of objectives rather than a portfolio providing higher benefits but a much lower probability of success? The optimal portfolio will likely contain some projects with high risk and high benefits as well as some with lower benefits and risk. Consider, too, that some portfolios such as those exploring new technologies—or firsts—have higher acceptable risk levels than other portfolios, including those containing projects that are enhancements to existing products. Organizations seek to balance risk across portfolios such that it achieves its objectives in terms of technology leadership, for example, while increasing market share by enhancing existing products.

9.5.2 Project Risk

In considering project risk we want to avoid projects with low benefit and high risk, or risks that reduce the anticipated benefits enough to eliminate their selection. Evaluation of risk can range from a simple consideration of the probability of occurrence and impact, with each having the characteristic high, medium or low, to developing and applying a full risk breakdown structure (RBS) that classifies and decomposes the types of risks that may arise. Levine listed seven categories for the first level of the risk work breakdown structure (WBS)—"time, people, costs, deliverables, quality, contract, and market"—while acknowledging that there could be others (Levine, 2005); one that comes to mind is environment.

With an appropriate risk WBS or other risk hierarchy, it is even possible to create an analytic hierarchy process (AHP) model with the risk hierarchy representing the objectives and the project candidates representing the alternatives and to produce a ratio-scaled risk assessment of the alternatives. This approach allows organizations to leverage the risk expertise of diverse decision makers. Regardless of approach, the organization determines and applies the effects of risk on the anticipated benefits for alternatives.

If ratio-scale measures of risk are available, their complement, probability of success, can be used to calculate the expected benefit by multiplying the anticipated benefit by the probability of success to yield the expected benefit. Note that this is a valid mathematical operation only when the measure of risk as probability of failure or success and the anticipated benefit are ratio-scale numbers. A project with a proposed benefit of 100 and a probability of success of 75%, for example, would have an expected benefit of $100 \times 0.75 = 75$. The expected benefits account for risk and can be used to select project portfolios considering both rewards and risks.

9.6 OPTIMAL PORTFOLIO WITH DEPENDENCIES, BALANCE, COVERAGE, AND RISK

When constraints, including dependencies, risk, and balance and coverage are identified, the organization is ready to select the optimal portfolio at a given funding level subject to these constraints. Since the process is iterative, any constraints not originally identified can easily be included in subsequent iteration if the results indicate there may be missing constraints. The constraints enable people to impose organizational realities on the selection process, yet too many constraints can unreasonably reduce the achievable benefits of the portfolio. Those involved must seek equilibrium between imposing organizationally necessary limitations and obtaining optimal benefits in terms of the organization's strategy.

The use of coverage helps to preserve the stability of organizational resources in keeping with the strategy and can ensure some support for all objectives. A company can't just develop new products and ignore the administration of employee benefits, for example. Using balance to achieve an appropriate mix of project types supports effective deployment of critical organizational resource. Dependencies are a fact of organizational life, so, too, is risk that must be considered in the context of reducing expected benefits. However, with each additional constraint, the mix of projects that are funded changes and the expected benefit of the portfolio is generally reduced with every additional constraint.

During the selection of the optimal portfolios, the Executive Review Board (ERB) is responsible for providing guidance to the PMB in terms of balance and coverage necessary for the organization, reviewing the portfolio scenarios presented, and providing authorization for funding. The PMB is also responsible for managing the portfolio models, analyzing portfolio-level critical resources, determining the impact of imposed conditions and risk on the portfolio scenarios, assessing the Efficient Frontier and various potential funding levels, and presenting its findings and recommendations to the ERB. The PMB creates and manages the risk model with guidance from organizational risk experts, and it administers the application of risk to the project portfolio candidates. The Project Management Office (PMO) is responsible for identifying project dependencies with assistance from the PMB, including assisting with the identification of portfolio-level resource constraints and supporting the organization's risk assessment models in addition to its regular responsibilities.

9.7 ALTERNATE SCENARIOS

To paraphrase the Roman author Pliny the Elder, the only certainty about the future is uncertainty. Alternate scenarios are a means to evaluate different project portfolio scenarios based on scenario specific parameters to rationalize portfolios against future expectations, conditions, and assumptions. That is, the organization performs what if analysis by constructing different project portfolio scenarios from various sets of underlying constraints, assumptions, and anticipated conditions. The aim is to select the best project portfolio to achieve goals and objectives based on what is anticipated with respect to the evaluated benefits, or as will be seen later (when risk is considered), the anticipated expected benefits. The advantage of alternate scenario analysis is the range of complexity for which scenarios can be developed; simple to complex. For instance, the organization may simply evaluate alternate scenarios for varying levels of funding before the current project portfolio budget is finalized or it can develop complex scenarios inclusive of both internal and external organizational factors such as constrained resources, expectations of consumers, estimated market conditions, and economic conditions, among many other factors. In addition to selecting the project portfolio, performing analysis of alternate portfolio scenarios enables the development of contingencies given various assumptions about the future.

Factors for establishing scenario parameters are only limited by the forces affecting the organization or creating the source of uncertainty. As Ian Wilson (2003) noted in his case study of Statoil, scenarios were used by Statoil to explore long-term research and development strategy for Statoil's Exploration and Production (E&P) Division. Much of Statoil's uncertainty stemmed from high-impact social, political, economic, and technological forces and the consequences they had for the business and thus on its technological needs. As Statoil is a gas and oil producer, estimates of future oil and gas prices are examples of assumptions and parameters that Statoil would use to develop alternate scenarios for its E&P Division. A project portfolio assumption of low oil prices would result in a different evaluation outcome compared to an assumption of high oil prices. Statoil's research and development investment and its benefits in offshore gas and oil projects would expectedly be affected by the anticipated fluctuations in oil and gas prices. For example, consider two project portfolio scenarios based on assumptions of $100 and $50 per barrel prices, respectively. At long-term price expectations of $100 per barrel, Statoil may be willing to increase the research and development portfolio budgets to maximize benefits compared to the amount of R&D spending with per barrel oil prices of $50. The different price assumptions or expectations can result in vastly different portfolio funding levels and benefits to the organization and illustrate the importance of underlying assumptions about market conditions from which the organization selects projects to include in the portfolio.

In developing alternate scenarios, the PMB collaborates and coordinates with the ERB to define scenario parameters and provide context for the portfolio being evaluated. Aside from providing project portfolio governance, the ERB provides linkage to the organization's strategic activities. Its members are better positioned, by virtue of their executive level or senior management perspectives, to define the bounds of alternate scenarios, in much the same way that they provided guidance on project categories and funding levels. In turn, the PMB's responsibility is to assist the ERB by developing the scenario parameters within the organization's PPM process and managing the process of evaluating various scenarios with review and approval by the ERB.

As will be seen in the ABU example, more than one optimal portfolio may exist. The advantage of using a software tool to support multiple scenarios is the ease with which these potential portfolios are viewed, analyzed, compared, and discussed. Once again we recommend that the reader follow along using the software to reinforce the learning experience, using the ABU model last saved during Chapter 8, or another real or hypothetical portfolio model of the reader's choosing.

9.8 ABU OPTIMAL PROJECT PORTFOLIO EXAMPLE

In the ABU example in Chapter 8, the Steering Committee led the development of the three initial portfolio scenarios requested by the Board of Trustees. The Steering Committee presented its process and the initial recommended portfolio of $86.5M that achieves 77.53% of the possible benefits at the monthly ABU Campus Revitalization Program status meeting, as shown in Figure 9.2.

During the meeting, the project manager for Project 8 (ABU Revitalization Program Regulatory & Environmental Approval Project—*Enabling Project*) notified stakeholders that in the course of the

AID	Alternative	Funded	Benefit	Cost	Partial	Min %	Must	Must Not
A1	1. Renovate Existing Student	NO	0.045	22.1	☐		☐	☐
A2	2. Renovate & Expand Davidson	YES	0.255	10.5	☐		☐	☐
A3	3. Construct Dr. Mary Haven Student	NO	0.051	8.7	☐		☐	☐
A4	4a. (GOLD) Renovate & Expand C.W.	YES	0.26	8.6	☐		☐	☐
A5	4b. (SILVER) Renovate & Expand C.W.	NO	0.058	6.5	☐		☐	☐
A6	4c. (BRONZE) Renovate & Expand C.W.	NO	0.025	4.2	☐		☐	☐
A7	5. Renovate Benjamin Stadium & Field	NO	0.208	44.5	☐		☐	☐
A8	6. Renovate Mason Hall Research	YES	0.114	7.4	☐		☐	☐
A9	7. Construct ABU Medical Clinic	YES	0.154	16.4	☐		☐	☐
A10	8. ABU Revitalization Program	YES	0.4	2.0	☐		☐	☐
A11	9. Construct Paisley Hall Student	YES	0.095	8.7	☐		☐	☐
A12	10. Renovate Deluth Hall Dining Facility	NO	0.05	8.5	☐		☐	☐
A13	11a. (GOLD) Construct ABU Indoor	NO	0.236	45.2	☐		☐	☐
A14	11b. (SILVER) Construct ABU Indoor	NO	0.05	35.5	☐		☐	☐
A15	11c. (BRONZE) Construct ABU Indoor	NO	0.019	24.2	☐		☐	☐
A16	12. Construct ABU Distance Learning	YES	0.311	9.3	☐		☐	☐
A17	13. Expand Campus Share Ride Services	YES	0.236	3.6	☐		☐	☐
A18	14. Construct Campus Theatre	YES	0.08	7.4	☐		☐	☐
A19	15. Construct ABU Faculty Technology	YES	0.131	12.6	☐		☐	☐

Figure 9.2   ABU initial portfolio based on Efficient Frontier

environmental study conducted on the northwest area building site, twenty red-haired woodpeckers' nests were discovered over a 30 acre area centrally located in the site. As a designated endangered species, the red-haired woodpecker is protected under the Endangered Species Act, thus, this area cannot be developed. As a result, Project 14 (Construct Campus Theatre) cannot be undertaken as it was sized and designated for this location. This means that Project 14 must not be selected for the portfolio.

In addition, the ABU Facilities Office expressed concern about its ability to provide project oversight for so many concurrent projects. ABU Project Management expressed concern that critical resources and project dependencies were not being considered in selecting the portfolio and might result in a project portfolio that was not executable with existing resources and capabilities. The ABU Facilities Steering Committee representative identified some dependencies among specific projects. He noted that Project 1 (Renovate Existing Student Dormitories) is dependent on Project 3 (Construct Dr. Mary Haven Student Housing Center) because the new housing must be available for students who will need to move out of the current dormitories during renovation. Therefore, it is not practical to select Project 1 unless Project 3 is selected. He also informed the group that Project 2 (Renovate & Expand Davidson Student Services Center) is mutually exclusive with Project 9 (Construct Paisley Hall Student Services Center). In other words, either renovate and expand the existing student services facility or construct the new facility, but not both; if Project 2 is selected, Project 9 must not be selected, and vice versa.

9.8.1 Project Dependencies and Mandatory Constraints

To impose these constraints, open the model in Expert Choice Desktop, go to the Data Grid, open the Resource Analyzer, and select the "ABU Initial Portfolio $86.5 Million" using the "Go To" menu and "Portfolio Scenarios" as shown in Figure 9.3, and then click on "OK." If the scenario had not been previously saved, then simply enter "86.5" in the "Budget Limit" then save the resulting scenario using the "Go To" menu.

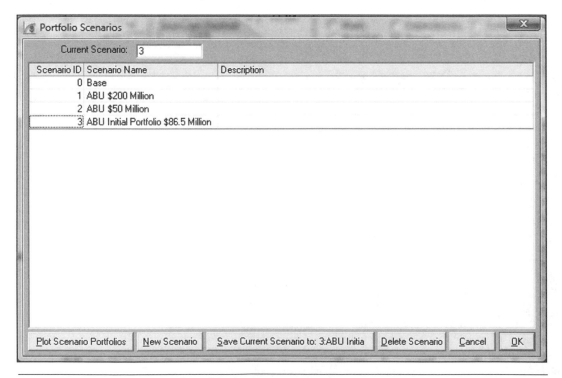

Figure 9.3   Open the ABU initial portfolio $86.5M scenario

The portfolio shown in the Resource Aligner should resemble the one in Figure 9.2 but, of course, your particular results differ because of the uniqueness of your evaluation results from Chapters 4 and 7.

Must and Must Not Constraints

To ensure that the habitat of the red-haired woodpecker is protected, impose the "Must Not" constraint on Project 14 (Construct Campus Theatre). To do so, select the appropriate box in the "Must Not" column of the Resource Aligner, as shown in Figure 9.4.

The only resulting change in the proposed portfolio is to eliminate Project 14 from the portfolio with a change in the funded cost dropping to $79.1M and a corresponding drop in benefits realized to 74.49%. No other eligible unselected project has a cost that can be accommodated within the portfolio budget specified as $86.5M. The next project in line to be funded, because it has the highest benefit of the eligible unfunded projects, is Project 3 (Construct Dr. Mary Haven Student Housing Center). This project can be funded for $8.7M, putting the portfolio just $1.3M over the recommended budget of $86.5M. Although it would add a benefit of only 0.051, it might be considered in conjunction with dormitory renovation (Project 1) in future discussions with the Board of Trustees, thus supporting the planned growth of the student population. Such considerations provide an example of the benefits of human analysis on the results produced by the software tool. In fact, it is the prerogative of people to make the decisions and the software tools simply enable better, more informed decisions.

The portfolio contains an enabler project, Project 8 (ABU Revitalization Program Regulatory & Environmental Approval Project) that must be funded regardless of its value for any of the other projects to be conducted. The evaluators recognized that during their evaluations, and chose it as the

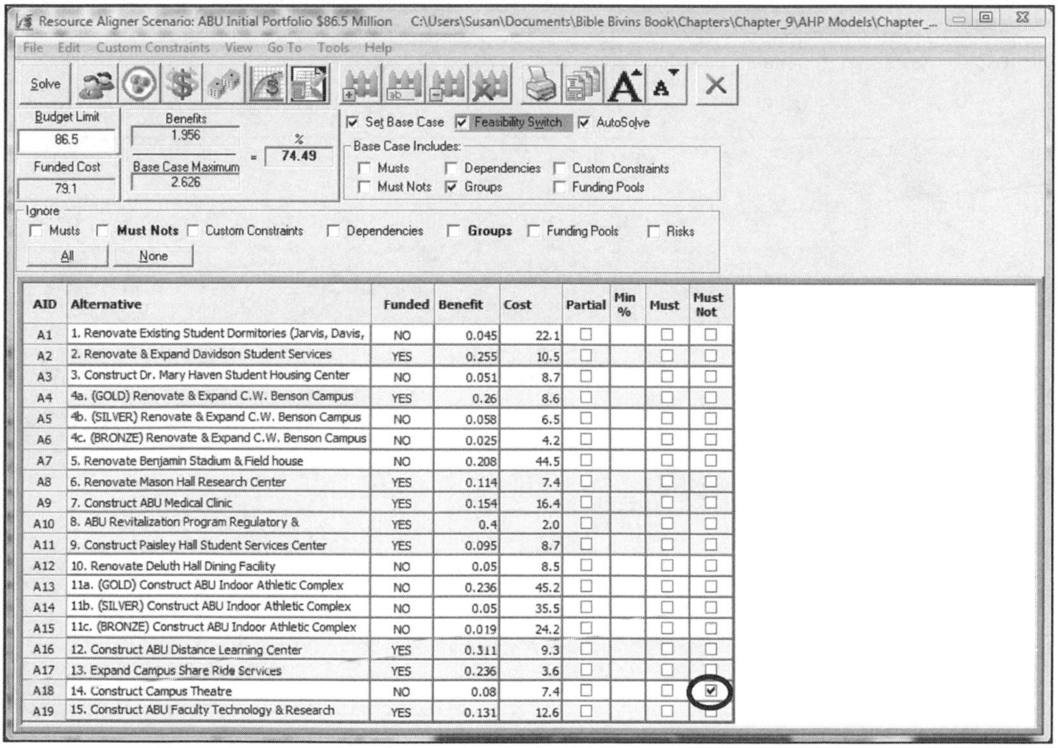

Figure 9.4   Impose "Must Not" constraint on Project 14 for environmental reasons

project with the highest benefit. If that had not been the case, and had Project 8 been in danger of de-selection, the Resource Aligner allows designation of a project as a "Must" by checking the appropriate box in the "Must" column. In such a case, if the solution is feasible, these mandatory projects are selected for funding regardless of benefit and cost.

Note that the "Base Case" includes a check in the "Groups" box, thus, the Resource Aligner considers them when calculating the maximum attainable benefit. To ask the Resource Aligner to ignore one or more checked constraint types to be considered in the "Base Case," check the appropriate box in the row under "Ignore," and the model will instantly recalculate without the ignored constraint types. The impact of changes imposed as a result of particular types of constraints can easily be seen by checking and unchecking the "Ignore" box next to each constraint type.

Project Dependencies

To impose the project dependencies identified by the facilities member of the Steering Committee, select the "Dependencies" icon as shown in Figure 9.5. Enter the dependency of Project 1 on Project 3 and the mutual exclusivity of Project 2 and Project 9 as shown in the matrix in Figure 9.6. Right click

File Edit Custom Constraints View Go To Tools Help
Solve
Budget Limit
86.5
Funded Cost
79.1
Benefits
1.956
Base Case Maximum
2.626
%
74.49
Set Base Case
Feasibility Switch
AutoSolve
Base Case Includes:
Musts
Dependencies
Custom Constraints
Must Nots
Groups
Funding Pools

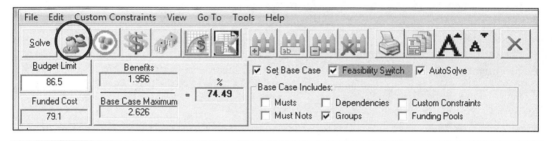

Figure 9.5 Select the dependencies icon to create project dependencies

File View OneClick Clear Tools Help
A1 1. Renovate Existing Student Dormitories (Jarvis, Davis, and Sewall Halls)
A2 2. Renovate & Expand Davidson Student Services Center
A3 3. Construct Dr. Mary Haven Student Housing Center (Off-Campus Facility)
A4 4a. (GOLD) Renovate & Expand C.W. Benson Campus Library (Alternatives Project)
A5 4b. (SILVER) Renovate & Expand C.W. Benson Campus Library (Alternatives Project)
A6 4c. (BRONZE) Renovate & Expand C.W. Benson Campus Library (Alternatives Project)
A7 5. Renovate Benjamin Stadium & Field house
A8 6. Renovate Mason Hall Research Center
A9 7. Construct ABU Medical Clinic
A10 8. ABU Revitalization Program Regulatory & Environmental Approval Project (Enabling Project)
A11 9. Construct Paisley Hall Student Services Center
A12 10. Renovate Deluth Hall Dining Facility
A1 1. Renovate Existing
D
A2 2. Renovate & Expand
X
A3 3. Construct Dr. Mary Haven
A4 4a. (GOLD) Renovate &
A5 4b. (SILVER) Renovate &
A6 4c. (BRONZE) Renovate &
Legend
D - The row element depends upon the column element. The row element is not funded unless the column element is funded.
M - The row and the column are mutually dependent; both must be funded or neither is funded.
X - The row and the column are mutually exclusive; funding one precludes funding the other.

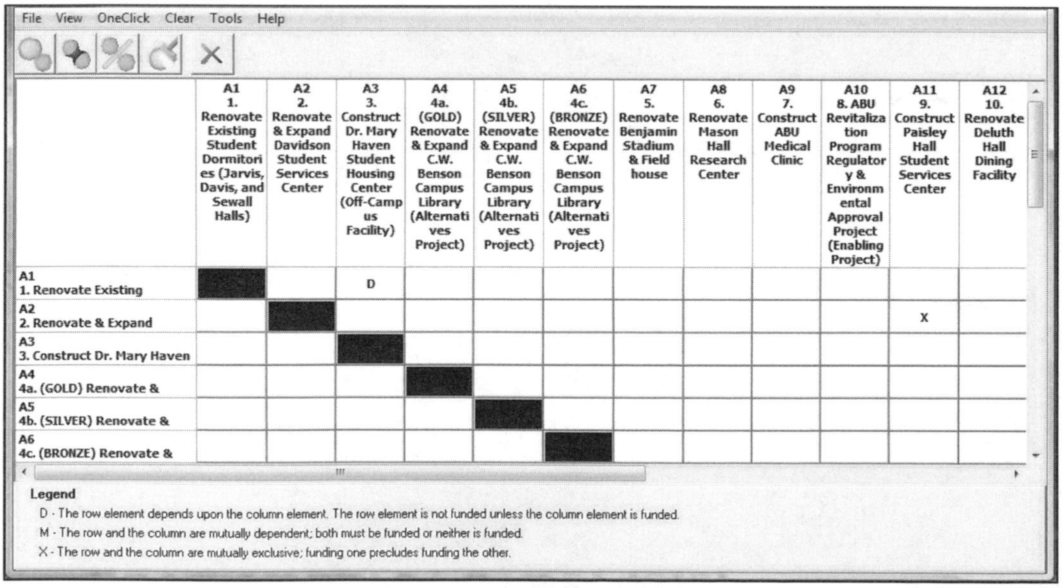

Figure 9.6 Project dependencies showing the row element depends on the column element

File View OneClick Clear Tools Help

Print ▶	Matrix
Print Preview ▶	Depends On
Close Ctrl+X	Dependent On
	Mutually Exclusive
	No Dependencies

	Re... E... S... Dormitories (Jarvis, Davis, and Sewall Halls)	Student Services Center	Student Housing Center (Off-Campus Facility)	A4 4a. (GOLD) Renovate & Expand C.W. Benson Campus Library (Alternatives Project)	A5 4b. (SILVER) Renovate & Expand C.W. Benson Campus Library (Alternatives Project)	A6 4c. (BRONZE) Renovate & Expand C.W. Benson Campus Library (Alternatives Project)	A7 5. Renovate Benjamin Stadium & Field house
A1 1. Renovate Existing	■		D				
A2 2. Renovate & Expand		■					

Figure 9.7   Example of menu functions in dependencies—printing dependencies

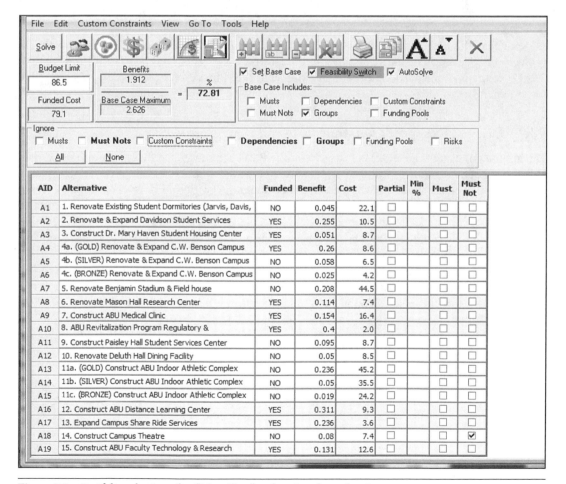

Figure 9.8   Portfolio selection after "Must Nots" and project dependencies

in the appropriate cell and select the desired type of relationship, "D," "M," or "X" as shown in the "Legend" at the bottom of the window.

These dependencies are intended to show project selection relationships, not schedule relationships. In this case a "D" indicates that the row element depends on the column element, and that the row element will only be funded if the column element is funded. This means that Project 1 will only be funded if Project 3 is funded. Note that the inverse is not true, for example, if Project 3 is funded, Project 1 may or may not be funded. An "X" indicates that two projects are mutually exclusive such that if one is funded the other cannot be funded. In this case designate that Project 2 and Project 9 are mutually exclusive. A third dependency type is "M" to indicate that the project in the row and the project in the column are mutually dependent such that both must be funded or neither must be funded.

Investigate the "Dependencies" menus to find helpful tools and reports, because project relationships in larger portfolios can become somewhat complex. As an example, use the File menu to access the ability to print the various dependencies, as shown in Figure 9.7.

When you are finished specifying dependencies and exploring the "Dependencies" menu options, close the window to see the impact on the selected portfolio, as shown in Figure 9.8.

Observe that because Projects 2 and 9 are mutually exclusive, Project 9 has been de-selected; both projects had previously been funded. Instead, Project 3 (Construct Dr. Mary Haven Student Housing [Off-Campus Facility]) has been funded which, coincidentally, has the same cost as Project 9. Project 3 is funded because it has the highest benefit of the remaining eligible projects with a cost that is accommodated by the specified budget limit. As before, no additional eligible projects could be accommodated within that limit and thus they remain unfunded.

Note that the cost remains as before, at \$79.1M, simply because the cost of the substituted project(s) happened to be the same as Project 9. However, the benefit has decreased from 74.49 to 72.81% of the possible portfolio benefit, because, with the elimination of Project 9, projects with a lower benefit are funded.

9.8.2 Critical Resource Constraints

During the same status meeting, the Director of the PMO acknowledged that the university is only able to support a maximum of three new construction projects, as opposed to renovation projects, because ABU facilities and the PMO are concerned about the greater need for project management resources and the degree of focus required by new construction projects. The Steering Committee had initially recommended that the portfolio contain a balance of renovation and new construction projects, including some projects of each type; it is clear that because of project management constraints no more than three new construction projects should be funded.

To support the resource constraints, it is necessary to classify each project as either "New Construction" or "Renovation." Our target is to ensure that at least one project of each classification is selected for balance, but also to honor the resource constraint by ensuring that no more than three projects classified as "New Construction" are selected. One way to do this is to create a user-defined column. Here we create a custom constraint to accomplish the classifications. Go to the Resource Aligner and select the "Custom Constraints" menu, "Add Constraint," and call it "New Construction" as shown in Figure 9.9.

A new frame appears at the right of the screen showing the list of alternatives, a column named "New Construction," and rows at the bottom for the user to specify the acceptable minimum and maximum number of alternatives (indicated by "Min" and "Max") for each custom constraint column. The Resource Aligner automatically calculates the "Total" and the number "Funded" as it manipulates the portfolio under relevant constraints. To enable this function, specify a "1" in the "New

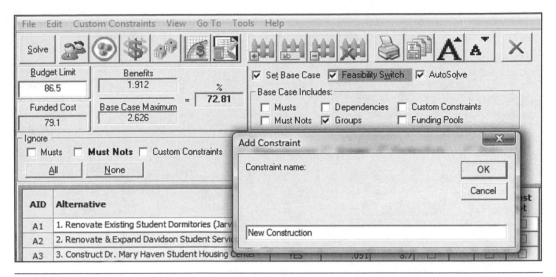

Figure 9.9 Insert a custom constraint called "New Construction" into the RA

Construction" column next to each alternative that represents a new construction project and leave the others blank, as shown in Figure 9.10.

Also, as shown in Figure 9.11, specify the maximum number of three new construction projects allowed by placing a "3" in the "Max" row for this constraint. Note that as soon as the value is entered, the funded projects change to reduce the number of new construction projects funded from 4.0 to 3.0.

The number of "Funded" projects changes to 3.0 and Project 3 (Construct Dr. Mary Haven Student Center) is no longer funded because it has the lowest benefit of the four new construction projects that were funded prior to adding the constraint. Project 10 (Renovate Deluth Dining Hall Facility), representing the highest benefit renovation project affordable within the budget limit is now funded instead with no remaining additional affordable and eligible renovation projects. The "Funded Cost" now stands at $78.9M, representing 85.93% of the possible benefits.

How is it possible that, with the addition of a constraint, the percent of possible benefits achieved goes up? The answer lies in the "Base Case Includes" check boxes that change the possible "Base Case Maximum." Recall that prior to imposing any constraints, the "Base Case Maximum" was the total budget required to fund all the alternatives. When a constraint is imposed, such as "Groups" for the GOLD, SILVER, and BRONZE alternate approaches to a project, the benefits for the SILVER and BRONZE alternatives are removed from the "Base Case Maximum," enabling the benefits anticipated from the funded projects to represent a more realistic percent of the total. Otherwise, with constraints such as "Groups," we would never achieve 100% of the potential benefits even if the budget limit was greater than the total funding needed for all projects. Constraints remove flexibility and possibilities from the portfolio and thus the "Percent Benefits" achieved (calculated by dividing "Benefits" by the "Base Case Maximum") is reduced to show the effect of imposing constraints.

As shown in Figure 9.11, a custom constraint to limit the number of new construction projects has been added. Why not check the box to include "Custom Constraints" in the base case calculation? If we were to consider this limitation in the base case, the effect would be to reduce the potential benefit achievable by removing the benefits of all new construction projects except the three with the highest benefit from the possible total. In the case of a constraint that would inappropriately inflate the benefits achieved by the selected portfolio such as this one eliminate it from consideration in the

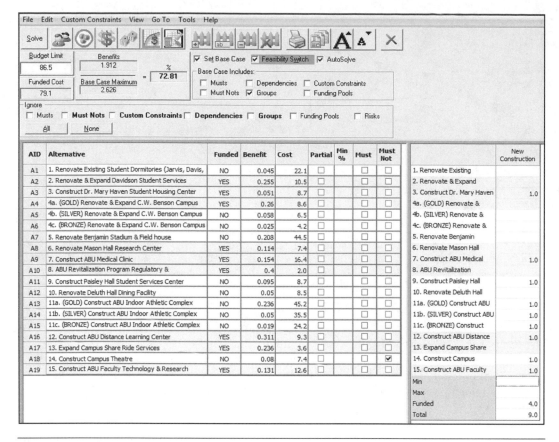

Figure 9.10   Adding a custom constraint column for new construction projects

base case by leaving the box next to "Custom Constraints" under "Base Case Includes" unchecked. (Expert Choice Resource Aligner provides the flexibility to include or ignore all such constraints within the base case; simply be aware of this fact and use this flexibility intelligently.) Thus, the "Base Case Maximum" (potential) benefits of 2.626 remain the same as they were before the constraint on new construction projects was introduced. Since the "Benefits" are slightly reduced, from 1.912 to 1.911, the percent of benefits attained by the selected portfolio is reduced to 72.77% from 72.81%. The difference in this case is small because the substituted project has a benefit of 0.050, nearly as high as 0.051. However, introducing this type of constraint, although certainly appropriate for the organization in this case, can reduce the achievable benefits.

Recall that the Steering Committee recognized that this initial portfolio, with the changes resulting from the monthly ABU Campus Revitalization Program status meeting, does not yet fully address the balance of project types and coverage across objectives that the Board of Trustees requested and does not include consideration of risk and the potential impact of risk on benefits.

9.8.3 Consideration of Balance and Coverage

Review of the portfolio against the objectives shows representation across only three of the objectives with no projects funded for the Residential objective or the Intercollegiate Athletics Facilities objective. At one point, before the introduction of the constraint on new construction projects, a

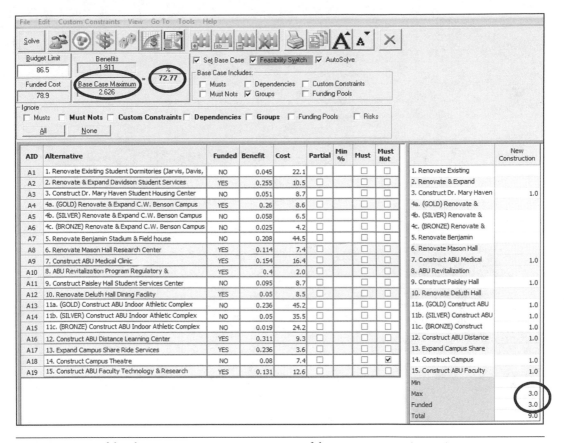

Figure 9.11 Portfolio changes on entering max constraint of three new construction projects

Residential project, Project 3 (Construct Dr. Mary Haven Student Housing) was funded; however, it was de-selected when the maximum number of new construction projects was limited to three. The Board of Trustees has specified that at least one project should be selected that supports each of the five objectives. In addition, although a constraint specifies selecting no more than three new construction projects because of critical resource constraints to manage them, it is still necessary to specify a constraint that requires selection of at least one new construction project and one renovation project. Because it builds directly on the "New Construction" custom constraint, requiring the selection of at least one new construction project is easy—type a "1" in the "Min" row for "New Construction."

Add another custom constraint column for "Renovation" by selecting "Custom Constraints," "Add Constraint," and typing "Renovation" in the "Constraint name" field, and then enter a "1" in that column for each project alternative that represents a renovation project, resulting in the new column. Type a "1" in the "Min" row for "Renovation," as shown in Figure 9.12. These specify that a minimum of one of each type of project must be funded. As expected, since this constraint was already met, no change is seen in the portfolio. However, should conditions change, the presence of this constraint in the model ensures that at least one each of the new construction and the renovation projects is included in the funded portfolio.

Save the model before moving to coverage of objectives. To do so, click the close button on the Resource Aligner window and respond "Yes" when asked whether to save the information as shown

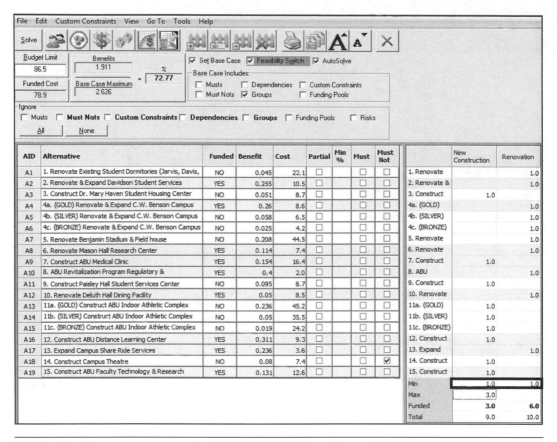

Figure 9.12   Custom constraint ensures at least one new construction and one renovation project

in Figure 9.13. Then save the model by selecting the "File" menu, and then "Save" and respond "Yes" when asked whether to save the changes. To preserve the steps performed in a separate version of the model, select "Save As" instead of save and respond "Yes" as shown in Figure 9.14. Then type a different file name in the "File Name" field, to preserve this set of changes without overwriting earlier versions of the model, and select "Save" as shown in Figure 9.15.

Recall that the Board of Trustees directed the Steering Committee to ensure that at least one project is funded to support each of the five objectives; the portfolio presently does not include any projects that support either the Intercollegiate Athletics or the Residential facilities objectives.

Building on the concept of custom constraints, it is possible to ensure coverage of all five objectives in the selected portfolio. Although we could proceed to create a new column in the Resource Aligner for each objective, there is a faster and more powerful way to accomplish this by creating a user-defined column called Category in the Data Grid. This column is then used to automatically create all five of the constraint columns, one for each objective, in the Resource Aligner. Recall that we have already created a Funded user-defined column to indicate, for each alternative, whether or not it is funded in the current scenario. To add the Category column from the Data Grid, select the "Edit" menu, "User-Defined Column," "Add," and choose "Categorical" as shown in Figure 9.16. A categorical user-defined column allows us to indicate in the resulting column the category to which each alternative belongs, in this case, which objective it primarily supports.

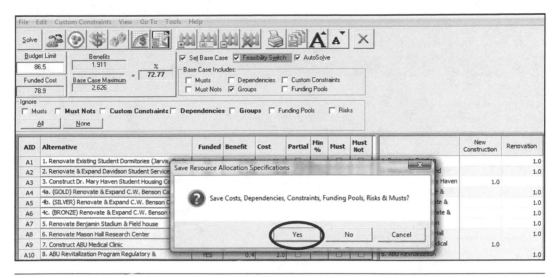

Figure 9.13 Saving the information generated in the Resource Aligner

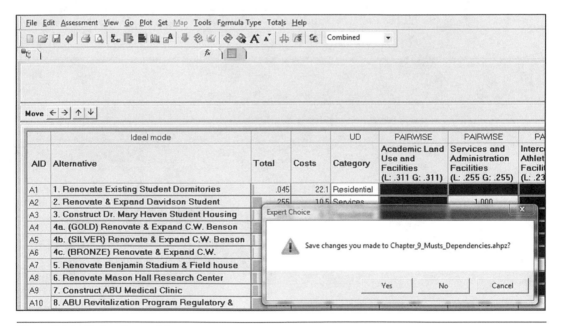

Figure 9.14 Saving the model

When a window to name the new column is shown, name it "Category" or other meaningful term and type a description to indicate that this column contains a short name for each objective that is used to introduce balance and coverage constraints. After the name and description are entered, a new window opens into which the category names are typed, as shown in Figure 9.17.

Next, select the category for each that represents the objective that each alternative best supports from the drop-down menu in the "Category" column, as shown in Figure 9.18. If an alternative supports multiple objectives, as does Project 8, the enabling project that in this case supports all

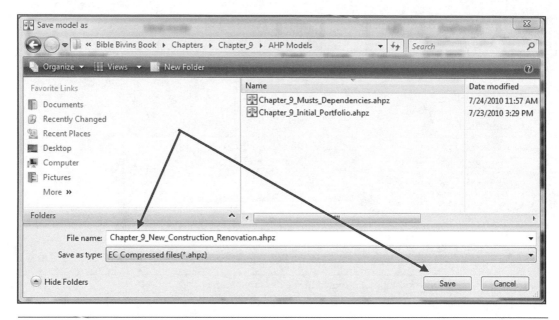

Figure 9.15   Change the file name to preserve earlier versions of the model

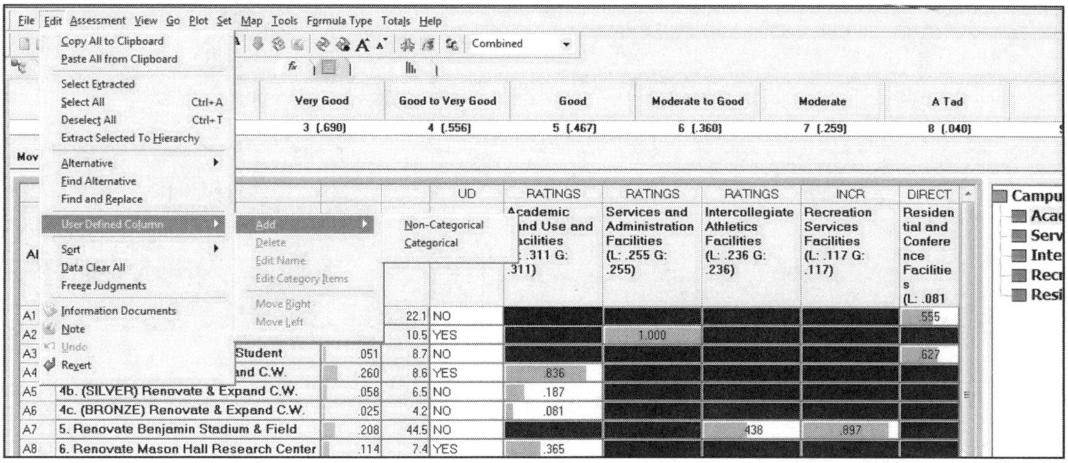

Figure 9.16   Add categorical User Defined Column in Data Grid

objectives, the category can be left blank. When the categories have been entered, use the Data Grid "Category" column to add five columns in the Resource Aligner, one for each objective as a separate custom constraint. To accomplish this, open the Resource Aligner and select the "Add Custom Constraint from User Defined Column" in the Resource Aligner "Custom Constraints" menu, as shown in Figure 9.19.

The Resource Aligner shows the available user-defined columns and allows the user to select the one for the custom constraint. Select "Category" and then "Add" and click "OK" as shown in Figure 9.20. This action results in the addition of five columns in the Resource Analyzer, one for each category (same as objectives, in this case, but not always), as shown in Figure 9.21. For each alternative,

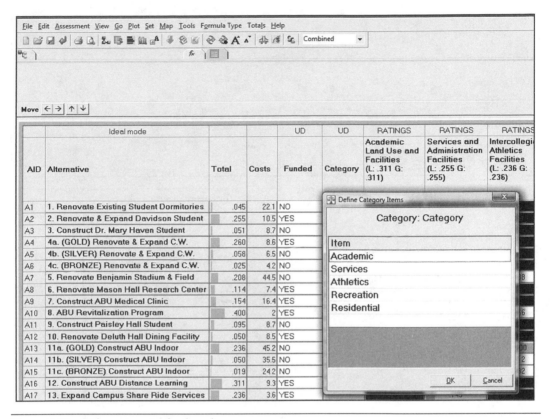

Figure 9.17 Define categories for the column

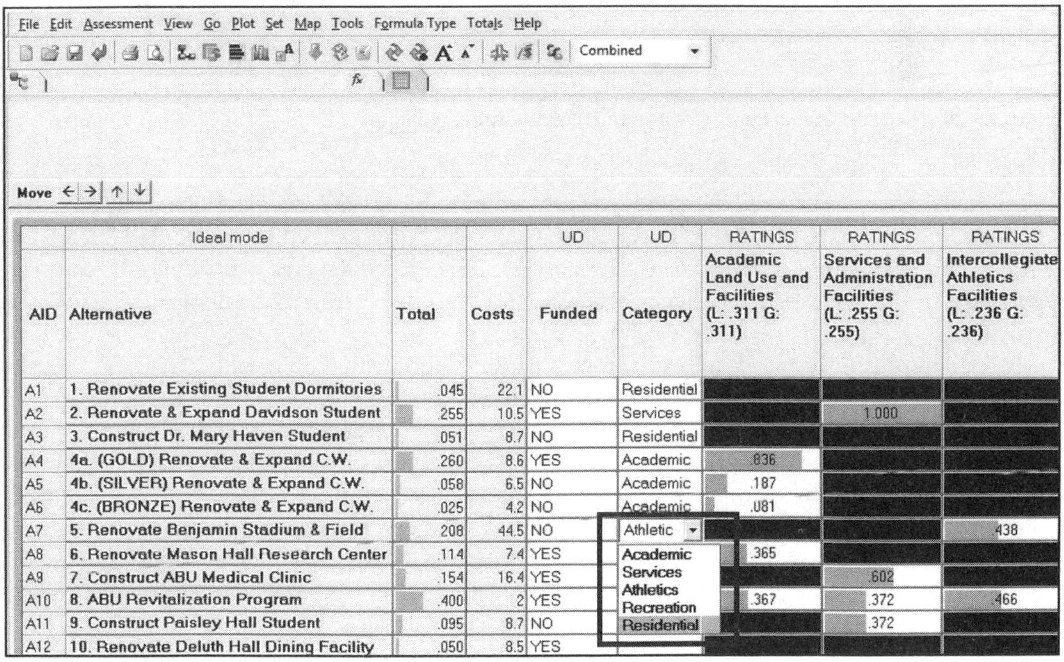

Figure 9.18 Select the primary supported objective from the category drop down menu

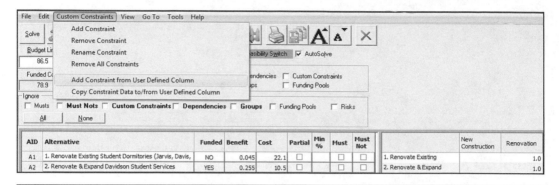

Figure 9.19   Use project categories to add a custom constraint for coverage across objectives

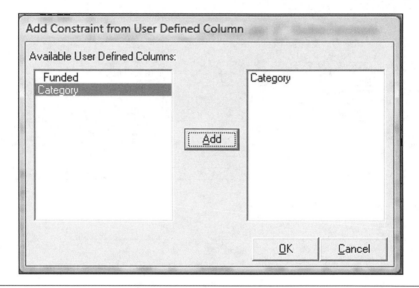

Figure 9.20   Select a User Defined Column to create a custom constraint

Resource Aligner has inserted the value 1.0 in the column for the objective that the alternative best supports in accordance with the text value in the Data Grid user-defined column called "Category." For cases in which a number of projects support multiple objectives, create a column for each category directly in the Resource Aligner, where a "1.0" can be entered manually for each covering objective.

Next, enter "1.0" for the "Min" row for each category to satisfy the Board of Trustees' directive that at least one project for each objective be funded, as shown in Figure 9.22. The Resource Aligner automatically counts the number of projects funded in the "Funded" row and the total number of projects in the "Total" row for each column. The user must explicitly specify the constraints in the "Min" row and the "Max" row, in accordance with the desired constraints. Enter a "1" in the "Min" row for each of the objectives columns to support the Trustees' request that at least one project be funded for each objective. While entering these constraints, watch the funded portfolio change. The column to indicate "Category" creates the custom constraint to ensure coverage across all five objectives, each of which is associated with a project category, or strategic bucket.

	New Construction	Renovation	Academic	Services	Athletics	Recreation	Residential
1. Renovate Existing		1.0					1.0
2. Renovate & Expand		1.0		1.0			
3. Construct Dr. Mary Haven	1.0						1.0
4a. (GOLD) Renovate &		1.0	1.0				
4b. (SILVER) Renovate &		1.0	1.0				
4c. (BRONZE) Renovate &		1.0	1.0				
5. Renovate Benjamin		1.0					1.0
6. Renovate Mason Hall		1.0	1.0				
7. Construct ABU Medical	1.0			1.0			
8. ABU Revitalization		1.0					
9. Construct Paisley Hall	1.0			1.0			
10. Renovate Deluth Hall		1.0				1.0	
11a. (GOLD) Construct ABU	1.0				1.0		
11b. (SILVER) Construct ABU	1.0				1.0		
11c. (BRONZE) Construct	1.0				1.0		
12. Construct ABU Distance	1.0		1.0				
13. Expand Campus Share		1.0				1.0	
14. Construct Campus	1.0					1.0	
15. Construct ABU Faculty	1.0		1.0				
Min		1.0					
Max	3.0						
Funded	**3.0**	**6.0**	4.0	2.0	0.0	2.0	0.0
Total	9.0	10.0	6.0	3.0	3.0	3.0	3.0

Figure 9.21   Column automatically created and populated per category in RA

	New Construction	Renovation	Academic	Services	Athletics	Recreation	Residential
1. Renovate Existing		1.0					1.0
2. Renovate & Expand		1.0		1.0			
3. Construct Dr. Mary Haven	1.0						1.0
4a. (GOLD) Renovate &		1.0	1.0				
4b. (SILVER) Renovate &		1.0	1.0				
4c. (BRONZE) Renovate &		1.0	1.0				
5. Renovate Benjamin		1.0					1.0
6. Renovate Mason Hall		1.0	1.0				
7. Construct ABU Medical	1.0			1.0			
8. ABU Revitalization		1.0					
9. Construct Paisley Hall	1.0			1.0			
10. Renovate Deluth Hall		1.0				1.0	
11a. (GOLD) Construct ABU	1.0				1.0		
11b. (SILVER) Construct ABU	1.0				1.0		
11c. (BRONZE) Construct	1.0				1.0		
12. Construct ABU Distance	1.0		1.0				
13. Expand Campus Share		1.0				1.0	
14. Construct Campus	1.0					1.0	
15. Construct ABU Faculty	1.0		1.0				
Min		1.0	1.0	1.0	1.0	1.0	1.0
Max	3.0						
Funded	**3.0**	**6.0**	3.0	1.0	1.0	2.0	1.0
Total	9.0	10.0	6.0	3.0	3.0	3.0	3.0

Figure 9.22   Portfolio including coverage of each objective by at least one funded project

If the user desires to see the columns in a particular order, the user-defined columns can first be created and moved to the desired order in the Data Grid using the "Edit" menu, "User-Defined Column," "Move Right" or "Move Left;" then copy the data into the Resource Aligner using the "Custom Constraints" menu, "Copy Constraint from User Defined Column."

The Resource Aligner has the capability to produce reports for documentation of the constraints entered and satisfied. To print or export one or more Resource Aligner reports, select the "File" menu, "Reports," and then select either the "Combined Report" as shown in Figure 9.23, or one or more of the single reports, and then select either "Preview/Export" or "Print."

Several changes were made to the portfolio of funded projects as a result of imposing the coverage constraints, as shown in Figure 9.24. Project 3 is now funded because it is the Residential objective project with the highest benefit. In addition, Project 11c is now funded because it satisfies the Athletics objective and the BRONZE alternative represented the first affordable such project. Because both of these are "New Construction" projects, two of the three new construction projects previously funded have been removed; they are Project 7 (Construct ABU Medical Clinic) and Project 15 (Construct ABU Faculty Technology Center). Project 12 (Construct ABU Distance Learning Center) is the only surviving new construction project.

With the coverage constraints imposed, the "Funded Cost" has risen from $78.9 to $82.8M. More importantly, the percent of possible benefits achieved dropped precipitously from 77.97 to just 64.58%. Such changes are indicative of the consequences of imposing constraints, but these constraints are often a reality in the organizations that must impose them. This portfolio represents the best portfolio that meets all the constraints specified by the Board of Trustees. Best, in this case, means that it provides the maximum benefit achievable within the budget and with all constraints specified.

9.8.4 Creating Charts Showing Costs versus Benefits

The Resource Aligner contains functions to plot benefits and costs, showing the benefits on the *y*-axis and cost on the *x*-axis. Once the benefits and costs have been determined, Expert Choice produces a

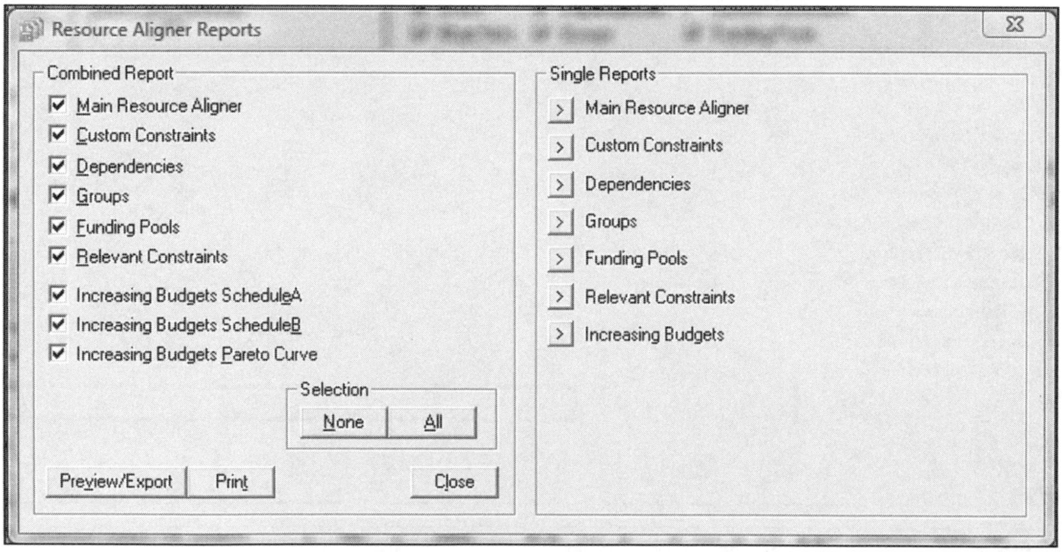

Figure 9.23 Printing or exporting Resource Aligner reports

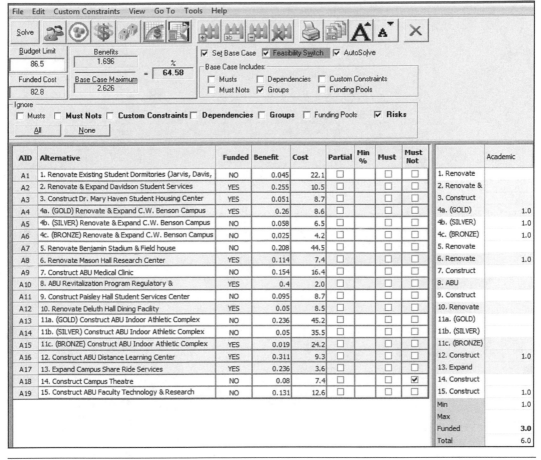

Figure 9.24 ABU facilities portfolio with maximum benefit under constraints

graphical representation of benefits and costs, but additional steps are necessary to make the benefit versus cost analysis more meaningful. In Chapter 6 during the discussion of the screening process, the concept of project categories, or strategic buckets, was discussed and guidance sought from the ERB about what those categories should be. In the case of ABU, the categories specified were:

- Academic
- Services
- Athletics
- Recreation
- Residential

To perform cost benefit analysis among projects in the same category, which are deemed to be more comparable, use the user-defined column "Category" created earlier in the Data Grid. Several plots are produced using the Data Grid, including alternatives against objectives. In this case choose to plot benefits versus costs. To accomplish this, from the Data Grid view select "Plot" and then "Benefits vs. Costs" as shown in Figure 9.25.

The bubble chart shown in Figure 9.26 appears. This chart provides a visual means to see why no Intercollegiate Athletics projects were selected initially—they are primarily in the lower right

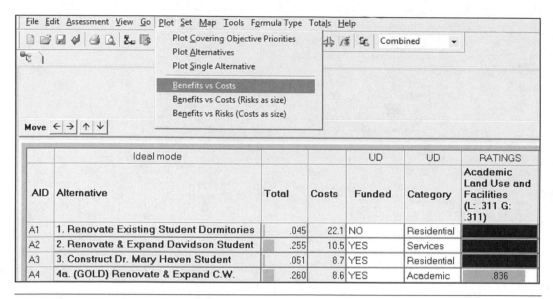

Figure 9.25   Plotting benefits versus costs from the Data Grid

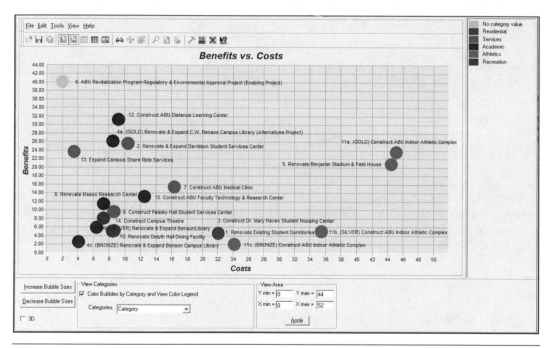

Figure 9.26   Plot of benefits versus costs for all alternatives with color coding by project category

quadrant, higher in cost, and, in some cases, lower in benefit than many projects in other categories. The Residential projects are also shown as low in benefit. When coverage is forced using the category constraints, one project of each of the two categories is funded.

When considering benefits versus costs, the most desirable projects in the plot are those in or near the upper left quadrant, because they represent the most benefit at the least cost. By the same token, projects in or near the lower right quadrant, all other things being equal, are the least desirable members of the chosen portfolio because they represent less benefit and higher cost. Charts such as this, if used properly, are helpful visuals for presentations and executive discussions.

At the bottom of the chart several options appear, enlarged and shown in Figure 9.27. We selected "Color Bubbles by Category" and "View Color Legend" by checking the box under "View Categories." In this case there is only one "Categorical" user-defined column that, coincidentally, is named "Category." If other categorical user-defined columns are defined, select the one to use for the color-coding from the drop-down list.

Note also that the button "All Selected" has been chosen in Figure 9.27. This option shows all the alternatives under consideration. To view a plot of only the funded alternatives, choose the "Funded" button, and only the funded projects appear in the resulting plot, as shown in Figure 9.28. Experiment with other options and menu items as well to learn the various capabilities for plotting.

By comparing the two plots it can be seen that the single "Athletics" project selected, the single "Services" project selected and the single "Residential" project chosen for funding were evaluated to have the lowest benefit among all the projects chosen, and that the "Athletics" project, Project 11c (BRONZE alternative) is the highest cost project funded. However, because of the Board of Trustees' desire to have all objectives (categories) represented, the constraints introduced ensure that these desires are met.

Figure 9.27 Options for display content for the plot

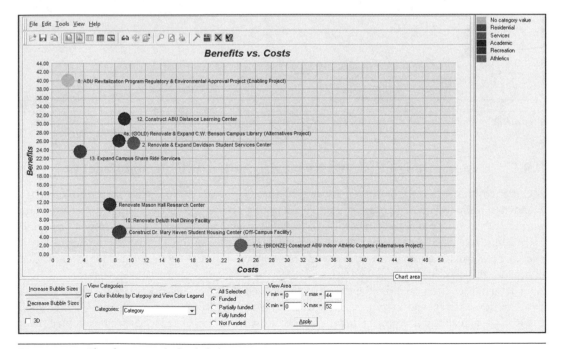

Figure 9.28 Plot showing only funded alternatives

Had we performed this plot after defining the categorical user-defined column, but before the introduction of the "Category" constraint to force at least one project for each objective, the plot would have been similar to Figure 9.29. Note how easy it is, using tools such as this, to see the imbalance in the portfolio with no representation for "Athletics" or "Residential."

It is difficult or impossible to manage a growing institution like ABU, where a high percentage of students live on campus, without suitable student residences. Likewise, ABU needs suitable modern athletic facilities, as a member of the Big Kahuna athletic conference with large endowments from alumni based on its athletic prowess. It is important for the evaluators to prioritize because that determines which alternatives are selected, subject to constraints. It is equally important for the perspective of executives to be applied in the form of constraints necessary for the organization to endure. In an organization with mature PPM processes, both the evaluators and the executives will operate with its best interest in mind rather than self-interest.

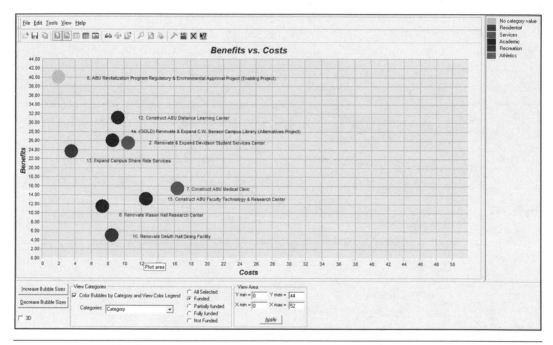

Figure 9.29   Plot of funded alternatives without coverage constraint

9.8.5 Consideration of Risk and Risk-Discounted or Expected Benefits

Members of the Steering Committee understand that to provide a more realistic portfolio recommendation to the Board of Trustees, the risks associated with the alternatives must be considered. The purpose of assessing project risk in portfolio selection is to assign a probability of success or a probability of failure to each alternative, and then to select a risk-adjusted optimal portfolio. The probability of success or failure is based on the qualitative and quantitative risk analyses performed for the individual alternative projects.

ABU facilities personnel developed a RBS to be used as the framework for assessing risk for all construction and renovation projects. A high-level view of the RBS is shown in Figure 9.30. To apply the RBS to each alternative project under consideration, a range of approaches can be adopted, from BOGSAT to a sophisticated AHP risk model. After review of each candidate project against the RBS,

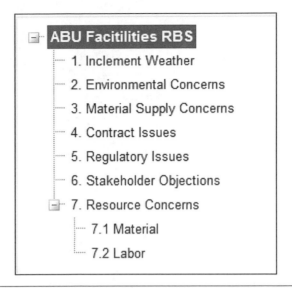

Figure 9.30   High-level RBS for ABU facilities construction and renovation projects

construction risk experts from the university facilities and the PMO identified the risks for each project, assessed the likelihood of occurrence and the degree of impact for each risk, and then estimated the total likelihood of failure for each project. Ideally, the risks in the RBS would be evaluated by a team of experts using AHP and Comparion to derive ratio-scale measures of the importance of each of the risks. The alternatives would likewise be evaluated against each potential risk for likelihood of occurrence and impact. The result is a ratio-scale assessment of the alternatives with regard to risk. Of course it is likely that the relative importance of the risks, and even the risks themselves, are different for different types of projects. For example, the risk of failing to be first-to-market for a new product development project is extremely high, while that risk does not even appear on the radar for a mandatory regulatory project. An actual organization would likely have multiple RBSs; in the case of ABU facilities, all are construction or renovation projects and can be served by a single RBS.

With assistance from the ABU construction risk experts, the Steering Committee created a risk model associated with the Expert Choice Model for the portfolio. A rating scale for the risk model was created in Comparion with eight intensity levels. The rating scale reflects a project's probability of failure. Based on the risk analysis for each project, ABU construction risk experts and members of the Steering Committee used the rating scale shown in Figure 9.31 to evaluate risk for the alternatives.

In this model, in addition to a rating scale, the Steering Committee could have chosen to allow direct priority input, possibly as the result of a separate risk evaluation. In reality, a much more complex risk model can be built to represent the organization's risk assessment capability. For example, we could construct the RBS and treat it as the objectives hierarchy, performing pairwise comparisons of the relative importance of the risks in the RBS. Then a rating scale could be applied to the alternatives with respect to each covering risk, thus producing a ratio-scale relative "Risk" value for the risks in place of a relative "Benefit" value for the objectives. If the alternatives were evaluated with respect to the risks first, the insight from the former could help in prioritizing the latter.

In this case an expert from the ABU Risk Management Team assisted selected members of the Steering Committee, ABU facilities, and the PMO to evaluate the risk of each project using the rating scale. The results of the ratings evaluation in the risk model are shown in Figure 9.32 by choosing

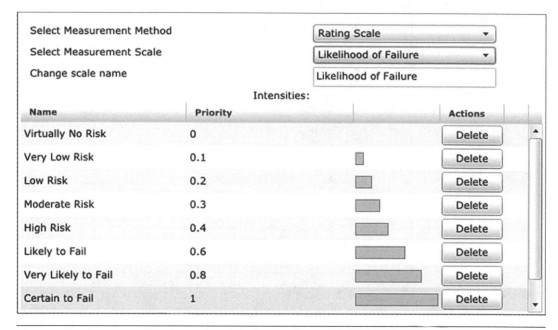

Figure 9.31   Rating scale for ABU project risks showing the probability of failure

Alternatives	Risk %
1. Renovate Existing Student Dormitories (Jarvis, Davis, and Sewall Halls)	20.00%
2. Renovate & Expand Davidson Student Services Center	15.00%
3. Construct Dr. Mary Haven Student Housing Center (Off-Campus Facility)	20.00%
4a (GOLD). Renovate & Expand C.W. Benson Campus Library (Alternatives Project)	10.00%
4b (SILVER). Renovate & Expand C.W. Benson Campus Library (Alternatives Project)	10.00%
4c (BRONZE). Renovate & Expand C.W. Benson Campus Library (Alternatives Project)	10.00%
5. Renovate Benjamin Stadium & Field House	20.00%
6. Renovate Mason Hall Research Center	40.00%
7. Construct ABU Medical Clinic	10.00%
8. ABU Revitalization Program Regulatory & Environmental Approval Project (Enabling Project)	5.00%
9. Construct Paisley Hall Student Services Center	15.00%
10. Renovate Deluth Hall Dining Facility	10.00%
11a. (GOLD) Construct ABU Indoor Athletic Complex (Alternatives Project)	10.00%
11b. (SILVER) Construct ABU Indoor Athletic Complex (Alternatives Project)	10.00%
11c. (BRONZE) Construct ABU Indoor Athletic Complex (Alternatives Project)	10.00%
12. Construct ABU Distance Learning Center	75.00%
13. Expand Campus Share Ride Services	5.00%
14. Construct Campus Theatre	20.00%
15. Construct ABU Faculty Technology & Research Center	10.00%

Figure 9.32   Risk evaluation results shown as relative probability of failure (risk)

the Comparion "Reports" tab, "Predefined Reports," and "Priority of Alternatives." There are other options for viewing the results in Comparion such as using the "Synthesize" tab, selecting "Overall Results," and then scrolling through the alternatives.

As seen in Figure 9.32, most of the projects have relatively low risk. However, Project 6 (Renovate Mason Hall Research Center) has a relatively higher risk, 40% probability of failure, because the existing building infrastructure may not support the state-of-the-art technology required for the faculty research center. Thus, the structure may need to be razed and rebuilt rather than merely being renovated. Also, Project 12 (Construct ABU Distance Learning Center) was deemed by the evaluators as likely to fail because the soil in the designated location is subject to liquefaction, requiring the insertion of foundational steel into bedrock at a depth that cannot be determined without a sophisticated geological investigation.

Risks can be entered into the Expert Choice Desktop Data Grid manually. They can also be entered automatically using a powerful capability in the software that allows the user to associate a separate Expert Choice Desktop risk model such as described earlier. Using a risk model created in Comparion, download the model from Comparion and save it in an Expert Choice format. Then navigate to the Data Grid in the portfolio model and bring up the "Risks" menu. To activate the "Risks" menu and see the "Risks" column, use the "View" menu and select the "Risks Column" as shown in Figure 9.33. Making the column visible also makes the menu visible.

To create an Expert Choice Desktop risk model and associate it with the portfolio model, use the "Risks" menu to "Create and Associate a Risk Model" shown in Figure 9.34 as the first selection in the menu. This automatically populates the risk model with the alternatives from the portfolio model. Then the risks are structured as the objectives hierarchy in the risk model, the alternatives associated with the risks, and the evaluation performed in either Expert Choice Desktop or Comparion; however, to associate the risk model and import risks, the model must reside in or have been downloaded to Expert Choice Desktop. The risk model can also be created separately and associated with the model later. To associate it later, choose the "Risks" menu and "Associate Risk Model" to associate the risk model with the evaluation model.

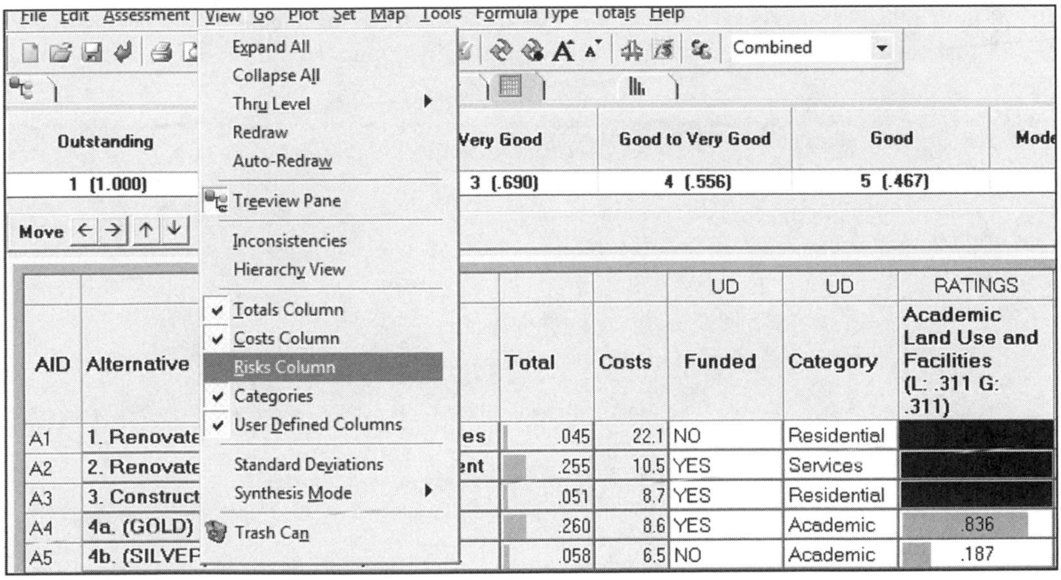

Figure 9.33 Viewing the Risks Column and Risks Menu in the Data Grid

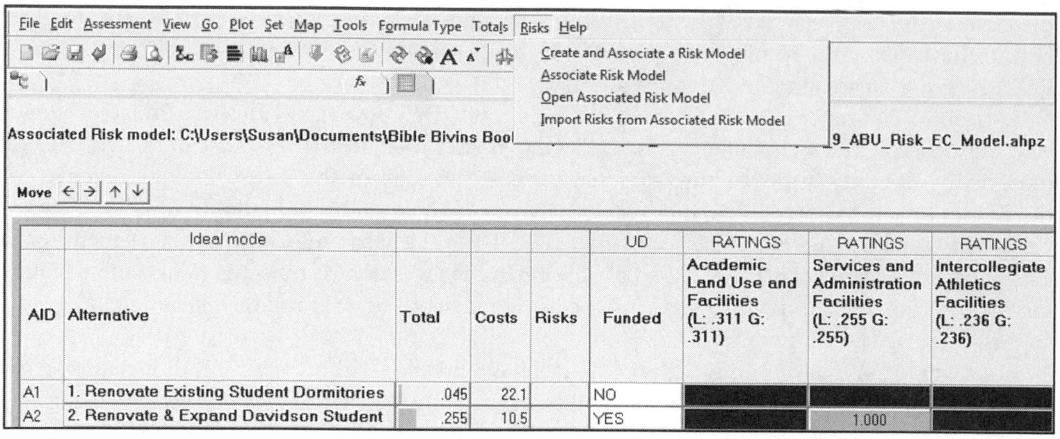

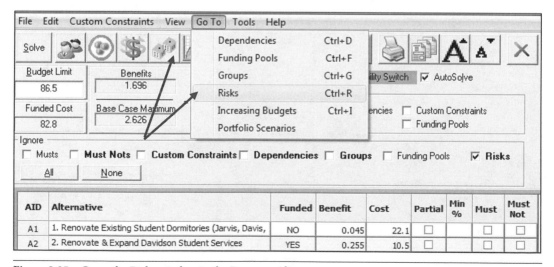

Figure 9.34   Associate or create and associate a risk evaluation model in the Data Grid

Once the risk model has been associated using the "Risks" menu in the Data Grid, open the Resource Aligner and, as shown in Figure 9.35, use the dice icon or the "Go To" menu and "Risks" to import the risks. The Resource Aligner risk window opens and asks you to specify whether the risk data in the associated model should be imported as probability of success or probability of failure (risk), as shown in Figure 9.36. After your selection is made, the risk data is imported into either the "Risks" column or the "Probability of Success" column, and the opposite column is calculated as well as the "Expected Benefits." Risk information can also be entered directly into the Resource Aligner to determine the discounted anticipated benefits. The discounted anticipated benefits for each project are shown in Figure 9.36.

In this case, we have chosen to enter the data shown in the Risks column in Figure 9.36 directly from the matrix shown in Figure 9.32. Once the risk data is entered through either method, the "Benefits" column in the Resource Aligner is replaced by the "E.Benefit" column, showing the product of probability of success and benefit. Because in this case we have entered the data as risk in the "Risks" column, the Resource Aligner has automatically populated the "Risks" column and has

Figure 9.35   Open the Risks window in the Resource Aligner

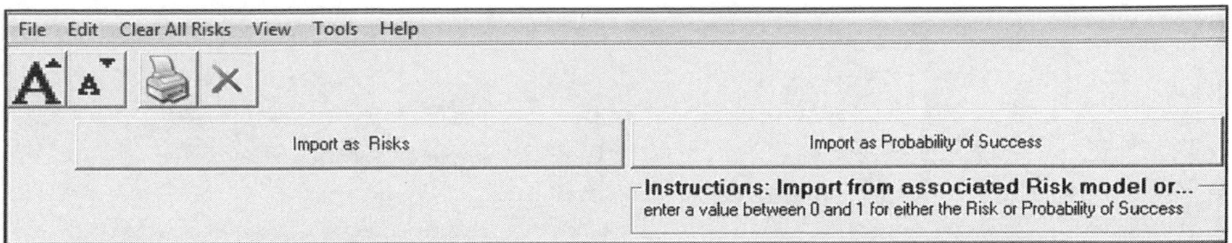

AID	Alternatives	Benefits	Risks	Probability of Success	Expected Benefits
A1	1. Renovate Existing Student Dormitories (Jarvis, Davis, and	0.045	0.20	0.8000	0.036
A2	2. Renovate & Expand Davidson Student Services Center	0.255	0.15	0.8500	0.217
A3	3. Construct Dr. Mary Haven Student Housing Center (Off-Campus	0.051	0.20	0.8000	0.041
A4	4a. (GOLD) Renovate & Expand C.W. Benson Campus Library	0.26	0.10	0.9000	0.234
A5	4b. (SILVER) Renovate & Expand C.W. Benson Campus Library	0.058	0.10	0.9000	0.052
A6	4c. (BRONZE) Renovate & Expand C.W. Benson Campus Library	0.025	0.10	0.9000	0.023
A7	5. Renovate Benjamin Stadium & Field house	0.208	0.20	0.8000	0.166
A8	6. Renovate Mason Hall Research Center	0.114	0.40	0.6000	0.068
A9	7. Construct ABU Medical Clinic	0.154	0.10	0.9000	0.139
A10	8. ABU Revitalization Program Regulatory & Environmental	0.4	0.05	0.9500	0.380
A11	9. Construct Paisley Hall Student Services Center	0.095	0.15	0.8500	0.081
A12	10. Renovate Deluth Hall Dining Facility	0.05	0.10	0.9000	0.045
A13	11a. (GOLD) Construct ABU Indoor Athletic Complex (Alternatives	0.236	0.10	0.9000	0.212
A14	11b. (SILVER) Construct ABU Indoor Athletic Complex	0.05	0.10	0.9000	0.045
A15	11c. (BRONZE) Construct ABU Indoor Athletic Complex	0.019	0.10	0.9000	0.017
A16	12. Construct ABU Distance Learning Center	0.311	0.75	0.2500	0.078
A17	13. Expand Campus Share Ride Services	0.236	0.05	0.9500	0.224
A18	14. Construct Campus Theatre	0.08	0.20	0.8000	0.064
A19	15. Construct ABU Faculty Technology & Research Center	0.131	0.10	0.9000	0.118

Figure 9.36 Entering or importing risk information into Resource Aligner from an associated risk model

calculated the "Probability of Success" for each alternative as 1.00 minus the risk value. In addition, it has populated the "Expected Benefits" column by multiplying the "Benefits" shown in the Data Grid by the "Probability of Success" for each alternative as shown in Figure 9.37.

Figure 9.37 also shows the optimum portfolio based on the evaluated risks in addition to constraints. When risk is considered, the portfolio is modified:

- Project 10—Renovate Deluth Hall Dining Facility is no longer funded because the reduction in expected benefit dropped enough such that it was no longer in the optimal combination.
- Project 11a—(GOLD) Construct ABU Indoor Athletic Complex is now funded instead of Project 11c, the BRONZE option for this project, because it became affordable and had the highest expected benefit of the affordable projects. The Resource Analyzer will solve for the optimal portfolio of benefits under constraints and within budget.
- Project 12—Construct ABU Distance Learning Center is no longer funded due to the aforementioned concern about the composition of the earth under the proposed foundation. Its expected benefit dropped 75% when risk was considered, and this reduction was enough so that it was no longer in the optimal combination.

The funded cost when risk is considered is $86.0M with 65.46% of the percentage of expected anticipated benefit if there was no budget limitation, as shown in Figure 9.38, as opposed to $82.8M funded cost with 69.2% of the benefits received when risks are ignored. To see the portfolio with and without risk, toggle the "Ignore" switch next to "Risks." The same capability is used to ignore or include any of the constraint types in the optimized results.

With the optimal portfolio selected subject to constraints and risk, at the $86.5M budget limit, save the model with a different name to enable revising risks while preserving the prior model, or

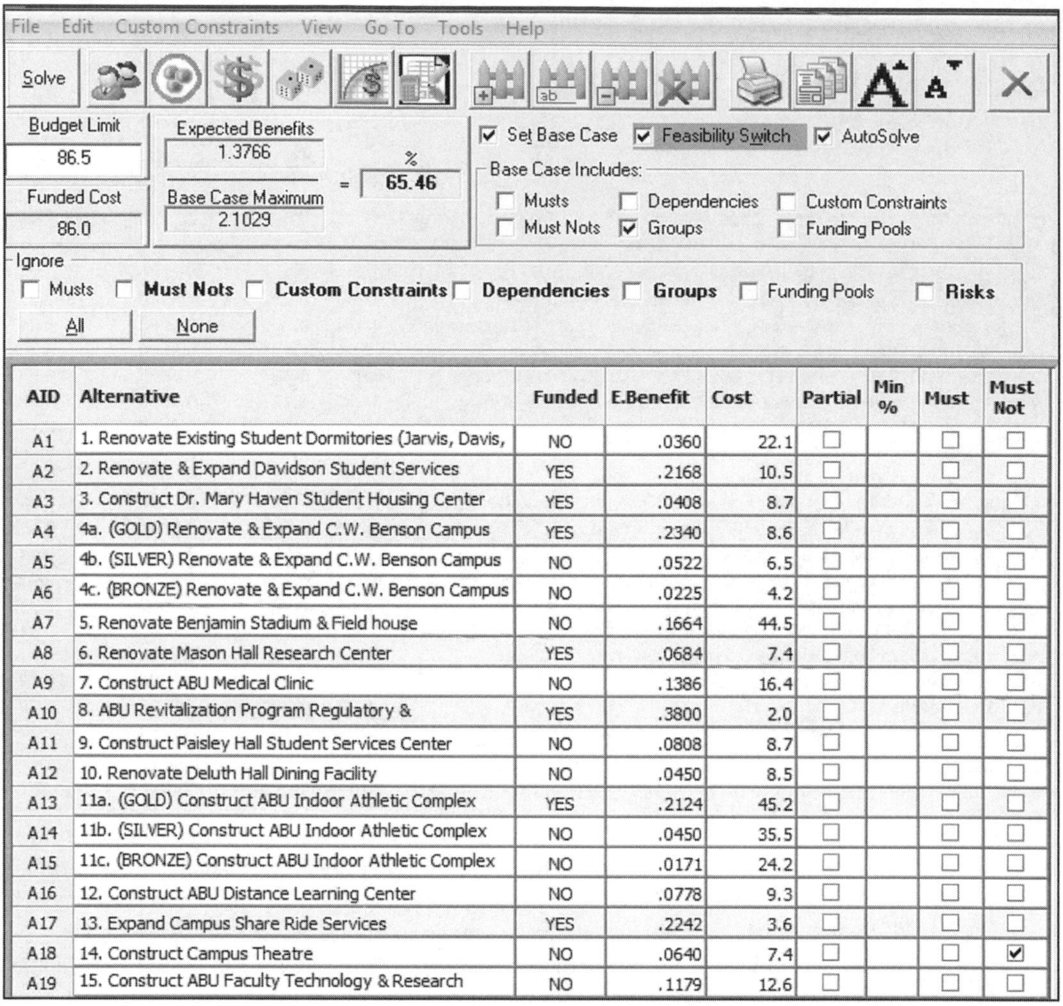

| File | Edit | Custom Constraints | View | Go To | Tools | Help |

Solve

Budget Limit **86.5**
Expected Benefits **1.3766**
Funded Cost **86.0**
Base Case Maximum **2.1029**

= **65.46** %

☑ Set Base Case   ☑ Feasibility Switch   ☑ AutoSolve
Base Case Includes:
☐ Musts   ☐ Dependencies   ☐ Custom Constraints
☐ Must Nots ☑ Groups   ☐ Funding Pools

Ignore
☐ Musts   ☐ **Must Nots**   ☐ **Custom Constraints**   ☐ **Dependencies**   ☐ **Groups**   ☐ Funding Pools   ☐ **Risks**
All   **None**

AID	Alternative	Funded	E.Benefit	Cost	Partial	Min %	Must	Must Not
A1	1. Renovate Existing Student Dormitories (Jarvis, Davis,	NO	.0360	22.1	☐		☐	☐
A2	2. Renovate & Expand Davidson Student Services	YES	.2168	10.5	☐		☐	☐
A3	3. Construct Dr. Mary Haven Student Housing Center	YES	.0408	8.7	☐		☐	☐
A4	4a. (GOLD) Renovate & Expand C.W. Benson Campus	YES	.2340	8.6	☐		☐	☐
A5	4b. (SILVER) Renovate & Expand C.W. Benson Campus	NO	.0522	6.5	☐		☐	☐
A6	4c. (BRONZE) Renovate & Expand C.W. Benson Campus	NO	.0225	4.2	☐		☐	☐
A7	5. Renovate Benjamin Stadium & Field house	NO	.1664	44.5	☐		☐	☐
A8	6. Renovate Mason Hall Research Center	YES	.0684	7.4	☐		☐	☐
A9	7. Construct ABU Medical Clinic	NO	.1386	16.4	☐		☐	☐
A10	8. ABU Revitalization Program Regulatory &	YES	.3800	2.0	☐		☐	☐
A11	9. Construct Paisley Hall Student Services Center	NO	.0808	8.7	☐		☐	☐
A12	10. Renovate Deluth Hall Dining Facility	NO	.0450	8.5	☐		☐	☐
A13	11a. (GOLD) Construct ABU Indoor Athletic Complex	YES	.2124	45.2	☐		☐	☐
A14	11b. (SILVER) Construct ABU Indoor Athletic Complex	NO	.0450	35.5	☐		☐	☐
A15	11c. (BRONZE) Construct ABU Indoor Athletic Complex	NO	.0171	24.2	☐		☐	☐
A16	12. Construct ABU Distance Learning Center	NO	.0778	9.3	☐		☐	☐
A17	13. Expand Campus Share Ride Services	YES	.2242	3.6	☐		☐	☐
A18	14. Construct Campus Theatre	NO	.0640	7.4	☐		☐	☑
A19	15. Construct ABU Faculty Technology & Research	NO	.1179	12.6	☐		☐	☐

Figure 9.37   Resource Aligner showing expected benefits or benefits reduced by risk

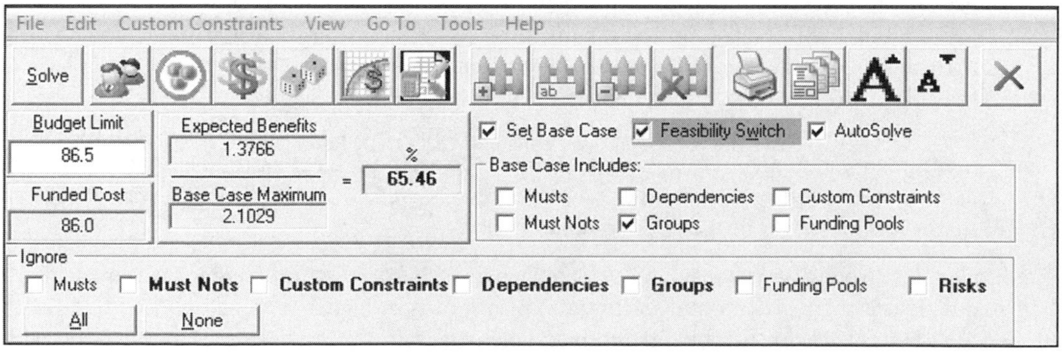

| File | Edit | Custom Constraints | View | Go To | Tools | Help |

Solve

Budget Limit **86.5**
Expected Benefits **1.3766**
Funded Cost **86.0**
Base Case Maximum **2.1029**

= **65.46** %

☑ Set Base Case   ☑ Feasibility Switch   ☑ AutoSolve
Base Case Includes:
☐ Musts   ☐ Dependencies   ☐ Custom Constraints
☐ Must Nots ☑ Groups   ☐ Funding Pools

Ignore
☐ Musts   ☐ **Must Nots**   ☐ **Custom Constraints**   ☐ **Dependencies**   ☐ **Groups**   ☐ Funding Pools   ☐ **Risks**
All   **None**

Figure 9.38   Funded cost and expected benefits percent considering all constraints and risk

save it as a scenario in the current model. Use the "File" menu, "Save As" command, but remember to select "No" when asked whether to save changes to the prior model to avoid overlaying it with the changes just made.

Of particular interest to the Board of Trustees is Project 7 (Construct ABU Medical Clinic) that is not funded at this budget level. They believe that a medical clinic is an important feature for a campus as large as ABU. Members of the Steering Committee, when revisiting the Efficient Frontier with what appears to be the optimal portfolio, can see that at the $81.5M interval, the Medical Clinic project becomes funded and, rather than selecting the GOLD option for Project 11a (Construct ABU Indoor Athletic Complex), the BRONZE option, Project 11c, is selected. In addition to Project 7, Project 6 (Renovate Mason Hall Research Center) is now funded. Since the maximum number of new construction projects is three, Project 15 (Construct ABU Faculty Technology Center) is eliminated. In addition to Project 7, Project 6 (Renovate Mason Hall Research Center) is now funded.

As seen in Figure 9.39, at a cost of only $81.4M—$4.6M less—Project 7 (Construct ABU Medical Clinic) is selected. Recall that to revisit the Efficient Frontier, use the graph icon in the Resource Aligner, change the approximate number of increments, if desired, and then click on "Solve." Figure 9.39 shows the result of solving with 50 increments and examining the "Budget, Benefit %, Cost" window on the upper right side of the screen.

When Resource Aligner is given a new budget limit of only $81.5M, the optimal selected portfolio is shown in Figure 9.40. Selecting this alternative portfolio results in a smaller expected benefit percent than the earlier proposed optimal portfolio at a budget limit of $86.5M, but the Steering Committee believes that the trade-offs should be considered by the Board of Trustees in comparison to the earlier proposed optimal portfolio.

Therefore, the Steering Committee elected to present two portfolios to the Board of Trustees, together with rationale. The first portfolio, shown in Figure 9.41, is the optimal portfolio at a budget limit of $86.5M, a funded cost of $86.0M, and an expected benefit of 65.46%, based on the evaluations, all constraints, and consideration of risk. It includes construction of the ABU Faculty Technology & Research Center rather than the ABU Medical Clinic.

Delta when optimizing for Increasing Budgets		
⊙ Approx. # of Increments [50] ○ Min Cost 2.0 □ 3D Plot		
○ Specified Amount ○ Min. Difference of Costs .1		

Budget	81.5	87.2
Benefit %	62.8%	65.5%
Cost	81.4	86.0
	2. Renovate & Expand Davidson Student Servi	2. Renovate & Expand Davidson Student Sern
	3. Construct Dr. Mary Haven Student Housing	3. Construct Dr. Mary Haven Student Housing
	4a. (GOLD) Renovate & Expand C.W. Benson (	4a. (GOLD) Renovate & Expand C.W. Benson
	6. Renovate Mason Hall Research Center	6. Renovate Mason Hall Research Center
	7. Construct ABU Medical Clinic	8. ABU Revitalization Program Regulatory & E
	8. ABU Revitalization Program Regulatory & Er	11a. (GOLD) Construct ABU Indoor Athletic C(
	11c. (BRONZE) Construct ABU Indoor Athletic (	13. Expand Campus Share Ride Services
	13. Expand Campus Share Ride Services	

Figure 9.39   Examining the Efficient Frontier to discover trade-offs or breakthroughs

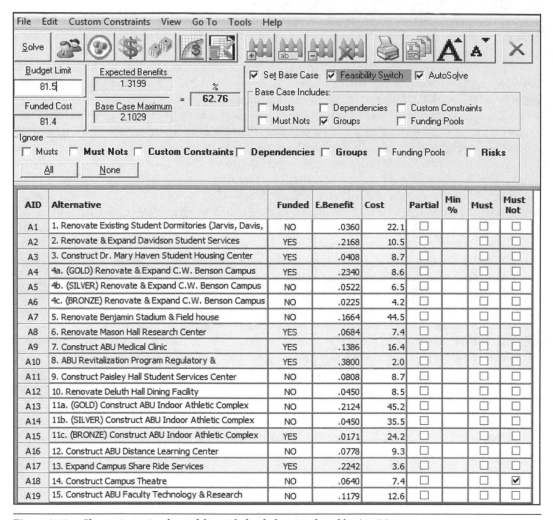

Figure 9.40   Change in optimal portfolio with funded cost reduced by $4.6M

The second portfolio that includes construction of the ABU Medical Clinic rather than the ABU Faculty Technology and Research Center is shown in Figure 9.42. It is based on the same considerations as the first portfolio but with a lower budget limit of $81.5M, a funded cost of $81.4M, and a lower expected benefit of 62.76%.

In Resource Aligner, use the "Go To" menu, "Portfolio Scenarios" to save both versions of the optimal portfolio so that you are able to quickly review either one. First, save the "ABU Initial Portfolio $86.5 Million" scenario, then change the budget limit to $81.5M and save the "ABU Trade-Off Portfolio $81.5 Million" scenario. When completed, the "Portfolio Scenarios" window should resemble Figure 9.43 if the earlier trial scenarios of $200 Million and $50 Million were retained.

Figure 9.44 shows the funded alternatives for the first optimal portfolio, "ABU Initial Portfolio $86.5 Million" using a bubble chart with the bubble size determined by risk. The larger the assessed risk for a given project, the larger the bubble representing it; for example, Project 6 has the largest bubble in Figure 9.44, so it is easy to see that it has the highest risk of the projects selected for funding. Note that Project 8 is selected and has a bubble color of gray, because it supports all objectives and thus was not assigned a category (or was assigned "No category value" in the legend).

AID	Alternative	Funded	E.Benefit	Cost	Partial	Min %	Must	Must Not
A1	1. Renovate Existing Student Dormitories (Jarvis, Davis,	NO	.0360	22.1	☐		☐	☐
A2	2. Renovate & Expand Davidson Student Services	YES	.2168	10.5	☐		☐	☐
A3	3. Construct Dr. Mary Haven Student Housing Center	YES	.0408	8.7	☐		☐	☐
A4	4a. (GOLD) Renovate & Expand C.W. Benson Campus	YES	.2340	8.6	☐		☐	☐
A5	4b. (SILVER) Renovate & Expand C.W. Benson Campus	NO	.0522	6.5	☐		☐	☐
A6	4c. (BRONZE) Renovate & Expand C.W. Benson Campus	NO	.0225	4.2	☐		☐	☐
A7	5. Renovate Benjamin Stadium & Field house	NO	.1664	44.5	☐		☐	☐
A8	6. Renovate Mason Hall Research Center	YES	.0684	7.4	☐		☐	☐
A9	7. Construct ABU Medical Clinic	NO	.1386	16.4	☐		☐	☐
A10	8. ABU Revitalization Program Regulatory &	YES	.3800	2.0	☐		☐	☐
A11	9. Construct Paisley Hall Student Services Center	NO	.0808	8.7	☐		☐	☐
A12	10. Renovate Deluth Hall Dining Facility	NO	.0450	8.5	☐		☐	☐
A13	11a. (GOLD) Construct ABU Indoor Athletic Complex	YES	.2124	45.2	☐		☐	☐
A14	11b. (SILVER) Construct ABU Indoor Athletic Complex	NO	.0450	35.5	☐		☐	☐
A15	11c. (BRONZE) Construct ABU Indoor Athletic Complex	NO	.0171	24.2	☐		☐	☐
A16	12. Construct ABU Distance Learning Center	NO	.0778	9.3	☐		☐	☐
A17	13. Expand Campus Share Ride Services	YES	.2242	3.6	☐		☐	☐
A18	14. Construct Campus Theatre	NO	.0640	7.4	☐		☐	☑
A19	15. Construct ABU Faculty Technology & Research	NO	.1179	12.6	☐		☐	☐

Figure 9.41   Optimal portfolio with $86.5M budget limit and funded cost of $86.1M

AID	Alternative	Funded	E.Benefit	Cost	Partial	Min %	Must	Must Not
A1	1. Renovate Existing Student Dormitories (Jarvis,	NO	.0360	22.1	☐		☐	☐
A2	2. Renovate & Expand Davidson Student Services	YES	.2168	10.5	☐		☐	☐
A3	3. Construct Dr. Mary Haven Student Housing Center	YES	.0408	8.7	☐		☐	☐
A4	4a. (GOLD) Renovate & Expand C.W. Benson Campus	YES	.2340	8.6	☐		☐	☐
A5	4b. (SILVER) Renovate & Expand C.W. Benson Campus	NO	.0522	6.5	☐		☐	☐
A6	4c. (BRONZE) Renovate & Expand C.W. Benson	NO	.0225	4.2	☐		☐	☐
A7	5. Renovate Benjamin Stadium & Field house	NO	.1664	44.5	☐		☐	☐
A8	6. Renovate Mason Hall Research Center	YES	.0684	7.4	☐		☐	☐
A9	7. Construct ABU Medical Clinic	YES	.1386	16.4	☐		☐	☐
A10	8. ABU Revitalization Program Regulatory &	YES	.3800	2.0	☐		☐	☐
A11	9. Construct Paisley Hall Student Services Center	NO	.0808	8.7	☐		☐	☐
A12	10. Renovate Deluth Hall Dining Facility	YES	.0450	8.5	☐		☐	☐
A13	11a. (GOLD) Construct ABU Indoor Athletic Complex	NO	.2124	45.2	☐		☐	☐
A14	11b. (SILVER) Construct ABU Indoor Athletic Complex	NO	.0450	35.5	☐		☐	☐
A15	11c. (BRONZE) Construct ABU Indoor Athletic Complex	YES	.0171	24.2	☐		☐	☐
A16	12. Construct ABU Distance Learning Center	NO	.0778	9.3	☐		☐	☐
A17	13. Expand Campus Share Ride Services	YES	.2242	3.6	☐		☐	☐
A18	14. Construct Campus Theatre	NO	.0640	7.4	☐		☐	☑
A19	15. Construct ABU Faculty Technology & Research	NO	.1179	12.6	☐		☐	☐

Figure 9.42   Trade-off portfolio with $81.5M budget limit and funded cost of $81.4M

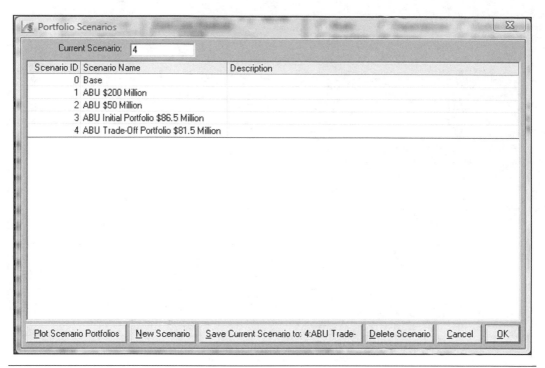

Figure 9.43   Portfolio scenarios window after saving initial and trade-off scenarios

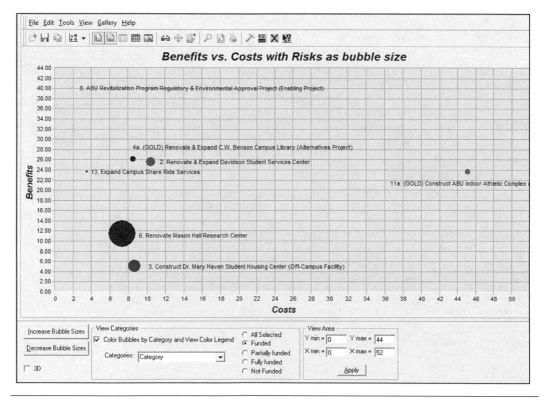

Figure 9.44   Original optimal portfolio benefits vs. costs with risks as bubble size

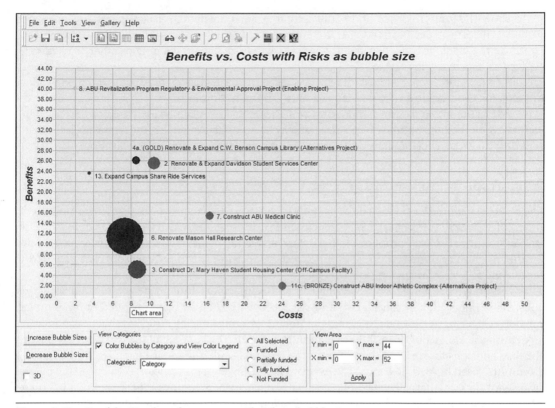

Figure 9.45   Portfolio Two benefits vs. costs with risks as bubble size

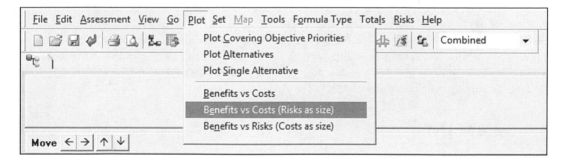

Figure 9.46   Preparing to plot trade-off portfolio

As described in Chapter 8, the location of a project on the chart is determined by increasing costs across the horizontal axis and increasing (expected) benefits along the vertical axis. The most desirable projects are thus found in the upper left quadrant with small bubbles; for the selected portfolio, the combination of projects shown is the most desirable portfolio with respect to the goal, given the specified constraints. Compare the chart positions of Project 11a and Project 11c in Figures 9.44 and 9.45, respectively, as an example of two of the alternative approaches to a project. Project 11a, the GOLD alternative, has considerably more expected benefit and, commensurately, considerably more cost than Project 11c, the BRONZE alternative.

To show the same information for the second optimal portfolio, select the scenario just saved named "ABU Trade-Off Portfolio $81.5M" to load it into the Resource Aligner. Then, in the Data Grid, use the "Plot" menu, "Benefits vs Costs (Risks as size)" and take note of other available plot choices, as shown in Figure 9.46.

Select the "ABU Trade-Off Portfolio $81.5M" scenario in the Resource Aligner and then produce the plot for the trade-off portfolio. To see only the funded projects with this scenario, select the "Funded" radio button as shown in Figure 9.45. The bubble sizes can be increased or decreased; review the options at the bottom of the screen. It may be necessary to move some of the labels for better legibility. To do so, click on the label to select it and then drag it to the desired position.

9.8.6 Approval to Proceed and Next Steps

The Steering Committee presented the portfolio scenario analysis process used and the results to the Board of Trustees at its regularly scheduled monthly meeting, for which the ABU Campus Revitalization Program Project Portfolio was a major agenda item. The Board of Trustees had been briefed on the program and interim project portfolio status in two prior meetings, so it was prepared to receive the final recommendation.

During the meeting the ABU Steering Committee members addressed the portfolio scenarios, constraints imposed, and consideration of risk along with the two recommended optimal project portfolios. During a previous Steering Committee meeting, the meeting facilitator conducted a structuring session using TeamTime to determine pros and cons of each of the two portfolios. Using the pros and cons to construct objectives for the portfolio (rather than for the projects), the Steering Committee used keypads to conduct an evaluation of the overall portfolio objectives and the relative priority of the two alternative portfolios. The Board of Trustees approved the recommended trade-off portfolio, "ABU Trade-Off Portfolio $81.5 Million." The portfolio includes the medical clinic for a total estimated cost of $81.4M. The Board provided the Steering Committee with the funding and the authority to launch the portfolio.

Additionally, the Board of Trustees requested that the Steering Committee, along with selected representatives from the facilities department, prepare a high-level schedule to be presented at the next monthly Board of Trustees meeting for each funded project, showing start and end dates, major milestones, and expected cash flow. Progress on the portfolio is to be reviewed with the Board of Trustees quarterly, while progress on each project is to be reported weekly to the Steering Committee by ABU facilities in conjunction with the PMO.

9.9 SUMMARY

Before this chapter, the strategic plan was developed or adjusted. Objectives were prioritized with respect to the goal, project proposals were solicited and pre-screened, business cases were screened to select a pool of candidate projects for the portfolio, and the initial portfolios were established, including various funding scenarios.

In this chapter we considered the effects of project dependencies and mandatory or prohibited projects, established resource constraints, applied balance and coverage to address executive guidance about distribution of projects across objectives and business areas, applied the concept of risk to benefits, and performed further portfolio scenario analysis. The output of the portfolio selection process is a portfolio (or multiple portfolios) of projects that best achieves organizational objectives, at a specified funding level, under constraints and risk. Further, to the extent possible, it satisfies competing demands within the organization.

Appropriate tools and a methodical process were used to produce rational, traceable, and defensible portfolio decisions. Ultimately, each organization determines what constitutes an optimal portfolio. With the optimal portfolio selected and funding authorized, the hard work of implementing the portfolio begins. In Chapter 10 we discuss the transition of the portfolio from selection to implementation and the iterative management of project portfolio cycles.

9.10 REFERENCES

Cohen, Allan R. (2002). "Power, Politics, and Influence: Savvy and Substance in Organizations" (Chapter 5). *The Portable MBA in Management*, 2nd ed. Hoboken, NJ. John Wiley & Sons.

Davidson Frame, J. (2002). "Selecting Projects That Will Lead to Success" (Chapter 9). *The New Project Management: Tools for an Age of Rapid Change, Complexity, and Other Business Realities*, 2nd ed. San Francisco, CA: Jossey-Bass.

Dupuit, J. (1844). "De la mesure de l'utilité des travaux publics," *Annales de Ponts et Chaussées*, 2nd series, vol. 8. Translated: Dupuit, J. (1952). "On the Measurement of Utility of Public Works," *International Economic Papers* 2, 83-110. English translation reprinted in K. J. Arrow and T. Scitovsky (1969). *Readings in Welfare Economics*, Homewood, IL: Richard D. Irwin, 255-283.

Lawrence, P. R. and J. W. Lorsch (1969). *Organization and Environment*. Homewood, IL: Richard D. Irwin.

Levine, Harvey A. (2005). *Project Portfolio Management: A Practical Guide to Selecting Projects, Managing Portfolios, and Maximizing Benefits*. San Francisco, CA: Jossey-Bass Business and Management Series.

Markowitz, H. (1952). *The Journal of Finance*, vol. 7, no. 1 (March), 77-91. Published by Blackwell Publishing for the American Finance Association.

Pinto, Jeffrey K. (1998). "What is Organizational Politics?" (Chapter 4). *Power & Politics in Project Management*. Newton Square, PA. Project Management Institute.

10

Implementing and Governing the Project Portfolio

With an approved project portfolio, the organization has successfully completed a major decision milestone by identifying and selecting the optimal project portfolio to meet strategic goals and objectives given specified constraints. As the portfolio moves into the implementation phase, the project portfolio management (PPM) system must shift to monitoring and controlling project and portfolio performance.

This chapter focuses on establishing a structure to collect relevant project and portfolio performance information as well as governance and roles and responsibilities, including the bounds of decision authority at each level of the PPM hierarchy. To effectively monitor project and portfolio performance, metrics must be identified, performance targets established, unacceptable variances determined, and performance information and reporting specified. This chapter establishes the process, infrastructure, governance, and roles and responsibilities necessary to effectively monitor, evaluate, and control projects and portfolios as described in Chapter 11. In Figure 10.1, the implementation phase and the evaluation phase appear to be sequential; in fact, these two phases are iterative and in a nearly constant state of overlap.

To effectively monitor performance and make appropriate controlling decisions, resulting in corrective actions, periodic measurements based on accurate and timely information are required. Corrective action in this context means implementing the project and portfolio decisions to bring performance back to baselines; for example, a project manager can elect to use crashing to bring schedule performance back to baseline, or a program manager can reallocate resources from a project performing ahead of plan to one performing behind plan. Corrective actions also include portfolio adjustments determined by the portfolio management board (PMB) such as termination of a project that is no longer expected to deliver its anticipated benefits. The decisions made during implementation and evaluation are governed by a reporting structure with well-defined roles, responsibilities, and limits of authority. The decision makers are supported by an infrastructure that gathers and reports consistent information about the progress of the projects in the current portfolio. In addition, the organization's PPM plan must define the measurement cycles and specify the performance deviations requiring corrective action. The process must deliver the *right* information to the *right* people at the *right* time to enable them to make the *right* decisions.

Project Portfolio Management (PPM) Model

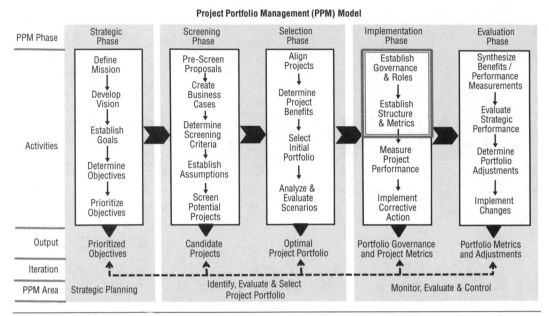

Figure 10.1   PPM model—Implementation Phase

10.1 PORTFOLIO PERFORMANCE REPORTING STRUCTURE

PPM decision making is influenced by the organizational context in which the decisions are made. The goal is to institute governance appropriate to both the structure of the organization and the maturity of the process. An expansive management structure creates unnecessary bureaucracy while a structure that is too limited may inhibit effective management. A conceptual PPM structure is presented in Figure 10.2 and shows a supportive sample structure. The organization shown has one set of goals and objectives and one project portfolio. Rarely is reality as simple as this illustration, but it shows a basis for establishing a management structure consistent with organizational goals and objectives. Each element of the structure shown is described briefly from the bottom to the top.

A project manager, supported by a project management team, manages one or more projects. The project manager leads the project team and is responsible for achieving the scope, the cost and schedule performance of the project as well as customer satisfaction for the project.

A program manager, often supported by a program management office (PgMO), manages one or more programs; a program is commonly described as a collection of related projects. The Project Management Institute (PMI, 2004) defines the PgMO as "the centralized management of a particular program, or programs, such that corporate benefit is realized by sharing of resources, methodologies, tools, and techniques, and related to high-level project management focus." (Note that the PMBoK used the abbreviation PMO instead of PgMO.) The program manager is responsible for achieving scope, cost and schedule performance of the program, as well as customer satisfaction for the program.

The project management office (PMO) manages the information systems and processes required to consolidate and report project and program performance, and to allocate resources across the projects and programs, among other functions.

Projects and programs that align to a common goal and its supporting objectives serve as a reasonable basis for grouping as a portfolio. Other bases for grouping include product lines, divisions, business areas, and markets. Organizations with multiple portfolios frequently designate portfolio

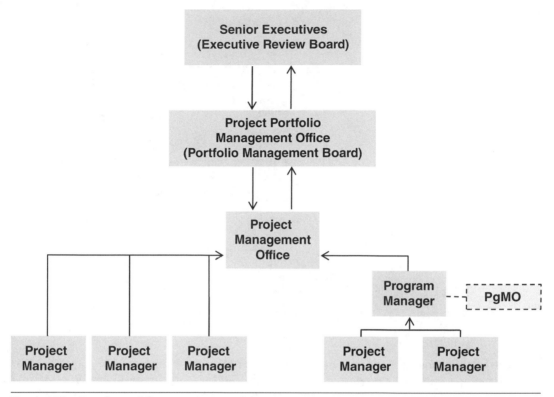

Figure 10.2   Sample portfolio management structure

managers who manage one or more portfolios. These portfolio managers often report to the executive responsible for the product line, division, or other grouping, along with their peers from operations. The portfolio manager is responsible for delivering the expected benefits of the portfolio and, further, those of the member projects, which is an important point to consider and is different from the responsibilities of the project manager. At the project level, the project manager is focused on pure project performance and successfully completing the project according to established baselines. However, at the portfolio level, the portfolio manager must also be mindful of how projects are performing in relation to the benefits they are expected to provide in addition to each project's respective performance. Therefore, decisions by the portfolio manager are made in a different context and from a different perspective than decisions made by the project manager.

A project portfolio management office (PPMO), like the PMB described in this book, is established to manage the selection, implementation, and evaluation of project portfolios. In some organizations the PMO and the PPMO may be a part of a single group or office that drives both project and portfolio management processes. It includes both project management and portfolio management expertise that can streamline reporting and controlling.

Senior executives, like the executive review board (ERB) described in this book, establish and drive the organization's mission, vision, goals, and objectives, prioritize the objectives, and review and approve project portfolios.

Larger, more complex organizations with multiple divisions or product lines may have multiple levels of strategic goals and objectives, each with one or more portfolios that contain projects that support them. Each portfolio contains the projects that support a subset of goals and objectives common to that part of the organization, as shown in Figure 10.3.

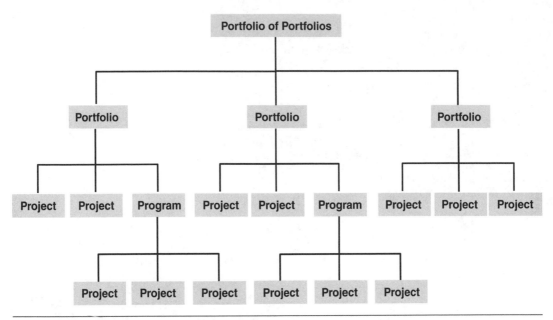

Figure 10.3   Sample structure for PPM in organizations with multiple portfolios

Some complex organizations may establish separate PMOs and PPMOs for each portfolio. Others with multiple portfolios may elect to establish a single PPMO with responsibility for PPM across the enterprise. Organizations with mature PPM processes and compatible governance models can achieve considerable economies of scale and consistency with a single PPMO.

Global or highly segmented organizations may establish a management structure to manage the portfolio of portfolios. In this book, and as shown in Figure 10.2, we have described the PMB as the group responsible for managing portfolios. As mentioned earlier, the name of the group is insignificant, but the roles and responsibilities must be carried out in any organization implementing PPM. Preferably, the PMB is comprised of highly experienced personnel who are intimately familiar with the organization's operating and cultural environment. Additionally, they must effectively interact with senior executives, understand the organization's strategic plan and the process of managing it, and be knowledgeable about its project management maturity and capabilities. As the PMB represents a critical transition point between strategy and tactics, its people must effectively collaborate with executives on strategic PPM decisions.

It is imperative to implement a PPM structure that is congruent with the organization's governance structure and unique business environment. Along with the management structure, clear governance must be established and communicated to identify who is responsible for what actions and decisions during the implementation and evaluation phases.

10.2 PPM GOVERNANCE DURING IMPLEMENTATION

Roles, responsibilities, and limits of authority define the governance that drives portfolio selection, monitoring, controlling, and adjustments within the organization's PPM system. Governance defines expectations, grants power, or verifies performance; it specifies the process of decision making by which decisions are implemented (or not implemented). Governance plays an important role within the PPM process by empowering decision makers within the organization's PPM hierarchy by providing guidance about the limitations or boundaries of the decisions that can and cannot be made at each hierarchical level.

Blomquist and Muller (2006) noted that corporate governance is defined by the Organization for Economic Co-operation and Development as involving ". . . a set of relationships between a company's management, its board, its shareholders, and other stakeholders. Corporate governance also provides the structure through which the objectives of the company are set, and the means of attaining those objectives and monitoring performance are determined." The Association for Project Managers (APM) in the United Kingdom introduces the subject of project management governance, including portfolio management. "Effective governance of project management ensures that an organization's project portfolio is aligned to the organization's objectives, is delivered efficiently and is sustainable. Governance of project management also supports the means by which the boards, and other major project stakeholders, are provided with timely, relevant and reliable information" (APM, 2004). Also in the United Kingdom, the Office of Government Commerce (OGC, 2010) suggests that portfolio management governance be integrated with existing senior management disciplines such as risk management, capital investment, and performance management and that appropriate processes are ". . . in place to support decision making at every level of the portfolio" (OGC, 2010). In other words, portfolio governance should be embedded in organizational governance rather than being separate from it.

During implementation, all management levels within the PPM process perform monitoring and controlling activities and are empowered to make decisions. However, each manager is bound by decision-making limitations. This important point is key to understanding who is responsible for making what decisions when interpreting the results from monitoring and evaluating activities. At the project level the project manager is traditionally empowered to make decisions necessary to maintain project performance to established baselines as long as these decisions do not negatively impact other projects' baselines. This empowerment comes in the form of guidance in the portfolio management plan and the project charter that assigns the project manager. Common decisions by the project manager include reallocating resources within the project, for example, to compress the schedule when a project falls behind the baseline schedule. However, other decisions such as terminating the project, acquiring resources or funding not otherwise assigned, or changing the baseline cost or schedule are not usually within the authority of the project manager.

Similarly, at the portfolio level, the portfolio manager is empowered to make decisions to maintain the portfolio's baseline performance. Resources from projects within the portfolio that are performing ahead of cost and schedule baselines may be reallocated to other projects that need them within the portfolio. Corrective action decisions made by the portfolio manager are made in the best interest of the entire portfolio without changing the relative benefits expected to be provided by the projects and the portfolio. While the project manager losing resources may not fully appreciate such decisions, they may be necessary to ensure portfolio success. Although the portfolio manager accommodates directed adjustments to the portfolio, he does not have the authority to determine whether or which projects are added or terminated. Nor does he have the authority to authorize adjustments to the anticipated benefit of the portfolio or any of its member projects, since the anticipated benefits are relative to the anticipated benefits of all other candidate projects and were established by prioritization within the organization's PPM process (Chapter 7). Of course, the portfolio manager is responsible for providing and is expected to provide appropriate supporting information and arguments affecting such decisions.

Project terminations, addition of new projects, and adjustments to baseline anticipated and expected benefits for projects and portfolios all rest with the PMB and ERB and are made within the organization's PPM process; these changes are known as portfolio adjustments. The difficult decision to terminate a project depends on information derived from monitoring and controlling activities when the termination is due to poor project performance. Completion or termination of existing projects can lead to the addition of new projects to the portfolio. Changes to the organization's strategic plan, based on either a new planning cycle or real time factors, can also result in portfolio adjustments, including project terminations, addition of new projects, and even reevaluation leading to the selection of another optimal portfolio under different constraints.

By assigning roles and responsibilities and establishing performance indicators, measurements can be documented and reported to the right people. Each reporting level in turn can evaluate performance information by comparing ongoing project and portfolio performance to baselines and determine whether the project or portfolio remains on track to achieve its expected benefits and contribute to strategic objectives. Deviations outside the limits specified in the PPM plan require portfolio adjustments or corrective actions that impact portfolio baselines. Roles and responsibilities as well as limits of authority ensure that the appropriate people are involved in critical PPM decisions during implementation and evaluation.

10.3 EVOLVING PPM ROLES AND RESPONSIBILITIES

As the PPM process progresses from the strategic phase through evaluation, the roles and responsibilities of groups within the organization continue to evolve and the focus and intensity of effort changes among the groups. Figure 10.4 shows the same structure as Figure 10.2 with the addition of sample responsibilities of each of the groups involved in PPM. For example, the ERB revises the strategic plan; prioritizes objectives; establishes major constraints such as funding, balance, and coverage; and approves the portfolios or directs further analysis.

Figure 10.5 shows the same diagram as Figure 10.4 with the annotations and directional arrows showing the flow of information among the groups. For example, information that flows from the

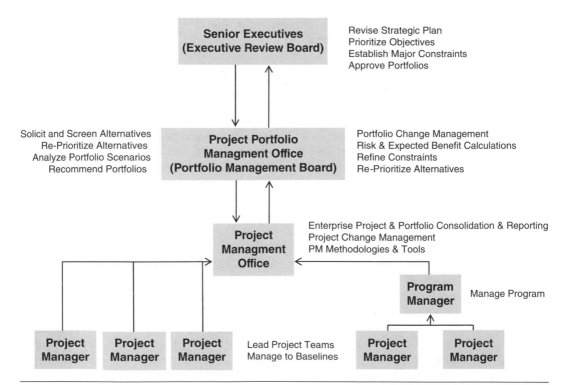

Figure 10.4   Sample portfolio management structure with high-level roles and responsibilities

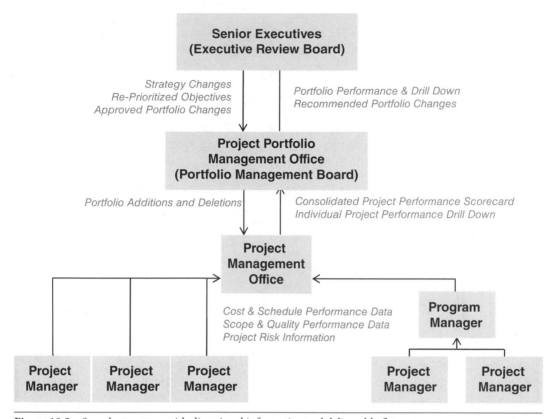

Figure 10.5 Sample structure with directional information and deliverable flows

ERB to the PMB includes strategy changes, reprioritized objectives, and approved changes to the portfolio. Information that flows from the PMB to the ERB includes portfolio performance information and recommended changes to the portfolio based on performance data or changes in strategy. In reality, information flows are bidirectional, but the arrows show the flow of decisions and recommendations.

Figure 10.6 combines Figures 10.4 and 10.5 and shows the roles and responsibilities as well as the flow of information and deliverables. Additionally, it provides an overview of a sample PPM structure, responsibilities, and information flow at a glance.

In the strategic phase, senior executives are the driving force behind the development of the strategic plan while PPM governance groups such as the ERB and PMB play a critical supporting role, in part by driving the process and by assisting executives to prioritize strategic objectives. Collaboration between executives and PPM groups during this phase results in the strategic plan (see Chapter 2) and prioritized objectives (see Chapter 4). As the PPM process progresses into the screening and selection phases, groups responsible for PPM oversight assume the central role in driving the process of selecting the project portfolio. The PMB, assisted by the PMO, develops a portfolio management plan that provides guidance about how the portfolio will be managed (the portfolio management plan is discussed in more detail later in this chapter). As the strategic plan is completed, the intensity of effort shifts from executives to the PMB and ERB who are now charged with identifying, selecting, and implementing the project portfolio. That is, the ERB and PMB perform the primary work necessary to solicit project proposals, organize and conduct the project evaluation process, and facilitate the selection of the optimal portfolio by appropriate management. After portfolio selection, when

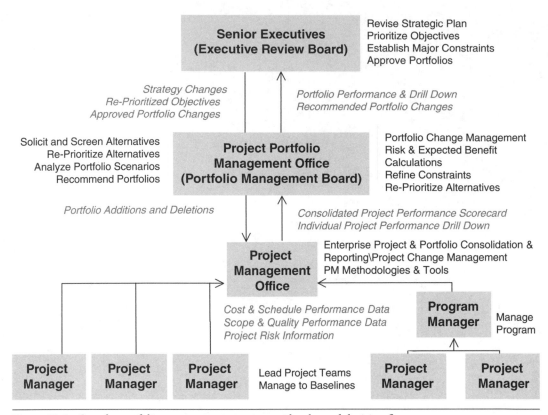

Figure 10.6   Sample portfolio management structure with roles and decision flow

the process moves into the implementation phase, roles and responsibilities continue to evolve and workload continues to change among groups.

During implementation project and program managers experience a dramatic increase in workload because they are responsible for effectively managing the selected projects, and the process of monitoring and controlling the projects is driven by the PMO or PgMO. (Of course, after any initial implementation, the workloads at all levels reach a relatively steady state.) While each project is unique, project management processes for all projects must be consistent to enable project teams to focus on delivery rather than on how to manage it. That consistency also enables coherent interpretation of progress across the organization. In most organizations the project management processes are developed, maintained, and communicated by the PMO, including the synthesis and reporting of project status.

Although the role of the PMO varies from organization to organization, for effective portfolio management the PMO or other responsible entity must establish and maintain the enterprise PPM system and integrate the selected portfolio into its database. This system provides for consistent project and portfolio performance reporting.

As projects are initiated and executed during implementation, the PMO is focused on monitoring and controlling to encourage completion within established performance indicator baselines. It directs corrective action when the performance indicators are outside documented acceptable variances. As projects within the portfolio near completion, the PMO works with the project teams and sponsors to ensure the project is transitioned into the organization's or the customer's operations and that the project is closed-out properly. It also documents the allocation of resources across the portfolio and coordinates changes to project cost and schedule baselines that do not affect expected benefit (i.e., benefits discounted for risk).

In contrast to the PMO's hands-on day-to-day operations, the ERB and PMB shift from identifying and evaluating candidates and recommending project portfolio(s) during the screening and selection phases to maintaining oversight of the chosen portfolios; that is, they manage, monitor, and control the portfolios and ensure the right mix of projects within the portfolio to achieve strategic objectives. While the PMO is concerned with ensuring that the projects in the portfolio perform to established baselines, the ERB and PMB focus on the delivery of expected benefits. The PMB manages the assessment of expected benefits and reports progress and changes to the ERB. The ERB, in turn, reports changes in strategy to the PMB. Either communication can cause a reevaluation of the portfolio. The ERB is well positioned to assess external or internal forces that might negatively (realized risks) or positively (unexpected opportunities) affect the portfolios. For instance, when an organization is unable to access adequate capital to fund planned organizational initiatives due to sudden changes in financial markets, a portfolio risk is realized. Such a realized risk forces the organization to make changes to its strategic plan, consequently requiring adjustment to project portfolios. In an organization using a robust PPM process, unforeseen circumstances can be addressed rapidly and effectively, as seen later in this chapter. As projects in the portfolios make their way through execution, the ERB and PMB assess portfolio performance data to evaluate the status of the organization's portfolios and make the necessary adjustments.

10.4 TYPES OF PORTFOLIO PERFORMANCE MONITORING AND CONTROL

The purpose of the implementation phase is not just to execute and deliver the projects within the portfolio, it is also to ensure that projects and portfolios are performing to plan and, if not, to identify and fix performance problems before they become severe enough to risk successful project and portfolio completion, thereby jeopardizing the accomplishment of strategic objectives. While all levels of the PPM structure rely on performance indicators for monitoring, the controlling decisions that apply corrective action are made from differing perspectives. In general, PPM decisions are derived from examining two forms of performance information flow: (1) bottom-up performance reporting and (2) top-down changes in strategy or priorities.

In bottom-up reporting, performance information flows up from individual projects to the PMO, through the portfolio manager, and up to the PMB and ERB. Controlling adjustment decisions are made at each level that are not expected to affect performance at the next higher level, as described in the decision flow shown in Figure 10.4. For example, a project manager can make decisions that result in conformance to baselines for the project and do not affect the performance of any other project, but must appeal any changes to baselines or resources to the next level. At the portfolio level, the portfolio manager can make decisions that result in the delivery of the portfolio at the expected benefit level, for example, reallocating resources from a project performing ahead of schedule and within budget to a project that is behind schedule; however, the portfolio manager cannot make decisions that will change the portfolio baselines, particularly any changes that impact expected benefit.

If a project's performance cannot be corrected or jeopardizes the portfolio's baselines, then corrective action recommendations are expected from the portfolio manager, but actual decisions rest with the PMB or ERB. In such a case, the PMB could decide to reallocate resources from one portfolio to another or recommend the termination of a project to the ERB, which must approve adjustments resulting from bottom-up performance reporting. Since termination of a project eliminates its anticipated and expected benefits, such a decision must be made by those owning the strategy. For smaller projects with inconsequential strategic impact, the organization can consider making such decisions at a lower level.

Changes in organizational strategies and the relative priority of the objectives flow down from executives and result in adjustments to the portfolio. This input from the top of the organization can be provided on a predictable basis, such as annually when the strategic plan is updated, or can happen at any time that the strategy is modified. In top-down information flow, portfolio adjustment decisions are based on factors influencing the organization's strategic plan. External or internal factors such as a new product offered by a competitor, changes in financial conditions, a merger or acquisition, and natural or man-made disasters can impact the organization's strategic plans. In the top-down portfolio performance decision process, executives can weigh the benefit of continuing to pursue underperforming portfolios or projects in the portfolios that no longer contribute to strategic objectives. When the strategy changes, the relative expected benefits change as well, often prompting reprioritization of the objectives and the projects that support their achievement.

Whether monitoring and controlling is bottom up or top down, decisions depend on accurate, complete, and timely information along with the tools and techniques to provide it. In addition to the infrastructure, clear definition of roles and responsibilities and articulated governance authorities and process must be in place.

10.5 FOUNDATION FOR MONITORING AND CONTROLLING THE PORTFOLIO

Sound project portfolio decision making is predicated on an infrastructure that facilitates the transfer and exchange of accurate information. In this section we explore the elements necessary to establish the foundation for PPM decision making, including the project portfolio management plan and the project portfolio management information system (PPMIS).

As stated, the central goal of the implementation phase is to successfully complete projects within the portfolio by effectively monitoring and controlling their performance, thus supporting the achievement of expected benefits. Whereas at the project level, success means completing projects within established baselines for the triple project constraints of cost, schedule, and specifications. Success in PPM means achieving anticipated expected benefits to support the achievement of organizational goals and objectives, which is the reason for undertaking the portfolio(s) in the first place. The primary management functions to achieve the central goal of the implementation phase are monitoring and controlling by establishing performance indicators, or metrics, and using them to apply judgment to determine corrective action or portfolio adjustments. By monitoring performance at regular intervals, performance problems can be identified early and controlling adjustments made to return performance to baseline expectations.

10.5.1 Project Portfolio Management Plan

Portfolios comprise multiple projects that can be performed in a single location or geographically dispersed. As a result, project teams can be collocated or distributed across multiple locations or even continents. For a portfolio containing a large number of projects, geographic diversity can pose numerous challenges to effective communication and management control. Rad (2006) describes the portfolio management plan as a document to guide the portfolio management staff in the establishment of portfolio management as well as its operation. He recommends that it include specific milestones and completion targets for each function to become fully operational. To add clarity of vision for project teams, when speaking of implementing PPM for the first time, Rad suggests that the implementation portion of the portfolio management plan include a schedule network diagram, bar chart, and a cost estimate. Additionally, the ongoing operation portion of the plan includes details of roles and responsibilities and specifics of interfaces with project managers, program managers, functional managers, stakeholders, and others. Although PMI does not specifically mention a project portfolio management plan in its standard for portfolio management, we strongly recommend that organizations establish such a plan.

We add that specifying levels of authority—who can make what decisions—is an important component of the project portfolio management plan, as is specifying the normal regular cycles for strategic plan revisions, portfolio reprioritization and adjustment, and portfolio and project performance reporting. Of course, these processes can be triggered at any time outside the normal cycles when a change in organizational conditions occurs.

The intent of the portfolio management plan is to increase clarity and uniformity while reducing ambiguity and inconsistency for portfolio decisions. The initial portfolio management plan must be completed early in the process of establishing PPM, prior to the implementation phase, and revised as necessary. Consistent and accurate information is vital to an effective PPM decision process, and the portfolio management plan is the primary document guiding managers about what information is required and when. While the portfolio management plan specifies what information needs to be exchanged and defines the governance criteria, the portfolio management information system provides the information infrastructure to facilitate effective documentation and the information exchange mechanism required to manage the portfolio.

10.5.2 Project Portfolio Management Information System

The Project Portfolio Management Information System (PPMIS) is the tool necessary to store and report project and portfolio performance information consistently. Projects, and project portfolios, generate enormous volumes of data that simply cannot be processed into actionable information efficiently or effectively without a PPMIS.

The PPMIS combines software, people, and processes to form an information collection and distribution system that provides the organization with an effective tool to manage project and portfolio performance. In some organizations, the PPMIS and the enterprise project management system are one and the same.

Additionally, the PPMIS provides the foundation to organize, store, exchange, process, analyze, report, and disseminate project and portfolio data and information among stakeholders. Its benefits include information processing, speed of communication, data and information exchange, analytical capabilities, increased productivity and, most importantly, decision support features.

The project and portfolio management software for the PPMIS is dictated by the organization's level of project and portfolio management maturity, the nature of projects undertaken, project management processes used by the organization, platforms supported, and organizational structure, among other factors. Large complex organizations relying heavily on projects and project portfolios benefit from robust enterprise project management software such as Microsoft's Enterprise Project Management, Oracle's Primavera, and PlanView among many other products. For effective portfolio management, important new features are needed to report project and portfolio performance with respect to anticipated benefits as well as traditional project cost and schedule performance. Regardless of other software tools used within the PPMIS, portfolio prioritization decisions are complex and require decision support software for structuring, measuring, and synthesizing evaluation results in a mathematically meaningful way. Likewise, portfolio optimization decisions require supporting tools that generate the combination of projects with the highest total benefit under specified constraints and that allow organizations to compare various scenarios. Such tools must be included in the PPMIS.

10.6 ITERATIVE NATURE OF PPM

Effective PPM is characterized by flexibility to iterate and respond rapidly to new information or strategic changes. Through the evaluation process, and integrated into the organization's strategic planning process and the PPM governance, organizations can rapidly adjust portfolios as conditions warrant. In this book the process is presented as strictly linear for purposes of presenting the material. However, in reality PPM activities overlap and, in many cases, are concurrent. Iteration is necessary due to changes in conditions, uncertainty about the future, response to realized risks, and to exploit emerging opportunities. Table 10.1 contains representative review and adjustment cycles and their suggested frequency of occurrence.

For organizations undertaking new product development projects, the PPM review cycles illustrated in Table 10.1 can be integrated with an organizational Stage-Gate process. This is the formal process or road map that many firms use to drive a new product projects from idea to launch (Cooper, 2001). This process is characterized by multiple stages, together with gates or decision points. It is also known in various forms as new product process, the gating process, or the phase-review process. This process is important to portfolio management because the stage gates are where Go/Kill decisions are made on individual new product projects.

As we'll describe in Chapter 11, decisions to kill, or terminate, a project require information about the project's current performance and its relative importance compared to other projects in terms of achieving strategic objectives. Thus, integrating the Stage-Gate process with the organization's PPM process provides the means to build confidence that continuing or terminating a new product development product is in the best interest of the organization. Stage-Gate is a registered trademark of R. G. Cooper & Associates Consultants. More information on this process can be located at http://www.stage-gate.com.

Determining how frequently review activities take place in a given organization includes consideration of the size, type, and duration of the projects it undertakes, its governance structure and processes, and the dynamics of the internal and external environments, in addition to other relevant factors. Specific guidelines for these cycles should be documented in the organization's project portfolio management plan. In Chapter 11 the cycles performed in the evaluation phase to report project and portfolio performance are described as well as cycles resulting from changes in organizational strategy.

Table 10.1 Representative review cycles for PPM activities

Project Portfolio Management Cycles	Week	Month	Quarter	Semi-Annual	Annual	Stage Gate	Strategy Change	Ongoing
STRATEGIC PHASE								
Define or Refine Mission / Vision / Goals /Objectives					X		X	
Prioritize Objectives					X		X	
SCREENING PHASE								
Prepare Business Cases				X	X			X
Revise Screening Criteria					X		X	
Screen Potential Projects				X	X		X	
SELECTION PHASE								
Prioritize Projects				X	X		X	
Define Constraints and Budget					X		X	
Perform Scenario Analysis								
Select or Revise Optimal Portfolio				X	X		X	
IMPLEMENTATION PHASE								
Report Project Performance (EVM)	X	X	X					
Report Benefits Performance (EVIPRO and EVI $_{PORT}$)		X	X				X	
EVALUATION PHASE								
Apply Project Corrective Action	X	X				X		X
Apply Portfolio Adjustment			X	X	X	X	X	

10.7 RESPONDING TO STRATEGIC CHANGE

As described in Chapter 2, the strategy of an organization is reviewed and updated on a regular basis, often annually. However, it can change at any time because of internal or external factors, including a merger or acquisition, the entry of a competitor into a market, new government regulations, and any number of other factors. In Chapter 4 the objectives from the strategic plan were prioritized, indicating their relative importance in terms of achieving organizational goals. In Chapter 7 the projects that successfully emerged from the screening process and became portfolio candidates were prioritized with respect to the objectives they support (local priority) and with respect to achieving the goal (global priority). Because strategy-changing events can occur suddenly and dramatically, the PPM process must be equally responsive.

The priorities of the objectives and the priorities (or benefits) of the alternatives are relative ratio-scale numbers that are only meaningful as long as the organizational strategy remains the same or the magnitude of the change is small enough that executives do not feel that reprioritizing objectives is required. When the strategy changes significantly, or when new objectives are introduced, reprioritization is required. This not only changes the relative priorities of the objectives and sub-objectives, it changes the relative priorities of the alternatives that support them as well. Such a change in strategy may also necessitate the introduction of new projects into the portfolio selection process. Additionally, the benefits (or relative priorities) of the alternatives continue to be meaningful only as long as the set of prioritized portfolio candidates—whether funded or not—and the priority of the objectives they support, remain the same.

Organizations can improve the responsiveness of the portfolio optimization process by anticipating various business or organizational scenarios such as different amounts of funding available, changing competitive positioning, and recent regulatory rulings; and then establishing portfolio scenarios that match them. Tools such as Expert Choice's Resource Aligner provide rapid access to such scenarios, as described in Chapters 8 and 9. All the activities highlighted under the column labeled "Strategy Change" in Table 10.1 may need to be performed when organizational goals and objectives change. With anticipated potential scenarios, these activities can be performed in advance. However, even with excellent planning, some events may occur without warning. An organization with disciplined PPM processes, roles, and responsibilities is more likely to adapt more rapidly and effectively than those with less PPM maturity, even to unanticipated changes, and they can perform the "Strategy Change" activities with greater agility.

10.8 SUMMARY

In this chapter we discussed the necessary prerequisites for effective implementation of the portfolio, the importance of monitoring and controlling the projects in the portfolio, governance and roles and responsibilities of major stakeholders, in other words, the infrastructure necessary to effectively manage projects and portfolios. By identifying which performance parameters to monitor and by collecting performance measurements periodically, performance deviations can be identified in a timely manner, allowing for appropriate corrective action or portfolio adjustment decisions to be applied. Analysis of reported data allows management to identify deviations from expected performance and to establish the significance of the deviations, helping determine the right corrective action or adjustment.

We also defined which decisions about projects and portfolios are within the authority delegated to project and portfolio managers and which are beyond their authority, including a termination of a project or restructuring a portfolio. Changes that affect the prioritized benefits of a project or the entire portfolio must also be addressed at a higher level. In addition, we described the iterative, cyclical nature of the PPM process and provided suggested sample frequencies for these cycles.

In Chapter 11 we focus on the PPM implementation and evaluation phases, including evaluating the performance of projects and making adjustments in terms of traditional measures, as well as rolling up those measurements to the portfolio level.

10.9 REFERENCES

Association for Project Managers (2004). *A Guide to Governance of Project Management*, United Kingdom.

Blomquist, Tomas and Ralf Müller (2006). "Introduction and Background" (Chapter 1). *Middle Managers in Program and Project Portfolio Management: Practices, Roles and Responsibilities*. Newton Square, PA. Project Management Institute.

Cooper, Robert G., Scott J. Edgett, and Elko J. Kleinschmidt (2001). "The Quest for the Right Portfolio Management Process" (Chapter 1). *Portfolio Management for New Products*, 2nd ed. New York, NY: Perseus Publishing.

Kerzner, Harold (2009). *Project Management: A Systems Approach to Planning, Scheduling, and Controlling*, 10th ed. Hoboken, NJ. John Wiley & Sons.

Meredith, J. R. and Samuel J. Mantel, Jr. (2006). *Project Management: A Managerial Approach*, 6th ed. Hoboken, NJ. John Wiley & Sons.

Office of Government Commerce (2010). *Portfolio Management Guide,* Final Public Consultation Draft, HM Treasury, London, UK.

Project Management Institute (2004). *The Guide to the Project Management Body of Knowledge* (PMBOK) Guide), 3rd ed. ANSI /PMI 99-001-2004.

Rad, Parviz F. and Ginger Levin (2006). "Project Portfolio Management Deployment Guidelines" (Chapter 3). *Project Portfolio Management Tools and Techniques*. New York, NY: IIL Publishing.

11

Implementing and Evaluating Project and Portfolio Performance

The critical component to managing during the portfolio implementation and evaluation phases is measuring the performance of individual projects in the portfolio and synthesizing these project metrics at the portfolio level to monitor project and portfolio performance and provide meaningful information for decision makers. As such, the major activities in this chapter are monitoring, evaluating, and controlling projects and portfolios. Monitoring is defined as "collecting, recording, and reporting information concerning any and all aspects of project performance that the project manager or others in the organization wish to know" (Meredith and Mantel, 2006). Evaluating is defined as the process of analyzing measurements recorded during monitoring activities to identify deviations from acceptable performance tolerances or to confirm continued acceptable performance by analyzing actual performance against planned performance. Controlling is defined as the actions taken to correct an unfavorable trend or to take advantage of an unusually favorable trend (Kerzner, 2006) and is typically governed by pre-established criteria to bound decision making.

In this chapter we discuss the use of traditional earned value management (EVM) metrics and other measurements to assess the performance of individual projects against their baseline values, and we describe the consolidation of these individual project metrics to produce the equivalent metrics at the portfolio level. We also show how these traditional metrics are used to create a strategically meaningful project and portfolio performance dashboard; such a dashboard displays project and portfolio performance information in terms of anticipated benefits at the time of selection and the objectives each project supports. In addition, we discuss changes to project and portfolio baselines and the circumstances under which they occur.

Figure 11.1 highlights the activities and results of the implementation and evaluation phases once metrics and governance are established. They include assessing project performance with respect to cost, schedule, and specification baselines and determining adjustments needed to maintain such performance. At the portfolio level, project performance is combined to assess performance at the portfolio level and to provide a foundation for evaluating strategic performance of the portfolio. When necessary, and as dictated by analysis during strategic performance evaluation, adjustments to the portfolio may be necessary to ensure the continued ability to deliver strategic benefits. Recall that the implementation and evaluation phases are iterative and their activities and results overlap and interact.

To effectively monitor performance and make appropriate corrective action decisions, periodic measurements based on accurate and timely information are required. As described in Chapter 10, the organization's project portfolio management (PPM) process must define the measurement

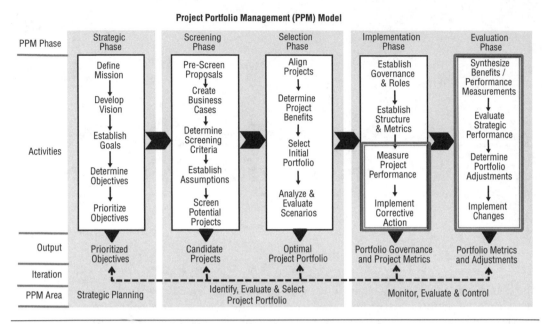

Figure 11.1 PPM model—Implementation Phase

cycles, identify which performance deviations require corrective action, and make the right information available to the right people at the right time to make the right decision. Decisions made during implementation are governed by a reporting structure with well-defined roles, responsibilities, and limits of authority. They are supported by an infrastructure that gathers and reports consistent information about the progress of the projects in the current portfolio.

During implementation and evaluation, the decision-making authority of project and portfolio managers is typically limited to changes that do not affect established performance baselines. Decisions in which adjustments require changes to baselines, or situations in which acceptable baseline deviation tolerances are breached, must be escalated through a formal change control process for action and approval at a higher level. At each level of the organization, information regarding the progress of projects in the portfolio or portfolios is gathered and reported to the next higher echelon. Every level of management, project through portfolio and even portfolio of portfolios, uses this information in differing degrees of detail but with the same purpose. The project and portfolio managers, as well as the PMB and executive review board (ERB), use performance indicators to ascertain the performance health of their projects and portfolios and ensure that they are performing at baseline levels or better.

11.1 PROJECT PERFORMANCE INDICATORS

To measure the progress of projects within the portfolio, performance indicators (also known as *key performance indicators*) must be established and distributed as guidance to project teams through the portfolio management plan. These indicators are objective and can be analyzed and evaluated quantitatively. Many organizations use EVM, a systematic means of evaluating project progress that combines schedule performance and cost performance to answer the question, "What have we received for the money spent?" In addition to specifying the indicators to measure and report, the project portfolio management plan (PPMP) contains tolerances to specify when action is necessary to bring performance back in alignment with the baseline and, further, defines who is responsible for making corrective action decisions. By collecting project data and synthesizing it into usable performance measurement information, the measurements can be compared to baseline performance parameters. Parameters within baseline expectations require no corrective action and the project continues to be monitored.

However, when a deviation from acceptable baseline ranges is observed, the project requires corrective action that can include schedule compression, cost reduction, and quality review. When deviations are severe, corrective action decisions may be escalated to a higher level and include reallocation of resources, possible project termination after analyzing the causes of and potential solutions for poor performance, and consequent adjustment of the portfolio. EVM is a primary tool for managing cost and schedule performance at both the project and the portfolio levels, but does not directly encompass scope or adherence to specifications, often known as quality. Thus, we also introduce a metric for assessing conformance to specifications, called the Quality Performance Index (QPI). The QPI is a measure of how well the product being produced by the project appears to conform to customer requirements (Nisenboim, 2002).

11.2 EARNED VALUE MANAGEMENT—MEASURING COST AND SCHEDULE PERFORMANCE

Earned value management is a system that combines schedule and cost performance and comprises four primary metrics: (1) budget at completion (BAC), (2) planned value (PV), (3) earned value (EV), and (4) actual cost (AC). These metrics are conceptually illustrated in Figure 11.2.

The project illustrated in Figure 11.2 is and has been reporting cumulative actual costs (AC) greater than planned while completing less work than planned (PV). This graphic illustrates the

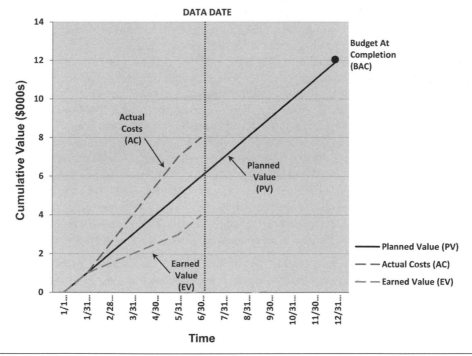

Figure 11.2   Earned value, planned value, and actual costs

capability of comparing a project's current progress to baseline expectations and showing cumulative progress. This comparison also provides the decision maker with information to evaluate whether a corrective action is needed and, if so, how severe the deviation is. Additionally, it helps the decision maker to determine the appropriate action to bring the project back within baselines. A relatively minor deviation in performance may result in a corrective action decision to apply additional resources or increase the effort of existing resources. A major deviation that is projected to negatively affect the project's cost and schedule baselines would likely result in a formal change control action and require elevation to decision makers at a level higher in the organization than the project manager. Of course, who can make what decisions is determined by the governance described previously.

As a brief explanation for those not familiar with the terms, EVM compares the earned value (EV) to both the planned value (PV) and actual cost (AC) to determine the cause and the magnitude of the cost variance and to aid in deciding whether corrective action is required.

- Budget at completion (BAC) is prepared during the planning phase and represents the total budget for the project, that is, how much is planned to be spent on the project. In the example in Figure 11.2, the BAC is $12,000.
- Planned Value (PV) represents how much of the project budget was planned to be spent to accomplish the work completed by the reporting date (data date). PV is calculated by multiplying the BAC by the planned percent complete (BAC × planned % complete) = PV. For instance, the BAC for the project is $12,000. As project work gets underway, Figure 11.2 illustrates the project progress measurement at the end of the sixth month of work. The schedule planned 50% of the work to be completed by the sixth measurement period (month). As a result, the PV was $6,000 ($12,000 × 50% = $6,000).
- Actual Cost (AC) is the total cost incurred in accomplishing the work completed by the reporting date. For instance, in Figure 11.2 our actual cumulative cost at the sixth performance reporting date (June 30) was $8,000. In comparing the PV ($6,000) to the AC ($8,000), we notice a negative cost difference or negative cost variance of $2,000. That is, our actual costs were $2,000 more than we planned and consumed 40% of the budget; the work required more money to complete than planned and we are thus over budget.
- Earned Value (EV) is the budgeted cost for the work that has actually been accomplished on the project and is calculated by multiplying the BAC by the actual percentage of work completed (EV = BAC × actual % complete). The actual percentage of work completed is determined by the organization's method for estimating work completed. Meredith and Mantel (2006) note the 50-50, 0-100, critical input use and the proportionality rule as common methods for estimating work package completion percentages. Using our example in Figure 11.2, as of the reporting date of June 30, presume we have completed approximately 33% of the work using one of the actual work completed estimating methods described by Meredith and Mantel. To calculate EV, we multiply BAC ($12,000) by actual percent complete (33%) which equals $4,000 in value earned. In comparing the PV ($6,000) to the EV ($4,000), we notice a negative schedule variance of $2,000, that is, the EV (budgeted cost of the work we actually completed) is less than the PV (budgeted cost of the work we scheduled). This indicates we have not earned as much value as planned and are thus behind schedule.

These metrics can be applied at any level in the deliverable work breakdown structure and rolled up to the project level. In the examples in this chapter, these EVM metrics are presumed to be reported at the work package level and consolidated at the project level to produce cost and schedule indices. The means of reporting percent work complete differs from organization to organization and even from project type to project type within an organization. For example, some organizations report 0% complete before a unit of work begins, 50% complete when it does begin, and 100% complete when the unit is complete. Projects that are labor intensive such as software development may report percent complete in terms of hours of effort invested compared to total planned hours for a module. Others estimate the percent complete and report the estimate, for example, cubic units of concrete poured divided by the total to be poured (sometimes known as *physical percent complete*).

11.2.1 Schedule and Cost Performance Indices

To provide context for earned value metrics we need a method to analyze cost and schedule performance. We can use two EVM measurements known as the schedule performance index (SPI) and the cost performance index (CPI).

Cost performance index (CPI) is calculated CPI = EV/AC. A value less than 1.0 indicates cost overrun while a value greater than 1.0 indicates a cost under run. Using our example from Figure 11.2, EV = $6,000 while AC = $8,000. Using our formula we derive a CPI = .75, indicating a major cost overrun.

Schedule performance index (SPI) is calculated SPI = EV/PV. Similar to the CPI, a value less than 1.0 indicates the project is behind schedule while a value greater than 1.0 indicates the project is ahead of schedule. Again, using our example from Figure 11.2, our EV equaled $4,000 while our PV equaled $6,000. Using our formula, we derive a SPI = .67, indicating the project is behind schedule. In addition to the indices, some organizations use cost and schedule variances that report the actual deviations from planned cost and schedule. When projects vary greatly in cost and duration, these metrics can be used to differentiate the magnitude of the variances that is not expressed simply by using indices. For example, a cost variance of −$1.2 billion and a cost variance of −$50,000 could both represent a CPI of 0.80 for their respective projects.

11.2.2 Combining Cost and Schedule Performance

SPI and CPI can be combined in various ways to yield a single index of performance for a project such as the schedule cost index (SCI) or a weighted index simply known as a composite index (CI).

The project's schedule cost index (SCI) represents the total project performance measurement using EV measures of schedule (SPI) and cost (CPI) as the basis. SCI is calculated by multiplying the project's current CPI by the SPI (Christensen, 1996). For instance, CPI = 0.80 and SPI = 1.20 would yield an SCI value of 0.96 (0.80 × 1.20 = 0.96).

However, instead of using SCI, measurement components can be weighted to form a composite index (CI) (Christensen, 1996) if the organization emphasizes either cost or schedule more than the other: CI = (w1 × SPI) + (w2 × CPI). For instance, CI can be weighted to 50% each for schedule and cost to produce an average when the organization deems both metrics of equal importance, or CI can be weighted more heavily on one metric than the other; for instance, cost at 70% and schedule at 30% when the cost is more critical and the schedule is flexible to maintain cost discipline. Determining the relative importance of these factors could be subjected to an analytic hierarchy process (AHP) evaluation. In our example of CPI = 0.80 and SPI = 1.20, the CI would be calculated to equate to {(0.80 × 0.70) + (1.20 × 0.30)} = 0.92.

It should be noted that SCI and CI produce different measurements. In Table 11.1, the CI was derived by weighting each performance index equally, and the SCI was calculated by multiplying the CPI by the SPI. As Table 11.1 shows, when using the SCI to measure project performance, the metrics result in a more pessimistic performance measurement when both CPI and SPI are less than 1.0, and it produces an overly optimistic performance measure when both CPI and SPI are greater than 1.0 when compared to an equally weighted CI. Comparing SCI and CI results for reporting Periods 1 and 2 against 3 and 4, we observe a larger disparity in the SCI measurement as compared to the CI.

In reviewing data from reporting Periods 1 and 4, we observe that the disparity increases as both CPI and SPI move further from 1.0 when both CPI and SPI are either greater than planned or less

Table 11.1   Schedule cost index versus equally weighted composite index

Reporting Period	Cost Index (CPI)	Schedule Index (SPI)	Schedule Cost Index (SCI)	Composite Index (CI)
1	0.80	0.80	0.64	0.80
2	0.90	0.90	0.81	0.90
3	1.00	1.00	1.00	1.00
4	1.10	1.10	1.21	1.10
5	1.20	1.20	1.44	1.20
6	1.20	0.80	0.96	1.00
7	1.10	0.90	0.99	1.00
Note 1: SCI = SPI x CPI Note 2: CI = CPI/2 + SPI/2				

than planned. When the CPI and SPI results are mixed, meaning one is larger than 1.0 and the other less than 1.0, the disparity is less obvious when compared to an equally weighted CI. It is for this reason we recommend using a composite index when combining CPI and SPI into a single project performance metric. Using the CI, the organization has the flexibility to weight the performance indices according to their preferences without overemphasizing the effect when both indices are less than or greater than 1.0 when using the SCI method. Also, the CI can include other metrics besides SPI and CPI. Accordingly, the authors have chosen to use the CI to illustrate project and portfolio performance in this chapter.

Table 11.1 illustrates two ways to use the same indices to derive significantly different performance results. The method used to calculate metrics and interpret the results is as important as which metrics are used.

11.2.3 Estimated Costs to Complete

Although we do not use them as examples to measure project performance in this chapter, two additional EVM metrics are addressed here because they are important in other ways in project portfolio management, including determining what cost to assign to projects in progress during a new portfolio selection process, a portfolio adjustment, or a new budgeting cycle:

- Estimate at completion (EAC) is a projected estimate of the total cost of the project when all of the work is complete. It can be calculated in multiple ways, depending on the perception of the cost performance rate at which remaining work will be completed. The formula used here presumes that the remaining work will be completed with the same cost performance as the project to date and is calculated as EAC = BAC/CPI.
- Estimate to complete (ETC) is a projected estimate of the cost of the remaining work and is calculated by the formula ETC = EAC − AC. ETC represents the cost to complete the project and is often used in project portfolio selection as the *cost* for a project that is underway as a result of having been funded in a prior portfolio or other selection process. This is in keeping with the concept that sunk costs, or costs already incurred, are irrelevant to the investment decisions made going forward (Higgins, 2007).

Our discussion of EAC and ETC is brief and simplistic because the estimates of cost at completion can be performed in multiple ways using cumulative or noncumulative indices; however, the concepts, when applied by an organization in a consistent manner, can be important measures of project performance and can be extrapolated as measures of portfolio performance.

EVM metrics provide a valuable mechanism from which to measure project performance and determine whether and what corrective action is required. Other EVM indicators are often used to assess project performance and for diagnostic and prognostic information; however, for our purposes in providing examples of project performance and synthesizing project performance to report performance at the portfolio level, we have excluded EAC and ETC from further discussion of project and portfolio performance in the remainder of this chapter.

11.3 QUALITY PERFORMANCE INDEX—MEASURING CONFORMANCE TO SPECIFICATIONS

While EVM provides a useful and powerful method for capturing project cost and schedule performance, it does not account for meeting specifications or the customer's expectations. A project can be performing well in terms of cost and schedule, but if the project is not meeting specifications or customer expectations, then project success is negatively affected. Nisenboim (2002) suggests the use of a QPI that measures how well the product appears to be conforming to specifications or customer requirements. Nisenboim suggests deriving this measure during project implementation using a simple rating review conducted informally by a peer or subject matter expert (SME). A rating of 0.90, for example, would mean that for the components of the developing product that are available for review, there is 90% conformance to requirements, in the opinion of the reviewer(s). Another more formal method could be comparing work package deliverables against contract specifications and assessing compliance directly or by using a rating scale.

Measuring and interpreting QPI results differs from EVM in that the QPI will rarely, if ever, exceed 1.0. That is, a QPI of 1.0 represents the project as delivering 100% of baseline specifications. A value higher than 1.0 would indicate the project is delivering more, in terms of specifications, than scope baseline—a rare occurrence in projects. A benefit of QPI is that this metric forces the project manager, and the organization's PPM system, to consider conformance to specifications when measuring project and portfolio performance. Delivering a work package and project within cost and schedule baselines will not result in a successful project if the project fails to achieve its intended purposes (e.g., meeting specifications).

While QPI does not specifically include customer satisfaction, the QPI metric could be expanded to include this element by combining both the compliance to specification rating and customer satisfaction rating into a single rating that considers both elements. Just like combining SPI and CPI results in a CI, QPI can be combined with SPI, and CPI can be weighted to form a project total performance index (TPI_{PRO}). A single number is thus derived to rate the project by adding the three weighted indices, that is, (w1 × SPI) + (w2 × CPI) + (w3 × QPI). Similar to the SCI, simply multiplying the three indices will result in an overly pessimistic measurement when all three indices are less than 1.0 and an overly optimistic measure when all three indices are positive (greater than 1.0). For this reason the authors suggest using the weighted CI method for purposes of measuring total project performance. While some practitioners suggest a metric for scope and a different metric for quality, the authors believe they are one and the same because quality means conformance to specifications.

11.4 MEASURING PROJECT PERFORMANCE

As illustrated in the EVM discussion, analysis of performance data to identify deviations from baselines is crucial for determining whether corrective action is required for the individual project. The parameters of PV, EV, and AC are reported on a period-by-period basis, for example, weekly, monthly, or bi-monthly. The frequency of reporting is often prescribed based on the duration or complexity of the projects.

Table 11.2 shows project performance measurements for American Business University's (ABU) Project 2 (Renovate & Expand Davidson Student Center) over the first six reporting periods while the project work is planned over 10 periods and comprises six work packages. For simplicity in illustrating EVM, work within each work package was evenly distributed over 10 reporting periods. PV, AC, and EV are noted under the "EVM Metric" column and are measured for each work package. To determine actual percent complete, ABU used the 50-50 estimating method. That is, tasks within each work package were credited with completing 50% of the work when the task started and the remaining 50% when the task was completed. This estimating method served as the basis for determining actual work completed, which is necessary to calculate EV (actual % complete × BAC). Another estimating method for percent complete could have been used, this was simply the method selected for the example, as documented at the bottom of the table.

The project's current EVM metric measurements are shown in the "Current Measure" column and equal the last reporting period measurements (reporting Period 6). As the most current, these measurements are used to calculate the project EV cost and schedule performance indices. While information across reporting periods is useful for identifying performance trends and EVM metrics are point-in-time indicators that can be used in cumulative plots, attempts to calculate and report an arithmetic mean for any of the work package EVM metrics across reporting periods will result in a mathematically meaningless number.

In Table 11.2, the project's current SPI, CPI, and CI are recorded at the bottom of the table noted by the project SPI (SPI_{PRO}), project CPI (CPI_{PRO}), and project CI (CI_{PRO}) columns. At the bottom of the reporting table, governance guidance has been annotated and extracted from the PPMP identifying the bounds of decision making for the project. In this example, the organization has authorized the project manager to make corrective action decisions for this project as long as the CI_{PRO} does not drop below 0.90. When the project's CI (CI_{PRO}) drops below 0.90, then corrective action decisions are

Table 11.2 Example ABU Project 2 project performance measurements (SPI, CPI, and CI)

Work Package #	EVM Metric	ABU Project #2 - Renovate & Expand Davidson Student Center										Current Measure	WP BAC ($000s)
		Project Performance Reporting Period											
		1	2	3	4	5	6	7	8	9	10		
1	PV	10.0	20.0	30.0	40.0	50.0	60.0	70.0	80.0	90.0	100.0	60.0	100
	AC	10.0	21.0	32.0	43.0	54.0	57.0					57.0	
	EV	10.0	20.0	28.0	37.0	47.0	55.0					55.0	
2	PV	20.0	40.0	60.0	80.0	100.0	120.0	140.0	160.0	180.0	200.0	120.0	200
	AC	22.0	41.0	63.0	84.0	103.0	112.0					112.0	
	EV	20.0	40.0	56.0	76.0	98.0	118.0					118.0	
3	PV	30.0	60.0	90.0	120.0	150.0	180.0	210.0	240.0	270.0	300.0	180.0	300
	AC	29.0	57.0	87.0	116.0	146.0	160.0					160.0	
	EV	36.0	66.0	96.0	129.0	159.0	189.0					189.0	
4	PV	25.0	50.0	75.0	100.0	125.0	150.0	175.0	200.0	225.0	250.0	150.0	250
	AC	25.0	50.0	75.0	100.0	125.0	125.0					125.0	
	EV	25.0	50.0	75.0	100.0	125.0	137.5					137.5	
5	PV	10.0	20.0	30.0	40.0	50.0	60.0	70.0	80.0	90.0	100.0	60.0	100
	AC	10.0	20.0	29.0	39.0	49.0	55.0					55.0	
	EV	10.0	20.0	28.0	38.0	48.0	60.0					60.0	
6	PV	5.0	10.0	15.0	20.0	25.0	30.0	35.0	40.0	45.0	50.0	30.0	50
	AC	5.0	10.0	14.0	19.0	22.0	22.0					22.0	
	EV	5.0	10.0	15.0	20.0	25.0	25.0					25.0	

Project Portfolio Management Plan (PPMP) Performance Metrics Guidance			
$CI_{PRO} \geq 1.0$ to .90 - Project Manager	Project SPI (SPI_{PRO})	0.9742	
< .90 to .80 - Portoflio Manager	Project CPI (CPI_{PRO})	1.1008	1,000
< .80 - Portfolio Management Board (PMB)	Project CI (CI_{PRO})	1.0754	

Note: "Actual % Completed" determined using 50-50 method. 50% credit given when task started and remaining 50% when task completed.

elevated to the portfolio manager. Finally, when the CI_{PRO} drops below 0.80, corrective actions are dictated by the PMB. This guidance prescribes authority limits for correcting project performance at each management level before project performance deficiency results in a likelihood of project failure. In the example in Table 11.2, the CI_{PRO} is well above 0.90 and the project manager retains corrective action decision-making authority.

In Table 11.2, cost has been weighted at 80% while schedule weight is 20%, indicating the organization's emphasis on cost over schedule. While not shown in the table, the CI_{PRO} was determined by the calculation $(1.1008 \times 0.80) + (0.9742 \times 0.20) = 1.0754$. When cost is heavily weighted, of course, it has a more significant impact than schedule on the performance result. As Table 11.2 illustrates, even though schedule performance is behind, overall performance is assessed as ahead of plan because the project is performing well with respect to the more heavily weighted factor, cost in this case. As stated earlier, the CI metric provides flexibility to combine and weight cost and schedule performance indicators.

The example in Table 11.2 used only EVM metrics. Project performance measurements can be expanded to include the QPI, resulting in a TPI as illustrated in Table 11.3. As mentioned previously, the QPI is a measure of how well the product appears to be conforming to customer specifications and can be determined using a simple rating by organizational SMEs or peers. The purpose is to devise a system to confidently assess current progress in meeting specifications whether using SMEs, peers, or some other method. Project 2's current QPI is assessed as 0.95, meaning that as of the sixth reporting period the project is on track to meet approximately 95% of specifications. As is the case with CPI and SPI, attempting to calculate the arithmetic mean across reporting periods for QPI will result in a meaningless result.

Although not shown in Table 11.3, Project 2's schedule index was weighted at 20%, the cost index at 20%, and the quality index at 60%, indicating that the QPI was significantly more important than cost or schedule performance. Project 2's TPI was determined by the calculation $(0.9742 \times 0.20) + (1.1008 \times 0.20) + (0.9500 \times 0.60) = 0.9850$. Given the guidance in the PPMP and noted at the bottom

Table 11.3 Example ABU Project 2 project performance measurements (EVM, QPI, and TPI)

Work Package #	EVM Metric	1	2	3	4	5	6	7	8	9	10	Current Measure	WP BAC ($000s)
		ABU Project #2 - Renovate & Expand Davidson Student Center											
1	PV	10.0	20.0	30.0	40.0	50.0	60.0	70.0	80.0	90.0	100.0	60.0	100
	AC	10.0	21.0	32.0	43.0	54.0	57.0					57.0	
	EV	10.0	20.0	28.0	37.0	47.0	55.0					55.0	
2	PV	20.0	40.0	60.0	80.0	100.0	120.0	140.0	160.0	180.0	200.0	120.0	200
	AC	22.0	41.0	63.0	84.0	103.0	112.0					112.0	
	EV	20.0	40.0	56.0	76.0	98.0	118.0					118.0	
3	PV	30.0	60.0	90.0	120.0	150.0	180.0	210.0	240.0	270.0	300.0	180.0	300
	AC	29.0	57.0	87.0	116.0	146.0	160.0					160.0	
	EV	36.0	66.0	96.0	129.0	159.0	189.0					189.0	
4	PV	25.0	50.0	75.0	100.0	125.0	150.0	175.0	200.0	225.0	250.0	150.0	250
	AC	25.0	50.0	75.0	100.0	125.0	125.0					125.0	
	EV	25.0	50.0	75.0	100.0	125.0	137.5					137.5	
5	PV	10.0	20.0	30.0	40.0	50.0	60.0	70.0	80.0	90.0	100.0	60.0	100
	AC	10.0	20.0	29.0	39.0	49.0	55.0					55.0	
	EV	10.0	20.0	28.0	38.0	48.0	60.0					60.0	
6	PV	5.0	10.0	15.0	20.0	25.0	30.0	35.0	40.0	45.0	50.0	30.0	50
	AC	5.0	10.0	14.0	19.0	22.0	22.0					22.0	
	EV	5.0	10.0	15.0	20.0	25.0	25.0					25.0	

The column header spanning row 1–10 reads **Project Performance Reporting Period**.

Bottom guidance section:

Project Portfolio Management Plan (PPMP) Performance Metrics Guidance		
$TPI_{PRO} \geq 1.0$ to .90 - Project Manager	Project SPI (SPI_{PRO})	0.9742
< .90 to .80 - Portfolio Manager	Project CPI (CPI_{PRO})	1.1008
< .80 - Portfolio Management Board (PMB)	Project QPI (QPI_{PRO})	0.9500
	Project TPI (TPI_{PRO})	0.9850
		1,000

Note: "Actual % Completed" determined using 50-50 method. 50% credit given when task started and remaining 50% when task completed.

of Table 11.3, the project manager would still retain decision-making authority for corrective action decisions, but given the determined weights, the project manager must be cognizant of the emphasis the organization places on the most important constraint and manage the project accordingly. Specifically, given the project's current QPI of 0.95, the project manager would investigate the areas of the project at risk of failure to meet specifications and take corrective action to bring performance back to the specifications baseline.

Monitoring project performance through EVM and other measurements such as QPI provides the project manager and the organization effective methods for evaluating project performance against project baselines and determining when a corrective action is necessary to bring the project back to baselines. Composite indices such as the CI and TPI allow the organization to derive a single metric to provide an assessment of the project's overall health as well as the flexibility to apply weights to each of the individual performance measurements.

While it is not necessary to use every project performance metric, it is important to establish the right metrics for the organization, portfolio, and the projects to provide performance measurements in the right context for decision makers. The examples illustrate that when appropriate performance metrics and baselines are established, timely and accurate project performance measurements can be effective in evaluating the performance of a project and in helping the project manager to make the right corrective action decisions. At the portfolio level, individual project performance information from across the portfolio must be synthesized to evaluate overall performance of the portfolio.

11.5 MEASURING PORTFOLIO PERFORMANCE

To derive meaningful portfolio level performance measures, we must consider the relative priority of the projects rather than simply averaging project portfolio performance measures without regard to the relative magnitude of their anticipated contribution. Since the priorities are ratio-scale numbers when using the AHP, and they represent the relative importance of the project in achieving strategic objectives, they can be used as weights to appropriately report performance at the portfolio level using traditional metrics. Using the ABU funded portfolio example, the first month's CPI, SPI, and CI are shown for each project in Table 11.4. To measure portfolio performance, individual project performance metrics such as SPI_{PRO}, CPI_{PRO}, and CI_{PRO} can be synthesized to produce the portfolio level

Table 11.4 ABU example—portfolio performance measurements (SPI_{PORT}, CPI_{PORT}, and CI_{PORT})

Project	Benefit	Normalized Benefit (Priority)	CPI_{PRO}	SPI_{PRO}	CI_{PRO}
2, Renovate & Expand Davidson Student Services Center	0.255	0.171	1.10	0.97	1.07
3. Construct Dr. Mary Haven Student Housing	0.051	0.034	1.13	1.02	1.11
4a. (GOLD) Renovate & Expand Benson Library	0.260	0.175	0.65	1.01	0.72
6. Renovate Mason Hall Research Center	0.114	0.077	0.89	0.97	0.91
7. Construct ABU Medical Clinic	0.154	0.103	0.90	0.90	0.90
8. ABU Revitalization Program Regulatory	0.400	0.269	1.14	0.89	1.09
11c. (BRONZE) Construct ABU Indoor Athletic Complex	0.019	0.013	1.07	0.90	1.04
13. Expand Campus Share Ride Services	0.236	0.158	0.98	0.90	0.96
		1.000	0.98	0.94	0.97
			CPI_{PORT}	SPI_{PORT}	CI_{PORT}
Project Portfolio Management Plan (PPMP) Performance Metrics Guidance					
$CI_{PORT} \geq .90$ - Portoflio Manager					
$CI_{PORT} < .90$ - Portfolio Management Board (PMB)					

metrics SPI_{PORT}, CPI_{PORT}, and CI_{PORT} that are calculated for the portfolio by summing the product of each index and the normalized anticipated benefits, as shown in Table 11.4.

In this example, the CPI, SPI, and CI for each project were calculated. The anticipated benefits (priorities) derived from the evaluation were normalized to 1.000 while maintaining their ratio-scale properties. To normalize benefits, divide the project benefits by the total benefits. The CPI_{PORT}, SPI_{PORT}, and CI_{PORT} were then calculated by multiplying each respective index by the priority for the project and adding them to arrive at the respective portfolio index. For example, the CPI_{PRO} of 1.10 for Project 2 was multiplied by the priority of Project 2 of 0.171; when this is done for all projects, their sum is the CPI for the portfolio, or CPI_{PORT}. In Excel this can be accomplished using the SUMPRODUCT function. Simply averaging the CPI, SPI, and CI numbers for the member projects yields different results for the portfolio indices and is incorrect because it does not take into account the project priorities. Thus, the differences become more dramatic when the performance of the highest priority projects is very high or very low.

When the organization prescribes one performance metric to be more important than another, as when cost is more important than schedule, then the portfolio composite index (CI_{PORT}) can be used to evaluate the performance health of the portfolio. In the example illustrated in Table 11.4, cost was weighted at 80% and schedule at 20% and calculated using the formula (CPI × 0.80) + (SPI × 0.20), indicating the organization's overwhelming emphasis on cost discipline. Analysis of the project cost and schedule performance information in Table 11.4 reveals that since the organization stresses cost over schedule, the single performance measure provided by the CI will be skewed in the direction of the CPI. For Project 2, although the schedule index measurement is noticeably lower than the cost measure, the project's overall health is assessed as only slightly below performance expectations (0.97). Given the organization's preference to maintain cost over schedule, the weighted CI_{PORT} metric depicts ABU's portfolio performance in the context of what the organization views as important.

Similar to project performance metrics, portfolio performance measurements can also be expanded to include the QPI_{PORT}. In Table 11.5, the QPI_{PORT} was determined by assessing the QPI for each project as discussed earlier and synthesizing the individual measurement by multiplying each project's QPI by its normalized benefits and summing the projects' QPIs to produce the QPI_{PORT}. As stated, this can be accomplished in Excel using the SUMPRODUCT function.

In addition, the three performance indices can be synthesized to produce a single portfolio level performance measure for the portfolio, the TPI_{PORT}. In Table 11.5, the TPI_{PORT} was calculated by summing the products of the weighted indices and each project's normalized benefits.

Table 11.5 Example—portfolio performance measurements (SPI_{PORT}, CPI_{PORT}, QPI_{PORT}, and TPI_{PORT})

Project	Benefit	Normalized Benefit (Priority)	CPI_{PRO}	SPI_{PRO}	QPI_{PRO}	TPI_{PRO}
2, Renovate & Expand Davidson Student Services Center	0.255	0.171	1.10	0.97	1.00	1.03
3. Construct Dr. Mary Haven Student Housing	0.051	0.034	1.13	1.02	0.98	1.05
4a. (GOLD) Renovate & Expand Benson Library	0.260	0.175	0.65	1.01	1.00	0.86
6. Renovate Mason Hall Research Center	0.114	0.077	0.89	0.97	0.95	0.93
7. Construct ABU Medical Clinic	0.154	0.103	0.90	0.90	0.90	0.90
8. ABU Revitalization Program Regulatory	0.400	0.269	1.14	0.89	1.00	1.03
11c. (BRONZE) Construct ABU Indoor Athletic Complex	0.019	0.013	1.07	0.90	0.95	0.99
13. Expand Campus Share Ride Services	0.236	0.158	0.98	0.90	0.93	0.94
		1.000	0.98	0.94	0.97	0.97
			CPI_{PORT}	SPI_{PORT}	QPI_{PORT}	TPI_{PORT}
Project Portfolio Management Plan (PPMP) Performance Metrics Guidance						
$TPI_{PORT} \geq .90$ - Portfolio Manager						
$TPI_{PORT} < .90$ - Portfolio Management Board (PMB)						

To this point in discussing project and portfolio evaluation, we have exclusively used SPI, CPI, and other project and portfolio performance measurements to evaluate the health of projects and the portfolio; however, these metrics do not address progress toward achieving strategic objectives or provide the organization a method to balance performance against the objectives the project portfolio supports. As *benefits* represent the anticipated relative contribution of a project toward achieving strategic objectives, benefits are important to consider when evaluating project performance, determining corrective actions, and assessing portfolio performance against the backdrop of strategic objectives. Although we have considered benefit by using priority to weight the portfolio level performance indicators, its impact is not easy to see in tabular form. EV, QPI, and composite indices can be used to produce a portfolio performance dashboard by assessing project performance against a rating scale developed within the organization and evaluating performance in the context of anticipated benefits provided by the project and portfolio.

11.6 PROJECT PORTFOLIO PERFORMANCE DASHBOARD

Poorly performing portfolios are less likely to achieve anticipated benefits and thus decrease the chances of achieving strategic objectives. One method to help decision makers monitor, evaluate, and control portfolio performance against strategic objectives is to use a project portfolio dashboard that incorporates benefits, as illustrated in Figure 11.3 with Expert Choice's Periscope software. The dashboard provides decision makers with a simple visual aid to evaluate how the portfolio is performing from a macro perspective and how the performance of individual projects impacts the strategic objectives they support. Figure 11.3 shows a performance hierarchy with the goal at the top of

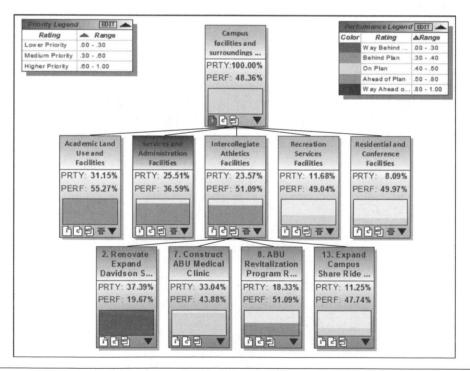

Figure 11.3   Example project performance dashboard (Expert Choice Periscope)

the hierarchy, objectives listed at the second level, and individual projects on the third (bottom) level. This hierarchy maintains traceability of projects to the objectives they support and objectives to the goals they support.

In addition, although we present colors as grayscale in the figures, on screen each box is color highlighted to visually display the current performance status of the goal, objectives, and individual projects. The basis for the color coding is an organizationally developed rating system, shown as the performance legend in Figure 11.3, with the various colors indicating performance within the specified range, from "Way Behind Plan" (red) to "Way Ahead of Plan" (blue). Further, each box provides the priority ("PRTY"), that is, the relative anticipated benefit or contribution to the goal or parent objective. This priority represents the ratio-scale evaluated contribution the project makes toward achieving each objective it supports. The height of the priority fill (color-shaded rectangle) within the box represents the relative priority or contribution to the parent level; the color-shaded rectangle of the highest priority project or objective fills the box, and the height of the other rectangles with the same parent are in proportion to the height of the full box with respect to their relative contributions. Finally, a quantitative performance measurement ("PERF") provides an assessment of the project, objective, and goal performance based on current performance measurements. In this example, project performance is traced through the objectives hierarchy up to the goal and uses traditional metrics as the basis for evaluating performance.

The benefit of such graphical displays is to quickly and simply illustrate the overall health of the portfolio and to quickly identify objectives that are not performing to baselines. By including the anticipated benefit of each project and objective to the goal, the decision maker is able to quickly understand the project's performance and its contribution to the objectives and goal it supports.

We can drill down to view the performance ratings for any given project, as shown in Figure 11.4 for Project 2 (Renovate and Expand Davidson Student Services Center). As can be seen, the

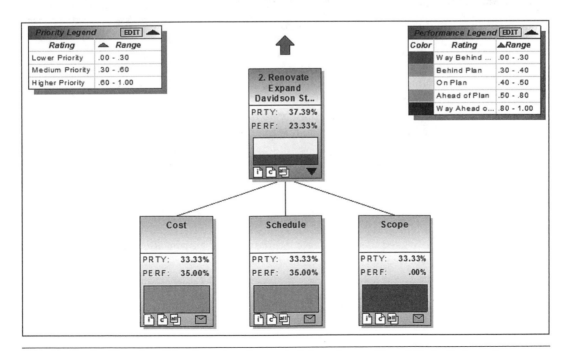

Figure 11.4   Dashboard traditional metrics of cost, schedule, and scope (Expert Choice Periscope)

traditional measures of cost (CPI), schedule (SPI) and scope (QPI) have been given equal weights (PRTY: 33.33%) in determining the performance of this project. Further, cost and schedule have been evaluated as "Behind Plan", while scope has been evaluated as "Way Behind Plan". Obviously this project is performing poorly and further investigation is warranted.

To translate project performance information, such as the CI or any other metric into meaningful and consistent measurements, the organization develops a ratings scale, an example of which is shown in Figure 11.5. A ratings scale can be developed using pairwise comparisons to derive the relative desirability of the intensity levels, and it represents the organization's perspective of performance given the project's current performance measurements. In essence, the ratings scale transitions the project's metrics into performance ratings (behind plan, ahead of plan, or other desired descriptors). By developing the ratings scale, the organization is specifying a uniform and consistent process to translate each project's metrics into the organization's performance categories. An organization-wide rating scale for each metric, and even for each type of project, also standardizes the interpretation of project performance information across portfolios and ensures greater common understanding and consistent interpretation throughout the organization while reducing ambiguities. Caution is advised when evaluating performance by color only, since a performance index of, for example, 0.91 would result in an On Plan color, while an index of 0.89 results in a Behind Plan color.

Color	CI Range		Rating	Periscope Range	
	Low	High		From	To
	0.00	0.75	Way Behind Plan	0.00	0.30
	0.75	0.90	Behind Plan	0.30	0.40
	0.90	1.10	On Plan	0.40	0.50
	1.10	1.25	Ahead of Plan	0.50	0.80
	1.25	2.00+	Way Ahead of Plan	0.80	1.00

Figure 11.5   Example project performance rating scale model (Expert Choice Periscope)

Evaluating project and portfolio performance trends over time is as important to decision makers as evaluating performance at specific points in time. A single performance report, at a point in time, may not provide a true indication of project performance. A project can be performing to baseline plan in the current performance report, but a chart showing multiple reporting periods can illustrate project performance trends. In turn, this trending performance impacts the performance of the supported objectives, as illustrated in Figure 11.6. In this example, we see that performance is beginning to trend downward for the Recreation and Services Facilities objective. Decision makers may want to drill down to individual projects or highlight this objective for further scrutiny during future performance reports, especially if this downward trend was not anticipated for the contributing projects' baseline schedules or costs. Drilling down and other dashboard features allow decision makers to evaluate which projects are contributing to this downward trend and also assess whether future performance is expected to stabilize or continue trending downward. An important element of this evaluation is proactive decision makers who identify potential problem areas early, before they become too serious.

Project Portfolio Dashboard Advantages

Dashboards can be prepared that show individual performance indices or multiple indices weighted and combined into composite performance measurements. From the perspective of the decision maker, this visual dashboard display helps provide context for how the overall portfolio(s) is performing relative to the goal. By providing a hierarchical representation of the strategic plan and supporting projects, decision makers can quickly identify problem areas and determine corrective

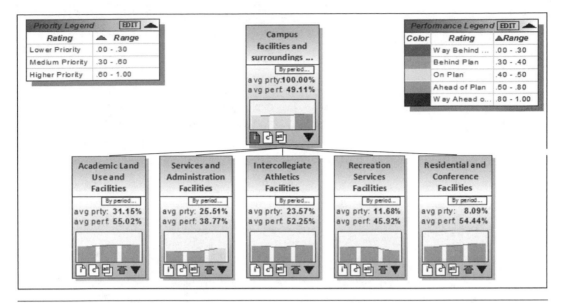

Figure 11.6　Example project performance dashboard trend chart (Expert Choice Periscope)

action by drilling down deeper into the portfolio and even into individual metrics. From Figure 11.3, it is easy to see that Project 2 (Renovate and Expand Davidson Student Center) is not performing well and is a major contributor to the Behind Plan status of the Services and Administration Facilities objective. As indicated in the dashboard, Project 2 is the most important project supporting the objective and accounts for 32.25% (local priority) of the benefits contributing to this objective. By presenting this information in a simple graphical display, the dashboard is a powerful decision support tool in aiding decision makers toward good questions and informed and reasoned decisions. This graphical display emphasizes that the relative priority, or benefit, of the member projects plays a necessary role in reporting portfolio performance.

11.7　EVALUATING PERFORMANCE AND DETERMINING PORTFOLIO CORRECTIVE ACTION

Monitoring performance is a key aspect of and contributor to the PPM process. Monitoring provides the information necessary for project and portfolio managers to evaluate performance and from which to take corrective actions within their decision authority, which is normally confined to changes not affecting cost, schedule, and specification baselines. Monitoring also provides valuable input to the evaluation phase to help decision makers determine changes affecting portfolio baselines.

As each project's performance information is reported to the portfolio, it is combined with other projects and reported to the organization (e.g., ERB and PMB) to provide a snapshot of the portfolio's health. Whether the strategic plan changes or remains the same, project portfolio monitoring, evaluating, and controlling activities yield useful information to support the strategic plan and from which to adjust the portfolio, if necessary. Figure 11.7 shows how portfolio performance, through effective monitoring, evaluating, and controlling in relation to the strategic plan, can support the PPM process and act as an input to the organization's strategic planning process. Recall the discussions from Chapter 10 about the iterative and cyclical nature of PPM, and responding to changes

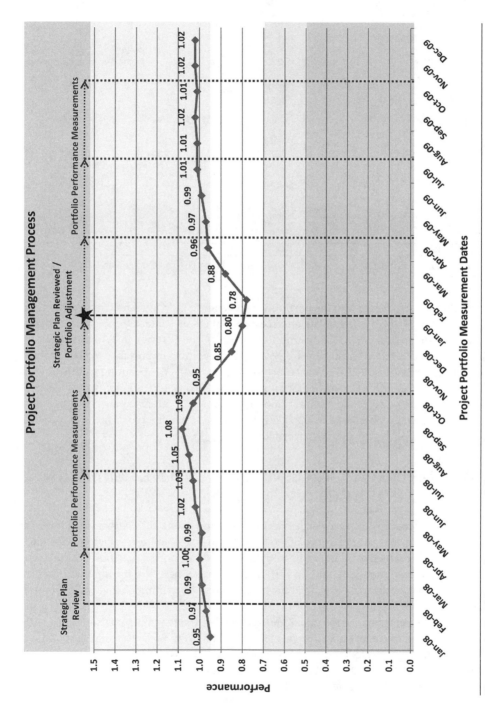

Figure 11.7   Portfolio performance trend chart implementing changes

in organizational strategy. Figure 11.7 also illustrates an example of a PPM review process overlaid on periodic performance measurements where the strategic plan is reviewed annually and current portfolio performance is evaluated quarterly using monthly project performance reports and real time strategic information.

Changes to the portfolio baseline can include a wide variety of corrective actions ranging from complete termination to simple reallocation of resources. The goal of portfolio adjustments is to maximize continued progress toward achieving strategic objectives by ensuring resources are applied to the projects most relevant to strategic objectives and having a reasonable chance of success. While a last resort, deciding to terminate a project is not an admission of defeat, but rather it is a proactive action to ensure success in achieving strategic objectives. Objectively identifying when a project no longer contributes to achieving objectives, or has minimal chance of success, is better accomplished as early as possible in the implementation phase to prevent the utilization of scarce resources that could be better applied to projects providing more value in achieving strategic objectives.

With poorly performing projects and portfolios, decision makers are better positioned to weigh the benefits of reallocating resources among projects and portfolios when evaluating their performance in relation to benefits. Other adjustments may include the addition of new projects to replace terminated projects. Terminating a project results in a change to the portfolio's total benefits and may necessitate reevaluation. Note that when portfolio reevaluation and reselection occurs, costs for existing projects represent remaining costs, or estimates to complete as described earlier, rather than total costs.

11.8 SUMMARY

This chapter described how performance information from projects and project work packages is combined to produce earned value and other project performance measurements; these measurements are used to monitor and evaluate project health by comparing current performance against baseline values and to help determine appropriate corrective actions. At the portfolio level we discussed methods to synthesize individual project performance measurements to produce portfolio level performance metrics and showed how these performance measures can be visually illustrated in a dashboard to compare project and portfolio performance to the strategic objectives they support. Throughout this process, governance guidelines specified in the project portfolio management plan provide the framework for establishing the limits of decision making and ensure the right level of management perspective is applied to decisions that affect baselines. By identifying which performance parameters to monitor and by collecting performance measurements periodically, performance deviations can be identified in a timely manner, allowing for appropriate corrective action decisions to be applied.

Project portfolio management does not guarantee success in achieving strategic goals and objectives. However, as this book illustrates, implementing an effective PPM process can increase the chances of successfully identifying, evaluating, and selecting the right projects for the portfolio, and those that, when completed successfully, best contribute to accomplishing objectives and achieving the organization's vision. Process effectiveness is achieved by developing an infrastructure to facilitate PPM throughout the organization, providing appropriate governance to oversee and guide the process, and by using the best tools and techniques to support better PPM decision making.

Even when an organization performs PPM properly, its assumptions and strategy must be right, and operations must deliver the results anticipated. PPM is the front end of the best chance of implementing the organization's strategy. In the best case, with the right strategy, effective PPM results in selecting the right projects, executing and delivering them successfully, thus driving the organization toward the achievement of its vision.

11.9 REFERENCES

Christensen, David S. (1996). "Project Advocacy and the Estimate at Completion Problem." *Journal of Cost Analysis* (Spring), 35-60.

Higgins, R. C. (2007). *Analysis for Financial Management.* New York, NY: Irwin/McGraw-Hill.

Kerzner, Harold (2009). *Project Management: A Systems Approach to Planning, Scheduling, and Controlling*, 10th ed. Hoboken, NJ. John Wiley & Sons.

Meredith, Jack R. Samuel J. Mantel, Jr. (2006). *Project Management: A Managerial Approach, Sixth Edition.* Hoboken, NJ. John Wiley & Sons.

Nisenboim, Shawn (2002). *The Practical Use of Earned Value.* http://www.timetiger.com/practicalev.asp (retrieved October 31, 2010).

INDEX